IB DIPLOMA PROGRAMME

English A: Literature

COURSE COMPANION

Hannah Tyson

Mark Beverley

OXFORD
UNIVERSITY PRESS

UNIVERSITY PRESS

Great Clarendon Street, Oxford OX2 6DP

Oxford University Press is a department of the University of Oxford.
It furthers the University's objective of excellence in research, scholarship,
and education by publishing worldwide in

Oxford   New York

Auckland   Cape Town   Dar es Salaam   Hong Kong   Karachi
Kuala Lumpur   Madrid   Melbourne   Mexico City   Nairobi
New Delhi   Shanghai   Taipei   Toronto

With offices in

Argentina   Austria   Brazil   Chile   Czech Republic   France   Greece
Guatemala   Hungary   Italy   Japan   Poland   Portugal   Singapore
South Korea   Switzerland   Thailand   Turkey   Ukraine   Vietnam

© Copyright Oxford University Press

British Library Cataloguing in Publication Data

Data available

ISBN: 978-0-19-913541-7

10 9 8 7 6 5 4 3 2 1

Printed in Great Britain by Bell and Bain Ltd, Glasgow

Paper used in the production of this book is a natural, recyclable product made
from wood grown in sustainable forests. The manufacturing process conforms to
the environmental regulations of the country of origin.

Acknowledgements
We are also grateful to the International Baccalaureate Organization for
permission to reproduce material from the IB Diploma Programme Psychology
subject guide and extended essay guide.

The publisher would like to thank the following for permission to reproduce
the following material:

Extract from *An Instant in the Wind* by Andre Brink, published by Vintage
reprinted by permission of The Random House Group Ltd.

"House by the Railroad, 1925," translated by Lawrence Venuti, from Edward
Hopper © 2006 Ernest Farres. Translation © 2009 by Lawrence Venuti.
Reprinted with the permission of Graywolf Press, Minneapolis, Minnesota,
www.graywolfpress.org

Extract from *Pistache* by Sebastian Faulks, published by Hutchinson. Reprinted
by permission of The Random House Group Ltd., and by Aitken Alexander

Quote from Jasper Fforde from *1000 Books to Change Your life*, Time Out Guides
2007 reprinted by permission of Time Out

Extract from *Lost in Translation* by Eva Hoffman reprinted by permission of
The Random House Group Ltd.,

Extract from the article 'Scan this book' by Kevin Kelly, published in The
New York Times Magazine. Used by permission

Quote from Hari Kunzru from *1000 Books to Change Your life* Time Out Guides
2007 reprinted by permission of Time Out

Extract from *Island* by Alistair MacLeod, published by Jonathan Cape / Vintage.
Reprinted by permission of The Random House Group Ltd., and by McClelland &
Stewart

Poem 'The Cyclist' from *Collected Poems* by Louis MacNeice. Reproduced by
permission of David Higham Literary Agents.

Extract from *The Levant Trilogy* by Olivia Manning used by permission of
David Higham

Extract from *Dreams of Trespass : Tales of a Harem Girlhood* by Fatima Mernissi
reprinted by permission of Edite Kroll Literary Agency and The Copyright
Clearance Center, USA

Extract from *Star of the Sea* by Joseph O'Connor, published by Secker & Warburg,
reprinted by permission of The Random House Group Ltd.,

Extract from 'A Hanging' from *A Collection of Essays* by George Orwell, (Copyright
© George Orwell, 1931). Reprinted by permission of Bill Hamilton as the Literary
Executor of the Estate of the Late Sonia Brownell Orwell and Secker & Warburg Ltd.

Extract from *Down and Out in Paris and London* by George Orwell, (Copyright
© George Orwell, 1933). Reprinted by permission of Bill Hamilton as the Literary
Execution of the Estate of the Late Sonia Brownell Orwell and Secker & Warburg Ltd.

Extract from 'Marrakech' taken from *A Collection of Essays* by George Orwell,
Copyright © George Orwell, 1939). Reprinted by permission of Bill Hamilton as
the Literary Executor of the Estate of the Late Sonia Brownell Orwell and Secker
& Warburg Ltd.

Extract from *Walsh* by Sharon Pollock reprinted by permission of Talon Books

Extract from Round Tehran from *Passenger to Tehran* by Vita Sackville-West ©
Estate of Vita Sackville-West reprinted by arrangement with Curtis Brown Group Ltd

Poem 'To the Desert' by Benjamin Alire Sáenz reproduced by kind permission of
the author;

"Baked Mud." by Juan Jose Saer translated by Sergio Waisman. First published
in *Words Without Borders: The World Through the Eyes of Writers*, edited by
Samantha Schnee, Alane Salierno Mason, and Dedi Felman. Published 2007 by
Anchor Books, a division of Random House. Copyright 2007 by Samantha Schnee,
Alane Salierno Mason, and Dedi Felman. Reprinted with the permission of Words
without Borders. All rights reserved.

Extract from *The Last Happy Occasion* by Alan Shapiro reprinted by permission of
the author

Poem 'Frogs' from *At the End of the Road* © 1963 by Louis Simpson reprinted by
permission of Wesleyan University Press

Extract from The Coast of Incense by Freya Stark, published by John Murray
Books. Reproduced by permission of John Murray.

Poem 'Question' by May Swenson reprinted by permission of the Literary Estate of
May Swenson. All rights reserved.

Extract from *The Unfinished Game* by Goli Taraghi translated by Zara Houshmand.
First published in *Words Without Borders: The World Through the Eyes of
Writers*, edited by Samantha Schnee, Alane Salierno Mason, and Dedi Felman.
Published 2007 by Anchor Books, a division of Random House. Copyright 2007 by
Samantha Schnee, Alane Salierno Mason, and Dedi Felman. Reprinted with the
permission of Words without Borders. All rights reserved.

Poem 'Artichoke' from *The Flying Change* by Henry Taylor reprinted by
permission of the Louisiana State University Press

Adapted poems 'The Second Coming' and 'The Wild Swans at Coole' by W B Yeats
from *Collected Poems* by W B Yeats reprinted by permission of A P Watt Ltd on
behalf of Gráinne Yeats

Extract from *The Common Reader: Second Series* by Virginia Woolf. Reprinted by
permission of the Society of Authors as the Literary Representatives of the Estate
of Virginia Woolf.

Cover: Autumn Leaves, 2005 (w/c on paper), Wolstenholme, Jonathan(b.1950)
(Contemporary Artist)/Private Collection/© Portal Painters/The Bridgeman Art
Library P7: Bernard Schoenbaum/The Cartoon Bank; P8: Billy Faulkner/Bigstock;
P10: Kurt/Dreamstime.com; P11t: The Mad Hatter's Tea Party, illustration from
'Alice's Adventures in Wonderland', by Lewis Carroll, 1865 (engraving)(b&w photo),
Tenniel, John (1820-1914)/Private Collectio /The Bridgeman Art Library; P11b:
Andy Goldsworthy/Thames and Hudson; P12: Joanna Jones; P16: Stage Fright by
Matthew Wetzler, http://thewmatt.com/; P18: Quentin Blake; P21: Christopher
Felver/Corbis; P23: Nostalgia/Getty Images; P28t: Ronald Grant Archive/Mary Evans
Picture Library; P28m: © Faber and Faber; P28b: SuperStock/Photolibrary; P30t:
Mary Evans Picture Library; P30b: SNAP/Rex Features; P34: Calvin & Hobbes; P35:
© 2011. Universal Uclick; P37: Sutton-Hibbert/Rex Features; P43: Max Palmer/Alamy;
P48: Photos 12/Alamy; P51: Paul Souders/Corbis; P57: Patrakov Fedor/Shutterstock;
P64: Nacivet/Photographer's Choice; P70: Ingram Publishing/Alamy; P79t: DBurke/
Alamy; P79b: Bettmann/Corbis; P83: OUP/Corbis/Digital Stock; P85: Brooks Kraft/
Sygma/Corbis; P89t: B Christopher/Alamy; P89b: © 1995 - 2011 Penguin Books
Ltd; P92: The Ronald Grant Archive; P99: The Print Collector/Photolibrary; P100:
Donald Cooper/Photostage; P101: Robbie Jack/Corbis; P113: Knopf Doubleday
Publishing Group; P114: The Ronald Grant Archive; P115: Everett Collection/
Rex Features; P116t Capital Pictures; P116m: c.CW Network/Everett/Rex Features;
P116b: Sophie Bassouls/Sygma/Corbis; P118: The Ronald Grant Archive; P122-124:
Alex McBride; P127t: Hiroshi Ichikawa/Dreamstime; P127b: Robert Fried/Alamy;
P129: The House by the Railroad, 1925 (oil on canvas), Hopper, Edward (1882-
1967)/Museum of Modern Art, New York, USA/The Bridgeman Art Library; P130:
Vintage Books; P131t: Librairie Artheme Fayard; P131b: Jose Olympio Editora; P132:
Sutton-Hibbert/Rex Features; P142l: Saul Steinberg/The Cartoon Bank; P142m:
Saul Steinberg/The Cartoon Bank; P142r: Saul Steinberg/The Cartoon Bank; P148t:
Juniors Bildarchiv/Alamy; P148b: Redmond Durrell/Alamy; P157: James Steidl/
Istockphoto; P166: Lance Bellers/Istockphoto; P171: John Janssen/Istockphoto; P177:
Zack Blanton/iStockphoto; P179-180: Diane Ackerman/The New York Times; P194t:
Blickwinkel/Alamy; P194b: Lessing J. Rosenwald Collection, Library of Congress.
Copyright © 2010 William Blake Archive. Used with permission; P195: Oscar
White/Corbis; P198: © 2008 The Pennsylvania Academy Of The Fine Arts; P199:
Guilherme Ferraz; P203: Marc Fischer/iStockphoto; P214l-r: Albright-Knox Art
Gallery/Corbis; The Print Collector/Photolibrary, Saluum, Self portait as a martyr,
c.1615 (oil on panel), Gentileschi, Artemisia (1597-c.1651)/Private Collection/
The Bridgeman Art Library; P215: Superstock/Getty Images; P226: Holdeneye/
Shutterstock; P228l: FPG/Taxi/Getty Images; P228r: Mary Evans Picture Library/
Photolibrary; P241: Serdar Tibet/Dreamstime; P249: Andrea Poole/Dreamstime;
P254: Rosie Brooks/Cartoonstock.com; P255t: Chepko Danil Vitalevich/Shutterstock;
P255b: Fancy/Alamy.

Course Companion definition

The IB Diploma Programme Course Companions are resource materials designed to support students throughout their two-year Diploma Programme course of study in a particular subject. They will help students gain an understanding of what is expected from the study of an IB Diploma Programme subject while presenting content in a way that illustrates the purpose and aims of the IB. They reflect the philosophy and approach of the IB and encourage a deep understanding of each subject by making connections to wider issues and providing opportunities for critical thinking.

The books mirror the IB philosophy of viewing the curriculum in terms of a whole-course approach; the use of a wide range of resources, international mindedness, the IB learner profile and the IB Diploma Programme core requirements, theory of knowledge, the extended essay, and creativity, action, service (CAS).

Each book can be used in conjunction with other materials and indeed, students of the IB are required and encouraged to draw conclusions from a variety of resources. Suggestions for additional and further reading are given in each book and suggestions for how to extend research are provided.

In addition, the Course Companions provide advice and guidance on the specific course assessment requirements and on academic honesty protocol. They are distinctive and authoritative without being prescriptive.

IB mission statement

The International Baccalaureate aims to develop inquiring, knowledgable and caring young people who help to create a better and more peaceful world through intercultural understanding and respect.

To this end the IB works with schools, governments and international organizations to develop challenging programmes of international education and rigorous assessment.

These programmes encourage students across the world to become active, compassionate, and lifelong learners who understand that other people, with their differences, can also be right.

The IB learner profile

The aim of all IB programmes is to develop internationally minded people who, recognizing their common humanity and shared guardianship of the planet, help to create a better and more peaceful world. IB learners strive to be:

Inquirers   They develop their natural curiosity. They acquire the skills necessary to conduct inquiry and research and show independence in learning. They actively enjoy learning and this love of learning will be sustained throughout their lives.

Knowledgable   They explore concepts, ideas, and issues that have local and global significance. In so doing, they acquire in-depth knowledge and develop understanding across a broad and balanced range of disciplines.

Thinkers   They exercise initiative in applying thinking skills critically and creatively to recognize and approach complex problems, and make reasoned, ethical decisions.

Communicators   They understand and express ideas and information confidently and creatively in more than one language and in a variety of modes of communication. They work effectively and willingly in collaboration with others.

Principled   They act with integrity and honesty, with a strong sense of fairness, justice, and respect for the dignity of the individual, groups, and communities. They take responsibility for their own actions and the consequences that accompany them.

Open-minded   They understand and appreciate their own cultures and personal histories, and are open to the perspectives, values, and traditions of other individuals and communities. They are accustomed to seeking and evaluating a range of points of view, and are willing to grow from the experience.

Caring   They show empathy, compassion, and respect towards the needs and feelings of others. They have a personal commitment to service, and act to make a positive difference to the lives of others and to the environment.

Risk-takers   They approach unfamiliar situations and uncertainty with courage and forethought, and have the independence of spirit to explore new roles, ideas, and strategies. They are brave and articulate in defending their beliefs.

Balanced   They understand the importance of intellectual, physical, and emotional balance to achieve personal well-being for themselves and others.

Reflective   They give thoughtful consideration to their own learning and experience. They are able to assess and understand their strengths and limitations in order to support their learning and personal development.

A note on academic honesty

It is of vital importance to acknowledge and appropriately credit the owners of information when that information is used in your work. After all, owners of ideas (intellectual property) have property rights. To have an authentic piece of work, it must be based on your individual and original ideas with the work of others fully acknowledged. Therefore, all assignments, written or oral, completed for assessment must use your own language and expression. Where sources are used or referred to, whether in the form of direct quotation or paraphrase, such sources must be appropriately acknowledged.

How do I acknowledge the work of others?
The way that you acknowledge that you have used the ideas of other people is through the use of footnotes and bibliographies.

Footnotes   (placed at the bottom of a page) or endnotes (placed at the end of a document) are to be provided when you quote or paraphrase from another document, or closely summarize the information provided in another document. You do not need to provide a footnote for information that is part of a 'body of knowledge'. That is, definitions do not need to be footnoted as they are part of the assumed knowledge.

Bibliographies   should include a formal list of the resources that you used in your work. 'Formal' means that you should use one of the several accepted forms of presentation. This usually involves separating the resources that you use into different categories (e.g. books, magazines, newspaper articles, Internet-based resources, CDs and works of art) and providing full information as to how a reader or viewer of your work can find the same information. A bibliography is compulsory in the extended essay.

What constitutes malpractice?
Malpractice is behaviour that results in, or may result in, you or any student gaining an unfair advantage in one or more assessment component. Malpractice includes plagiarism and collusion.

Plagiarism is defined as the representation of the ideas or work of another person as your own. The following are some of the ways to avoid plagiarism:

- Words and ideas of another person used to support one's arguments must be acknowledged.
- Passages that are quoted verbatim must be enclosed within quotation marks and acknowledged.
- CD-ROMs, email messages, web sites on the Internet, and any other electronic media must

be treated in the same way as books and journals.

- The sources of all photographs, maps, illustrations, computer programs, data, graphs, audio-visual, and similar material must be acknowledged if they are not your own work.
- Works of art, whether music, film, dance, theatre arts, or visual arts, and where the creative use of a part of a work takes place, must be acknowledged.

Collusion is defined as supporting malpractice by another student. This includes:

- allowing your work to be copied or submitted for assessment by another student
- duplicating work for different assessment components and/or diploma requirements.

Other forms of malpractice include any action that gives you an unfair advantage or affects the results of another student. Examples include, taking unauthorized material into an examination room, misconduct during an examination, and falsifying a CAS record.

About the authors

Hannah Tyson teaches English at the United World College in Montezuma, NM. She has participated in the revisions of the courses in English A and is the faculty member for the IB Online Curriculum Center. Her special interest in the current course is literature in translation. She is a senior examiner and moderator, as well as an online and live workshop leader.

Mark Beverley currently teaches English and theory of knowledge at Sevenoaks School in the UK, having recently returned from 11 years (8 of those as Head of English Department) at the United World College of South East Asia. He is an examiner, Paper Setter and workshop leader for *Language A: literature* and, with Hannah Tyson, has recently led the online training in the new course.

Contents

Introduction

The aim of this book is to provide support for students studying the Language A: Literature program in English, either at standard or higher level. It will take you through the various course components, exploring the requirements of each one in turn, provide an introduction to the different kinds of literary works you will encounter, as well as highlight the types of skills ultimately being assessed. There are many examples of student writing alongside comments and advice from examiners, and it is packed with activities that will develop good practice. The book *does not* seek to prescribe formulae that guarantee success. What it *does* is draw attention to the kinds of techniques and approaches that are the hallmarks of successful students.

Literature presents us with different ways of seeing the world, and in a connected sense the Language A: Literature course invites response from you in a variety of ways. As you might well expect, you will be called upon to speak, listen and write about literary works, but perhaps more importantly, you will be asked to *think* about them – what they are about, how they work and what significance they have in the world. In this sense the course will highlight many points of connection with theory of knowledge, and this book makes use of those connections as it goes along. It also offers guidance on the extended essay and places emphasis on the importance of *international-mindedness* through examples of works from other cultures and traditions.

Fundamentally, the Language A: Literature course asks you to engage *actively* with the literature you will encounter, to embrace a working methodology that highlights independence of thought and creative, imaginative analysis of traditional and modern literary works. It is perhaps with this spirit in mind that much of the book has been written. Our hope is that as a course companion it will help you 'see' literary works in a slightly clearer light. In this respect, it is very much concerned with demands of the IB, but it also aims to provide a broader preparation for successful reading, writing, speaking and listening in university courses and beyond.

1 Nine propositions about reading

Objectives
- to orient you to some of the values and approaches that you will find in this book
- to spur your interest in wide and critical reading of the kinds of literary works appropriate to this stage of your education

This introductory unit is meant to engage you in some collaborative 'play'. This word is not just meant as a kind of cover for what is essentially 'work'. The National Institute for Play proposes that play "shapes our brains, creates our competencies, and ballasts our emotions". As we examine some proposals about reading in this chapter, and then about writing in Chapter 2, we would like to look at these familiar parts of our schooling in a new light: the play that "sculpts our brains… makes us smarter and more adaptable" (National Institute for Play, http://www.nifplay.org/vision.html).

So we begin the collaboration by throwing out some ideas to you about reading, asking you to take them on board, wrestle with them and follow some activities that question them and see what they have to say.

"Now you're probably all asking yourselves, 'Why must I learn to read and write?'"

Reading, in its many forms

While you have the luxury of being a student, it's a good time to consider what reading involves: how it can challenge you, change you, and make you a person who is interesting to converse with… even find a partner and certainly a circle of friends at different points in your life.

On the following pages are nine proposals about reading that might make you think more widely or deeply about reading; you are invited to examine them, argue with them, and refine them. They are not 'truths' but proposals.

Proposition 1: there are two kinds of reading
At the very least, here is one way to classify reading:

- Everyday reading.
- Artful reading.

In his DVD course *The Art of Reading* (The Teaching Company, 2009), Professor Timothy Spurgin makes this useful distinction between types of reading. He describes 'everyday reading' as the kind of reading we do in our daily life to acquire information, follow instructions, get directions, see what's going on in the world: what we find in news reports, recipes, emails, blogs and tweets.

Some of the reading we will do in this course will involve everyday kind of reading – in fact, this book itself is that kind of reading. It will provide answers to the following questions:

- What's this course about?
- What is the course asking me to do?
- How will I get my marks for the course?
- What kind of work have other students done?
- How have examiners responded to students' work?

'Artful reading' is not quite the same thing. In fact, it can be very different from everyday reading and that may possibly be the very reason for its existence: to provide us with something that takes us beyond the 'everyday'.

Professor Spurgin cites some of the differences; artful reading is:

- reading to encounter things we have not yet or may not experience. For example, what would it be like to be stranded on a desert island with only a group of our peers, male, as in *The Lord of the Flies* or female as in *John Dollar*?
- reading to become aware of words themselves and their potential. What difference from our everyday words do we see in the first part of W. B. Yeats' poem 'The Second Coming'?

The Second Coming

Turning and turning in the widening gyre
The falcon cannot hear the falconer;
Things fall apart; the centre cannot hold;
Mere anarchy is loosed upon the world,
The blood-dimmed tide is loosed,…

W. B. Yeats

To these purposes, we can add:

- reading to compare to or understand our own experiences through those of others; how similar or different is your experience to that of Holden Caulfield of *The Catcher in the Rye* or to anyone in the Harry Potter books?

- reading to escape from our immediate surroundings, to enter other worlds or to participate in imagining them as in *Ender's Game*.

Maryanne Wolf in *Proust and the Squid: The Story and Science of the Reading Brain* offers some interesting ideas about humans reading. She talks about reading as a remarkable invention, something that is neither a necessity nor a natural evolution. "We were never born to read," says Wolf. She also argues that reading can cause a rewiring of the brain (Wolf 2007). On the other hand, Nicolas Carr and others are quite concerned that our habit of skimming and our "hyperactive online habits" are doing damage to our mental faculties (quoted by Patrick Kingsley, *The Guardian*, 15 July 2010). These issues are discussed further on pages 14–15.

Proposition 2: there are some special aspects about artful reading and probably some special skills connected to it

One of the features about artful or aesthetic writing and artful reading that you are already familiar with, if not especially aware of, is that there is more going on than the delivery of information.

So we could ask how do we artfully read things that are artfully written? We are talking, of course, about poetry, novels, plays, short stories, as well as travel narratives, essays, autobiographies and even letters.

Artful reading could be said to be reading that listens to words in several ways:

- first, to hear the **content** created by the words, such as the imaginary lives and events of the novel, the tragic choices or comic sequence of events of plays, the impressions of human feeling in poems.

- second, to hear the **molding of words and their music**, to find words used in new ways, in eye- and ear-catching ways; to be able to hear "the brightness of the present tense" (Corrado Minardi) or the music of the "still unravished bride of quietness / Thou foster child of silence and slow time" (John Keats, 'Ode on a Grecian Urn').

- third, to listen for what Charles Baxter calls "the half-noticed and the half-heard," the meanings that are playing beneath the words. Students often talk about this aspect of writing and reading as "the deeper meaning", but the more sophisticated term today is "the subtext". Baxter also calls this "the realm of what haunts the imagination: the implied, the half-visible, the unspoken" (Baxter 2007).

To open yourself to all of these levels will equip you quite well to become an 'artful reader'. When you set yourself to read the words and hear the words and speak the words, you begin to evolve towards the adult reader that we hope you will become.

Proposition 3: there are reasons why there are so many bookstores, varieties of e-book devices and readers who read these artful kinds of writing

If you were one of the many lucky children who were read to before they could read on their own, you probably value the memory of reading aloud and of being read to. Many people continue to extend that experience by listening to audio books. It's not by accident that people like to write (sometimes artfully) about their memories of books and being read to early in their lives and learning to read. Sven Birkert has written a book with a title worth thinking about. It's called *The Gutenberg Elegies: The Fate of Reading in an Electronic Age*. In it, Birkert writes:

From the time of earliest childhood, I was enthralled by books. First, just by their material mysteries. I studied the pages of print and illustration, stared myself into the wells of fantasy that are the hallmark of the awakening inner life. Mostly there was pleasure, but not always. I remember a true paralytic terror brought on by the cartoon Dalmatians pictured on the endpapers of my Golden Books. For a time

I refused to be alone in the room with the books, even when the covers were safely closed… But that was the exception… A page was a field studded with tantalizing signs and a book was a vast play structure riddled with openings and crevices I could get inside…

Birkert, S. 1994. *The Gutenberg Elegies: The Fate of Reading in an Electronic Age.*

Whatever may happen to the 'fate of reading', it seems that books, reading and readers may be around for a while. What do you think?

Activity

All of us are likely to have some memory of being read to or learning to read – or a reason why we don't remember. After making a list with your class of some of the earliest books you encountered, write a short piece about one aspect or memory. Try to give it as much individuality as Birkert does in his account.

Proposition 4: reading books can change your life

In spite of the fact that this statement seems like the worst of easy platitudes, there are many people who claim that reading a particular book 'changed their life', so many of them in fact that in 2007 Time Out Guides published a book called *1000 Books to Change Your Life*. Quite a lot of people were willing to tell the publishers about reading that had had this dynamic effect. A good many of these books would come under the category of what we have called here 'artful reading' (or, in our case, IB reading).

Here is what Hari Kunzru, a novelist himself, has to say about his reading of a long and complicated novel called *Gravity's Rainbow*:

This is the one, the paperback that is held together with tape and probably won't stand another reading; this enormous novel about the chaos of the last days of World War II, with its weird concerns about pigs and bananas and plastics manufacture, its occult structure, its hokey songs, disconcerting scope and flagrant disregard for literary taste. *Gravity's Rainbow* is a book dumb enough to call a German spa town Bad Karma and clever enough to induce in me, as a 19-year-old would-be writer, a sense of quasi-religious awe that I find slightly embarrassing now, if only because it's not really gone away. After I first read it, I decided most of my considerable problems would be solved if only I could learn to make something as pleasurable and complex as this book. It made me abandon most of the other options I was considering to make the time pass, which in retrospect was a good thing.

Time Out Guides. 2007. *1000 Books to Change Your Life.*

Getting back to first experiences with books and reading, here is Jasper Fforde's recollection of encountering the two books about Alice by Lewis Carroll. Here, he touches not only on life-changing through books, but two other significant elements of personal reading: the first encounter with reading and the later pleasures of re-reading.

Learning to read, like learning to walk and talk, is one of life's Great Expanders. I can remember acquiring this skill, and also the realization that this was something pretty important. I set about finding a book in my parent's library to flex this newly found power. I didn't want the boring stuff that grown-ups read, but a proper book, with chapters, dialogue and pictures. And there it was – *The Complete Alice*. I fell into the books and was immediately dazzled by the virtuosity of the nonsense and the humorous warmth that runs through the pages – from the Red Queen to the Cheshire Cat to the *Jabberwocky*, possibly the finest piece of nonsense poetry ever written… a decade or two later… I discovered to my amazement that the books had changed. Yes, the old stuff I remembered was there, but there was something else. Something new, subtle, clever and wonderful, hovering in the shadow of the subtext – puzzles of logic, physics and metalanguage. I can't think of a book that has influenced me more. Not simply as an author but as a person: the value of humour, the boundlessness of the human imagination and how rich life's experience can be, as long as one is willing to look – and be receptive enough to notice it when you find it. I still have that same volume in my library today, and do you know, I think it's still changing.

Time Out Guides. 2007. *1000 Books to Change Your Life.*

Activity

Write a short piece about a book that changed your life in some way.

Proposition 5: 'analysis' in relation to 'artful reading' is not an ugly word

Often, students complain about what they see as one of the primary activities of English classes: **the analysis of artful reading**. Words students may apply to this activity, often with disgust, are 'dissecting' and 'picking apart'. Well, there is perhaps some truth to these descriptions, but looking at the bigger picture sometimes makes the smaller elements of it more reasonable and easily understood.

Sometimes the best analogy or comparison to use when trying to rationalize the close reading or analysis of artful texts is to look at visual artists at work. Often, we feel more spontaneous about responding to visual art than to texts.

Here is both an illustration of a work and a comment on the shaping of the work by the artist, Andy Goldsworthy, who shapes and plays with natural objects, turning them into artful constructions. Goldsworthy's work, in installations around the world, often includes snake-like images or extensions of the natural forms. In the one opposite, constructed as a part of the 100th anniversary celebration of the Dutch Forestry Commission in 1999, first look at the images, play with some ideas about the interaction of the natural and the handmade, and then read what Goldsworthy has to say about his pieces.

Goldsworthy writes:

> There is so much to this place that I can't see. Trees that I cannot find and places that I do not know. I cannot explain what I am looking for, but feel there is something here.
>
> Seven days may not be enough to get anywhere close to it (Tuesday 16 March).
>
> Worked among the dunes in the woods; white holes in the dark woods… I found two large birch trees growing together. The trees may even grow below ground and be the same tree. I extended the forms of the trunks into, and then along, the surface of the sand. I enjoyed making this piece and have never worked with sand so connected to trees, taking form, energy and movement from the trunks (Wednesday, 17 March).
>
> Goldsworthy, A. 2000. *Time*.

Activity

How did reading about Goldsworthy's intentions and feelings affect your response to his work? Could you have made some conjectures about what the artist was intrigued by or trying to express without his help?

In most of our viewing of visual art, we do not have such access, and yet we can appreciate both the parts as well as the whole, and often can express the reasons why we respond as we do.

Now look at the painting opposite for which we have provided no comment. Compare your two responses and your perceptions of what might be beautiful, intriguing or satisfying. Do you think a work of visual art can be 'life-changing' in the way a piece of writing might change your life?

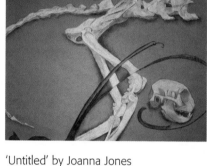

'Untitled' by Joanna Jones

We don't know what ideas or feelings Jones was trying to convey, but it's possible you were willing to make some proposals, both about what the artist had on her mind and in her eye, and what aspects you appreciate or have some feelings about. We are equally free to make such conjectures about writing, even when we have no guidance from the writer about what they were thinking or wanting to articulate. Often this initial response evolves into some close analysis of style, technique, or overall impact, or how the work connects with other things we have seen or like.

Usually when we talk about literature – when we analyse – we have no access to what the writer intended, but occasionally we do.

Activity

Compare your responses to the two poems that follow; in the first case, the poet has given us some clues, but in the second we have only the words of the poem.

The first poem is by Jane Kenyon, an American poet:

> **Once There Was Light**
>
> Once, in my early thirties, I saw
> that I was a speck of light in the great
> river of light that undulates through time.

I was floating with the whole
human family. We were all colors – those
who are living now, those who have died,
those who are not yet born. For a few

moments I floated, completely calm,
and I no longer hated having to exist.

Like a crow who smells hot blood
you came flying to pull me out
of the glowing stream.
"I'll hold you up, I never let my dear
ones drown!" After that, I wept for days.

Jane Kenyon

In an interview, Kenyon talks about the origins of the poem:

I really had a vision of that once. It was like a waking dream.

My eyes were open and I saw these rooms, this house, but in my mind's eye, or whatever language you can find to say these things, I also saw a great ribbon of light and every human life was suspended. There was no struggle. There was only this buoyant shimmering, undulating stream of light. I took my place in this stream and after that my life changed fundamentally. I relaxed into existence in a way that I never had before.

Kenyon, J. 1999. *A Hundred White Daffodils*.

A bit later, when asked about the end of the poem, Kenyon indicates that the image at the end of the poem, however, stands for the depression with which she had struggled throughout life.

Now consider this second poem without any addition of comment from the poet:

To the Desert

I came to you one rainless August night.
You taught me how to live without the rain.
You are thirst and thirst is all I know.
You are sand, wind, sun, and burning sky,
The hottest blue. You blow a breeze and brand
Your breath into my mouth. You reach – then *bend*
Your force, to break, blow, burn, and make me new.
You wrap your name tight around my ribs
And keep me warm. I was born for you.
Above, below, by you, by you surrounded.
I wake to you at dawn. Never break your
Knot. Reach, rise, blow, *Sálvame, mi dios,*
Trágame, mi tierra. Salva, traga*, Break me,
I am bread. I will be the water for your thirst.

*Save me, my God; take me, swallow me, earth. Save me, take me.

Benjamin Alire Sáenz

Do you feel more secure about the way you read and understood the first poem than the second? What do we do about the question of what the author 'intended'? How do we appreciate literary works if we know nothing about the author or the context? Can we, in fact, *really* come to understand the works without help from the writer?

For most aesthetic or artful writing that we will read in this course, we will not have this kind of access: what sort of person did Shakespeare want us to see in Hamlet? Did Chinua Achebe in *Things Fall Apart* support Okonkwo's choices or emphathize with them or condemn them?

Collaborating to interpret, to analyse

What moves Hamlet to take action? What kind of a person is he? Do we find reasons in the text to emphathize with or question Okonkwo's choices? Such questions, if changed a little, can sometimes be best explored if we 'play' with them in collaboration with others. This collaboration will involve looking carefully at the **words**, the **context**, the **structuring** of the **events**, the **response of other readers** and a good many other features as well, especially how the writer has shaped the meaning.

The whole point of the 'analysis', the collaboration, is that we can return to the texts with renewed appreciation of what we are reading. We are not dissecting some hapless dead frog, whose parts, even well identified, cannot be put back together and appreciated in all his 'frogness'. We are able to return to the whole literary work and see it in a new way – that's the whole point of analysis.

Proposition 6: reading alone, and reading with others are the same and different

People who like to read, or think about the human activity of reading, like Maryanne Wolf (see page 8) and those who simply love books, have some interesting ideas connected to reading.

Reading by yourself

Most of us do our reading as a solitary activity and, though we may listen to music at the same time, are usually focused deeply on that reading. Katherine Hayles, a scholar and student of the ways and whys of reading, likes to think about the interface between the past and the present in terms of such things as reading and computer language. She distinguishes two kinds of attention that impact the solitary reading experience.

Hayles makes a distinction between **hyper** and **deep attention** and she sees it as a generational divide. That is, she sees a difference between you, the IB student, and the people who are writing and editing this book.

As you may guess, the shift between generations is one she attributes to the development of "networked and programmable media", which changes the way people who have such access "do business, conduct their social lives, communicate with one another, and – perhaps most significant – think" (Hayles 2007).

When you settle down to read Toni Morrison's *Beloved* or Emily Brontë's *Wuthering Heights* (because a number of chapters are expected for your class tomorrow), you will probably need to be focused on, maybe even 'lost' in, the events of the story. This is what Hayles calls **deep attention**.

However, if you are completing a short piece of reading for a class discussion tomorrow, say just one section of this chapter, you may allow yourself to give attention to it only as one of the "multiple information streams" or tasks that take up your time after the school day: texting or tweeting, checking your email, washing your hair, fixing a snack. This kind of attention is different; Hayles calls it **hyper attention**, and it's not particularly useful if you have a long reading assignment in *Wuthering Heights*.

Clearly, both kinds of attention are important to anyone living in today's environment, but it might be good to think carefully when choosing which kind to use in different activities and parts of your day, and, particularly for this course, how you will apply the ideas to your work (or play) that involves artful reading.

Reading as a social activity

As a student in an actual school setting (and some of you could be doing this course in a distance learning environment), you have a built-in group of readers with whom to collaborate. Even online, you have a group with whom to 'play' in terms of bouncing ideas off each other. In fact, many adult readers who want to talk about books they have read do so online. Some groups are even set up with a simultaneous discussion going on as people read through the book. David Foster Wallace's 1079 page novel, *Infinite Jest,* is just one example of a group set up online so that people can share their ideas. (Perhaps the group functioned as a support group to help everyone get to page 1079?)

As an IB student in this course, you have both immediate and online opportunities to exchange ideas about books, to analyse and play with texts both alone and collaboratively. The more you take advantage of these the more you are likely to learn, or to reassemble the 'frog' with increased appreciation… or turn it into a prince.

Due to the divide between deep attention and hyper attention, and their relation to reading, many people today are so worried about the future of reading that a 'slow reading' movement is growing up. If you have ever heard of the 'slow food' movement (as opposed to the 'fast food' so widely available today), you will hear its echo in this impulse to 'slow reading'. If you are interested in this lively debate, you can find Patrick Kingsley's article at http://www.guardian.co.uk/books/2010/jul/15/slow-reading/print. You can also check the slow reading blog at http://tracyseeley.wordpress.com/.

Social reading is such an integral part of human life that scholars are now beginning to study the phenomenon. One website where people are thinking about what is happening with reading in the present and could happen in the future is The Institute for the Future of the Book: http://www.futureofthebook.org/.

An interesting posting here is called 'The Taxonomy of Social Reading: a proposal' by Bob Stein, which sets up a chart showing all the permutations of reading practice that take place in today's world. If you are interested, you can read his article at: http://futureofthebook.org/social-reading/introduction/. He will very likely publish a book one day about his findings.

Activity

There are a growing number of websites where IB and other students are talking about books, and many where you can join people of all ages in discussing, annotating and sharing ideas about literary works.

As an exploratory exercise, go to http://www.bookglutton.com/ and see how things are organized and shared.

You might want to set up a blog within your class where people can post their results or respond as well as in class about books you are studying and 'analyzing'. Above all, take the opportunity to talk about books with your classmates.

Proposition 7: 'talking' about books requires listening and 'hearing'

> Do you ever get stage fright?

> No, I'm not afraid of the stage. It's the audience that frightens me.

Discussion in your IB class, discussion that often centers on what the class is reading, is likely to happen almost every day. Whether or not this is really collaborative depends a lot on you.

Some people feel very at home in class discussions; some do not. Some of us are ready to comment at almost every opportunity; some prefer to listen. All positions are respected in a good collaborative classroom, and for some people speaking up in a discussion doesn't resemble their idea of 'play', but is closer to the anxiety of stage fright.

However, if everyone is to contribute to your group's success in the IB assessment, everyone needs to work at speaking, listening and really hearing. The best way for everyone to 'read' well is for everyone to make a contribution.

Proposition 8: we need to learn the language people use when talking about artful reading

David Lodge, a novelist and a writer about literature, has produced a very enjoyable and informative book about fiction called *The Art of Fiction* (1992). In short and lively chapters, he talks about particular features of fiction, usually just one, and how it appears in that writer's work. If, however, you look at the Contents, you will see that there is a certain kind of language involved in 'literary talk'. Here are the first entries:

- Beginnings
- The Intrusive Author
- Suspense
- Teenage *Skaz* (Holden Caulfield!)
- The Epistolary Novel
- Point of View

As you can see, there are some terms here that you might need to investigate or learn more about.

If you are going to carry out interesting conversations about reading, and if you are going to succeed in this IB literature course, you will need to acquire a working vocabulary of at least some of these terms – the conventional vocabulary used to identify, compare and closely analyse literary works.

A special point about proposition 7:

This IB course puts a high value on students being able to talk about what they have read or are reading. You will have two assessments that involve you as a speaker and even more often as a listener.

These are two oral assessments: a presentation to the whole class and an individual oral commentary, which at higher level is focused on poetry followed by an interview with your teacher about another work.

Both students who are traditionally eager speakers and those who are reluctant speakers need to use the classroom exchanges to practise for these assessments. The first group needs to slow down a little and listen more, and the second group needs to hear themselves speaking aloud about literature.

Activity

Below are a few assorted sentences from other writers talking about "books that changed my life".

a Pick out the literary terms that you recognize and compare them with the words other people in your class would have chosen to say.

b Can you offer definitions of these literary terms?

c Some of the terms may be familiar, but can you precisely define or paraphrase these writers' views of other writers in the following selections?

i Of Murakami's *South of the Border, West of the Sun*, Julie Myerson writes: "I am haunted by this novel. It's told in an apparently passive, reasonable, deadpan prose, yet it's one of the most emotionally shattering things I've ever read. It has all the stillness and lyricism of a poem…"

Time Out Guides. 2007. *1000 Books to Change Your Life.*

ii Andrew O'Hagan finds Fitzgerald's *The Great Gatsby* "a perfect marriage of style and subject." He says, "Like the best tragedies, *The Great Gatsby* is also a romance…"

Time Out Guides. 2007. *1000 Books to Change Your Life.*

iii Talking about Raymond Carver's short stories, Will Napier immediately identifies the attraction: "It's the conversational tone of the narrative that gets me."

Time Out Guides. 2007. *1000 Books to Change Your Life.*

Working with terms in the IB guide to the course will, hopefully, increase your fluency with 'literary talk' and make you an even better reader. As an added benefit, you will certainly improve the way you write about literature.

Proposition 9: artful reading demands a wide-angle lens

Our final proposition takes in a great deal, and the wide-angle lens of a camera is used to suggest this.

Firstly, we need to think about the text itself and about ourselves in relation to the text as deeply and widely as we can. We sometimes need to widen our lens to consider the following:

● Where am I in relation to this piece of artful writing in terms of time, space, gender, ethnicity, class and other elements that define and shape both myself and the text?

● How many ways can we read this text? Are there layers of meaning we may not see at first reading: issues of power, class and politics, for example?

● How do I hear the author's attitude to what's in the text?

For example, will you and I understand the following poem by Gwendolyn Brooks, written around 1960, in the same way if I am a white female lawyer working in Paris today and you are an African-American male student in Atlanta, Georgia or a Chinese female student in an IB classroom in Singapore?

We Real Cool

The Pool Players
Seven at the Golden Shovel

We real cool. We
Left school. We

Lurk late. We
Strike straight. We

Sing sin. We
Thin gin. We

Jazz June. We
Die soon.

Gwendolyn Brooks

Secondly, we need to recognize that this IB literature course will ask us to venture into the larger world of reading by including some works of literature that are part of the literary traditions of places and language traditions that are different to our own.

The Rights of the Reader
by Daniel Pennac
illustrated by Quentin Blake

1 The right not to read.
2 The right to skip.
3 The right not to finish a book.
4 The right to read it again.
5 The right to read anything.
6 The right to mistake a book for real life.
7 The right to read anywhere.
8 The right to dip in.
9 The right to read out loud.
10 The right to be quiet.

Activity

What works have you read that come from language traditions other than English? Can you think of attitudes that affect your reading from the wider world? Unit 3 considers these issues in more depth.

Another thought about reading:

The French novelist Daniel Penac believes that you, as a reader, have some rights. What do you think about his ideas? Do you as readers in this IB literature course have rights? Or is this just a fanciful notion demonstrated in Quentin Blake's illustration?

This reading will widen the angle of vision even further. We will need to adopt an attitude of both openness and curiosity, a practice of investigation and adaptation.

The connections of your English course to your theory of knowledge course

One aspect of your English A literature course that will emerge as you go through this book is the inter-relatedness of two aspects of your IB curriculum: your English course and your theory of knowledge course.

As in this chapter, you will find exercises at the end of some chapters that ask you to consider these connections. As we have been exploring reading particularly in this chapter, Maryanne Wolf who has written *Proust and the Squid* offers some more interesting ideas:

> …our brain presents a beautiful example of open architecture. Thanks to this design, we come into this world programmed with the capacity to change what is given us by nature so that we can go beyond it… Reading can only be learned because of the brain's plastic design. And when reading takes place, the individual brain is forever changed, both physiologically and intellectually. For example, at the neuronal level, a person who learns to read in Chinese uses a very particular set of neuronal connections that differ in significant ways from the pathways used in reading English.
>
> Wolf, M. 2007. *Proust and the Squid: The Story and Science of the Reading Brain*.

At the end of her book, Wolf quotes Kevin Kelly, who takes us into another area of consideration about reading, now and in the future:

> In the clash between the conventions of the book and the protocols of the screen, the screen will prevail. On this screen, now visible to one billion people on earth, the technology of the search will transform isolated books into the universal library of all human knowledge.
>
> *New York Times* Magazine, 14 May 2006.

In a work called *The Future of the Book,* now almost out of date having been written in 1996, the Italian thinker and writer Umberto Eco, in the 'Afterword', speaks of screens versus books, images versus words. Eco takes the view that though many feared that photographs would displace paintings (and did not) the screen and the book will learn to live together harmoniously, that images and 'alphabetic' culture will both be important parts of human experience, that reading will endure as a significant part of life (Nunberg 1996).

Activity

As your final engagement with the 'play' of ideas about reading, consider some of the following questions:

a What kind of knowledge comes through reading?

b How does the knowledge derived from reading books measure up against other kinds of knowledge: what we gain through sensory perception or what we learn of the actual experience of emotions through events, for example?

c Could we do without the kind of reading we do in books?

d Will books disappear in the future? What kinds of knowledge would be lost, if any?

e Would the disappearance of books make a difference to human development?

19

The Golden Triangle: three vectors for writing with style

> **Objectives**
> - to suggest some useful angles for academic writing in general to highlight some aspects of evaluation that will apply to your writing for the IB programme

Very often, when students who are following the IB literature course are asked what they want to get out of it, their response is "I want to learn to write better". In fact, if you were to ask a successful writer the same question, their answer might very well be similar. Once you get really interested in that question and are sure you are ready to act on your answer, you have embarked on a process that might take up some of your energies for a lifetime.

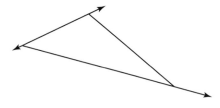

Three vectors

One way to approach an improved writing style that will help you to succeed in this IB literature course is to look at three factors:

1 Voice.

2 Audience.

3 Occasion.

In the simplest terms, if you can develop a lively personal **voice** that takes account of both the **audience** you intend as the receiver(s) or addressee(s) and the particular **occasion** for which you are writing, you will be able to establish a confident foundation that you can continue to develop throughout your life. Of course, all of these features are intertwined in any piece of writing and, although we can give them separate labels, it's not always possible to clearly separate them in a given piece of writing. Still, we can separate them out, theoretically, so that we can direct some attention and effort towards each.

There are almost infinite sources of advice about how to write well. Your teacher should be a major source of instruction and practice; you can also find books of advice, websites for tutoring and instruction.

There is no question that at the very root of an evolution in your writing style is the need to master the technical elements of writing English prose. In the early stages of your IB literature course, it's very likely that some class time will be spent on being sure you have a good grasp of the elements of sentence and paragraph construction, as well as some of the trickier elements of grammar, punctuation and spelling.

In this chapter, however, there is a short synthesis of some broader ideas about writing gathered from people who create and teach IB programmes. In addition, you will find some quotes in the margin that come from a well-known article by the novelist Kurt Vonnegut, in which he talks, in a very straightforward way, about "how to write with style".

> **Six tips from Kurt Vonnegut on writing:**
> 1 Find a subject you care about.
> 2 Do not ramble.
> 3 Keep it simple.
> 4 Have the guts to cut.
> 5 Sound like yourself.
> 6 Say what you mean to say.

Reading: a path to better writing

In spite of the attention we are about to give to developing a voice in your writing, it's important to remind you that *good writing grows out of good reading*. And, yes, good writers learn by reading other good writers.

The reading that you gravitate to may be in fact a kind of unconscious impulse towards the kind of style you would like to develop. So, in fact, your set of 'good writers' may be quite different to that of your friends. You may like Barbara Kingsolver and Douglas Adams and someone else may decide that John Grisham and Malcolm Gladwell make the best reading.

Whatever style you might aspire to, if you want to make your reading a tool for improving your writing, then you need to move into a more analytical mode; you need to re-read, and study how your writer chooses words and makes sentences out of them. You need to see how they open a piece and how they close, and also how they sustain a reader's interest along the way. There are many small and large elements of a good writing style; these are only a few.

"Why should you examine your writing style with the idea of improving it? Do so as a mark of respect for your readers, whatever you're writing. If you scribble your thoughts any which way, your readers will surely feel that you care nothing about them."
Kurt Vonnegut

Kurt Vonnegut

Activity

One of the tried and true ways that many prose writers have learned to write like the 'greats' is to engage in exercises that involve imitation. While doing this sort of exercise may seem like minute and trying work, it can also be viewed as quite a creative and challenging endeavour.

1 Read carefully through the two short extracts that follow, one by Henry James and one by Cormac McCarthy. Choosing either or both, change the subject and write about it imitating the style of the original. In order to become closely familiar with the prose style of these two very different stylists, you must:

- write about *your* subject (try to choose something quite different)
- follow the exact placement of words and the very same sentence structure
- where there is a noun, substitute your own noun; where there are several clauses, or where there is a simple sentence, you must imitate these also
- end up with exactly the same number of words as the original.

2 As a second version of the same exercise, try doing the same with a writer whom you admire. You may discover that there is a great deal more to a writer's stylistic choices than first meets the eye.

The Beast in the Jungle

He had thought himself, as long as nobody knew, the most disinterested person in the world, carrying his concentrated burden, his perpetual suspense, ever so quietly, holding his tongue about it, giving others no glimpse of it nor of its effect upon his life, asking of them no allowance, and only making on his side all those that were asked.

He hadn't disturbed people with the queerness of having to know a haunted man, though he had moments of rather special temptation on hearing them say they were forsooth "unsettled."

Henry James

The Big Two-Hearted River

He came down a hillside covered with stumps into a meadow. At the edge of the meadow flowed the river. Nick was glad to get to the river. He walked upstream through the meadow. His trousers were soaked with the dew as he walked. After the hot day, the dew had come quickly and heavily. The river made no sound. It was too fast and smooth. At the edge of the meadow, before he mounted to a piece of high ground to make camp, Nick looked down the river at the trout rising. They were rising to insects come from the swamp on the other side of the stream when the sun went down. The trout jumped out of the water to take them. While Nick walked through the little stretch of meadow alongside the stream, trout had jumped high out of the water. Now as he looked down the river, the insects must be settling on the surface, for the trout were feeding steadily all down the stream. As far down the long stretch as he could see, the trout were rising, making circles all down the surface of the water, as though it were starting to rain.

Ernest Hemingway

Voice in academic writing

What does it mean to develop a personal voice in your academic writing? It's worth considering what a personal voice is not, to help you develop a notion of what it is.

- A personal voice is not scribbling "thoughts any which way".
- A personal voice is not filled with inaccurate uses of words.
- A personal voice does not invent its own rules of grammar, punctuation or spelling.
- A personal voice is not the one you use in your most informal daily conversation.
- A personal voice is not one that is ambiguous and hasty.

What does it take to create a voice that:

- engages the reader and makes that reader want to go on reading what you have written?
- is identifiably yours?

The simple answer is: a great deal of hard work. Some of you will give that aspiration a high priority, and some will not.

Everyone, however, develops a personal voice to some extent, deliberately or not. Think about your emails or your texts: isn't it likely that yours differ from those of other people, that your closest friends might be able to identify what comes from you, partly because of *what* you talk about, but also *how* you talk about it? The same thing can happen with your own academic writing.

Choosing your words, the order in which you arrange them, the choice and variation about how you construct sentences, and the connecting and length of your paragraphs: all of these are or can be deliberate choices you make to deliver your thoughts and feelings in a written form. **Choice** is, in fact, the essence of what is often called **style**. Style is the whole set of choices a writer makes; you can make these with or without a lot of deliberation, but you *will* make choices and one of the outcomes will be the **voice** that you create in your writing.

Activity

Here's an experiment in choosing how to put some words together into several sentences, and perhaps even paragraphs, in your own individual way.

a The following are some words used to describe a setting. Use them to create your description of a setting.

ravines	precipice	red	primeval	crescents
thundering	slushing	caves	roots	wind
green	coast	waves	protruding	decayed
baboons	gullies	eagle	shaped	finding
pockmarked	grotesque	yellow	beaches	

b Compare your work to that of another student and see if you can see differences and similarities; see if you can find some evidence of a particular way of combining words, making sentences and paragraphs – a style, in other words.

c Finally, turn to the end of this chapter on page 27 to see how the writer Andre Brink has actually incorporated all of these words into his two paragraphs from a novel set in his native South Africa.

Whatever voice emerges in your writing, it's important that it is *your* voice. One mistake IB students often make when they are writing their materials for assessment is to try to create or imitate a kind of 'high' voice that they imagine is demanded by serious academic work. In this case, their version of the Little Red Riding Hood story (a famous folktale of a little girl who goes to visit her grandmother and encounters a wolf) would probably look like Russell Baker's version:

Once upon a point in time a small person named Little Red Riding Hood initiated plans for the preparation, delivery and transportation of foodstuffs to her grandmother, a senior citizen residing in a place of residence in a wooded area of indeterminate dimension.

Baker, R. quoted in Adams, M. 1984. *The Writer's Mind: Making Writing Make Sense.*

23

People who try to get students to write successfully in their academic work often talk about some common misconceptions about "how you're supposed to write". In a chapter from their book about argument written for students, *They Say/I Say: The Moves that Matter in Persuasive Writing*, Gerald Graff and Cathy Birkenstein speak of the issue of "writ[ing] effective academic arguments while at the same time holding on to some of your own voice… you may well become turned off from writing if you think your everyday language practices have to be checked at the classroom door."

What most teachers and readers of student writing are hoping to help students develop is a voice that seems 'natural': one that is appropriate to their age and experience. But by 'natural' they do not mean informal or colloquial, although there is certainly room, as these authors observe, for an occasional mix of both the academic and the informal (Gerald Graff & Cathy Birkenstein 2007).

Here's an example of a sentence that combines both, while at the same time talking about our subject, student writing:

"And certainly our noting of errors on student papers gives no one any great joy; as Peter Elbow says, English [the course] is most often associated *either* with grammar or with high literature – two things designed to make folks feel most out of it."

Note the colloquial "out of it". What do you think the intention of the writers is here? Is this an encouragement to plant jargon and colloquial phrases throughout your academic writing? No, but it does acknowledge that a well-chosen colloquial phrase can be acceptable. As new writers producing your IB assessments, it's a good idea to follow that route with great restraint, even to the point of putting the colloquialisms in quotation marks. Use very few, if any, and use them for deliberate purposes. If English is not your first language, be especially careful, as what may seem formal may indeed be considered colloquial by native speakers.

Michael Adams uses a good example in *The Writer's Mind* to make a further point about appropriate voice in your academic writing:

> *"No matter what your first language, you should treasure it all your life. If it happens not to be Standard English, and it shows itself when you write Standard English, the result is usually delightful, like a very pretty girl with one eye that is green and one that is blue."*
>
> Kurt Vonnegut

A student tells me he wants to write a paper on Shakespeare's use of imagery in Sonnet 73. "I noticed that Shakespeare uses a dying fire and falling leaves and fading twilight to suggest his own passing years." And yet when the student writes his paper he talks like this:

"A careful reader of Shakespeare's Sonnet 73 will perceive that the poet carefully articulates his fundamental metaphor by manipulating the integration of images concerning death or dying with his own emotional and intellectual state that is projected onto nature and natural phenomenon."

Adams, M. 1984. *The Writer's Mind: Making Writing Make Sense.*

Adams goes on to point out that, "Such prose impresses no one but the author. Too many people write not to communicate, but to impress – to sound intelligent and well educated. They end up, however, sounding stuffy, pompous and mechanical" (Adams 1984).

Audience

One of the most urgent questions that IB students ask in relation to their writing for their courses is: "What kind of writing (or voice) do my teachers and IB examiners want to 'hear' (or read)?"

Whether or not the question is expressed in exactly those terms, a successful IB student is one who is aware that there are different styles for different audiences. Often, you will hear students make comparative judgments along the lines of:

- "Mr. A wants you to follow this format, or that line of argument and he never wants you to use the word 'quote' instead of 'quotation'…"
- "Ms. B. wants everything lined up in a five-paragraph essay, but she likes a lot of details."

This kind of lore or legend reflects accurately that all of us, as students, are aware of the assumed preferences of our audience when we are writing to meet a demand set by someone else. It is sometimes hard to decide how far an audience should govern our choices about style, but that, of course, is part of developing as an independent thinker (one of the attributes of the learner profile) and writer.

So since the audience for our writing assessments in this course is an unknown person, how do we negotiate the matter of audience?

First of all, examiners are governed by sets of criteria for each piece of assessment that you are going to write. Generally, these criteria focus on:

- the degree of knowledge and understanding that you show about the works you have read
- the appreciation you show for the stylistic choices writers have made in these works and how those choices affect the delivery of their works
- the degree to which you deliver your ideas in a clear and easy-to-follow way
- the quality of the language you use to express your ideas and feelings.

Therefore, examiners have 'rules' that they need to follow. This does not mean that they are likely to be free from personal preferences about styles of writing, but they must not allow these preferences to override the criteria by which your work is to be marked.

All of these criteria, or 'descriptors' as they are sometimes called, will be explored in various ways in the following chapters, but the last two are especially relevant to our discussion of audience.

One criterion is called "Organization" and here are the chief elements of that feature across the assessments:

Ideas are effectively organized, with very good coherence.

What, then, would an examiner – your audience – be looking for in order to give you the marks earned at this level of the criterion, which is the top level?

> *"Sound like yourself. The writing style which is most natural for you is bound to echo the speech you heard when a child. I myself grew up in Indianapolis, where common speech sounds like a bandsaw cutting galvanized tin and employs a vocabulary as unornamental as a monkey wrench… All these varieties of speech are beautiful."*
> Kurt Vonnegut

Activity

It would be very useful for your whole class to arrive at some agreement about how an essay, for example, would demonstrate effective organization and what is meant by "coherence" in an essay. It would also be useful to work on a student essay, maybe one of your own, evaluating these features above all.

Another criterion is called "Language" and that is certainly relevant to our consideration of developing a style that will work for this course.

For top marks in "Language" for this course, the descriptor will be like this:

Language is very clear, effective, carefully chosen and precise, with a high degree of accuracy in grammar, vocabulary and sentence construction; register and style are effective and appropriate to the task.

This is a very rigorous demand, obviously. One unfamiliar word may be "register", but this is really another way of talking about formality and informality in the way you write for these assessments. This descriptor also raises the third factor to be considered in this chapter – occasion.

Occasion

By the time you are a few months into this course you will be aware of two different types of 'occasion' or situation in which you will be asked to write.

On some 'occasions' you will have ample time to plan, draft, and polish your work; on others you will be writing under some time constraints. All the more reason, perhaps, to think through what you would like to have emerge as your particular 'style', the way you speak and the way you address and interest your audience. In the midst of answering an examination paper will not be the time to decide the best way to deliver your ideas.

What is most important about occasion is that you recognize it for what it is. In the case of this IB literature course, the examiner wants to hear:

● how you have grasped and appreciated the works you have read

● how you have thought about these works and can speak about them with some degree of individuality

● how well you have organized your views so that the examiner can easily follow your line of argument

● how correct and precise your language is.

As one final element relating to occasion, it would be good to highlight the word 'argument'. Very often, students fail to see that every one of their written assignments involves a kind of argument. In fact, that 'academic conversation', as they call it, is the central concept in the publication *They Say/I Say: The Moves that Matter in Persuasive Writing* by Graff and Birkenstein. The 'occasion' for all your written assessments in this course is, yes, the 'academic conversation' between you and the examiner.

In your commentary, you are going to argue the reasons why the piece before you is a good piece of writing. In your work in literature in translation, you will argue that a particular literary feature in a work you have studied 'matters', that it represents some conscious choices by the writer and achieves certain effects or purposes. In your Paper 2 essay, you will be arguing that there are interesting comparable features in two works that are worth looking at and these have achieved certain effects.

Everyone likes to read what has been written by a writer who, first, has a clear sense of the audience and the occasion, who is fully focused on what is being put down on the paper, but more than that, even, a writer who seems to enjoy a chance to speak those ideas to an audience – which brings us back to the development of your own personal voice. As examiners will tell you, a lively engaged response can cover a multitude of other minor weaknesses.

An Instant in the Wind
(Original extract by Andre Brink for the activity on page 23.)

The ravines run down to the sea where the continent ends abruptly. Overland, too, one reaches the coast, suddenly finding oneself on the edge of a dark red precipice stained yellow and green with lichen, decayed into grotesque patterns shaped by wind and water, pockmarked by caves; down to the primeval chaos of rocks and protruding tree-roots, and, in between, small crescents of beaches, sand or shingle.

Sound: the deep thundering of the waves against the resplendent rock of the cliffs; the slushing of water though sluices and gullies and tidal caves; the barking of baboons high up on the cliffside among the trees; the piercing scream of a fishing eagle; the screeching of gulls.

Andre Brink

---

3 Close reading as a practice

Objectives

- to understand the importance of close, detailed reading as it applies to various components of the course
- to recognize the role played by analysis and interpretation in the practice of literary commentary
- to explore practical strategies for responding to unseen texts

Some preliminaries

Before we get going on some details in this chapter, it is worth drawing attention to some underlying ideas that will help you to make sense of three important components of the course:

- The unseen literary analysis.
- The individual oral commentary.
- The individual oral presentation.

Whenever you encounter a work of art, whether it is reading literature, seeing a painting, listening to a piece of music or watching a film or theatre performance, something will *happen*. Perhaps you might *feel* something – be moved, excited, confused, bored or made to laugh. Perhaps you might *think* of something – an idea, a memory, a point of comparison. You might experience a sense of involvement with the work, or distance from it. You might like it or hate it. Whatever the nature of the response, the important thing to remember is that you *have* one. Good practice in all aspects of the IB literature course, and the commentary in particular, comes in part from developing an awareness of *how* and *why* a work of art makes you respond in the way that you do.

Think of any novel, poem or drama text that has made an impact on you, either recently or some time ago.

- *What* was your reaction to it?
- *How* did it provoke this reaction?
- *Why* do you remember it?

Being aware of the different ways in which literary works can operate is an important step in breaking them down and making sense of them. In part, this involves a fairly objective, even scientific, analysis of the way texts are created, but it is as much an introspective exploration of the way our own feelings and thoughts are generated or influenced by the works with which we come into contact.

Take any literary work that happens to be nearest to you right now – a poetry book, a play, a novel or work of non-fiction, preferably one that you have never read before. Open the book to any page and read 5–10 lines of text. Then take a minute to think about what you have just read and your response to it. Jot down your thoughts.

The more you get into this as a practice – thinking about the way a literary work has affected you in whatever small or large way – the better equipped you will be to demonstrate skills of independent engagement in all aspects of this course.

Finding and creating meaning in texts

An interesting feature of the way we read, think and talk about works of art has to do with the role that *we* play in making sense of them. The question, 'What do you think the author *meant*?' is often asked by both students and teachers, and it makes the assumption that our role is to somehow 'discover' this meaning, which is sometimes thought to be hidden somewhere in the text. In some respects, however, the IB literature course asks you to re-think this idea, and to consider the role that *you* play when you read, think and talk about literary works. *Making* meaning is in some ways a more appropriate description of the process that goes on rather than *finding* it.

In pairs or small groups, find a film or TV drama that you have both/all seen. On your own, spend five minutes writing down what you consider to be the most important/interesting, most/ least enjoyable aspects of the film. Tell your partner or the rest of the group what you have written.

- Do you agree on the most important components?
- Do the things others pick out and the way they talk about them tell you anything about *them as individuals* as well as the film?

A connection with theory of knowledge

At some point in your theory of knowledge course, perhaps when you address the topic of perception, you will spend some time thinking about the role played by your own mind in the way we come to understand the world. You will probably have already heard, for instance, of the slightly clichéd problem of whether a fallen branch from a tree in a forest makes any noise when there is no one there to hear it. You will also consider the issue of colour, and indeed any kind of sense experience – coming to recognize the complex physiological process that takes place when such things as light and sound waves are transferred to our brains in the form of neuron activity and the firing of synapses. Much of what we think is 'out there' in the world we see, feel, smell, touch or taste, is really only a construction – an interpretation. Our brains, quite literally, *make* sense out of experience and present a version of the world to us.

Consider this optical illusion, for instance. When you look at it, are you seeing what is *actually* there, or what your brain is *telling* you is there? For this reason, we can never really be sure of what the world *is* like, only what it *seems* to be; in a way, our brains tell us stories – just like literature!

Furthermore, just as we are individuals who live in a particular space and time, as members of communities, so our cultural background plays a role in the way this process of *making sense* actually happens. For example, the things we know about totalitarian states in the 21st century inevitably shape the way we read and interpret *1984* by George Orwell in a way that they could not have when the novel was first released. We might wonder how Shakespeare's audiences might have responded to a play like *Macbeth* or *Richard II* when the majority of individuals would have believed whole-heartedly in such things as the existence of witches or the divine right of kings. *Waiting for Godot* by Samuel Beckett has experienced a number of infamous productions in prisons; how might spending significant amounts of time behind bars make sense of the concept of 'waiting' in that play, or the identity of 'Godot'? Or consider Arthur Miller's play *Death of a Salesman,* a play seemingly so obviously located in the cultural milieu of the time and place in which it was produced: typically the downfall of the figure Willy Loman is read as the inevitable outcome of a flawed, misguided 'everyman' and the play as an indictment on the shallow ideology of capitalist post-war America. When Miller produced the play in China in the 1980s however, it was 'read' by those at the first Beijing production in quite a different way:

Timebends

Willy was representative everywhere, in every kind of system, of ourselves in this time. The Chinese might disapprove of his lies and his self-deluding exaggerations as well as his immorality with women, but they certainly saw themselves in him. And it was not simply as a type but because of what he wanted. Which was to excel, to win out over anonymity and meaninglessness, to love and be loved, and above all, perhaps, to *count.* When he roared out, "I am not a dime a dozen! *I am Willy Loman, and you are Biff Loman!*" it came as a nearly revolutionary declaration after what was now thirty-four years of leveling. (The play was the same age as the Chinese revolution.) I did not know in 1948 in Connecticut that I was sending a message of resurgent individualism to the China of 1983 – especially when the revolution had signified, it seemed at the time, the long-awaited rule of reason and the historic ending of chaotic egocentricity and selfish aggrandizement.

Arthur Miller

Our own lives and the places and cultures we inhabit are clearly vital to the way we exist in a relationship to literary works.

Critical positions

In the late 20th century, an acceptance of the centrality of the reader and their culture in the formulation of meaning in literature led to some critics taking up particular 'positions'. This means that they elect to examine literary works in terms of particular ideological stances. Read through the following:

Willy Loman in *Death of a Salesman*: American production

Feminist criticism tends to read literature in terms of gender, with a particular emphasis on the representation of women and female identity. It is concerned with the ways social and cultural attitudes towards women are expressed in texts, as well as the issues arising from the adoption of male or female narrative voices. Patriarchy is often an important consideration.

Feminist

Reader-response criticism is interested in the role played by the reader in creating meaning in literary works. It is interested in the way the reader's cultural values and attitudes can lead us to make assumptions about characters and ideas, as well as to 'fill gaps' that are either ambiguous or contradictory – as a means to interpret and explain them.

Reader-response

Race/post colonial readings of literary works look in depth at the representation of ethnicity. Emphasis is placed on the way literature deals with issues associated with race and injustice, with particular regard for works that are written or set in colonial places and periods. Power is a recurring motif in such readings. Criticism will often highlight western attitudes towards nationality and ethnicity, as they are expressed within texts but also by them in terms of authorship and publication. The values encoded within the language of literary works are of particular concern, as well as assumptions and associated paradigms expressed implicitly or explicitly by authors and their characters.

Race/post colonial

Critics from this school of thought seek to organize works of literary fiction into categories defined by the various genres: fiction; non-fiction; detective; thriller; comic; tragic; and so on. They examine texts in terms of the extent to which they embody characteristics and conventions associated with these particular categories.

Genre theory

Cultural/historical critics tend to read literary works as they portray aspects of the periods and cultures in which they are set. Writers like Tolstoy or Shakespeare are of course of particular interest, but critics will also look at the extent to which any literary work expresses facts and opinions about periods of history and their associated cultural values and practices. Fundamentally, such criticism argues that texts cannot be read and interpreted as if they 'stand alone' but as products of times and places.

Cultural/historical

Structuralist criticism is not particularly concerned with the context, content or 'meaning' of a literary work so much as the way it is put together. It recognizes that writers present 'constructions' of the world in the way they organize their ideas. Structuralist critics will often find interest in the way the language and form of a particular work might depend on such things as important oppositions or contrasts, for instance, or key motifs around which a work might find the means to create patterns.

Structuralist

Marxist criticism is interested in the way literature explores the issues of social class and power, with particular emphasis on the treatment of working-class people and the poor. It highlights political, cultural and social contexts, both in terms of the way they are embodied in the writing of a particular work, as well as the way our reading of it is affected by time and place.

Marxist

Psychoanalytic critics are concerned with the way literature reflects the operation of the mind. Since the time of Sigmund Freud, the last 100 years have witnessed enormous development of interest in the way aspects of human behaviour are either completely or in part repressed by social and cultural ethical attitudes. The characters and relationships of literary texts are often reflective of the complexity of human psychology, and psychoanalytical criticism will tend to center on internal and external conflicts between and within characters.

Psychoanalytic

Activity

Work in pairs with one of the above critical positions on a text you are currently studying.

a How different would your reading be of the work in comparison with a pair with a different position?

b Is one stance easier to argue than another?

c To support your point of view, which features of the text are you focusing on or ignoring?

d How does this compare with another pair with a different position?

Paper 1: literary analysis and the practice of commentary

Whether standard or higher level, there are two main components of the course that test your ability to respond to texts in a close, detailed way.

The first of these is Paper 1 of the final exam, in which you are asked to write about either a poem or prose extract that you will not have seen before. At standard level, the paper is referred to as 'guided literary analysis', so called because you are provided with two questions on the passage: one on aspects of 'understanding and interpretation'; the other on aspects of style. Higher level students, however, write a 'literary commentary'. At this level, you are not given guiding questions and so will need to show a more independent control of structure and general response to both the content and craft of the poem or extract in front of you.

In addition, both standard and higher level students must perform an individual oral commentary, which amounts to a 10-minute oral on an extract from one of the works you will have studied for Part 2.

We will go into more detail about these oral assessments in Chapters 4 and 5, but they are mentioned at this stage because of the similar kinds of skills you are required to demonstrate in both.

Tackling unprepared texts: developing skills of analysis

The importance of detail

Examiners of all components of the literature course frequently comment on the presence, or absence, of **detail** as a major factor in determining the success of a written or oral assignment. A practice worth adopting as much as you can is to focus attention on individual words, phrases or lines from any text you happen to be studying, or even ones you are reading in your spare time. When doing this, try not to worry too much about the 'meaning' of the extract; instead, try to concentrate attention on the many and varied ways in which the craft of writing can be broken down.

Consider, for example, the opening to Ted Hughes' poem, 'Wind':

> This house has been far out at sea all night,
>
> The woods crashing through darkness, the booming hills

Write down the things that strike you in this extract.

What did you notice first? Perhaps the striking initial metaphor of the house being described as a boat? You might also have picked up the figurative use of "crashing" and "booming" in the second line as a means to **personify** the storm, and the imagery of sound? You might also have noted the onomatopoeia – the way the particular repeated sounds (for example, the sibilance of "s" and "sh" or the harsh, plosive sounds in the words beginning with "b" and "c") or the predominance of vowel sounds provide a sense of size and scope to the storm. What about the contrast between the largely monosyllabic diction in line 1 and the polysyllabic words in line 2? You may even be able to talk about the present participle verb forms and the **structure** of the two lines? Or what about the **narrator**? How does the simple phrase "This house" place the narrator right at the center of the storm and give the poem an intimate, personal voice?

The key, perhaps, is to be able to respond to the art of writing on many and varied kinds of levels, as well as to be able to explore the **effects** of particular features or literary devices. If you can do this often, and informally, you will quickly acquire the right kinds of skills for success in the exam.

Do not limit yourself to literary works; newspaper articles, advertisements, political leaflets and even instruction booklets for a TV or DVD player all use language in particular ways. They may not be as rich in use of specifically literary features, but the writers of each will have thought carefully about choices of diction, syntax and general register in order to communicate with the reader as effectively and as appropriately as possible.

The importance of critical rigour

Another idea that you will encounter in your theory of knowledge course concerns the way in which different areas of knowledge (mathematics, human sciences, ethics, history, etc.) address problems of knowledge in different ways. The issue of how *different* they are in the practices they adopt will frequently be a topic of consideration. That being said, you might also find yourself addressing some surprising points of similarity. For instance, the natural sciences and the arts are often described in opposition to each other. After all, science is 'objective', logical, dealing with tangible proof, whereas art is 'subjective', interested in the irrational, the unpredictable and is a matter of opinion, isn't it?

Well, perhaps it's not quite so clear cut. As a human endeavour, science can often either get it wrong, or depend much on the imagination and creativity for its development and discoveries. Similarly, when we write and talk about art, don't we apply analytical tools of reason and logic – like science? When we explore literary works, don't we look for evidence, 'data' in the form of text information?

In many ways, therefore, the analysis of literature has its roots in more 'objective' practices than perhaps we might at first think. So how can we bring some of the critical rigour and methodology typically associated with science to the exploration of unseen literary texts?

Breaking the text down

What is the 'smallest' component in a line of text about which we could offer some legitimate analytical comment? A phrase? A word? A sound? Perhaps even a single beat of rhythm in poetry? In some ways, seeing yourself as a camera with a lens that can zoom in on the smallest possible detail, as well as pan out to consider the meaning of the whole work, can be a useful practice to employ.

In this way, we can break down the text into various aspects so as to create a kind of strategic 'checklist' as we prepare to write about it:

Checklist

- **Subject**: what is the subject of the text? Quite simply, what is it about? It might be a childhood memory, a father's relationship with his son, a wasp's nest, the First World War, outer space – we could go on for ever. The point here is to recognize the literal content of the text rather than any kind of thematic or metaphorical meaning being explored by it.
- **Action**: what *happens* in the text? Are the events important?
- **Character/relationship**: does it focus on a character or relationship?
- **Setting**: does setting play a role? Think in terms of physical setting – rural/urban, inside/outside, etc. but also in terms of time, geographical place and culture.
- **Narrator**: who is speaking? What kind of narrator? First or third person? Involved with the narrative or detached?
- **Themes and ideas**: what themes/ideas does the text explore? Why has it been written?
- **Imagery**: in what ways does the text make use of descriptive, sensory detail?
- **Figurative language**: what role do similes/metaphor/symbolism play?
- **Sound**: how does the text make use of sound? Consider alliteration, rhyme, assonance, onomatopoeia, and so on.
- **Diction**: comment on the vocabulary of the text. What kinds of words have been chosen? Simple or complex? Are there any elements of repetition?
- **Structure**: how has the extract been constructed? Stanzas or paragraphs? Does each deal with a different idea, or represent a point of development? In other words, does the layout contribute to the meaning? What kinds of syntax are employed? Are the lines or sentences long or short? End-stopped or run-on? Are there any uses of caesurae or types of pattern?
- **Tone**: what kinds of feelings does the narrator express towards the subject(s) of the text?

This is a list of some of the possibilities; your text might make use of some or many of them – or there may well be others not referred to here.

Recognizing the impact of literary features

It's important to remember that any kind of commentary practice, whether oral or written, must *not* simply identify a range of literary features. You have to think about their *effects*, and it is here that what we said on page 28 about developing an awareness of the way a text has an impact on you comes into play. Let's put this point to the test.

Activity

Read the poem 'Ancestral Photograph' by Seamus Heaney on the next page and apply the above checklist to it. What kinds of literary features can you identify? What can you say about their effects?

Ancestral Photograph

Jaws puff round and solid as a turnip,
Dead eyes are statue's and the upper lip
Bullies the heavy mouth down to a droop.
A bowler suggests the stage Irishman
Whose look has two parts scorn, two parts dead pan.
His silver watch chain girds him like a hoop.

My father's uncle, from whom he learnt the trade,
Long fixed in sepia tints, begins to fade
And must come down. Now on the bedroom wall
There is a faded patch where he had been –
As if a bandage had been ripped from skin –
Empty plaque to a house's rise and fall.

Twenty years ago I herded cattle
Into pens or held them against a wall
Until my father won at arguing
His own price on a crowd of cattlemen
Who handled rumps, groped teats, stood, paused and then
Bought a round of drinks to clinch the bargain.

Uncle and nephew, fifty years ago,
Heckled and herded through the fair days too.
This barrel of a man penned in the frame:
I see him with the jaunty hat pushed back
Draw thumbs out of his waistcoat, curtly smack
Hands and sell. Father, I've watched you do the same

And watched you sadden when the fairs were stopped.
No room for dealers if the farmers shopped
Like housewives at an auction ring. Your stick
Was parked behind the door and stands there still.
Closing this chapter of our chronicle
I take your uncle's portrait to the attic.

Seamus Heaney

Seamus Heaney

You might have noted some or all of the following:

- **Subject**: the poem is about a photograph of Heaney's great uncle, through which the speaker weaves comment about both his great uncle and his father, and explores various memories associated with them.
- **Action**: while looking at the photograph and thinking about its significance, the speaker has taken it off the wall. Describing the "faded patch" that is left "As if a bandage had been ripped from skin" gives the experience an organic quality, suggesting a degree of physical, perhaps emotional pain that the action of removing the picture from the wall incurs. At the end of the poem, the speaker takes it "to the attic", which suggests moving on and leaving the past behind.
- **Character**: the poem obviously describes both the figure of the uncle as well as his father in considerable detail. Through close physical details such as "Jaws puff round and solid as a turnip" and "the upper lip / Bullies the heavy mouth" the uncle is portrayed as a rather

self-assured, perhaps even somewhat arrogant man. The presentation of his father, however, is more interested in characteristics associated with personality than physical appearance; the lines "Until my father won at arguing" and "Bought a round of drinks to clinch the bargain" communicate his sense of expertise and pride in his work, which then gives way to sadness "when the fairs were stopped".

- **Relationship**: through the description of both men as they set about their work, the speaker in the poem expresses a feeling of admiration for them. In the lines, "I herded cattle / Into pens or held them against a wall" there is a sense in which the speaker feels at one with a familial history and tradition. His action at the end of the poem perhaps indicates his present sense of distance and detachment from both men, as well as a break from the past.

- **Setting**: the house and the attic, as well as the cattle market he imagines in the past, are given some importance in the poem, largely as a means to represent the nature of both men and the contrast between past and present.

- **Narrator**: the poem communicates a personal voice and the use of pronouns in lines such as "where he had been" and "Father, I've watched you do the same" register an intimate, 'involved' speaker. At the same time, the presence of physical detail establishes a degree of distance and objectivity to the speaking voice.

- **Themes and ideas**: a number of ideas are explored by the poem, including both involvement and separation from family tradition, the relationship between the past and the present and the passing of time, and the value of agricultural traditions. One key idea that perhaps underlies the poem is a degree of tension between past and present, himself and his family. The speaker seems to want to hang on to the past by writing about it, at the same time as let go; he seems to feel a sense of security in the family history that precedes him as well as the desire to forge his own path. Family and tradition are therefore a source of inspiration and comfort as well as a constraint.

- **Imagery and figurative language**: the speaker's uncle is referred to figuratively through similes and metaphors such as "solid as a turnip", which registers his substantial physical presence when alive, in contrast to "Dead eyes are statue's" through which his image in the photograph captures a sense of absence and stillness in his death. In "Empty plaque to a house's rise and fall" Heaney communicates the impact of passing time, and the image of the father's stick "parked behind the door" says something about when the agricultural fairs "were stopped", as well as commenting on the paradox of time having moved on while yet being preserved. The stick is still and yet "there still".

- **Sound**: Heaney uses a preponderance of assonance and vowel sounds generally in the first stanza; words and phrases such as "round and solid", "Dead eyes" and "down to a droop" enhance the sense of the great uncle's physical presence. There are a number of examples of alliteration in "Heckled and herded" and "stick… / …still", which have the effect of bringing alive the memories and the poignant reflection the speaker undergoes.

- **Diction**: of note here, perhaps, are words that capture the physical presence of the various concerns of the poem, whether in the descriptions of the uncle or father, the house, the photograph or the agricultural fair. Active verbs such as "Bullies", "ripped", "herded", "groped", "handled", "Heckled" and "smack" draw attention to the physicality of the work undertaken by both men and the speaker's reminiscence in sense experience. Adjectives such as "Dead", "heavy", "penned", "jaunty" and "parked" are equally vivid.

- **Structure**: the poem is divided into stanzas of regular length, each of which systematically takes us from the present, then ever further back into the past, before coming back to the present again. The syntax is irregular; some lines make use of caesurae, while others are continuous; some are end-stopped, others run on and there is a loose sense of organization in an irregular rhyme scheme. In this way, Heaney provides a sense of structure while at the same time an informal 'speaking' voice.

- **Tone**: much of the poem is expressed in a fairly detached voice as the speaker portrays his great uncle and father with an exact, almost scientific visual precision. At the same time, key images suggest a sense of sadness at time having passed and distance from a heritage, a world that the speaker no longer feels a part of. The last two lines are fairly insistent in their tone, as if the desire to move on is undertaken with purpose.

Tackling unprepared texts: developing skills of interpretation

Up to now, much of what we have covered deals with a fairly 'objective' process of identifying various aspects of literary craft and exploring their effects. In all aspects of the IB literature course, however, you are also expected to demonstrate skills of interpretation, which effectively means examining the way that a text makes sense to you, and the way you make sense of the text – as we began to think about on pages 29–30. In the preceding notes on 'themes and ideas', for instance, there is one level of interpretation provided – which is that the poem communicates a degree of tension, between past and present, the personal and the familial.

Activity

Read the following statements of interpretation about the poem 'Ancestral Photograph'. Arrange them in rank order, with number 1 being the statement you most agree with, number 5 the least.

a The poem is concerned with the passing of time. It expresses a sense of nostalgia for a world that has passed, at the same time as a recognition of the need to look forward.

b Above all, the poem is concerned with the speaker's feelings towards his father and great uncle. It is a celebration of their lives and a means to explore his roots in an agricultural tradition.

c The poem gains its power from the ambiguity of the speaking voice. The narrator of the poem communicates a deeply personal account of his own intimate history, as well as an objective detachment from it.

d The motif of the photograph is the key to the poem. As an image, it encapsulates everything the speaker feels about his great uncle and the past. In the action of taking it to the attic at the end, the photograph as a symbol of preserving the past comes to an end. Perhaps it is replaced, however, by the poem itself? Heaney does not forget the past; he re-lives it in the act of writing the poem.

e 'Ancestral Photograph' is a poem whose life comes from attention to close, largely visual, detail. In writing about the image of his great uncle, the actions of his father at the agricultural fair and the act of putting the photograph away, the speaker makes considerable visual imagery and so brings the whole experience alive.

How do *you* 'read' 'Ancestral Photograph'?

Interpreting an extract, whether known or unseen, is in some respects simply a matter of deciding which of the features listed in the checklist on page 36 are more important than others. Setting, for instance, may or may not be an important feature of a short piece of writing. You need to select the features which for you carry the most weight and allow those to come to the foreground, while others stay in the background, or are hidden altogether. In order to add flesh to any one of the statements listed in the activity on page 39, you would need to make more of some features of the poem than others. It is an act of selection and evaluation of the features that you regard as important. This is something we could refer to as 'active reading'. By doing this, you will be consistently showing independent critical thinking skills.

How do I come up with a line of interpretation – a 'thesis'?

There is no easy answer to this but try to think of a thesis as the washing line on which the rest of your points are going to hang. Hopefully, the following might provide you with some starting points:

- Identify the **most important feature of content** and ask yourself what is being suggested about that feature of content.

- Alternatively, what is the **most important aspect of style**? In two of the statements in the previous activity, imagery and structure are highlighted as features of literary craft that arguably contribute a great deal to the way a particular theme is presented.

- Look for **contrasts**. More often than not, short extracts will make use of significant oppositions – whether between ideas, sections of the text or perhaps such things as strands of imagery.

- **Development**: is there an underlying sense of transition in the poem or extract – whether in terms of its ideas, the content, or its language and style?

- **Conflict**: our interest in prose, poetry and drama very frequently comes from the establishment of some kind of central tension, whose resolution (or lack of it) is often responsible for maintaining our interest.

- Why, in essence, do you think this is a good piece of writing?

By now, you will have come to understand the interactive nature of the reading process. The text presents itself in the form of black shapes on the page, and you find meaning in those black shapes by responding to the denotations of the words, their connotative implications and the various literary features through which everything is crafted. What *you* bring to the text is every bit as important as the way the text works on its own. Indeed, it is perhaps true to say that the text wouldn't 'mean' anything without you there to make sense of it – just as the tree in the forest can't make any noise unless there is someone there to hear it.

A word on annotating

It is sometimes surprising how few students engage regularly in the habit of carefully annotating text, and perhaps this is in part because it is a skill that needs developing. Annotating is important because it is a record of the reading journey that you take as you see, think and feel your way through a piece of literary text.

A few pointers to consider:

1 There is something to say about any text from the second you cast your eye on it: if it is a poem, you can comment on its shape on the page, whether it is divided into stanzas, and if prose, whether it is one block of text or a series of paragraphs. If it is a drama text, you

can quickly see whether one person speaks more than another, whether there are significant stage directions and, as with poetry, whether or not the lines are regular in length.

2 First read the text through completely to get your initial impressions, writing down such things as:

- words and phrases that strike you as important, or that stand out for whatever reason

- points of development – to show where the text seems to undergo a kind of shift or change

- questions – things you do not understand, or that seem at first confusing

- the main concerns of the piece of writing as they appear to you on a first reading.

3 Read for **content**: decide on which key aspects of the text's content are important and allow those to come to the foreground. Then read through, underline and add notes *only* on such matters as characterization and relationships, setting, action, themes and ideas.

4 Read for **style**: again, which stylistic properties of the text seem more significant than others? You will always have things to say about diction, syntax and structure, but what about imagery and figurative language, rhyme and rhythm and sound? Focus on the most important aspects of literary craft.

> Using **colour** can be helpful here: why not complete all annotations on aspects of content in one colour, and all aspects of style in another?

An important consideration, then, is the idea of reading for different purposes – focusing on a different aspect each time you go through the text.

Whether preparing for the unseen text in Paper 1 or the individual oral commentary for Part 2, successful students are almost always the ones who demonstrate independent exploration of the text, and an active involvement with it. As much as possible, therefore, make your annotations a detailed, visual record of your reading journey through the extract (just as one student has tried to do on page 42).

Asking questions of texts: an alternative strategy

As we have said, annotations are a record of the journey you take through a particular piece of writing. On the whole, students tend to write down things they are fairly sure of – answers to questions they have mentally set themselves. In other words, they have applied the checklist of possibilities covered on page 36 and gone through it in a fairly systematic way. While there is nothing inherently wrong with this, it can sometimes lead to a slightly formulaic kind of response and a lack of personal engagement with the text.

As an alternative approach, more active 'involvement' with the text can come from processing the questions you might have about it. What would you like to know? What seems confusing or difficult? What are the effects of some of the literary features you have identified?

To test this approach, read through the poem 'Winter' on page 43. As you read, or afterwards, write down the questions that have occurred to you.

The Sleepout

Childhood[1] sleeps[2] in a verandah room[3]

in an iron bed[4] close to the wall[5]

where the winter over the railing[6]

swelled the blind on its timber boom

and splinters picked lint[7] off warm linen[8]

and the stars were out over the hill;

then one wall of the room was forest[9]

and all things in there were to come. [10]

Breathings[11] climbed up on the verandah

when dark[12] cattle rubbed at the corner

and sometimes dim towering rain[13] stood

for forest, and the dry[14] cave hunched[15] woollen.

Inside the forest was lamplit[16]

along tracks to a starry creek bed

and beyond lay the never-fenced country,[17]

its full billabongs[18] all surrounded

by animals and birds, in loud crustings,[19]

and[20] sometimes kept leaping up amongst them.

And[20] out there, to kindle[21] whenever

dark found it, hung the daylight moon. [22] [23]

Les Murray

- A very atmospheric poem.
- Uses contrasts:
  light/dark
  inside/outside
  security/insecurity
  realist/fantasy
  sleep/waking.
- Nature as a living,
  breathing force.
- Childhood as an
  imaginative/magical
  experience.
- Tone = calm/reflective –
  even celebratory?
- Lots of sense imagery.
- Effective use of sound.

---

[1] The subject of the poem?

[2] A kind of personification?

[3] Outside or inside? Perhaps a slight tension?

[4] Suggests something hard/uncomfortable

[5] Security

[6] Suggests nature as an influential/controlling/
organic force

[7] Assonance. Vowel sounds predominate in the poem.
Room seems dilapidated

[8] Sense of warmth/richness

[9] Transition. Darkness descends and division between
inside/outside evaporates

[10] Sense of expectancy

[11] Personification – whose?

[12] Darkness again, sense of mystery?

[13] Visual image

[14] Contrast to rain

[15] Visual image

[16] Where is the speaker now? Has moved, perhaps
imaginatively, into forest. Light and dark another
opposition

[17] Boundless – like his imagination?

[18] Australian term? (Pond? Lake? Not sure!)

[19] Surprising! Original way to describe sounds of nature

[20] Repetition moves us forwards

[21] Light?

[22] Another opposition/paradox – darkness is not frightening

[23] He 'sees' all this but only in his imagination?

Winter

The ten o'clock train to New York;
coaches like loaves of bread powdered with
    snow.
Steam wheezes between the couplings.
Stripped to plywood, the station's cement standing
    room
imitates a Russian novel. It is now that I remember
    you.
Your profile becomes the carved handle of a letter
    knife.
Your heavy-lidded eyes slip under the seal of my
    widowhood.
It is another raw winter. Stray cats are suffering.
Starlings crowd the edges of chimneys.
It is a drab misery that urges me to remember
    you.
I think about the subjugation of women and
    horses,
Brutal exposure. Weather that forces, that strips.
In our time we met in ornate stations
arching up with nineteenth-century optimism.
I remember you running beside the train waving
    goodbye.
I can produce a facsimile of you standing
behind a column of polished oak to surprise me.

Am I going toward you or away from you on this
    train?
Discarded junk of other minds is strewn beside
    the tracks.
Mounds of rusting wire. Grotesque pop-art of dead
    motors.
Senile warehouses. The train passes a station.
Fresh people standing on the platform;
their faces expecting something.
I feel their entire histories ravish me.

Ruth Stone

Here are some questions to start you off:

1 Who is the narrator speaking to?

2 What's the effect of the "loaves of bread" simile?

3 Why does this poem make you think about death?

4 How is a rather depressing and somber mood created, and does this change as the poem goes on?

5 How important are setting and the season of winter to the poem?

6 Why "Grotesque pop-art"?

7 How does the speaker remember the person to whom she is speaking?

8 What are the "entire histories" she mentions at the end?

Activity

Below is a prose extract.

a In pairs, write five questions that you think draw attention to the extract's most noticeable features.

b Swap your questions with another pair and see if you can answer each other's questions.

c Did you focus on similar or different components?

The Rings of Saturn

No matter whether one is flying over Newfoundland or the sea of lights that stretches from Boston to Philadelphia after nightfall, over the Arabian deserts which gleam like mother-of-pearl, over the Ruhr or the city of Frankfurt, it is as though there were no people, only the things they have made and in which they are hiding. One sees the places where they live and the roads that link them, one sees the smoke rising from their houses and factories, one sees the vehicles in which they sit, but one sees not the people themselves. And yet they are present everywhere upon the face of the earth, extending their dominion by the hour, moving around the honeycomb of towering buildings and tied into networks of a complexity that goes far beyond the power of any one individual to imagine, from the thousands of hoists and winches that once worked the South African diamond mines to the floors of today's stock and commodity exchanges, through which the global tides of information flow without cease. If we view ourselves from a great height, it is frightening to realise how little we know about our species, our purpose and our end, I thought, as we crossed the coastline and flew out over the jelly-green sea.

W. G. Sebald

A final point on the importance of asking questions

There will often be details of extracts, whether in the unseen Paper 1 commentary or the extract you are given for the individual oral commentary in Part 2, which are confusing or hard to understand. When this happens, try to turn the problem into a question. Ask yourself *why* a particular aspect is confusing or difficult, and then try to answer that question. Perhaps it is because there is a word or phrase that could mean a number of things, or perhaps there seems to be a contradiction with something that is said earlier in the poem or extract. But this might well be the point: perhaps the poem contains elements of contradiction because it is *about* something contradictory. Perhaps the poem is *meant* to be ambiguous. Let's face it, life is more often contradictory, confusing or ambiguous, and why should literature not reflect this?

It is important, therefore, not to resist difficulty. Don't try to explain things that are not clear because it might well lead you into unhelpful speculation and 'gap filling' as a result – 'reading' the text in an inappropriate way.

Commentary practice and creative writing

To this point, we have adopted fairly traditional means of unpicking extracts for commentary practice, and looking at short 'unknown' extracts as often as possible is the best way to keep your skills ticking over.

There are other ways, however. Writing creatively, for example, is sadly all too infrequent among IB literature students – often for good reasons of coursework pressure, and so on. However, playing with texts, and especially trying to emulate the styles of particular writers, is a really effective way of sensitizing yourself to their stylistic characteristics.

Here are a few ideas you might like to try; your teacher may well have more:

Pastiches

This is a particularly enjoyable, often very productive, activity to try. A pastiche is an imitation of a writer or work, making use of similar kinds of diction, syntax or literary techniques and features – sometimes to comic effect.

Take a look at this clever example by the writer Sebastian Faulks:

Franz Kafka tries to keep up with the world of Mr Gates

Hans T awoke one morning after a troubled dream to find his right hand had turned into a large mouse. 'Good boy, Hans,' said his mother when she came into his bedroom. 'Now you can book our holiday on the Internet.'

Two large men in raincoats sat Hans in front of a screen.

'Who sent you?' he asked.

'Never mind,' said the first man. 'Click your fingers.'

'Mmm,' said the second man. 'Microsoft Word has experienced an unexpected error.'

'What?' said Hans.

'Did your browser stop working?' said the first policeman.

'Or', said the second man, 'did you recently add a new item to your active desktop?'

'Or did you restart your computer without shutting it down first?'

'I don't know,' said Hans. 'But what shall I do now?'

'Do this,' said the first man brusquely. 'Right-click the desktop to show the desktop menu, point to the active desktop, click customise my desktop.'

'Clear the checkbox for the item you added most recently,' said the second man, more gently. 'Right-click the desktop, point to the active desktop, then click show web content. Did you want to turn off your active desktop?'

'No,' said Hans. 'I want to buy a coach ticket for my mother.'

An hour later Hans had reached the site of Castle Tours. The screen froze, while a small egg timer whirled in fixed mockery.

Eight hours after this, his mother came into the room. 'Will you get off the line, Hans,' she said, 'I'm expecting a call from your Aunt Gudrun.'

'This thing doesn't seem to work,' said Hans.

'Get up,' yelled the first man, 'your message has permanent fatal errors. Come with us.'

'Where to?' said Hans.

'You will see,' said the second man softly. 'You have performed an illegal operation.'

Sebastian Faulks

Below is an example from a student seeking to emulate some of the conventions of the poetry of Sylvia Plath:

Lunch Queue

Time brings us toward each other
Eating each other's words,
And feet
Crushing hands and granite paving stones.

Gnarled faces pushing,
Pushing, pushing.
Watchful tigers searching for their
Pre-cooked prey.

Wiser monkeys
Block the path of chaotic lives,
Yelling at the walls,
Smashing windows with highest decibels.

Let us in! Let us in!
Beat of drumming propels us
Onwards Outwards
Glistening tongues wrap themselves
In loops
Over tiny daggers, pitchforks, spears.

Hunger satisfied,
Jack and Jill
Lick their fingers to the bone.

Inspired by Sylvia Plath

Although both of these extracts 'play' with the characteristics of two distinct writers for comic effect, in composing them the writers have had to think very carefully about what makes a writer's style recognizable. Try it with an author you are currently reading or studying – just a few lines. It can be great fun, as well as incredibly useful.

Connect paragraphs

This is connected to the pastiche idea. Read through paragraphs a and b below and write one that connects them. Again, try to identify the features of the original style that make it notable. When you have written your paragraph, compare it with others in the group and then with the original taken from *Cat's Eye* on page 49.

a Some of the euphoria I once felt in falling snow comes back to me; I want to open my mouth and let the snow fall into it. I allow myself to laugh, like the others, trying it out. My laughter is a performance, a grab at the ordinary.

b She opens her eyes and reaches up her hands, which are damp and reddened, and we pull her upwards so she won't disturb the image she's made. The snow angel has feathery wings and a tiny pin-head. Where her hands stopped, down near her sides, are the imprints of her fingers, like little claws.

Turn poetry into prose (and vice versa)

Any kind of work that you do in which your attention is focused on the **details** of literary language, thereby sensitizing you to the way it works or creates particular effects, is a helpful means of developing commentary skills. Try taking any short poem and re-writing it as prose. What are the differences? Alternatively, try it the other way round: look closely at a few paragraphs of any text and underline what you regard as the words or phrases that carry the most weight. Write these out. Next, play with laying them out on a page: where would you put in the line breaks in order to create a poem from them?

Here is one example, from the last chapter of *Great Expectations* by Charles Dickens:

Great Expectations
(The original paragraph with 'important' parts underlined.)

There was <u>no house now</u>, <u>no brewery</u>, <u>no building</u> whatever left, but <u>the wall of the old garden</u>. The cleared space had been <u>enclosed</u> with a rough fence, and, looking over it, I saw that some of the old <u>ivy</u> had struck root anew, and was <u>growing green on low quiet mounds of ruin</u>. <u>A gate</u> in the fence standing ajar, I pushed it open, and went in.

<u>A cold silvery mist</u> had <u>veiled the afternoon</u>, and the moon was not yet up to scatter it. But, the <u>stars were shining beyond</u> the mist, and <u>the moon was coming</u>, and the evening was <u>not dark</u>. I could trace out <u>where</u> every part of <u>the old house had been</u>, and <u>where the brewery had been</u>, and where the gates, and where the casks. I had done so, and was looking along the <u>desolate garden walk</u>, when I beheld <u>a solitary figure in it</u>.

The figure showed itself <u>aware of me</u>, as I advanced. It had been <u>moving towards me</u>, but <u>it stood still</u>. As I drew nearer, I saw it to be the figure of a woman. As I drew nearer yet, it was about to turn away, when it stopped, and let me come up with it. Then, it faltered as if much surprised, and uttered my name, and I cried out:

<u>'Estella!'</u>

Charles Dickens

The 'important' parts without the rest:

no house now no brewery no building the wall of the old garden enclosed ivy growing green on low quiet mounds of ruin A gate A cold silvery mist veiled the afternoon stars were shining beyond the moon was coming not dark where the old house had been where the brewery had been desolate garden walk a solitary figure in it aware of me moving towards me it stood still Estella!

> **Add line breaks and you have a new poem:**
>
> No house now
> No brewery
> No building
>
> The wall of the old garden
> Enclosed
> Ivy
> Growing green
> On low quiet mounds of ruin
>
> A gate
> A cold silvery mist
> Veiled the afternoon
> Stars were shining beyond
> The moon was coming
>
> Not dark
> Where the old house had been
> Where the brewery had been
>
> Desolate garden walk
> A solitary figure in it
>
> Aware of me
> Moving towards me
> It stood still
>
> Estella!

Film still from the ending of David Lean's film of *Great Expectations*

One last suggestion: keep a reading journal

Hopefully, you will have seen by now that thinking, talking and writing about literature does not have to be a dry, formal, analytical exercise. You can engage with the works in your course in many different kinds of ways.

Having a reading journal is a really enjoyable means of developing some of the suggestions for responding to the works we have made in this chapter, as well as providing you with the potential for developing *independent thinking* about them. Try using a journal in the following ways:

- To write down your independent thoughts about character, setting, theme and style as you read through a text; do you *like* or *sympathise* with a character? Does the text remind you of people, places or events that *you* have experienced? Does the text ask questions that you want to know the answers to? What do you think is going to happen?

- Write creatively: we have suggested some ways in which you can engage with the content and style of a literary work by writing in response to it. Short pieces of creative writing, whether successful or not, can be really helpful as a means to maintain your sensitivity to writing as a *craft*.

- Background research: whether or not your teacher asks you to, getting some background information on the writer's biography and/ or the time and place in which a work is set, can be really important to the work you do on it.

- Relevant experience: recording your response of other works that you happen to be reading, films you have seen, art galleries you have visited or places you have travelled to, can also be really helpful. In part, you will find yourself reminded of the relationships the works you are studying on the course have to 'real life', but also as a record of the personal and imaginative journey you have taken through these two years. It might be nice to look back on these exciting periods of your life in the years to come!

Cat's Eye
(Original paragraph – see page 46.)

Cordelia throws herself backwards onto a blank front lawn, spreads her arms out in the snow, raises them above her head, draws them down to her sides, making a snow angel. The flakes fall onto her face, into her laughing mouth, melting, clinging to her eyebrows. She blinks, closing her eyes against the snow. For a moment she looks like someone I don't know, a stranger, shining with unknown, good possibilities. Or else a victim of a traffic accident, flung onto the snow.

Margaret Atwood

Tackling Paper 1

Objectives

- to develop strategies for tackling Paper 1
- to respond to poems or extracts of prose in the exam
- to use creative writing to develop analytical skills

Part 1: poetry

Up to now, we have explored some important general ideas that influence the way we read and find meaning in any text. Hopefully, we have succeeded in breaking down the operation of critical analysis. If you can understand the way this works, you should then be in a position to develop and fine-tune your responses in a more deliberate, targeted way.

Keeping these things in mind, let's now turn our attention more fully to the demands of Paper 1.

The first exam paper (which counts for 20 per cent of the final grade) is referred to as 'guided literary analysis' at standard level, and 'literary commentary' at higher level. The most important thing is that, unlike the individual oral commentary you will deliver for Part 2, the Part 1 exam presents you with texts you will almost certainly not have seen before. You are given the choice of either a poem or extract of prose and in 1.5 hours at standard level and 2 hours at higher level are asked to write an analysis of whichever one you choose.

In the second half of this chapter, we'll go through some poems and prose extracts, drawing attention to the things you need to remember as you prepare to sit the paper.

Activity

Remembering the advice provided in Chapter 3 on 'active reading', annotation as a record of this process and the importance of asking questions, apply the appropriate strategies to the poem 'Jaguar'.

1 Read through the poem on the next page and record your response to the following areas, as suggested in Chapter 3.

    a Visual appearance on the page.

    b The title.

    c First impressions: what strikes you most immediately?

    d Read for aspects of **content**.

    e Read for aspects of **style**.

    f What questions do you have of the poem?

2 When you have completed your annotations, spend some time thinking about:

- aspects which strike you as **more important** – which you might seek to foreground in a commentary
- underlying principles through which you might be able to establish some kind of **unifying argument**.

Jaguar

The apes yawn and adore their fleas in the sun.
The parrots shriek as if they were on fire, or strut
Like cheap tarts to attract the stroller with the nut.
Fatigued with indolence, tight and lion

Lie still as the sun. The boa constrictor's coil
Is a fossil. Cage after cage seems empty, or
Stinks of sleepers from the breathing straw.
It might be painted on a nursery wall.

But who runs like the rest past these arrives
At a cage where the crowd stands, stares, mesmerized,
As a child at a dream, at a jaguar hurrying enraged
Through prison darkness after the drills of his eyes

On a short fierce fuse. Not in boredom –
The eye satisfied to be blind in fire,
By the bang of blood in the brain deaf the ear –
He spins from the bars, but there's no cage to him

More than to the visionary his cell:
His stride is wildernesses of freedom:
The world rolls under the long thrust of his heel.
Over the cage floor the horizons come.

Ted Hughes

Compare the notes you have made in the above activity with these:

- **Subject:** the poem is interested in the exploration of a particular animal, the jaguar, whose power is registered largely through making comparison with other, 'inferior' creatures.

- Important aspects of **content:**

  - The opening two stanzas of the poem focus on animals other than the jaguar, which are depicted as lazy, disengaged or conceited. The apes seem to spend their time picking fleas and tiger and lion "Lie still as the sun", in a passive, nonchalant state. The parrots are compared to "cheap tarts" in their rather desperate attempts to attract the attention of "the stroller with the nut" and the comparison of the boa constrictor's coil to "a fossil" seems to represent the seemingly empty, shallow existence of all these animals. They seem reduced to a purely biological condition, uninspiring, without energy and without any sense of character.

  - The introduction of the jaguar in stanza three represents a dramatic point of **contrast.** The crowd is "mesmerized", compared to "a child at a dream" as the people watch a creature that seems everything the aforementioned animals are not. The phrases "hurrying enraged / Through prison darkness" and "He spins from the bars" convey the jaguar's energy and restlessness, as well as providing him with an emotional life in "the drills of his eyes / On a short fierce fuse". The jaguar is portrayed with a kind of vitality and spirit that the cage it is in almost fails to contain. Hughes writes, "His stride is wildernesses of freedom" and in the line, "The world rolls under the long thrust of his heel" his power is presented such that he seems almost to have dominion over the whole world.

- The poem makes use of the **setting** of the zoo and its cages, as well as the anonymous human "crowd" to reinforce the individuality of the jaguar. In all respects the creature is set apart. The poem becomes an attempt on the part of the narrator to write himself into the 'life' of the jaguar, to imaginatively interact with its physical, almost metaphysical presence. In this way, the poem is both objective description and more subjective, imaginative celebration.

- The **language** of the poem is rich and detailed. Diction is chosen carefully to communicate the physical characteristics of each creature. Verbs such as "yawn", "shriek", "hurrying" and "spins" actively depict the essential character of each animal, and these are reinforced with adjectives such as "breathing", "fierce" and "blind". Both human and animal worlds are described in very tangible ways, so that we can feel, hear and see them.

- The **structure** is regular in its four-line stanzas, and as we move through the poem so we move from one cage to the next until, like the crowd, we are asked to stop in front of the jaguar. Lines are a mixture of end-stopped and run-on so that there is a sense of organization, as well as fluidity in the lines. The speaker comments with an almost scientific precision on what he sees, and yet allows himself moments of more spontaneous expression in response, for instance, to more unpredictable traits of the animals.

- There is a host of **literary** elements to the poem. Hughes makes use of figurative language and imagery throughout. The "shriek" of the parrots is compared to "fire", tiger and lion "Lie still as the sun" and the crowd stands "As a child at a dream". The similes reveal the speaker's imaginative operation as he seeks to find a language through which to describe these animals. This sense of empathy really takes off when he comes to the jaguar. The "drills of his eyes" in the "prison darkness", for example, use metaphor to detail the creature's sinister, determined nature. At the end of the poem, the phrase "Over the cage floor the horizons come" suggests that the cage no longer exists, and the jaguar becomes one with the wilderness. There is considerable **visual** and **aural imagery** in the poem's exploration of the physicality of each animal.

- Other literary features worthy of comment might include the use of features of **sound**. There is alliteration in the phrases "bang of blood in the brain" and "Stinks of sleepers", and assonance in "prison... drills" and "world rolls... long". These examples each illustrate the way the poem seeks to describe the animals as vividly and as 'real' as possible, and thereby once again convey the speaker's imaginative connection with the creatures.

– Finally, the tone of the poem varies as the speaker moves from one animal to the next. Monosyllabic **diction** in the earlier part of the poem conveys the speaker's sense of boredom and disinterest in the first group of animals, but by the time he gets to the jaguar the **rhythm** of the lines picks up and more complex, polysyllabic diction gives expression to the vitality of the jaguar. He seems to regard the animal with wonder and admiration, as well as almost a sense of fear in response to the jaguar's power and potential. The superlative expressions in the last stanza, where he is "More than" the cell that seeks to contain him, elevate the jaguar's status to the point where the speaker's imagination and the jaguar itself are almost united at the end of the poem. It is as if the rest of the world has ceased to exist.

These are just some responses to a number of aspects of the poem. How far did they agree with yours? There are, of course, other things we could talk about but in focusing more on some, rather than others, you are, in effect, starting to construct a reading.

> Keep in mind the techniques explained on pages 34–6, which will help you to tie your points together as your commentary moves on. Where could you get your ideas from?

Activity

Here are two possible statements of interpretation of the poem 'Jaguar':

a This poem elevates the status of the jaguar above all other creatures, including humans. Its central concern is the way the physical characteristics of the creature transcend the constraints of its cell and imaginatively inspire the speaker.

b The poem's main strength is its use of imagery and figurative diction to communicate the physicality of the animal kingdom. Senses predominate in a poem above all concerned with the operation of animal instinct.

Write two more statements that could be said of this poem, focusing on such things as the most important idea, a fundamental contrast or opposition, a key use of language, and so on.

Let's now put some of the ideas we have covered into practice and start to consider how to turn these preparatory reading activities into writing about the text.

As noted earlier, standard level and higher level students are faced with a slightly different task in Paper 1, and the notes presented in the following pages take the differences into account. That being said, the essential focus on analytical skills remains the same so, if you are a higher level student, do not think you cannot take heed of the ensuing advice for standard level students on their 'guided literary analysis' and, likewise, standard level students may gain a lot from the points made later about 'structuring a literary commentary' and deriving a thesis.

The standard level guided literary analysis

At standard level, you will be given two questions on the poem or prose extract. One will tend to focus on matters to do with content and the other form, language or style. Your response will then consist of answers to these two questions, but you do not have to answer them in sequence. As long as answers are presented in your analysis, it is up to you to organize your ideas in the way you see fit.

Activity

Refresh your memory of the approach to unseen work that was suggested by our exploration of 'The Jaguar' and spend some time annotating a copy of the following poem.

The Birds

I'll miss the small birds that come
for the sugar you put out
and the bread crumbs. They've

made the edge of the sea domestic
and, as I am, I welcome that.
Nights my head seemed twisted

with dreams and the sea wash,
I let it all come quiet, waking,
counting familiar thoughts and objects.

Here to rest, like they say, I best
liked walking along the beach
past the town till one reached

the other one, around the corner
of rock and small trees. It was
clear, and often empty, and

peaceful. Those lovely ungainly
pelicans fished there, dropping
like rocks, with grace, from the air,

headfirst, then sat on the water,
letting the pouch of their beaks
grow thin again, then swallowing

whatever they'd caught. The birds,
no matter they're not of our kind,
seem most like us here. I want

to go where they go, in a way, if
a small and common one. I want
to ride that air which makes the sea

seem down there, not the element
in which one thrashes to come up.
I love water, I *love* water –

but I also love air, and fire.

Robert Creeley

Now read through these two questions:

Question 1: What is the relationship that the narrator here explores between himself and the landscape?

Question 2: How do language, imagery and structure contribute to the poem's mood?

How would you set about answering these questions? Clearly, the first one is interested in a matter of content – the relationship between the narrator and the landscape, and the second one form and style – the means through which the poem generates atmosphere and mood.

The questions provide you with a way of organizing your points around these two main ideas. You need to think about whether to directly address them and present your analysis as an answer to the two questions more or less in sequence, or whether to write an analysis that *includes* the answers within it.

Read the following student response and discuss with a partner what you feel are its strengths and weaknesses.

Standard level student response

'The Birds', by Robert Creeley, portrays the internal conflict of a character who finds himself torn between two types of setting, one that is known and familiar, and one that is more distant and elusive.

The poem opens with a sense of nostalgia as the anonymous central character recollects the sources of familiarity in his past that had once provided him with comfort and security. His statement that he will "miss the small birds that come" suggests the character's hesitation in leaving the landscape in which he currently exists and has been accustomed to. Furthermore, his allusion to another figure, referred to merely as "you", implies that this familiar landscape also embodies some kind of relationship that he is reluctant to abandon. Creeley further develops the idea of his character at a point of transition through imagery of him at "the edge of the sea", which holds both connotations of an end to his current existence and a sharp turning point in his life. His past experiences, or his past in general, are also at the "edge" of the landscape – they are "domestic" and calm. Irregular syntax of the subsequent line, as the character remembers, "Nights my head seemed twisted / with dreams and the sea wash" that came "quiet, waking" reflects his confused state of mind. The contrast between "quiet" and "waking" evokes a sense of the narrator's peaceful hopes and 'dreams' that are quickly disrupted by the sea wash that brings him back to his harsh reality, prompting him to desperately reminisce and count "familiar thoughts and objects" for comfort.

Creeley then moves into a second kind of landscape through imagery of one of the narrator's memories. He explores his deep desire to "rest" as he reaches the "edge of the sea", which represents the transition area between the two settings. Further contributing to this sense of the narrator's impending transition is his allusion to his memory of "walking along the beach / past the town till one reached / the other one, around the corner / of rock and small trees". This parallels the author's intention to leave his current existence in search of a sense of freedom in another realm, one that is "clear, and often empty, and / peaceful". Creeley's use of vowel sounds as he depicts the "lovely ungainly / pelicans" that "fished" generates a soothing tone as he takes delight in their simple act of catching fish. And yet there is still a sense of tension; he juxtaposes "dropping / …rocks" with "grace" in portraying the creatures as both "lovely" and "ungainly". Similarly, he yearns to go "where they go", but only in a "small and common way". Rather than fighting for survival in the sea as an "element / in which one thrashes to come up" in his present landscape, the narrator longs to "ride that air" and be in harmony with the former. In this way he yearns for the idea of entering a landscape that represents freedom, much like the natural world that the birds thrive in, but he remains hesitant to leave all that is "domestic" to him.

The tone of the poem is affected considerably by Creeley's choice of diction and expression. On the one hand, he adopts a simple and direct kind of diction in reference to such ordinary objects as "sugar" and "bread crumbs", as well as actions such as "walking along the beach". On the other hand, more abstract expression in phrases like "I let it all come quiet", "Nights my head seemed twisted" and "I want / to ride that air" provide a more imaginative, emotional dimension to the poem. The tone therefore varies from moments when he seems calm and contented to expressions of longing and a kind of spiritual thirst.

This sense of tension and contrast is also found in the structure of the poem. At first glance, the structure appears to be very regular, with three-line stanzas and lines of roughly equal length, with one lone line at the end. However, on closer reading, the structure of the poem is actually very loose, with extended use of enjambment. For example, the first word of one sentence is put at the end of

the first stanza – "They've" – and then this sentence is continued in the next stanza with "made the edge of the sea domestic". Examples like these of cross-stanza enjambment occur regularly throughout the poem, perhaps reflective of the way the narrator tries to see nature in terms of his 'familiar' world, as if trying to 'organize' it, at the same time as yearning to be free from that which is regular and 'known'.

'The Birds' concludes with the central character remaining undecided over which of the two landscapes, representing freedom and familiarity respectively, to choose. He presents a paradox alluding to three conflicting elements – water, air and fire – that serve as metaphors for the freedom, and passion for which he yearns. His emotive use of repetition, for instance, in the statement "I love water, I *love* water" is seen to conflict with the separate final line, "but I also love air, and fire" and so the poem ends on a note of ambiguity. It is as if he wishes neither to lose himself in the beauty of the natural world, nor to remain fully part of the human dimension, but to engage imaginatively with both.

The examiner will mark your analysis according to four strands of criteria:

1 Understanding and interpretation.

2 Appreciation of the writer's choices.

3 Organization.

4 Language.

Marked out of 5 in each, what final mark out of 20 would you award this candidate? Discuss your reasons with a partner.

The higher level commentary: providing a sense of structure

Unlike standard level, higher level extracts are not accompanied with questions. This means that you can perhaps be a little freer in the way you construct your analysis and interpretation, but you will have to think more carefully about how to organize your points.

It is perhaps fair to say that the majority of detailed analyses of extracts will tend to broadly follow one of two structural principles:

● **The linear approach**: this is a commentary that moves sequentially through the extract, analysing its progression in sections. This can often work well when there is a very clear sense of development in the extract. Your topic statements (the first sentence of each paragraph) can then center on the points of transition – but, remember, these may not always occur between stanzas or paragraphs. The danger with this way of organizing your ideas is falling into re-telling the story. Remember, your job is to analyse and interpret the text, not describe it.

- **The conceptual**: this is a commentary that divides the extract not into sections of development, but into different aspects of content and different aspects of language. You may find yourself talking about the character of the narrator in paragraph one, her relationship with x in paragraph two and the setting in paragraph three, etc. You may either look at language as you go along in support of your points, or save discussion about language for the later stages of the commentary (generally speaking, however, the essay will usually be driven by points about content, with language in support). This kind of structure will look at the extract more holistically. It is perhaps more challenging than the linear approach, but tends to enable you to show more independent control over your central line of argument, and to develop ideas more coherently as you go along.

This being said, you should not think that there is a formula to guarantee success, and careful thinking *for yourself* about the best way to structure your essay will be a crucial means through which to demonstrate understanding of the extract or poem, and independent critical ability.

Have a look at the following poem, 'The Cyclist'. Annotate a copy of the poem carefully in as much detail as you can, using all or some of the strategies suggested in Chapter 3.

The Cyclist

Freewheeling down the escarpment past the unpassing horse
Blazoned in chalk the wind he causes in passing
Cools the sweat of his neck, making him one with the sky,
In the heat of the handlebars he grasps the summer
Being a boy and to-day a parenthesis
Between the horizon's brackets; the main sentence
Waits to be picked up later but these five minutes
Are all to-day and summer. The dragonfly
Rises without take-off, horizontal,
Underlining itself in a sliver of peacock light.

And glaring, glaring white
The horse on the down moves within his brackets,
The grass boils with grasshoppers, a pebble
Scutters from under the wheel and all this country
Is spattered white with boys riding their heat-wave,
Feet on a narrow plank and hair thrown back

And a surf of dust beneath them. Summer, summer –
They chase it with butterfly nets or strike it into the deep
In a little red ball or gulp it lathered with cream
Or drink it through closed eyelids; until the bell
Left-right-left gives his forgotten sentence
And reaching the valley the boy must pedal again
Left-right-left but meanwhile

For ten seconds more can move as the horse in the chalk
Moves unbeginningly calmly
Calmly regardless of tenses and final clauses
Calmly unendingly moves.

Louis MacNiece

Look through your annotations. What things did you notice? What key features of content, language and style struck you as **most** significant? What questions did you ask yourself?

Now start thinking about how you might turn your annotations into a plan for an actual commentary:

- What kind of 'reading' have you come up with? Does it highlight a particular aspect of content or style? Does it ask from where the poem gains its main strength? Does it focus on a contrast or conflict, or a significant development?

- What kinds of structure might you follow? One that traces the linear development of the poem, or perhaps one that breaks the poem's features down into concepts?

- Try and put together some kind of plan.

Now read through this commentary.

Higher level student response

In 'The Cyclist', Louis MacNiece creates an evocative depiction of the fleeting summer days of childhood. This elaborate, perhaps somewhat romanticized account seemingly describes a single cyclist on a summer day. However, MacNiece's attempt to fully capture the atmosphere of a summer bicycle trip allows him to also explore the various ways in which this isolated incident connects both to the boy described and to more general aspects of human experience.

In the poem's opening stanza, MacNiece describes the physical details of cycling, referring to the way in which the boy holds the handlebars, the breeze caused by the "passing" of the bicycle, and even the sweat on the boy's neck. He is not presently constrained or limited in any way, moving so quickly that he can paradoxically pass the "unpassing" horse, and be "Freewheeling" across such a vast expanse that he is at "one" with the all-encompassing sky. Summer becomes a tangible quantity which the boy "grasps" as eagerly as he does the handlebars, imbuing even the description of a mere dragonfly with childlike wonder, as it rises like "peacock light". In a different sense, however, the boy is also confined; being young, he exists in "parenthesis" between much larger "brackets" and has yet to pick up his role or place in what is to come. This becomes an ongoing metaphor throughout the poem, comparing life to a sentence or story, of which this young boy represents only a few punctuation marks. The fact that this "summer" may last only "five minutes" hints at the fleeting nature of this carefree childhood.

The second stanza broadens the subject to include other young boys. The stanza is primarily atmospheric, although a reference to the horse, too, being contained "within his brackets" suggests that the similar brackets of the first stanza are a more universal affiliation, and the limits they place on the horizon are not unique to this boy. The stanza uses diction with connotations of heat and even anger such as "glaring", repeated for emphasis, and "boils" as well as sibilance in "grass boils… grasshoppers" to suggest heat and movement. This experience of summer cycling is no longer limited to one child or the group; it is a "wave" of boys that is spreading to cover or engulf "all this country".

This rapid expansion of the poem's main subjects, combined with unsettling and even potentially dangerous vocabulary, such as "glaring", "heat-wave" and "boils" create tension as to what the resolution of all this movement and energy compared to bracketing control will be.

The third stanza returns to the initial references to summer, which is effectively personified. The active verbs throughout this sequence, such as "chase", "strike" and "gulp" further emphasize the activity of these youths. However, in line 5 of the third stanza, the flowing run-on sentences of the previous stanzas are brought to a halt by the "Left-right-left" order and repetition of a bell. At this point, the "main sentence" that the boy has yet to join is reintroduced, even if it has become almost forgotten. In this case, the tolling of the bell and the return of the "sentence" could refer to an inevitable transition between youth and maturity, despite the apparent desire to "meanwhile" continue "For ten seconds more" on the bicycle of youth. Alternatively, the poem could be making summer analogous to a bicycle ride – when the boy reaches "the valley" at the end, he must resume the "Left-right-left" steady pedalling work of school with all its confusing "tenses and final clauses". Or the poem could be referring to any kind of brief escape, where "five minutes" become "all to-day and summer" coming to an unfortunate end. The poet's intention is left ambiguous, perhaps intentionally, by the uncertain ending, where enjambment and the repetition of "Calmly" make it difficult to discern what is so calm.

Although it does not have an obviously clear intended meaning, Louis MacNiece's 'The Cyclist' does capture the atmosphere of summertime recreation in a detailed manner, which leaves tantalizing suggestions, never fully explored, of the range of ideas and activities that the activity of cycling could metaphorically represent.

What are your impressions of this commentary? What are its strengths and weaknesses? It is certainly a commentary with many strengths. The student has engaged effectively with the poem, referring to the text in support of their points, and there is comment on stylistic components as well as aspects of content. Aspects of content include the **subject** of the cyclist and of cycling itself, the **setting** of summer and some comment on nature, as well as some analysis of **thematic ideas** such as the nature of childhood, the concepts of freedom and of time and the fact that the poem is open to multiple interpretations. On the negative side, the commentary doesn't really delve into the representation of summer in very much depth, commenting on personification but not really saying much about how or why, nor things like the chalk horse – and perhaps there is more to say about such things as the contrasts between movement and stillness in the poem, or the way the atmosphere and mood change as the poem goes on. Also, what, exactly, is meant by "more general aspects of human experience"? A bit vague, isn't it?

In terms of language and style, there is comment on the central metaphor of writing a sentence and some reference to diction, but not much more. What other things could the student have made reference to? There are quite a few further examples of figurative language ("he grasps the summer", "in a sliver of peacock light", "drink it through closed eyelids" for example), there are things to say about the sense imagery, the free-verse structure and what about tone?

What further things would you have brought to the foreground as well as, or in place of, the points in this student's answer? In this example, the central argument seems to be that there are a number of ways of reading this poem. Do you agree? Or would you have centralized such things as the key contrast between movement and stillness, what the poem 'says' about summer – or childhood, or even writing, its celebration of freedom and the imagination – as possible lines of interpretation?

A word on introductions

Getting introductions right can be one of the hardest but most significant things in your commentary. Partly because it is the first thing the examiner reads, but also because it is the place in which your essay is provided with a clear sense of direction.

Read through the three introductions to commentaries written under exam conditions in response to the poem 'Magician'. What do you think are the strengths and weaknesses of each?

Magician

What matters more than practice
is the fact that you, my audience,
are pulling for me, want me to pull
it off – this next sleight. Now
you see it. Something more than
whether I succeed's at stake.

This talk is called patter. This
is misdirection – how my left
hand shows you nothing's in it.
Nothing is. I count on your mistake
of caring. In my right hand your
undoing blooms like cancer.

But I've shown you that already –
empty. Most tricks are done
before you think they've started – you
who value space more than time.
The balls, the cards, the coins – they go
into the past, not into my pocket.

If I give you anything, be sure
it's not important. What I keep
keeps me alive – a truth on which
your interest hinges. We are like
lovers, if you will. Sometimes even
if you don't will. Now you don't.

Gary Miranda

Introduction 1

'Magician', by Gary Miranda, is a poem in which the mental processes of a magician are being explored immediately before, during and after he has performed a magic trick for an audience. While this task would seem to be quite innocent, Miranda is able to make the task appear quite sinister by setting a tone that evokes both fear and uncertainty in the reader. This is done primarily through the controlling of pace with caesurae and enjambment, and also by Miranda's choice of menacing vocabulary.

Introduction 2

The poem 'Magician' is as clever and deft as the tricks it describes. Through the use of concealed metaphor, combined with terse and logical language, Miranda exposes the human desire to hide from the harsh realities of life and conveys to the reader that people cannot turn to 'magic' for answers – we must discover them for ourselves.

Introduction 3

This poem, 'Magician', by Gary Miranda, focuses on the relationship between a magician and his audience. He compares this relationship to that of 'lovers' and in doing so explores the tension between truth and deception. The first-person narrative is important to the poem as we gain a glimpse into both the public identity of this entertainer, as well as the somewhat disturbing exploration of his private thoughts and feelings.

Although the three introductions are fairly different in nature, the second being quite 'personal' in its reading, the first and third a little more objective, perhaps, they seem nevertheless to include similar things:

- A statement of the subject of the poem and some brief comment on the way the poem develops the subject.
- A reference to one or two key features of language and style.
- A 'signpost' that indicates the direction, the line of argument and/ or interpretation the commentary is going to follow.

It would be wrong to suggest that you should always adopt this formula in your approach to writing introductions to commentaries, but at least you now have a sense of the kinds of things which might be considered appropriate.

By now, you will have developed an understanding of some of the ways in which poetry commentaries can be tackled.

Now read and annotate a copy of the following higher level poem:

Later in this chapter on page 69 we will explore conclusions.

Behaviour of Fish in an Egyptian Tea Garden

As a white stone draws down the fish
she on the seafloor of the afternoon
draw down men's glances and their cruel wish
for love. Slyly red lip on the spoon

slips in a morsel of ice-cream; her hands
white as a milky stone; white submarine
fronds, sink with spread fingers, lean
along the table, carmined at the ends.

A cotton magnate, an important fish
with great eyepouches and a golden mouth
through the frail reefs of furniture swims out
and idling, suspended, stays to watch.

A crustacean old man clamped to his chair
sits coldly near her and might see
her charms through fissures where the eyes should be
or else his teeth are parted in a stare.

Captain on leave, a lean dark mackerel,
lies in the offing; turns himself and looks
through currents of sound. The flat-eyed flatfish sucks
on a straw, staring from its repose, laxly.

And gallants in shoals swim up and lag,
circling and passing near the white attraction;
sometimes pausing, opening a conversation;
fish pause so to nibble or tug.

Now the ice-cream is finished, is
paid for. The fish swim off on business
and she sits alone at the table, a white stone
useless except to a collector, a rich man.

Keith Douglas

Below is a student's response to the poem 'Behaviour of Fish in an Egyptian Tea Garden'. Read the essay through and, with a partner, discuss what you think are its strengths and weaknesses.

Keith Douglas' 'Behaviour of Fish in an Egyptian Tea Garden' is a poem describing an extended metaphor comparing a beautiful woman (presumably in an Egyptian tea garden, as suggested by the title) to an attractive white stone and the men who see her to passing fish. The usage of extremely rich, provocative, and highly metaphoric language in this poem enhances the quality and effect of the poem.

The poem opens by setting the scene – it establishes the white stone on the seafloor, the woman in the afternoon who catches men's attentions. As fish are drawn to a white, luminescent stone, so are men attracted to this woman. It should be noted that the only instance in which a stanza does not end with a period is the first, and the second stanza is a continuation of the description of this woman.

By combining provocative and marine terms and adjectives, Douglas simultaneously transmits the appeal of the woman while maintaining the underwater-like impressions of the poem. Words like "red lip", "milky", "sink", and "carmined" have a connotation of luxurious femininity designed to appeal to men, and the image created by the "Slyly red lip on the spoon" and pronounced by the new stanza which "slips in a morsel of ice-cream" further serves to establish the woman's sexual appeal. However, Douglas maintains the constant connection to the sea by describing the woman's hand as a stone with submarine frond-like fingers.

The third stanza sets up the action in this poem; it describes a fish, the first man who "swims out" to watch. This particular "fish" has the least human characteristics of all the fish described in the poem. This further helps Douglas set him apart as an observer. The following stanzas describe other fish with human traits and actions, or men with fish-like actions and characteristics. The "crustacean old man" who is "clamped to his chair" like a clam or an oyster, the "Captain on leave, a lean dark mackerel", the "flat-eyed flatfish [who] sucks / on a straw", and "gallants in shoals [that] swim up and lag…/ …opening a conversation". Douglas describes all of these other fish with language that creates an active interaction between the woman (the stone) and the men (the fish). The old man sits next to her; the captain turns to look at her; the man sitting in his place is content to stay there sucking on his straw and staring at her; groups of brave young men try to interact with her, "circling and passing near the white attraction". The close descriptions of the men and the woman and the intertwinement of their descriptions, along with references to marine terms, serve to set up and maintain the aquatic atmosphere throughout the entirety of the poem.

The emphasis placed on the importance of the woman's action of eating ice-cream is further emphasized in the final stanza, when the ice-cream has been finished. While she is eating, she has a human-like quality which makes her approachable. However, once she has finished, she is more like the non-responsive and non-interactive white stone that is beautiful, but useless. The eating of the ice-cream serves to humanize the woman and to allow the interaction (or attempts at such) between her and the men. Once she has finished the ice-cream, she returns to being a non-interactive, beautiful object that is "useless except to a collector, a rich man".

It is interesting to see the combination of the appeal of the woman with the marine/aquatic atmosphere of the poem. While Douglas describes human actions, he does so using adjectives and terms used in marine terminology. This serves to have an overall effect of submerged passion, even an almost scientific look at love. The constant maintenance of the aquatic metaphor makes the reader's ability to connect and empathize with the characters and their interaction within the poem limited. However, perhaps this is the desired effect – a highly artistic way of presenting what might otherwise be considered a mundane situation in order to elevate it, while at the same time preventing emotional attachment to, or empathy with, the characters in the poem.

Examiner's comments

This commentary has much strength, showing reasonable understanding of the poem and some close reference to the text. The candidate has got to grips with the essential extended metaphor of the poem, commenting on the presentation of the woman and the various male admirers, though there is room for more sensitive response to phrases such as "white submarine / fronds" and the student omits to comment on a number of phrases, such as "their cruel wish / for love". There is a tendency to describe the action, in place of analysis – particularly in the third paragraph, but more interesting interpretive thinking occurs towards the end, particularly in the comment about the use of marine imagery to "have an overall effect of submerged passion, even an almost scientific look at love". Perhaps it is a shame that they didn't make more of this line of interpretation, as there is considerably more to say about the issue of the objectification of the woman and the themes of the poem.

In terms of style, comment is made on imagery, diction and metaphor – with some analysis of the effects of literary features. Analysis could also have been made, however, of the structure of the poem, its use of sound and, perhaps most importantly, the ironic tone with its humorous, objective detachment, while at the same time communicating a fairly personal, involved – and arguably also quite serious – attitude towards the action.

The criteria for assessment of Paper 1 are presented at the end of this chapter on pages 74–7. Imagine you are an examiner. What marks would you award this commentary for the different criteria?

Why not have a go at either a guided literary analysis or a commentary on your own. If you are a higher level student, simply ignore the questions.

Summer Solstice, Batticaloa, Sri Lanka

The war had turned inward until it resembled
suicide. The only soothing thing was water.
I passed the sentries, followed the surf out of sight.
I would sink into the elements, become simple.

Surf sounds like erasure, over and over.
I lay down and let go, the way you trust an animal.
When I opened my eyes, all down the strand
small crabs, the bright yellow of a crayon,

had come out onto the sand. Their numbers, scattered,
resembled the galactic spill and volume of the stars.
I, who had lain down alone, emptied,
waked at the center of ten thousand prayers.

Who would refuse such attention. I let it sweeten me
back into the universe. I was alive, in the midst
of great loving, which is all I've ever wanted.
The soldiers of both sides probably wanted just this.

Marilyn Krysl

Question 1: What attitude towards war is reflected in the poem?

Question 2: In what ways and to what effect does the poem use comparison?

Part 2: prose

We need to remember, of course, that you also have the option of writing about prose in the exam.

Essentially, the practices we have been discussing are no different with a prose extract. The only key difference that does apply is that poems tend to be complete works, while the prose option will, in all likelihood, be an extract from a longer work.

In analysing prose there is the same expectation of focus on language and style as there is content. However, students often find that exploring the effects of literary features in prose is more challenging than with poetry. Perhaps this is because prose can appear to be less 'concentrated' than poetry in this way, or perhaps it feels easier to talk at greater length about matters of content. Whatever the reason, there is just as much to say about *how* prose writers communicate their ideas – *what* they say – as the writers of poetry.

Let's consider some of the tools prose writers use to generate different kinds of narrative voice:

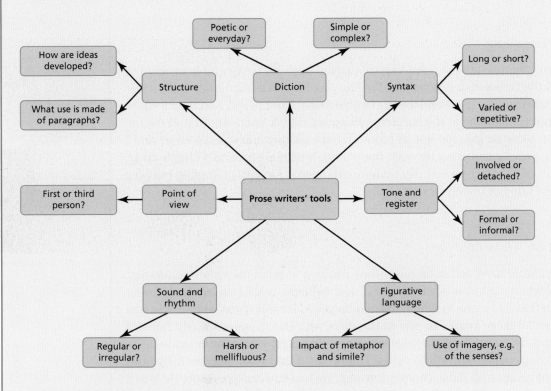

1 Read through the following five extracts of prose and annotate them on your own.

   a What different 'voices' have been created?

   b Which of the above tools are important to **the way** these voices are created?

   c How do these voices affect the way we read the content?

   d Which extract do you like best and why?

2 Swap your ideas with a partner, or in small groups. Do you agree or disagree? What key points of similarity or difference can you find?

Extract A From: *Venice*

It is not altogether an easy city for children to live in. It has no dangerous traffic and few unspeakable rascals; but Venice is inescapably urban, and only lucky children with gardens, or with parents indulgent enough to take them to the distant park, have somewhere green to play. Blithe but pathetic are the groups of urchins to be found entertaining themselves, in hot dry squares or dripping alleyways, with their inexplicable Venetian games – the most popular is governed by the accuracy with which a child can throw the old rubber heel of a shoe, but is so hedged about with subtleties and qualifications that for the life of me I have never been able to master the rules. The State schools of Venice are excellent and lavishly staffed, but they generally occupy tall, dark, overheated buildings, heavily decorated with potted plants. There are no playing fields or yards, and even the mid-morning break (or so my own children lugubriously assure me) is celebrated indoors, with a biscuit or an orange at a blank brown desk.

Jan Morris

Extract B From: *Breath*

I hurtle on too long through the pounding submarine mist. End over end in my caul of bubbles until the turbulence is gone and I'm hanging limp in a faint green light while all the heat ebbs from my chest and the life begins to leach out of me. And then a white flash from above. Someone at the surface, swimming down. Someone to pull me up, drag me clear, blow air into me hot as blood. He spears down and stops short and I recognize my own face peering through the gloom, hesitating an arm's length away, as if uncertain of how to proceed. My own mouth opens. A chain of shining bubbles leaks forth but I do not understand.

Tim Winton

Extract C From: *A Small Good Thing*

Although they were tired and in anguish, they listened to what the baker had to say. They nodded when the baker began to speak of loneliness, and of the sense of doubt and limitation that had come to him in his middle years. He told them what it was like to be childless all these years. To repeat the days with the ovens endlessly full and endlessly empty. The party food, the celebrations he'd worked over. Icing knuckle-deep. The tiny wedding couples stuck into cakes. Hundreds of them, no, thousands by now. Birthdays. Just imagine all those candles burning. He had a necessary trade. He was a baker. He was glad he wasn't a florist. It was better to be feeding people. This was a better smell anytime than flowers.

"Smell this," the baker said, breaking open a dark loaf. "It's a heavy bread, but rich." They smelled it, then he had them taste it. It had the taste of molasses and course grains. They listened to him. They ate what they could. They swallowed the dark bread. It was like daylight under the fluorescent trays of light. They talked on into the early morning, the high, pale cast of light in the windows, and they did not think of leaving.

Raymond Carver

Extract D From: *Spring Day*

In the fresh-washed sunlight, the breakfast table is decked and white. It offers itself in flat surrender, tendering tastes, and smells, and colours, and metals, and grains, and the white cloth falls over its side, draped and wide. Wheels of white glitter in the silver coffee-pot, hot and spinning like catherine-wheels, they whirl, and twirl -- and my eyes begin to smart, the little white, dazzling wheels prick them like darts. Placid and peaceful, the rolls of bread spread themselves in the sun to bask. A stack of butter-pats, pyramidal, shout orange through the white, scream, flutter, call: "Yellow! Yellow! Yellow!" Coffee steam rises in a stream, clouds the silver tea-service with mist, and twists up into the sunlight, revolved, involuted, suspiring higher and higher, fluting in a thin spiral up the high blue sky. A crow flies by and croaks at the coffee steam. The day is new and fair with good smells in the air.

Amy Lowell

Extract E From: *Vernon God Little*

I sit waiting between the shafts of light from a row of doorways, naked except for my shoes and Thursday's underwear. Looks like I'm the only one they rounded up so far.

I ain't in trouble, don't get me wrong. I didn't have anything to do with Tuesday. Still, you wouldn't want to be here today. You'd remember Clarence Somebody, that ole black guy who was on the news last winter. He was the psycho who dozed in this same wooden hall, right on camera. The news said that's how little he cared about the effects of his crimes. By 'effects' I think he meant axe-wounds. Ole Clarence Whoever was shaved clean like an animal, and dressed in the kind of hospital suit that psychos get, with jelly-jar glasses and all, the type of glasses worn by people with mostly gums and no teeth. They built him a zoo cage in court. Then they sentenced him to death.

I just stare at my Nikes. Jordan New Jacks, boy. I'd perk them up with a spit-wipe, but it seems kind of pointless when I'm naked.

D. B. C. Pierre

Now let's look at a longer prose extract for comment. Once again, thinking back to the advice in Chapter 3 on pages 34–6 about how to tackle unseen extracts, read through the following and record your response in the form of annotations, questions and selection of aspects you regard as most important.

The Boat

There are times even now, when I awake at four o'clock in the morning with the terrible fear that I have overslept; when I imagine that my father is waiting for me in the room below the darkened stairs or that the shorebound men are tossing pebbles against my window while blowing their hands and stomping their feet impatiently on the frozen steadfast earth. There are times when I am half out of bed and fumbling for socks and mumbling for words before I realize that I am foolishly alone, that no one waits at the base of the stairs and no boat rides restlessly in the waters by the pier.

At such times only the grey corpses on the overflowing ashtray beside my bed bear witness to the extinction of the latest spark and silently await the crushing out of the most recent of their fellows. And then because I am afraid to be alone with death, I dress rapidly, make a great to-do about clearing my throat, turn on both faucets in the sink and proceed to make loud splashing ineffectual noises. Later I go out and walk the mile to the all-night restaurant.

In the winter it is a very cold walk, and there are often tears in my eyes when I arrive. The waitress usually gives a sympathetic little shiver and says, "Boy, it must be really cold out there; you got tears in your eyes."

"Yes," I say, "it sure is; it really is."

And then the three or four of us who are always in such places at such times make uninteresting little protective chit-chat until the dawn reluctantly arrives. Then I swallow the coffee, which is always bitter, and leave with a great busy rush because by that time I have to worry about being late and whether I have a clean shirt and whether my car will start and about all the other countless things one must worry about when one teaches at a great Midwestern university. And I know then that that day will go by as have all the days of the past ten years, for the call and the voices and the shapes and the boat were not really there in the early morning's darkness and I have all kinds of comforting reality to prove it. They are only shadows and echoes, the animals a child's hands make on the wall by lamplight, and the voices from the rain barrel; the cuttings from an old movie made in the black and white of long ago.

I first became conscious of the boat in the same way and at almost the same time that I became aware of the people it supported. My earliest recollection of my father is a view from the floor of gigantic rubber boots and then of being suddenly elevated and having my face pressed against the stubble of his cheek, and of how it tasted of salt and of how he smelled of salt from his red-soled rubber boots to the shaggy whiteness of his hair.

When I was very small, he took me for my first ride in the boat. I rode the half-mile from our house to the wharf on his shoulders and I remember the sound of his rubber boots galumphing along the gravel beach, the tune of the indecent little song he used to sing, and the odour of the salt.

Alistair MacLeod

How did you get on? Look back through your annotations. What kind of reading journey took place?

If you haven't already done so, try to organize your ideas into categories. What key aspects, for instance, would you nominate for **content**? Perhaps:

- the presentation of the **character of the narrator**: his sense of isolation and unease. What is the nature of his experience of identity? Why does he seem afraid, especially of death?
- the narrator's **relationship with his father**: how does he experience grief at his loss? What role does his father continue to play in his memory? What do physical details of his father's appearance tell us about him?
- the **setting**: there are things to say about the presentation of the seascape and the sense of winter
- the **image of the boat**: as a motif it seems to carry literal and figurative significance
- the past and the **contrast** between the past and the present: the narrator's attitude towards the past seems a little ambiguous. Does he find refuge in recollection or does he want to be free from it? Past and present worlds are presented quite differently.
- important **thematic ideas** concern the significance of death and the exploration of grief and loss.

What about stylistic concerns? Key components that may have struck you could have included:

- the narrator's 'voice': a first-person narrative, sensitive and reflective
- **diction** and **syntax**: varied uses of language and structure. A 'real' and honest speaking voice.
- **imagery**: mixing literal and figurative, incorporating imagery of death. There is a considerable amount of sense imagery.
- the importance of the use of present tense
- the attention to physical detail.

So what is this extract 'about'?

- The past and identity: the narrator's attempt to make sense of the difference between child and adult worlds.
- Grief: the extract is concerned with the narrator coming to terms with his father's death.
- The inter-weaving of past and present; the sense of temporal confusion. What role does the writing of the narrative itself have to play?
- The extract's general concern with the subject of death.
- Something else.

What do I write in a conclusion to my commentary?

Before we look at a student commentary in full, it is worth taking a brief look at conclusions. Earlier in this chapter on pages 60–1, we noted that students often find writing introductions and conclusions quite a challenge and, although it is important not to treat them as all the same, you could consider a number of things that might help.

In the past, you may have been told to treat your conclusion as a summary of your main ideas. While there is an element of truth in this, just to repeat the things you have already said seems rather pointless and repetitive. Try to think of your conclusion as a means to address some of the following:

- In summary, what is the **most important** thing your commentary has attempted to say? For instance, take us back to your basic line of argument: what have you tried to argue in this commentary?
- What has the poem or prose extract in essence suggested about its central subject?
- What do you feel is the **most significant strength** of the poem or prose extract? Is there a key component from which it gains its main effect?
- Does the poem or prose extract have any kind of 'message'? What does it fundamentally say about human experience or the human condition?
- What's the **main effect** of the poem or prose extract in terms of the reader?

Activity

Read through the following three concluding paragraphs of a commentary written in response to the poem 'Magician' (on page 60). What do you feel are the strengths and weaknesses of each conclusion?

Conclusion 1

The poem, 'Magician', by Gary Miranda, is one of rising and falling tension as the sinister inner-thoughts of a performing magician are explored. The very clever way in which Miranda associates fear with the magician is highlighted by his use of structuring to affect tone. The excitement created throughout the initial stanza entralls the reader into a poem that at first sight seems shallow. The depth of the poem is however made clear by the final message presented in the last lines. This message being of the importance of understanding that which is happening around us, not just in the physical world that we can see but also in regard to those important things we cannot always see.

Conclusion 2

Ultimately, it is the absence of poetry in 'Magician' that makes its message so effective, and shows the reader that God does not exist. Miranda's deft and adroit language both exposes human weakness and points to where the real answers can be found.

Conclusion 3

To conclude, 'Magician' ends up being a poem concerned with the nature of human flaws – the willingness of people without power to be manipulated and controlled, and the weakness of those in power who depend on commendations given to them for their sense of security. The apparent simplicity of the language and form of the poem reinforces its basic theme: it is in fact quite a complex work, and so the reader – like the audience – has also been deceived.

How do examiners assess the commentary?

Let's now take a look at a full commentary written by a higher level student under exam conditions. In order to make the most sense of the exercise, tackle the prose extract below yourself first and then compare your annotations with the student's commentary on pages 71–2.

If you are a standard level student, perhaps you could come up with some questions that would draw attention to the extract's key features of content and style.

Read through the extract and spend up to 30 minutes making annotations and planning your answer.

The In-Between World of Vikram Lall

I felt a tremor in my sister's arm.

Before us, at the intersection, the mosque stood towering in all its grandeur, outlined in a brilliant series of decorative light bulbs in honour of some celebration; its clock tolled the half hour at ten-thirty. A dog barked somewhere, and in perverse reply came the sound of a bicycle bell. The image of old Mwangi was floating in my mind, of him tending the garden patiently, when suddenly a terrifying, unearthly squeal came from the shadows, followed by a hoot. My sister and I froze in our tracks. Oh God, Oh Rabba, she whispered, digging her fingers into my arm. Out leapt before us six youths, howling like wild dogs, gesturing like demons, mouthing all manner of obscenities; they surrounded us. I took hold of Deepa's hand and made a dash for it in the direction we had come, only to meet a leering Elvis face, shirt open, pants crotch-tight, wielding a tree branch. I lurched sideways, ran forward, to no avail. We should have screamed, but terror froze our throats. Backwards, sideways, forwards again, and our paths were blocked in a horrifying checkmate and what awaited was only the kill. But then at the intersection appeared a white Mercedes; it turned left onto the main road, swerved left again toward the gate where we stood trapped, and the six scampered away into the dark like cockroaches. The man at the wheel was a local millionaire, Mr. Bapu; he rolled down a window and asked us who we were and what was the matter. We explained our predicament, and he told us to spend the night in his house, he would have us driven to the campus the next morning.

There was no doubt in my mind, from the obscenities I had heard – in a mixture of Cutchi and Swahili, that Tanzanian specialty – and the faces I had seen – that buck-toothed horse, the curly-haired half-caste chotara – that our attackers had known me, and most likely seen my sister before. I, a Nairobi Punjabi Hindu, was dating one of their girls; to make matters worse, I had a sister who was going out in the open with an African. When men develop contempt for a woman, the vilest, filthiest language escapes their lips. All night I smarted from those insults. Deepa was close to hysteria and I spent the night in the same room with her.

The next morning Mr. Bapu drove us in his white Mercedes to the campus, but not before a lavish breakfast and a tour of his quite wonderful garden, which he obviously had a hand in tending, though there was an elderly gardener with whom he chatted amiably. Mr. Bapu cut for Deepa a red rose. On the way he hummed a tune, some sort of bhajan, which we could not quite figure out, but it seemed completely out of key and Deepa and I had a job keeping up straight faces.

I realize that my contempt for those nocturnal attackers has not waned a bit; I have called them names, but this is how I have always recalled them and that terror-filled eternity that must actually have been two or three minutes. Mahesh Uncle comes to mind: when we were little he once said to us, in his typical manner, Henh, henh – see how memory makes monkeys out of our enemies, as one of my teachers used to say. And what does it make out of our friends, Uncle? we asked. He said, It gives them a tint of rose, or it saves them in amber – do you know what amber is, children?

Mr. Bapu, whom we never saw again, is preserved in amber.

Moyez Vassanji

Take a moment to look through your annotations and the plan you have sketched for yourself. Think it through and make sure it will work. If you have time, you could even write the commentary out in full.

Now look at this student's response. As you read, jot down things that you like and don't like about the way this commentary has been written.

When subjected to the selective nature of memory, traumatic experiences can become black and white in their extremity, making "monkeys out of our enemies" and remembering our friends with "a tint of rose". In this extract from *The In-Between World of Vikram Lall*, M. G. Vassanji writes from the narrative perspective of a young "Nairobi Punjabi Hindu" male as his account of a terrifying attempted attack confronts racism and sexism in culturally diverse Tanzania.

The reader is immediately alerted to an apparently tense situation at the start of the extract, as the narrator feels "a tremor in my sister's arm". The suspense is left to simmer as the narrator deviates to describe the landscape. The mosque "towering in all its grandeur" suggests that religion is a large part of this culture, although the narrator does not appear to be Muslim as he ponders "some celebration". His lack of local knowledge and nostalgia for "old Mwangi" suggests that he does not belong to this community – the "campus" that he and his sister return to later reaffirming this.

The dark silence, marred only as "a dog barked" and by the "sound of a bicycle bell", is broken by an "unearthly squeal… followed by a hoot"; the unnatural squeal contrasting the animalistic youths as they are "howling like wild dogs" and "gesturing like demons", although it is clear that the narrator believes them to be responsible for both noises.

Deepa's whispers of "Oh God, Oh Rabba" echo the confusion of culture which seems so prevalent in this town. The terrifying memory intensifies as the narrator describes "a leering Elvis face, shirt open, pants crotch-tight, wielding a tree branch". The overtly sexual nature of the boys' attire seems to threaten Deepa with their power in an obviously masculine society. The atmosphere becomes even more hostile and as the "youths" wield their "tree branch[es]" even nature plays a hostile role. Empathetic and horrified from the graphic descriptions, the reader feels buffeted "backwards, sideways and forwards" with the two victims as they try desperately to avoid their "checkmate". The "awaited… kill" also uses animal imagery, helping to describe their cruelty and barbaric nature of the attack.

However, a turning point in this extract arrives simultaneously with "a white Mercedes", the colour white symbolizing a hope to juxtapose with the despair and futility of their "checkmate". To the narrator, with a newfound confidence and hope, the "wild dogs" and "demons" quickly become "cockroaches". Their alliterative retreat as the "six scampered" emphasizes their meek and childlike presence in view of authority, this contrasting with their entry as "out leapt before us six youths" – the syntax adding to the suspense and terror of their entry. The narrator's recollection of Mr Bapu's civilized and kind questioning "who we were and what was the matter" seems especially heroic after the "howling" and "gesturing" of the youths.

While the narrator realizes that he and his sister have been attacked due to racial differences, "I, a Nairobi Punjabi Hindu, was dating one of their girls; to make matters worse, I had a sister who was going out in the open with an African", he is not above returning the insults, labelling his attackers "that buck-toothed horse" and "the curly-haired half-caste chotara". His bitter but also cruel tone suggesting to the reader that this is perhaps not a one-sided victimization, the lack of dialogue in this first-person recount adding to its subjectivity. Sexism also seems to be rife in Tanzania, as the narrator reflects that "when men develop contempt for a woman, the vilest, filthiest language escapes their lips". This crudity contrasts Mr Bapu's gentleman-like gesture as he presents Deepa with "a red rose" from his garden. These on-going comparisons between the obviously favoured behaviour of Mr Bapu, representing possibly either the same cultural group as the narrator or simply an objective stance from these cultural clashes, and the attackers aid the narrator in his portrayal of his attackers as completely heinous, animalistic and cruel.

As he reflects, the narrator comes to the conclusion that his "contempt for those nocturnal attackers has not waned a bit" as his horrific and intense imagery and similes describe the way in which he "has always recalled them". The metaphorically "terror-filled eternity" being much more real and important to him than the literal "two or three minutes" of the attack. However, the narrator does somewhat qualify his feelings, gaining some perspective as Mahesh Uncle's words come "to mind"; "see how memory makes monkeys out of our enemies". The narrator does admit the subjectivity and imposed extremity of his memory as "Mr. Bapu… is preserved in amber". "A tint of rose" and "amber" as a method of preservation being images of the sometimes deceptively good light that our memories place our friends and allies in. The narrator's hero, Mr Bapu, will always be an entirely good person to the narrator, with his "lavish breakfast" and "wonderful garden", rather than the man of many faults and many virtues that he in all likelihood is. Similarly, the narrator's attackers will always be evil and cruel tormentors in this version of this event, their side of the story not recounted for the reader.

Throughout the extract, Vassanji's young male narrator recounts a particularly horrifying attack due to a clash in cultures and lack of understanding or empathy. His rather selective memory gives the reader a one-sided view, aligning them with him but also making them aware of the different viewpoints from the extract that they are both able to hear; this lack of understanding and communication is possibly one of the underlying reasons for this conflict and the racism and sexism in Tanzania.

Now read the examiner's comments. Do you agree with the assessment?

> ### Examiner's comments
>
> This is a well-structured response to the extract that maintains close attention to detail. The opening paragraph is effective, providing an interesting introduction to the key ideas and signposting the direction in which the candidate will eventually go with the argument about memory.
>
> In the essay's main body, the candidate explores many key aspects of content, including the presentation and role played by physical and social setting, the key characters and their relationships, as well as showing sensitivity to the action of the extract and the creation of tension. There is more to say, however, about the shifts and contrasts in the extract – particularly the portrayal of Mr Bapu in the second half. There are also one or two moments of speculation, when points assume certain things without real justification; the 'confusion' of culture comment is one example. The candidate weaves some thoughtful interpretive comments on the subjects of culture, gender and memory, managing to say interesting things also about the relationship between the 'selective nature of memory' and the first-person narrative.
>
> In addition, the candidate comments perceptively on various literary components, including imagery, some uses of sound ('alliterative retreat'), syntax, tone and narrative voice. There are occasions when more analysis of the effects of these features would be helpful.
>
> Technically, the essay maintains an appropriately analytical register, with some flashes of quite sophisticated writing. The candidate pays close attention to the need for supporting detail, although sometimes quotations are not properly integrated into the lines. The essay is well organized, and shows a sense of development. The candidate shows confidence with analytical writing and, at the same time, allows a sense of independent voice to emerge.

> Look at the official higher level assessment criteria for literary commentary at the end of this chapter on pages 76–7. What marks would you have awarded this candidate?

Activity

Write an analysis of the following prose extract. Refer to the questions if you are a standard level student, or ignore them and write a commentary if you are a higher level student.

Star of the Sea

The music of the ship was howling around him. The low whistlings; the tortured rumbles; the wheezy sputters of breeze flowing through it. The clatter of loose wainscoting. The clank of chains. The groaning of boards. The blare of wind. Never before had he felt rain quite like it. It seemed to spew from the clouds, not merely to fall. He watched the wave rise up from a quarter of a mile away. Rolling. Foaming. Rushing. Surging. Beginning to thicken and swell in strength. Now it was a battlement of ink-black water, almost crumpling under its own weight; but still rising, and now roaring. It smashed into the side of the bucking *Star*, like a punch thrown by an invisible god. He was aware of being flung backwards into the edge of a bench, the dull crack of metal against the base of his spine. The ship creaked violently and pitched into a tilt, downing slowly, almost on to beam ends. A clamour of terrified screams rose up from steerage. A hail of cups and splintering plates. A man's bellow: 'Knockdown!

Knockdown!' One of the starboard lifeboats snapped from its bow-chain and swung loose like a mace, shattering through the wall of the wheelhouse.

The boom of the billows striking the prow a second time. A blind of salt lashed him; drenched him through. Waves churning over his body. The slip of his body down the boards towards the water. A shredding *skreek* of metal on metal. The grind of the engine ripped from the ocean. The ship began to right itself. Snappings of wood filled the air like gunshots. The wail of the klaxon being sounded for clear-all-decks. The man with the club-foot was helping a sailor to grab a woman who was being swept on her back towards the broken rail. She was screaming in terror; grasping; clutching. Somehow they seized her and dragged her below. Hand by hand, gripping the slimy life-rope like a mountaineer, Dixon made it back to the First-Class deckhouse.

Two stewards were in the passageway distributing canisters of soup. Passengers were to retire to their quarters immediately. There was no need for concern. The storm would pass. It was entirely to be expected. A matter of the season. The ship could not capsize; it never had in eighty years. The lifebelts were merely a matter of precaution. But the Captain had ordered everyone to remain below. Laura looking pleadingly at him from the end of the corridor, her terrified sons bawling into her skirts. The three of them being grabbed by an angry-faced Merridith and dragged into her cabin like sacks.

'Inside, sir. Inside! Don't come out until you're called.'

He had found dry clothes and eaten all his soup. After an hour, the storm had levelled down a little. The Chief Steward had knocked on his door with a message from the Captain. All passengers were strictly confined for the rest of the day. No exceptions whatsoever were permitted. The hatches were about to be battened down.

Joseph O'Connor

Question 1: What impression is generated of the atmosphere of the storm?

Question 2: How does the author use diction and syntax to create a sense of tension?

Paper 1 assessment criteria: guided literary analysis (standard level)

Criterion A: understanding and interpretation
- How well does the student's interpretation reveal understanding of the thought and feeling of the passage?
- How well are ideas supported by references to the passage?

Marks	Level descriptor
0	The work does not reach a standard described by the descriptors below.
1	There is very basic understanding of the passage, with mainly irrelevant and/or insignificant interpretation.
2	There is some understanding of the passage but little attempt at interpretation, with few references to the passage.
3	There is adequate understanding of the passage, demonstrated by an interpretation that is mostly supported by references to the passage.
4	There is good understanding of the passage, demonstrated by convincing interpretation that is fully supported by references to the passage.
5	There is very good understanding of the passage, demonstrated by sustained and convincing interpretation that is supported by well-chosen references to the passage.

Criterion B: appreciation of the writer's choices

● To what extent does the analysis show appreciation of how the writer's choices of language, structure, technique and style shape meaning?

Marks	Level descriptor
0	The work does not reach a standard described by the descriptors below.
1	There is virtually no reference to the ways in which language, structure, technique and style shape meaning.
2	There is some reference to, but no analysis of, the ways in which language, structure, technique and style shape meaning.
3	There is adequate reference to, and some analysis and appreciation of, the ways in which language, structure, technique and style shape meaning.
4	There is good analysis and appreciation of the ways in which language, structure, technique and style shape meaning.
5	There is very good analysis and appreciation of the ways in which language, structure, technique and style shape meaning.

Criterion C: organization

● How well organized and coherent is the presentation of ideas?

Marks	Level descriptor
0	The work does not reach a standard described by the descriptors below.
1	Ideas have little organization and virtually no coherence.
2	Ideas have some organization, but coherence is often lacking.
3	Ideas are adequately organized, with some coherence.
4	Ideas are well organized and coherent.
5	Ideas are effectively organized, with very good coherence.

Criterion D: language

● How clear, varied and accurate is the language?

● How appropriate is the choice of register, style and terminology? (Register refers, in this context, to the student's use of elements such as vocabulary, tone, sentence structure and terminology appropriate to the task.)

Marks	Level descriptor
0	The work does not reach a standard described by the descriptors below.
1	Language is rarely clear and appropriate; there are many errors in grammar, vocabulary and sentence construction, and little sense of register and style.
2	Language is sometimes clear and carefully chosen; grammar, vocabulary and sentence construction are fairly accurate, although errors and inconsistencies are apparent; the register and style are to some extent appropriate to the task.
3	Language is clear and carefully chosen, with an adequate degree of accuracy in grammar, vocabulary and sentence construction despite some lapses; register and style are mostly appropriate to the task.
4	Language is clear and carefully chosen, with a good degree of accuracy in grammar, vocabulary and sentence construction; register and style are consistently appropriate to the task.
5	Language is very clear, effective, carefully chosen and precise, with a high degree of accuracy in grammar, vocabulary and sentence construction; register and style are effective and appropriate to the task.

Paper 1 assessment criteria: literary commentary (higher level)

Criterion A: understanding and interpretation

- How well does the student's interpretation reveal understanding of the thought and feeling of the passage?
- How well are ideas supported by references to the passage?

Marks	Level descriptor
0	The work does not reach a standard described by the descriptors below.
1	There is basic understanding of the passage but virtually no attempt at interpretation and few references to the passage.
2	There is some understanding of the passage, with a superficial attempt at interpretation and some appropriate references to the passage.
3	There is adequate understanding of the passage, demonstrated by an interpretation that is supported by appropriate references to the passage.
4	There is very good understanding of the passage, demonstrated by sustained interpretation supported by well-chosen references to the passage.
5	There is excellent understanding of the passage, demonstrated by persuasive interpretation supported by effective references to the passage.

Criterion B: appreciation of the writer's choices

- To what extent does the analysis show appreciation of how the writer's choices of language, structure, technique and style shape meaning?

Marks	Level descriptor
0	The work does not reach a standard described by the descriptors below.
1	There are few references to, and no analysis or appreciation of, the ways in which language, structure, technique and style shape meaning.
2	There is some mention, but little analysis or appreciation, of the ways in which language, structure, technique and style shape meaning.
3	There is adequate analysis and appreciation of the ways in which language, structure, technique and style shape meaning.
4	There is very good analysis and appreciation of the ways in which language, structure, technique and style shape meaning.
5	There is excellent analysis and appreciation of the ways in which language, structure, technique and style shape meaning.

Criterion C: organization and development

- How well organized, coherent and developed is the presentation of ideas?

Marks	Level descriptor
0	The work does not reach a standard described by the descriptors below.
1	Ideas have little organization; there may be a superficial structure, but coherence and development are lacking.
2	Ideas have some organization, with a recognizable structure; coherence and development are often lacking.
3	Ideas are adequately organized, with a suitable structure; some attention is paid to coherence and development.

| 4 | Ideas are effectively organized, with very good structure, coherence and development. |
| 5 | Ideas are persuasively organized, with excellent structure, coherence and development. |

Criterion D: language

- How clear, varied and accurate is the language?
- How appropriate is the choice of register, style and terminology?
  (Register refers, in this context, to the student's use of elements such as vocabulary, tone, sentence structure and terminology appropriate to the task.)

Marks	Level descriptor
0	The work does not reach a standard described by the descriptors below.
1	Language is rarely clear and appropriate; there are many errors in grammar, vocabulary and sentence construction, and little sense of register and style.
2	Language is sometimes clear and carefully chosen; grammar, vocabulary and sentence construction are fairly accurate, although errors and inconsistencies are apparent; the register and style are to some extent appropriate to the commentary.
3	Language is clear and carefully chosen, with an adequate degree of accuracy in grammar, vocabulary and sentence construction despite some lapses; register and style are mostly appropriate to the commentary.
4	Language is clear and carefully chosen, with a good degree of accuracy in grammar, vocabulary and sentence construction; register and style are consistently appropriate to the commentary.
5	Language is very clear, effective, carefully chosen and precise, with a high degree of accuracy in grammar, vocabulary and sentence construction; register and style are effective and appropriate to the commentary.

The individual oral commentary

Objectives

- to recognize the importance of speaking, as much as writing, about texts
- to understand the components of Part 2: detailed study
- to acquire practical skills in preparation for the assessment of Part 2: the individual oral commentary

In the next two chapters, we will take a look at the parts of the literature course known as detailed study (Part 2) and options (Part 4). These two components are internally marked, which means that your teacher undertakes the assessments and marks are then moderated by someone else outside your school. Both of these two components are each worth 15 per cent of the overall grade.

What makes internal assessment different?

Parts 2 and 4 of the course are characterized by the fact that assessment takes place through oral work, as opposed to written. In Part 2, you will need to complete an individual oral commentary, with a subsequent discussion if you are taking higher level, and in Part 4 an individual oral presentation.

We will cover the details of Part 4 in Chapter 6. First, let us take a look at the significance of talking about literature.

Speaking and listening

Question: How much do you involve yourself in class discussion? Do you take an active role, making frequent contributions, adding ideas or questioning others? Or do you prefer to listen, and only volunteer points when you feel particularly strongly about something, or when your teacher asks you to?

Whatever the nature of your personality, in terms of the IB literature course, it is important that in some capacity you get used to talking about the works you are studying. This is because in Parts 2 and 4, marks can be gained more easily if you are used to voicing your opinions and exploring ideas in an oral rather than a written form.

Activity

1 Thinking back to the work you did in Chapter 4 on developing commentary skills, read through the four lines of poetry at the top of the next page. Instead of writing down your annotations, however, just talk to the person sitting next to you about them.

   a What strikes you as interesting?

   b What are the lines 'about'?

   c What kinds of literary elements are important?

   d Do you like the lines of poetry?

   e Do you agree on the most salient or notable things?

Preludes

The winter evening settles down
With smells of steaks in passageways.
Six o'clock.
The burnt-out ends of smoky days.

T. S. Eliot

2 Remaining in your pairs, give yourselves the letter A or B. The As will read the first three stanzas of 'Morning Song', and the Bs the next three. Take a minute to read through your lines, thinking about the same kinds of questions as in Activity 1, and then talk to your partner about your extract for three minutes. You will need to try and use the maximum amount of time available, so be as detailed as you can.

Sylvia Plath

Morning Song

A

Love set you going like a fat gold watch.
The midwife slapped your footsoles, and
   your bald cry
Took its place among the elements.

Our voices echo, magnifying your arrival.
   New statue.
In a drafty museum, your nakedness
Shadows our safety. We stand round
   blankly as walls.

I'm no more your mother
Than the cloud that distills a mirror to
   reflect its own slow
Effacement at the wind's hand.

B

All night your moth-breath
Flickers among the flat pink roses. I wake
   to listen:
A far sea moves in my ear.

One cry, and I stumble from bed, cow-
   heavy and floral
In my Victorian nightgown.
Your mouth opens clean as a cat's. The
   window square

Whitens and swallows its dull stars. And
   now you try
Your handful of notes;
The clear vowels rise like balloons.

Sylvia Plath

3 Now take a minute to annotate the extract you *didn't* talk about with the points made by your partner. See how much of what they said you can remember. Then swap notes. Did you get it all down? Or were there things you missed?

The last part of this activity focuses attention on how much you listened. It's perhaps true to say that teachers often place emphasis on contributing to discussion in class, but of course success in this depends as much on being able to **listen** carefully and actively, as being able to talk with confidence.

In preparing both for your Part 2 and Part 4 oral assessments, time spent listening and responding to points made by other people is extremely important, not least because it is a crucial way of developing your own ideas. In both assessment tasks, the more you can demonstrate a sense of independent exploration of the texts, the better.

Part 2: detailed study

What is an individual oral commentary?

The individual oral commentary, undertaken at the end of your study of the Part 2 works, is a recorded talk that lasts around 10 minutes in response to an extract from one of these works. The extract will be accompanied with guiding questions set by your teacher and you will not know in advance which extracts have been selected for the exam. After 20 minutes of preparation time, you will be expected to talk independently for around eight minutes, and your teacher will then ask questions in the final two minutes.

If you are a higher level student, you must perform your commentary on poetry, and in a second part of the assessment (also lasting 10 minutes) engage in a discussion with your teacher about one other Part 2 work. You will not know in advance which work has been chosen for discussion.

Which extracts will be selected?

Although you are not allowed to know the extract in advance, your teacher will select one that provides you with a significant amount of material to talk about. You will have plenty to say about the content and style, as well as its relationship either to the whole work, or to other works you have studied by that author.

The extract's length will be around 20–30 lines, depending on its complexity. In the case of poetry, the extract will sometimes be a complete poem, but otherwise be taken from somewhere in the work that you will have studied. This will give you the opportunity to explore the context.

What are the guiding questions?

Both higher and standard level extracts will be accompanied by two guiding questions, designed to focus your attention on some key elements. Often, one question will focus on an aspect of content and the other style, but not always. Below are two examples of guiding questions, taken from the subject guide to the course.

> **Guiding questions**
> 1 How does stanza structure reflect the development of the poem's subject?
> 2 In what ways does the final line/stanza change your understanding of the poem as a whole?

> Please note that you are **not obliged to answer these guiding questions**; they are there simply to keep you on track, and stimulate your thinking in case you get stuck.

Notice that the questions are reasonably specific, without giving things away. They will not:

- provide you with points of explanation or interpretation for which you can then gain credit

- focus on the **effects** of particular words, phrases or literary features, thereby limiting your ability to demonstrate independent response to the extract's details.

What kinds of things should I talk about in my commentary?

In many ways, the individual oral commentary is quite similar to the Paper 1 written commentary covered in Chapter 4. You are expected to explore features of **content**, **language** and **style** in considerable detail, demonstrating an ability also to organize your ideas and show some sense of independent thinking.

The key difference, of course, is that you will know the work from which the extract comes, and part of what you comment on (unless it is a complete poem) might be the place of the extract in its immediate **context**, as well as its relationship to the whole work.

Another key difference from the unseen extract for your written commentary will be that the extract is significantly shorter. Therefore, you will have room to talk about it in significant detail, and this is something you should take full advantage of.

The key areas you will be expected to show proficiency in are as follows:

- **Understanding the content**: what does the extract reveal about matters such as character, relationship, theme, action and setting? Are there elements of conflict, contrast or development? Why is it an *important* extract?

- **Understanding the style**: what key features of language and style are present in this extract? The crucial thing to remember, as we said before, is to explore the effects of these features. How do they affect our reading of the material?

- **Organization of ideas**: there needs to be a sense of structure to your commentary, an attempt to present your ideas with some degree of purpose. It would perhaps be unreasonable to expect the same kind of structural rigour in an oral, with 20 minutes preparation time, as a full 1.5 or 2-hour exam, but nevertheless, there should be some evidence of structure.

- **Language**: once again, although the demands on your use of language might be slightly less formal than in written work, there is an expectation that you maintain an appropriate register, and avoid lapsing into unhelpfully colloquial expression.

How do I prepare and deliver my commentary?

In the 20 minutes of supervised preparation time, you should make sure you are fully prepared by undertaking the following tasks:

- Read the extract and guiding questions through extremely carefully.

- Following the advice you have been given in Chapter 3 about annotating extracts in preparation for Paper 1, take time to explore the extract in terms of content, style and context. Read and re-read for different purposes.

- After 10–15 minutes, you should be in a position to decide on what the important features of the extract are. Use these as a means to organize your ideas and write down the order of your main points on a separate piece of paper.

One of the most important things to remember in your commentary is the requirement that you **refer in detail back to the text**. There is no excuse for not doing this as the extract is right there in front of you.

Experience suggests that the majority of your ideas should be written on and around the extract itself. The reason for this is that if you write them on a separate piece of paper, you will then have to keep looking back at the extract in search of the supporting text details. This will be difficult to do and time consuming. That being said, writing down the main sections of your commentary, perhaps in bullet-point form, on a separate sheet is a helpful way of reminding yourself of what you have covered and where you are going next.

How should I approach the delivery?

Keep calm! It is likely that you will feel a little nervous, so slow down and take time to think about what you are saying. If you make mistakes, just carry on. To get top marks, you do not need to deliver a flawless commentary.

You will be expected to talk for around eight minutes, during which time your teacher should not interrupt. At the end of that time, they will ask you some questions on such things as details you may have missed, points that could use some further elaboration or aspects of style or content that you need to show you have fully understood. Unless you have already done so in the commentary itself, your teacher might also ask you about the context of the extract, or the relationship between the poem and others you have studied by the same author. Try to answer the questions as fully as you can, and don't be frightened to ask for clarification if you are asked something that you do not fully understand.

Should I worry about an introduction and conclusion?

Introductions and conclusions are important means of creating a sense of structure. Any **introduction** to an individual oral commentary ought to cover some or all of the following:

- Your name, candidate number, and details of the extract that you have in front of you, such as title and author.

- A brief summary of the context. What is going on in the extract and what has just happened? If it is a poem, you could perhaps say something about its main subject.

- Briefly state the main features of content and language/style that you think are the most important in this extract.

- It is also not a bad idea to explicitly state the structure you intend to follow. There is nothing wrong, for instance, in saying something like: "In this commentary, I would first like to talk about x, and then go on to cover y and finally explore the significance of z." This will force your brain to process and hopefully remember the structure you intend to follow.

It is also important to bring your commentary to some kind of end. A **conclusion** should be brief, and could address all or some of the following:

- A statement as to what is the most important element of the extract – either an aspect of content or style, or both.

- A summative statement as to where the extract's importance lies in terms of the rest of the writer's work, or the text as a whole.

- Some kind of comment about the main way the extract or poem influences the reader.

The individual oral commentary in practice

Let's now turn our attention to various extracts and think about how you might prepare to deliver a commentary on them. There is obviously a strong possibility that you won't know the works from which they come, so commenting on context will be difficult, but at least you can gain a sense of where the majority of marks are earned.

Activity

W. B. Yeats is one of the early 20th-century's most famous writers. His poetic career covered many years of turbulent social and political history in Ireland and throughout Europe, and his style developed considerably throughout his long career. 'The Wild Swans at Coole' was written in 1916.

Read the poem carefully and spend 5–10 minutes making notes on the most interesting features. Try to think about how you would organize your points if you had to do a commentary on the poem for real.

The Wild Swans at Coole

The trees are in their autumn beauty,
The woodland paths are dry,
Under the October twilight the water
Mirrors a still sky;
Upon the brimming water among the stones
Are nine-and-fifty swans.

The nineteenth autumn has come upon me
Since I first made my count;
I saw, before I had well finished,
All suddenly mount
And scatter wheeling in great broken rings
Upon their clamorous wings.

I have looked upon those brilliant creatures,
And now my heart is sore.
All's changed since I, hearing at twilight,
The first time on this shore,
The bell-beat of their wings above my head,
Trod with a lighter tread.

Unwearied still, lover by lover,
They paddle in the cold
Companionable streams or climb the air;
Their hearts have not grown old;
Passion or conquest, wander where they will,
Attend upon them still.

But now they drift on the still water,
Mysterious, beautiful;
Among what rushes will they build,
By what lake's edge or pool
Delight men's eyes when I awake some day
To find they have flown away?

W. B. Yeats

What did you note down?

If possible, talk through your ideas with a partner. Did the same things stand out for you both? Have you started to build similar or contrasting lines of interpretation?

Perhaps you will have given some consideration to the following:

1 The **subject** of the poem being the "Wild Swans", Yeats explores their literal and figurative significance. The **tone** is personal and reflective as Yeats deliberates on the facts of time, aging and beauty.

2 The poem adopts a fairly formal **structure**, with five even stanzas and lines that follow a reasonably regular syntax and iambic rhythm, although this is not consistent. There is also a fairly regular rhyme scheme – all of which serves to create a lyrical, euphonic feel to the poem.

3 The first stanza focuses on the natural beauty of the autumn setting. Water "mirrors" the sky, creating a sense of unity and harmony in the natural world; an atmosphere of stillness and tranquillity is carefully established, so as to create a significant contrast with the movement and noise of the next stanza, signalled perhaps through the use of the word "brimming". The tone is fairly neutral and distant. Simple **diction** is used to depict the position of the swans on the "brimming water among the stones" and the specific number of "nine-and-fifty" reinforces the sense of narrative detachment.

4 In the second stanza, the poem becomes more personally reflective in tone. The speaker, presumably Yeats himself, uses the personal pronouns "me" and "I" as he thinks about the 19 years he has been coming to count the swans. The line, "The nineteenth autumn has come upon me" places him in a somewhat passive position and this is reinforced when the swans "suddenly mount / And scatter..." There is a contrast here between the tranquil, peaceful mood of the opening stanza and adjectives such as "broken" and "clamorous", which suggest a sense of disorder and dissonance.

5 The third and fourth stanzas focus on the subject of change over time. Yeats adopts a somewhat melancholic, nostalgic tone as he reflects on the difference between the present and the past. "All's changed", he says, since the first time he heard the "bell-beat" of the swans flying overhead. Interestingly, he now 'sees' the swans less in visual terms and more in auditory terms. He does not specify exactly *what* has changed, however, until the next stanza. It seems Yeats himself is tired and has "grown old" in comparison with the "unwearied" swans which continue to experience "passion or conquest".

6 In the final stanza, Yeats returns to the present and the words, "Mysterious, beautiful" recapture the mood of the opening stanza. This gives way, however, to a speculative ending in which he questions how long they will remain at the lake, the moment when he wakes up "To find they have flown away?" The poem has thus undergone a development from 'objective' fascination with the beauty of the swans in their natural setting to a more introspective exploration of the problem of time and aging. The swans too have been transformed in a sense, from a literal image to a more figurative symbol of beauty and passion, perhaps even immortality – an experience of stillness and permanence for which the speaker longs in his own life, but is unable to achieve.

7 The poem's adoption of a regular syntax, rhythm and rhyme scheme is, in a sense, reflective of the poem's initial creation of a perhaps slightly artificial, 'romantic' natural landscape, which is then increasingly broken – giving way to a more 'realistic' and intimate deliberation on the problem of time and change. Nature is at once a distant, ethereal symbol of beauty and, at the same time, a present reminder of the physical properties of aging and the fact of dying.

8 Perhaps the poem's publication date might also lead us to deliberate about the kinds of social and political change in Ireland and Europe at the time. The 1916 revolt in Dublin, the First World War, as well as the revolution in Russia, might well have played a part in Yeats' exploration of contrasts between stillness and movement, silence and noise, order and chaos – oppositions that lie at the heart of this poem and emerge even more forcibly in others.

You may well have noted a variety of other things too.

Look again at the order of the numbered notes on pages 83–4. There is a sense, perhaps, of an introduction stating the main ideas; this subsequently opens up to a more detailed linear analysis of the features of individual stanzas and, as the notes go on, more attention is given to things that arguably lie at the heart of this poem. In the mind of the student making these notes, for instance, the significance of the poem's use of contrasts becomes more pronounced, and this is what they foreground at the end in a kind of conclusion.

These were ideas we talked about in the section in Chapter 4 on general commentary practice, weren't they? Remember the key things:

- Detailed reference to the poems.
- Equal analysis of form and content.
- A sense of structure.
- Some degree of interpretive 'reading'.

Activity

Let's look now at a different poem, but this time leave the note-making exercise to you, using the following prompts to get you thinking. When you have finished, think about the best way to structure your ideas.

1 What would you say is the key subject of the poem 'Sea Canes'? Friendship, loss, nature or death? Or the relationship between them? Perhaps something else?

2 How does the poem use structure to bring about the development of its ideas?

3 How does Walcott incorporate the concept of dialogue in the poem?

4 What kinds of imagery and figurative language does Walcott use, and to what effect?

5 In what way(s) does the motif of the canes themselves change as the poem progresses?

6 What use does Walcott make of sound?

7 How would you describe the tone of the poem? Are there any shifts in tone as the poem develops?

8 In what sense does the poem reach a kind of 'conclusion'?

Sea Canes

Half my friends are dead.
I will make you new ones, said earth.
No, give me them back, as they were, instead
with faults and all, I cried.
Tonight I can snatch their talk
from the faint surf's drone
through the canes, but I cannot walk
on the moonlit leaves of ocean
down that white road alone,
or float with the dreaming motion
of owls leaving earth's load.
O earth, the number of friends you keep
exceeds those left to be loved.
The sea canes by the cliff flash green and silver;
they were the seraph lances of my faith,
but out of what is lost grows something stronger
that has the rational radiance of stone,
enduring moonlight, further than despair,
strong as the wind, that through dividing canes
brings those we love before us, as they were,
with faults and all, not nobler, just there.

Derek Walcott

Derek Walcott

Guiding questions

In many ways, the prompts asked about the poem 'Sea Canes' are similar to the guiding questions you will receive on your individual oral commentary extract. Remember that it is not compulsory to answer the guiding questions, but it is likely that you will address their implications at some point in the commentary.

As was suggested in Chapter 4, getting used to asking questions of an extract *yourself* is a good thing to do. Why not practise writing your own guiding questions in response to a poem or extract from a work you have studied?

Responding to extracts from other genres

If you are a standard level student, you will study two works for Part 2, and if you are a higher level student, you will study three works. Each work, must be from a different genre, whether drama, prose or prose other than fiction. At higher level, poetry is required as the basis for the individual oral commentary, and understanding of the other two works is assessed through a discussion between you and your teacher, conducted after your 10-minute individual oral commentary is completed. We address this second assessment component on page 97.

At standard level, assessment is carried out through the individual oral commentary only, but extracts chosen by your teacher may come from either of the two works that they have chosen.

We have looked at the genre of poetry, so let's now look at some extracts from other genres.

Prose other than the novel and short story

In many respects, what you say about this kind of prose will not be any different from the kinds of things you might say about the novel and short story. Perhaps you might find yourself spending a little longer on the role of narrative voice, the relationship between 'reality' and fiction in the extract, the question of political and/or social background, but not necessarily. Don't forget that prose other than the novel and short story is just as varied in content and style as fiction itself.

Although the following exercises on each of the other genres will be of particular relevance to those doing standard level, higher level students might see them as a means to think about the characteristics of other genres in a more general sense – to help them with the discussion, or other areas of the course.

Activity

The first extract is from an essay by George Orwell. Read it through, and make careful notes in response to the following questions:

1 In what way is the description of the dog significant?

2 How does Orwell describe the prisoner?

3 What importance does Orwell attach to details such as avoiding the puddle of water?

4 What attitudes towards life and death does the extract communicate?

5 How does the extract use different kinds of imagery?

6 How would you describe the tone of the extract?

7 What role is played by narrative point of view in the extract?

8 How would you describe the uses made of diction and syntax?

A Hanging

'Who let that bloody brute in here?' said the superintendent angrily. 'Catch it, someone!'

A warder, detached from the escort, charged clumsily after the dog, but it danced and gambolled just out of his reach, taking everything as part of the game. A young Eurasian jailer picked up a handful of gravel and tried to stone the dog away, but it dodged the stones and came after us again. Its yaps echoed from the jail walls. The prisoner, in the grasp of the two warders, looked on incuriously, as though this was another formality of the hanging. It was several minutes before someone managed to catch the dog. Then we put my handkerchief through its collar and moved off once more, with the dog still straining and whimpering.

It was about forty yards to the gallows. I watched the bare brown back of the prisoner marching in front of me. He walked clumsily with his bound arms, but quite steadily, with that bobbing gait of the Indian who never straightens his knees. At each step his muscles slid neatly into place, the lock of hair on his scalp danced up and down, his feet printed themselves on the wet gravel. And once, in spite of the men who gripped him by each shoulder, he stepped slightly aside to avoid a puddle on the path.

It is curious, but till that moment I had never realized what it means to destroy a healthy, conscious man. When I saw the prisoner step aside to avoid the puddle, I saw the mystery, the unspeakable wrongness, of cutting a life short when it is in full tide. This man was not dying, he was alive just as we were alive. All the organs of his body were working – bowels digesting food, skin renewing itself, nails growing, tissues forming – all toiling away in solemn foolery. His nails would still be growing when he stood on the drop, when he was falling through the air with a tenth of a second to live. His eyes saw the yellow gravel and the grey walls, and his brain still remembered, foresaw, reasoned – reasoned even about puddles. He and we were a party of men walking together, seeing, hearing, feeling, understanding the same world; and in two minutes, with a sudden snap, one of us would be gone – one mind less, one world less.

George Orwell

Guiding questions

1 In what ways does Orwell present the figure of the condemned man?

2 How does Orwell use imagery in this extract?

If you were to deliver a commentary on this extract, how would you structure it?

- You could adopt a **linear approach**, identifying the following as the main topics of your commentary:

  - The first two paragraphs, which focus on the dog.
  - The third paragraph and the presentation of the condemned man.
  - The last paragraph, which focuses on the narrator and his reasoned approach to the impact of the man's death.

- The tone of voice and role played by point of view.
- The importance of imagery in the extract.
- The extract's place within the context of the rest of the story.

- Alternatively, a more **'conceptual' organization** of ideas could proceed as follows:

  - The 'realism' of the extract, as portrayed through such things as use of concrete detail, imagery and the intimacy of the narrative voice.
  - The extract's sympathy for the condemned man.
  - The exploration of the finality of death.
  - The tone of voice and role played by point of view.
  - The use of paragraph structure and syntax as a means to generate tension.
  - The extract's significance in the context of the rest of the story.

Which do you think would work better? Remember, there is never only one way of organizing your ideas. You need to structure your commentary in a way that reflects your assessment of the character of the extract – for instance, one that depends on a strong degree of development, or one that treats various ideas that can be separated.

Activity

Below is a second extract. This is taken from an autobiographical work by Eva Hoffman. It is a memoir of her life growing up in Canada, in exile from her native Poland. The work is particularly poignant about subjects of childhood and cultural dissonance, as well as in its central exploration of the relationship between language and identity.

Read the extract through carefully, thinking about the different areas of significance. Compose some questions like the ones on page 86 which you feel would draw attention to these areas.

When you have written your questions, hand them to your partner. Both of you can then spend some time answering them. It might be interesting to compare the ideas you choose to foreground.

Lost in Translation

When the brass band on the shore strikes up the jaunty mazurka rhythms of the Polish anthem, I am pierced by a youthful sorrow so powerful that I suddenly stop crying and try to hold still against the pain. I desperately want time to stop, to hold the ship still with the force of my will. I am suffering my first, severe attack of nostalgia, or *tesknota* – a word that adds to nostalgia the tonalities of sadness and longing. It is a feeling whose shades and degrees I'm destined to know intimately, but at this hovering moment, it comes upon me like a visitation from a whole new geography of emotions, an annunciation of how much an absence can hurt. Or a premonition of absence, because at this divide, I'm filled to the brim with what I'm about to lose – images of Cracow, which I loved as one loves a person, of the sun-baked villages where we had taken summer vacations, of the hours I spent poring over passages of music with my piano teacher, of conversations and escapades with friends. Looking ahead, I come across an enormous, cold blankness – a darkening, an erasure, of the imagination, as if a camera eye has snapped shut, or as if a heavy curtain has been pulled over the future. Of the place where we're going – Canada – I know nothing. There are vague outlines of half a continent, a sense of vast spaces and little habitation. When my parents were hiding in a branch-covered forest bunker during the war, my father had a book with him called *Canada Fragrant with Resin* which, in his horrible confinement, spoke to him of majestic wilderness, of animals roaming without being pursued, of freedom. That is partly why we are going there, rather than to Israel, where most of our Jewish friends have gone. But to me, the word "Canada" has ominous echoes of the "Sahara." No, my mind rejects the idea of being taken there, I don't want to be pried out of my childhood, my pleasures, my safety, my hopes for becoming a pianist. The *Batory* pulls away, the foghorn emits its lowing, shofar sound, but my being is engaged in a stubborn refusal to move. My parents put their hands on my shoulders consolingly; for a moment, they allow themselves to acknowledge that there's pain in this departure, much as they wanted it.

Eva Hoffman

Guiding questions

1 How does the character of the narrator emerge during this extract?
2 How would you describe the tone of voice?

The novel and short story

On the next page is an extract from the novel *Heart of Darkness* by Joseph Conrad. Published in 1902, it tells the story of a central narrator's journey on a trade mission in Belgian Congo, who, along the way, confronts some highly-disturbing events and characters, most notably a figure named Mr Kurtz; the novel works on a number of levels, providing comment on the inhumanity of colonial exploitation, as well as describing a journey into the darkness of the self and a confrontation with the reality of evil. In this particular section, Marlow (the narrator) describes an anonymous native woman in the camp that Kurtz has established in the heart of the Congolese jungle:

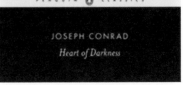

JOSEPH CONRAD
Heart of Darkness

Heart of Darkness

She walked with measured steps, draped in striped and fringed cloths, treading the earth proudly, with a slight jingle and flash of barbarous ornaments. She carried her head high; her hair was done in the shape of a helmet; she had brass leggings to the knee, brass wire gauntlets to the elbow, a crimson spot on her tawny cheek, innumerable necklaces of glass beads on her neck; bizarre things, charms, gifts of witch-men, that hung about her, glittered and trembled at every step. She must have had the value of several elephant tusks upon her. She was savage and superb, wild-eyed and magnificent; there was something ominous and stately in her deliberate progress. And in the hush that had fallen suddenly upon the whole sorrowful land, the immense wilderness, the colossal body of the fecund and mysterious life seemed to look at her, pensive, as though it had been looking at the image of its own tenebrous and passionate soul.

She came abreast of the steamer, stood still, and faced us. Her long shadow fell to the water's edge. Her face had a tragic and fierce aspect of wild sorrow and of dumb pain mingled with the fear of some struggling, half-shaped resolve. She stood looking at us without a stir, and like the wilderness itself, with an air of brooding over an inscrutable purpose. A whole minute passed, and then she made a step forward. There was a low jingle, a glint of yellow metal, a sway of fringed draperies, and she stopped as if her heart had failed her. The young fellow by my side growled. The pilgrims murmured at my back. She looked at us all as if her life had depended upon the unswerving steadiness of her glance. Suddenly she opened her bared arms and threw them up rigid above her head, as though in an uncontrollable desire to touch the sky, and at the same time the swift shadows darted out on the earth, swept around on the river, gathering the steamer into a shadowy embrace. A formidable silence hung over the scene.

Joseph Conrad

Guiding questions
1 What thematic significance does the figure of the woman have?
2 How does Conrad make use of figurative language?

In many respects, this extract is typical of the kind you will often see in an individual oral commentary exam, as it is rich in literary devices and highly detailed in its portrayal of content.

Activity

Having read the extract above taken from *Heart of Darkness*, answer the following questions, with reference to the notes on literary features that follow on the next page:

1 How does the narrator present the figure of the woman? You could consider such things as descriptions of her clothing, her isolation from others, her beauty, her sense of sadness, her power, as well as her vulnerability, her relationship with the landscape, etc.

2 In what ways does the extract make use of contrasts, for example between the woman and other 'pilgrims', real and illusory, civilized and barbaric?

3 What kinds of developments take place within the extract?

4 What kinds of attitudes and feelings does the narrator convey towards his subjects?

5 How important is sense description in the extract?

6 In what ways does the extract incorporate ambiguity and/or paradox?

Literary features

Some or all of the following notes might be of relevance:

- Look carefully at the **diction** of the extract, and the way detailed description is used. Adjectives such as "barbarous", "savage" and "ominous" contrast with adverbs such as "proudly" and "stately", creating a complex figure who is both secretive, perhaps frightening, and yet regal and proud.

- You might consider **descriptions** of the woman's clothes as both lavish and decorative, reflective perhaps of the esteem in which she is regarded, and yet she is associated with "wild sorrow" and "dumb pain". At the same time, the repetition in "brass leggings", and "brass wire gauntlets" as well as the word "helmet" suggest a kind of body armour, like a soldier or warrior.

- The woman is therefore depicted in relation to a very 'civilized' imagery of clothes, and yet she is associated also with nature. She commands a "hush" over the "whole sorrowful land"; "fecund and mysterious life" and the "immense wilderness" seem to see in her a mirror image of "its own tenebrous and passionate soul".

- Various kinds of **syntax** are used in the extract, from the layered descriptions in long sentences with multiple clauses to the very short and simple, for example in "Her long shadow fell to the water's edge" and "The young fellow by my side growled". Some sentences are also structured to create a kind of grammatical balance, for example in "She was savage and superb, wild-eyed and magnificent".

- **Sense imagery** is incorporated throughout, from the strikingly visual opening descriptions through to references to sound in "jingle", "growled" and "murmured" and "silence". There are various references to darkness and light. The extract also mixes together imagery of movement and stillness. The opening paragraph concentrates on the woman's actions: she walks in a very "measured", "stately" manner, whereas in the second paragraph she "stood still" and stares at the narrator with his entourage. Finally, the image of her holding up her arms "rigid above her head, as though in an uncontrollable desire to touch the sky" reinforces her status, as well as her "inscrutable" nature as she seemingly holds everyone and everything in her power.

- The extract incorporates significant use of other **figurative language,** from the description of the woman "treading the earth" through to the **personification** of the land, the "swift shadows… gathering the steamer into a shadowy embrace" and the "formidable silence" that "hung over the scene" in the final sentence.

- **Setting** and landscape generally play an important role in the extract – both as a means to reinforce the presentation of the woman, as well as to suggest the active, living character of the natural world. The sense of a wilderness predominates, and it is described as something "mysterious", "brooding" and "inscrutable" – much like the woman herself.

- There are **contrasts** in content and language between the first and second paragraphs as the woman is, at first, in motion, then still. As the narrative voice becomes more personal, these contrasts generate

> Remember that success in this exercise, as hopefully the notes opposite will reinforce, depends on close and detailed analysis of the text and its stylistic features. No reference has been made to the rest of the novel: even though some sense of the extract's contextual significance might be brought in at some point in your commentary, the focus is predominantly on the text in front of you.

an increasing tension as we are drawn into the woman's power and mystery, just as those observing her.

Once again, there will be more things on which you could have commented. Why not have a go at organizing your ideas into sections and then doing the commentary 'for real'?

Perhaps it would be a good idea to look now at an actual commentary, completed under exam conditions. The following text and transcript is a standard level commentary on an extract from a short story by Edgar Allan Poe. You may well have heard of this American writer, who was a champion of a gothic style – a bit like Joseph Conrad, choosing to delve into the darker recesses of the human psyche. One of the great things about Poe is that content and style in his writing are inextricably linked. A bit like music, where form and content are arguably one and the same thing, Poe likes to write in such a way as to generate an 'experience', that makes you feel and imagine as much as think. In this way, perhaps, his writing works like poetry.

Read through the following extract. Then make notes and think about how you would set about delivering a commentary on it.

> Gothic literature focuses on death, decay, ruin, chaos and terror. It originates from the late 18th and early 19th centuries and arose in response to the historical, political, sociological and pyschological contexts of the period.

The Pit and The Pendulum

I was sick – sick unto death with that long agony; and when they at length unbound me, and I was permitted to sit, I felt that my senses were leaving me. The sentence – the dread sentence of death – was the last of distinct accentuation which reached my ears. After that, the sound of the inquisitorial voices seemed merged in one

5   dreamy indeterminate hum. It conveyed to my soul the idea of revolution – perhaps from its association in fancy with the burr of a mill wheel. This only for a brief period; for presently I heard no more. Yet, for a while, I saw; but with how terrible an exaggeration! I saw the lips of the black-robed judges. They appeared to me white – whiter than the sheet upon which I trace these words – and thin even to

10   grotesqueness; thin with the intensity of their expression of firmness – of immoveable resolution – of stern contempt of human torture. I saw that the decrees of what to me was Fate, were still issuing from those lips. I saw them writhe with a deadly locution. I saw them fashion the syllables of my name; and I shuddered because no sound succeeded. I saw, too, for a few moments of delirious horror, the soft and

15   nearly imperceptible waving of the sable draperies which enwrapped the walls

of the apartment. And then my vision fell upon the seven tall candles upon the table. At first they wore the aspect of charity, and seemed white and slender angels who would save me; but then, all at once, there came a most deadly nausea over my spirit, and I felt every fibre in my frame thrill as if I had touched the wire of a galvanic
20 battery, while the angel forms became meaningless spectres, with heads of flame, and I saw that from them there would be no help. And then there stole into my fancy, like a rich musical note, the thought of what sweet rest there must be in the grave. The thought came gently and stealthily, and it seemed long before it attained full appreciation; but just as my spirit came at length properly to feel and entertain
25 it, the figures of the judges vanished, as if magically, from before me; the tall candles sank into nothingness; their flames went out utterly; the blackness of darkness supervened; all sensations appeared swallowed up in a mad rushing descent as of the soul into Hades. Then silence, and stillness, night were the universe.

Edgar Allan Poe

Guiding questions

1 What importance does Poe attach here to experience of the senses?

2 What role does imagery play in this extract?

- What are the key features of content, language, form and style that you think you would comment on?

- The extract is one continuous paragraph. How could you provide a structure to your commentary?

Below is a transcript from an actual examined standard level commentary on the Poe extract.

- Read it through and compare it with the approach you think you would have made.

- What are its strengths and weaknesses?

A transcript of an IB formal individual oral commentary on an extract by Edgar Allan Poe

This extract is taken from the beginning of the story 'The Pit and the Pendulum'. In it we see the central character, who is also the narrator, being unbound and in a courtroom finding himself sentenced to death for reasons unknown. The main aspects of language in the extract are imagery, repetition, use of varied types of syntax and it very much appeals to the use of the senses. In my commentary I am going to follow a linear structure because the passage is quite progressive – the character goes through a series of frightening discoveries in his emotional and spiritual descent, and the reader effectively goes through the experience with him as the senses come increasingly into play.

The passage begins with the phrase, "I was sick, sick unto death with that long agony." This provides us with an immediate sense of the central character's experience of fear – and the feeling is conveyed through the emotive diction, "sick" and "long agony". The use of dashes and repetition communicates a sort of realistic feel to the narrator's voice, as if he is speaking to us – and this creates a sense of intimacy with him, which is important to the way the story develops. In this opening section of the story there is no real depiction of setting – we are positioned inside the narrator's head. He simply tells us that he was under "the dread sentence of death" and there is no physical sense of where he actually is or how he got there. The fact that he also says, "my senses were leaving me", places us very much in a kind of metaphysical realm, and it is one characterized by a sense of fear and foreboding. Indeed, fear and a feeling of something ominous would seem to be the 'effect' that the entire story is built around.

We then move on to further sensuous aspects; the narrator says that the voice that proclaimed his death "was the last of distinct accentuation which reached my ears" and from this point there is an ambiguity as to whether the events he describes are actually real, or simply taking place in his head – in his imagination. There is, for example, quite a hallucinogenic quality in the line "the sound of the inquisitorial voices seemed merged in one dreamy indeterminate hum" and it is something he seems almost aware of when he says "perhaps from its association in fancy". The blurring of lines between the real and the metaphysical or supernatural is very much a feature of Poe's work, and we see it throughout this passage.

Moving on now to the second section of my commentary, the phrase, "This only for a brief period..." establishes the importance of time, which becomes a significant motif in the extract – especially with the swinging pendulum itself later adding to a sense of tension and suspense. The two sentences here are split into short phrases, the second one mirroring the structure of the first. The varied types of syntax help to vary the pace of the passage as well as reinforce the realism of the narrator's voice. The phrase "presently I heard no more" indicates a shift in his experiences of the senses as he now encounters only silence, but it is silence disturbed by seeing the image of "the lips of the black-robed judges". I think we sort of feel his sense of panic – in not being able to hear or see anything, except for the judges' lips. This is an example of synecdoche – when a part of something is used to stand for the whole – and in this case is particularly terrifying – much more than the complete image of the judges would be – because they are depersonalised through it, made almost inhuman. There are also continuous references to the senses, in for example, the "white" lips – "whiter than the sheet upon which

I trace these words" as well as in the words "thin" and "firmness", all of which work to create physical details of a kind of horrifying picture. His feeling of terror in response to the image is marked with the phrases "the intensity of their expression of firmness – of immoveable resolution – of stern contempt of human torture". And here we have an example of the way Poe's writing uses the same kind of devices as poetry typically does; for instance, the repeated "t" sounds in the line are particularly harsh, using sound to reinforce the meaning of the phrases being said. We then move on to "I saw them writhe with a deadly locution". This is another short phrase and the diction "writhe" and "deadly" once again reinforce the emotional intensity of the writing.

The next section of my take on the passage begins with the narrator saying that he sees his name being spoken but that "no sound succeeded". There is almost a degree of synaesthesia here, mixing up the senses to create a sense of disorientation. The glimpse of the "sable draperies which enwrapped the walls of the apartment" fails to offer him any comfort, though, as he states that he experiences "delirious horror" at seeing them. The word "delirious" only reinforces his feeling of uncertainty, as if there is nothing he sees, hears or feels that he can be certain of. This is, of course, an idea that the rest of the story goes on to develop when he wakes up in the torture chamber with the pit and the swinging pendulum. Having said that, there is almost a feeling of hope when he introduces us to the image of the "seven tall candles upon the table". This is extended when he remarks that "they wore the aspect of charity, and seemed white and slender angels". The connotations of "white" as opposed to "black", as well as the obvious implications of "slender angels" provide him briefly with the thought of something light and good in and among all the horror. Any possibility of relief, however, is quickly dismissed with the words "all at once, there came a most deadly nausea over my spirit" and we return to the experience of fear and terror. Also, I would point out that the mention of angels makes us think of a supernatural element to the story; but when he writes that the "angel forms became meaningless spectres", there is once again that sense of ambiguity as to whether he is actually seeing anything 'for real', or whether it is all happening inside his head. Whether real or fantasy, however, any possibility of hope now leaves him; he says "I saw that from them there would be no help" and returns to the thought that he will certainly die.

The final section that I would like to talk about in my commentary begins with the line "And then there stole into my fancy, like a rich musical note, the thought of what sweet rest there must be in the grave." Here we see the idea of the foreboding of death but it seems a good thing; for the first time there is almost positive imagery – in the simile, for instance of "like a rich musical note" and the line "what sweet rest there must be in the grave" but it is ironic that the sense of longing he experiences, and the positive implications of "rich musical note" and "sweet rest" are associated with nothing other than death itself.

Just as this thought comes to him, however, the vision of the judges ends, he says "as if magically" and from here he seems to dissolve into a sense of "nothingness", a complete loss of the senses. The candle flames "went out utterly; the blackness of darkness supervened" and he ends with "Then silence, and stillness, and night were the universe". At the end he loses consciousness, and describes this as a "mad rushing descent as of the soul into Hades". The connotations of evil and the supernatural in the "Hades" reference reinforce the supernatural darkness of the passage and the feeling of a kind of pure, absolute terror.

To conclude, this passage is important to the rest of the story as it really builds a sense of suspense and tension right from the beginning. The portrayal of the fear of the central character, which gets even worse later on – seems to me the most overriding point, and it is one that many of the other stories – 'The Tell Tale Heart', 'The Black Cat', 'The Fall of the House of Usher' and so on also portray. Furthermore, the repetition of words and phrases, the emotive language, the richness of the imagery and examples of exaggerated expressions are kind of typical of Poe's style. As you read, you kind of experience things with him – the intimacy of the writing means that you kind of get drawn into the same kinds of darkness and psychological terror as the narrator himself.

Drama

It is likely that you will study Shakespeare at some point in your course and, if your teacher chooses a Shakespeare play for Part 2, you should feel pleased rather than anxious. No one would, of course, refer to Shakespeare as an 'easy' writer, but with effort, the rewards are tremendous. This could be said for lots of reasons, but not least because of the variety of things he presents you with for exploration.

Just like any good novel, Shakespeare's plays are filled with an array of fascinating and complex characters, relationships and themes. In other words, the content of the plays provides you with tremendous analytical scope. In addition, there is the language: the poetry and prose of a Shakespeare play makes use of the full range of literary characteristics that define the greatest poetry. Finally, we must not forget that Shakespeare is perhaps above all a wonderful dramatist. This is a man who knows how to act, how to write dialogue and how to engage his audience through all kinds of dramatic and theatrical ideas – many of which set him miles ahead of his contemporaries. For this reason, it is always a good idea to read and talk about Shakespeare as much in theatrical terms as straightforward 'literary' ones.

The upshot of all of this, from your point of view, is that an extract from one of Shakespeare's plays presents you with a great deal of material to talk about. Therefore, try to see discussion of his work as an exciting and rewarding challenge, rather than something to discourage you.

Activity

Below is an extract from Act 2, Scene 2 of *Measure for Measure*. The character of Angelo has been given temporary governance of the city of Vienna, and in a rather draconian way he has re-instigated a law that punishes sex outside of marriage with death. One character, Claudio, has been found guilty of the 'crime' of fornication and is condemned to die. His sister, Isabella, is a nun, and learning the news has come to Angelo to beg for mercy. In this extract, Angelo confronts the fact that he finds himself having fallen in love – or lust with Isabella.

Make some notes on the extract and divide your notes into three main sections:

1 Content (character, relationship, action, theme, etc.)

2 Language and style.

3 Dramatic features.

Measure for Measure

Angelo		What's this, what's this? Is this her fault or mine?
		The tempter or the tempted, who sins most?
		Ha!
		Not she: nor doth she tempt: but it is I
	5	That, lying by the violet in the sun,
		Do as the carrion does, not as the flower,
		Corrupt with virtuous season. Can it be
		That modesty may more betray our sense
		Than woman's lightness? Having waste ground enough,
	10	Shall we desire to raze the sanctuary
		And pitch our evils there? O, fie, fie, fie!
		What dost thou, or what art thou, Angelo?
		Dost thou desire her foully for those things
		That make her good? O, let her brother live!
	15	Thieves for their robbery have authority
		When judges steal themselves. What, do I love her,
		That I desire to hear her speak again,
		And feast upon her eyes? What is't I dream on?
		O cunning enemy, that, to catch a saint,
	20	With saints dost bait thy hook! Most dangerous
		Is that temptation that doth goad us on
		To sin in loving virtue: never could the strumpet,
		With all her double vigour, art and nature,
		Once stir my temper; but this virtuous maid
	25	Subdues me quite. Even till now,
		When men were fond, I smiled and wonder'd how.

Guiding questions

1 How does Shakespeare present Angelo's tortured state of mind in this extract?

2 In what ways does the extract make use of imagery?

For **section 1**, you could explore:

- the shift in Angelo's character from earlier in the play. He recognizes now that he is susceptible to the same instincts from which he has so far declared himself free.
- Angelo's sense of internal division and conflict – between what he *feels*, instinctively, and what he 'knows' is morally wrong
- Angelo's recognition of Isabella's purity (somewhat ironically) as the source of his lust
- the presentation of private 'reality' beneath the public mask
- the thematic concerns with corruption, vice and mercy or redemption.

For **section 2**, you could comment on:

- the structure of the speech – the way it moves from one idea into the next in a fairly 'reasoned' way
- the contrast between this sense of development with exclamatory, spontaneous outbursts – "O, fie, fie, fie!" etc.
- the significance of Angelo's self-questioning
- the use of contrasts and oppositions 'tempter – tempted', 'violet – carrion' (flora versus fauna), 'thieves – judges', etc.
- the disjointed, irregular syntax to reflect Angelo's confused and desperate state of mind
- the repetition – of diction and motif
- the imagery of corruption and disease.

For **section 3**, you might note:

- conflict between the two sides of Angelo's personality
- heightened tension
- the contrast between the public role in which we have so far seen Angelo and the priviate self he now reveals
- the dramatic effect of raising the audience's interest in what will happen next.

There will almost always be elements of conflict and contrast in Shakespeare's extracts, whether in place (countryside, city, etc.), character and relationship, language and voice, and so on. Therefore, a strong line of interpretation could well come from centralising one of these conflicts, arguing that much of the dramatic interest in the extract or scene comes from it.

The higher level discussion

As we noted earlier on page 86, assessment of higher level students requires the completion of an additional oral exam. Once your individual oral commentary is complete, your teacher will ask the same kinds of subsequent questions as at standard level, but then initiate a transition into a discussion on one of your other works. At higher level, poetry is prescribed for your commentary, so the discussion will focus on one of your two other texts, be they drama, fiction or non-fiction prose. You cannot know which of the texts will be chosen, nor of course the questions you will be asked, but the fact that discussion will not center on an extract means that you are likely to be talking more generally about the whole work.

What additional skills will I need to demonstrate?

At the start of this chapter, we spent some time thinking about *speaking* as opposed to writing about literature, and we also addressed the issue of *listening*. Being able to think critically about the points made by others and respond appropriately, as well as answer questions in a meaningful and productive way, are skills that can often take some time to develop. In the higher level discussion, you are going to need to make use of these skills as effectively as you can in order to earn the best possible mark for the assessment task.

Look ahead to pages 104–6 of this chapter, where you will find the official marking criteria for the internal assessment component. At higher level, Criteria D and E focus specifically on the subsequent discussion and call upon teachers to mark candidates on their 'knowledge and understanding of the work used in the discussion' and their 'response to the discussion questions'. Read through the criteria and think about the skills required of you. Notice that in Criterion B, for example, to score 3 marks or more, you need to demonstrate some degree of 'appreciation' in your response to the questions.

Activity

a Imagine for a moment that you are the teacher of a higher level literature group. Choose any work you are currently studying, or have studied relatively recently, and write some questions that you think would be appropriate ones to ask of your students (as if you were conducting the discussion part of the assessment). Remember what you are trying to elicit from them in terms of knowledge of the work, as well as the more general skills addressed by the marking criteria.

b In pairs, read through each other's questions and use them as the basis for a 10-minute discussion.

c Think and talk about:
- how easy or difficult this exercise was
- any difficulties to do with:
  - understanding the question
  - showing understanding of the work
  - avoiding long pauses or 'fillers', such as 'errr', 'umm' or 'like'
  - providing answers to the questions that were substantial enough without drifting off topic.
- In what ways could you practise to get better?

A sample discussion

Here is a transcript of an extract from an assessed higher level discussion on Shakespeare's play *Hamlet*. If you know the work, you will be able to comment on the degree to which the student shows 'knowledge and understanding'; if not, perhaps you will at least be able to remark on whether the student answers the questions appropriately, provides supporting evidence from the text and whether they use an appropriate language and register.

> The beginning of any literary work is, of course, very important. What do you think of the way Shakespeare chooses to begin this play?
>
> **Teacher**

Student

Well, I guess most writers would see the beginning of their particular work as the place where the reader's or audience's interest is captured. In the case of this play, you have the sense of tension established right at the opening. It's night time, Bernardo and Francisco are outside the castle and it is clear that something is wrong. At first, they don't recognize each other and there's almost a sense that they are frightened to talk about the appearance of the ghost the night before. This creates a sense of expectation because, like them, we wonder if it is going to appear again. When the ghost does appear, provided the director makes it work effectively, there is a big increase in the degree of tension, and this is only made worse by the fact that it looks like Hamlet's father. There is an emotional intensity in the sense of fear and awe in response to the supernatural appearance, but there are also questions being raised – why does the ghost appear, for instance? If it is indeed Hamlet's father, then how has he died? And what does it all have to do with the story of Fortinbras? That last part is important too; there is a threat of war. It all adds up, I think, to create a sense of foreboding. All is not well in Denmark, and the audience can't help but be caught up in this atmosphere of fear and trepidation.

Teacher

Are there contrasts, do you think, between the way the ghost is presented here and in subsequent scenes?

Student

The next time we see the ghost is in Scene 5 – the last scene of Act I. The most important difference here is that this time the ghost speaks. Its silence in the first scene makes it mysterious and more frightening, but here it almost becomes more real, more human, because we find out the story of how it – or he, as King Hamlet, died – or should I say, was murdered?

> What do you think of the way Hamlet responds to the ghost in that scene?
>
> **Teacher**

> It's interesting that he refers to him more as a ghost or a spirit than his actual father and in fact he is fairly terrified throughout the scene. There's some ambiguity there, perhaps. But then I think that so much of the ghost's role is kind of ambiguous.
>
> **Student**

> What do you mean?
>
> **Teacher**

> Well, one thing, for instance, is the moral issue. The supernatural is typically presented as something frightening, something associated with evil, and yet here we have the ghost asking – or telling – Hamlet to perform an act of retributive justice. Is he or it evil or good? And is the act of revenge that he asks for actually a moral one? In effect, he is asking Hamlet to commit to an act of violence, which in itself is certainly morally questionable. I think the ghost is presented almost as two things at the same time – a divine figure that represents justice and morality at the same time as a rather selfish, flawed individual who is simply angry about what Claudius did.
>
> **Student**

> What about the ghost's appearance in Act 3?
>
> **Teacher**

> I actually think this is the most powerful scene in the play. You have Hamlet confronting his mother after the truth of Claudius' guilt has been made evident – at least to Hamlet, and I guess the audience, in the prayer scene. The way he attacks her and especially his apparent obsession with her sexual relationship with Claudius makes us wonder what his motives actually are. We have the killing of Polonius and then of course the appearance of the ghost – which Gertrude apparently does not see. Why was the ghost visible to the soldiers in the first scene of the play and yet not to Gertrude? Does Shakespeare intend us to think, at this point, that Hamlet has in fact gone mad for real? Or is this just another way of presenting ambiguities in the play? For me, that was the most interesting and frustrating thing about this play as we studied it. It seems to defy any attempt to explain or find consistency. In terms of the content of the play – the characters, relationships and so on, there is so much that is contradictory and confusing, and I think Shakespeare sort of mirrors this ambiguity in the form of the play – the mix of reality and the supernatural, the contrasts between public and private scenes, and to me the ghost plays a key role in that. You know – you can't make sense of the play very easily!

Student

- Although this is only an extract from the discussion, what do you think of it?
- With reference to the criteria for this part of the higher level assessment (see pages 105–6), what mark would you award this response?
- Discuss your ideas with a partner or others in the group.

Sample discussion questions

The following examples of discussion questions are ones provided by the official subject guide for this course. How do you think you might fare if you were asked these? Talk about them as a group or you could use them as a means to prepare for your assessment.

Prose: the novel and short story

- What fictional character did you find most interesting? Can you account for that effect based on some choices you see that the writer has made in constructing the character?
- Did you observe any contrivances in the novel that were in some way distracting, such as coincidences, or unresolved questions, unconvincing resolutions, chance meetings and the like?

- How powerfully – or not – would you say the setting affected the events or action of the novel?
- How emotionally or intellectually satisfying did you find the conclusion of the novel or short story?
- How enthusiastic were you about the novel or short story in the opening pages or paragraphs?

Drama

- Did you find the dramatist using different kinds of tension in the play in order to engage and hold the audience?
- What, for you, was the most riveting or satisfying moment in the play? Can you account for how the playwright managed to achieve that effect?
- What do you consider to be the strengths and weaknesses of the protagonist and what effect do you think these have on the believability of the play?
- Who was your favourite or least favourite secondary character in the play? Can you see how the playwright elicited such a response?
- Do you think any profound human truths are being considered in this play, or do you see its main purpose as keeping an audience interested in human behaviour?

Prose other than fiction

- What cultural aspects of the context do you think had the strongest impact on the writer's story?
- Is there any person in the work, other than the writer, whose presence you found to be forceful or memorable?
- Were there some aspects of life that you found significantly omitted in the writer's story of experience?
- What features of the work most attracted you, for example, the history or the geography, the encounters with people or the personal reactions of the writer?
- What is the role of anecdote in the work and how well do you think this writer handled that feature?
- Do you have any reservations about the writer's responses or attitudes to the places/people/ideas?
- What human issues form the subjects of the work? Did you find any of them particularly well handled?
- Did you find the essayist skilled in bringing the work to a particularly satisfying conclusion?

Internal assessment criteria: individual oral commentary (standard level)

Criterion A: knowledge and understanding of the extract

- How well is the student's knowledge and understanding of the extract demonstrated by their interpretation?

Marks	Level descriptor
0	The work does not reach a standard described by the descriptors below.
1–2	There is virtually no knowledge, demonstrated by irrelevant and/or insignificant references to the extract.
3–4	There is some knowledge, demonstrated by very limited interpretation, but with some relevant references to the extract.
5–6	There is adequate knowledge and understanding, demonstrated by interpretation supported by mostly appropriate references to the extract.
7–8	There is good knowledge and understanding, demonstrated by interpretation supported by relevant and appropriate references to the extract.
9–10	There is very good knowledge and understanding, demonstrated by careful interpretation supported by well-chosen references to the extract.

Criterion B: appreciation of the writer's choices

- To what extent does the student appreciate how the writer's choices of language, structure, technique and style shape meaning?

Marks	Level descriptor
0	The work does not reach a standard described by the descriptors below.
1–2	There is virtually no reference to the ways in which language, structure, technique and style shape meaning in the extract.
3–4	There is some reference to the ways in which language, structure, technique and style shape meaning in the extract.
5–6	There is adequate reference to, and some appreciation of, the ways in which language, structure, technique and style shape meaning in the extract.
7–8	There is good appreciation of the ways in which language, structure, technique and style shape meaning in the extract.
9–10	There is very good appreciation of the ways in which language, structure, technique and style shape meaning in the extract.

Criterion C: organization and presentation

- To what extent does the student deliver a structured, well-focused commentary?

Marks	Level descriptor
0	The work does not reach a standard described by the descriptors below.
1	The commentary has virtually no structure and/or focus.
2	The commentary has limited evidence of a planned structure and is only occasionally focused.
3	The commentary shows some evidence of a planned structure and is generally focused.
4	The commentary has a clearly planned structure and is focused.
5	The commentary is very clearly structured and the focus is sustained.

Criterion D: language

- How clear, varied and accurate is the language?
- How appropriate is the choice of register and style? (Register refers, in this context, to the student's use of elements such as vocabulary, tone, sentence structure and terminology appropriate to the commentary.)

Marks	Level descriptor
0	The work does not reach a standard described by the descriptors below.
1	The language is rarely clear and appropriate, with many errors in grammar and sentence construction and little sense of register and style.
2	The language is sometimes clear and appropriate; grammar and sentence construction are generally accurate, although errors and inconsistencies are apparent; register and style are to some extent appropriate.
3	The language is mostly clear and appropriate, with an adequate degree of accuracy in grammar and sentence construction; the register and style are mostly appropriate.
4	The language is clear and appropriate, with a good degree of accuracy in grammar and sentence construction; register and style are effective and appropriate.
5	The language is very clear and entirely appropriate, with a high degree of accuracy in grammar and sentence construction; the register and style are consistently effective and appropriate.

Internal assessment criteria: individual oral commentary and discussion (higher level)

Criterion A: knowledge and understanding of the poem

- How well is the student's knowledge and understanding of the poem demonstrated by their interpretation?

Marks	Level descriptor
0	The work does not reach a standard described by the descriptors below.
1	There is limited knowledge and little or no understanding, with poor interpretation and virtually no relevant references to the poem.
2	There is superficial knowledge and some understanding, with limited interpretation occasionally supported by references to the poem.
3	There is adequate knowledge and understanding, demonstrated by interpretation supported by appropriate references to the poem.
4	There is very good knowledge and understanding, demonstrated by careful interpretation supported by well-chosen references to the poem.
5	There is excellent knowledge and understanding, demonstrated by individual interpretation effectively supported by precise and well-chosen references to the poem.

Criterion B: appreciation of the writer's choices

- To what extent does the student appreciate how the writer's choices of language, structure, technique and style shape meaning?

Marks	Level descriptor
0	The work does not reach a standard described by the descriptors below.
1	There are few references to, and no appreciation of, the ways in which language, structure, technique and style shape meaning in the poem.

2	There is some mention, but little appreciation, of the ways in which language, structure, technique and style shape meaning in the poem.
3	There is adequate appreciation of the ways in which language, structure, technique and style shape meaning in the poem.
4	There is very good appreciation of the ways in which language, structure, technique and style shape meaning in the poem.
5	There is excellent appreciation of the ways in which language, structure, technique and style shape meaning in the poem.

Criterion C: organization and presentation of the commentary

- To what extent does the student deliver a structured, well-focused commentary?

Marks	Level descriptor
0	The work does not reach a standard described by the descriptors below.
1	The commentary shows little evidence of planning, with very limited structure and/or focus.
2	The commentary shows some structure and focus.
3	The commentary shows evidence of a planned structure and is generally focused.
4	The commentary is clearly structured and the focus is sustained.
5	The commentary is effectively structured, with a clear, purposeful and sustained focus.

Criterion D: knowledge and understanding of the work used in the discussion

- How much knowledge and understanding has the student shown of the work used in the discussion?

Marks	Level descriptor
0	The work does not reach a standard described by the descriptors below.
1	There is little knowledge or understanding of the content of the work discussed.
2	There is some knowledge and superficial understanding of the content of the work discussed.
3	There is adequate knowledge and understanding of the content and some of the implications of the work discussed.
4	There is very good knowledge and understanding of the content and most of the implications of the work discussed.
5	There is excellent knowledge and understanding of the content and the implications of the work discussed.

Criterion E: response to the discussion questions

- How effectively does the student respond to the discussion questions?

Marks	Level descriptor
0	The work does not reach a standard described by the descriptors below.
1	There is limited ability to respond meaningfully to the discussion questions.
2	Responses to the discussion questions are sometimes relevant.
3	Responses to the discussion questions are relevant and show some evidence of independent thought.
4	Well-informed responses to the discussion questions show a good degree of independent thought.
5	There are persuasive and independent responses to the discussion questions.

Criterion F: language

- How clear, varied and accurate is the language?

- How appropriate is the choice of register and style? (Register refers, in this context, to the student's use of elements such as vocabulary, tone, sentence structure and terminology appropriate to the commentary.)

Marks	Level descriptor
0	The work does not reach a standard described by the descriptors below.
1	The language is rarely clear and appropriate, with many errors in grammar and sentence construction and little sense of register and style.
2	The language is sometimes clear and appropriate; grammar and sentence construction are generally accurate, although errors and inconsistencies are apparent; register and style are to some extent appropriate.
3	The language is mostly clear and appropriate, with an adequate degree of accuracy in grammar and sentence construction; the register and style are mostly appropriate.
4	The language is clear and appropriate, with a good degree of accuracy in grammar and sentence construction; register and style are effective and appropriate.
5	The language is very clear and entirely appropriate, with a high degree of accuracy in grammar and sentence construction; the register and style are consistently effective and appropriate.

6 The individual oral presentation

Objectives

- to understand the components of Part 4: options
- to get to grips with the assessment demands of the individual oral presentation
- to consider techniques for effective presentations

As mentioned in Chapter 5, the second component of your mark for internal assessment (which also counts for 15 per cent of the overall grade) comes from a presentation you complete in response to the study of one or more of your Part 4 works. Unlike the individual oral commentary, the presentation is based on a topic that you can choose and prepare – so in many ways the individual oral presentation represents a slightly less daunting task than the individual oral commentary. It is a part of the course where you can afford to really let your creative juices flow, so take advantage of the opportunity it represents.

This chapter provides you with more detail on the options and kinds of texts your teacher is 'free' to choose, and suggestions for the variety of topics and approaches that might work best.

Part 4: options

What is an individual oral presentation?

We began Chapter 5 by drawing attention to the literature course's interest in oral as much as written responses to the various works you study. The Part 4 assessment is based on a prepared oral presentation that lasts between 10 and 15 minutes. The topic and format is largely up to you, but will be worked on in consultation with your teacher.

If you wish, you can work with a partner or even in a small group, provided that each of you is responsible for an equal amount of presentation time. More often than not, students choose to work on their own because you are then free to develop ideas in the way you want.

On the day of the exam, you will present your topic with no interruptions from the teacher, but when you have finished they will most likely ask you one or two questions. This discussion might be between the teacher and you, or may possibly involve the whole class.

What kind of topic might be appropriate?

The individual oral presentation is a chance for you to talk about a subject from your Part 4 works in which you have a particular interest. Therefore, it is important that, as you go through your Part 4 texts, you get used to reading and thinking about them for yourself. Making notes as you study each work on aspects that particularly engage your interest is a good thing to do, as well as recording possible presentation ideas.

The following list of potential areas of focus comes from the official subject guide:

- Cultural setting of the work(s) and related issues.
- Thematic focus.
- Characterization.
- Techniques and style.
- Author's attitude to particular elements of the work(s) such as character(s), subject matter.
- Interpretation of particular elements from different perspectives.

Your idea might come from one of these areas, or a combination of them. It's important to remember, however, that the topic should be fairly defined and specific, so that you get a chance to demonstrate detailed understanding of the work(s) and a degree of independent thinking.

What should I do for the presentation?

The good thing about Part 4 is that it represents an opportunity for something a little different. Your teacher may well select texts that are slightly less known, or more contemporary, or in some other way perhaps less 'established' than works in the other parts. In the same way, you are set free in this component to select the kind of presentation you want. Official examples from the subject guide of the kinds of appropriate activities are as follows:

- A critique of your own writing that has been produced in the style of one of the literary genres studied.
- An explanation of a particular aspect of an author's work.
- The examination of a particular interpretation of a work.
- The setting of a particular writer's work against another body of material, for example details on social background or political views.
- A commentary on the use of a particular image, idea or symbol in one text or in a writer's work.
- A performance or a pastiche of a poem being studied – this activity should be followed by some explanation of, and discussion on, what you have attempted to do.
- A comparison of two extracts, two characters or two works.
- A commentary on an extract from a work studied in class, which has been prepared at home.
- An account of your developing response to a work.
- The presentation of two opposing readings of a work.
- A monologue or dialogue by a character at an important point in the work.
- Reminiscences by a character from a point in later life.
- An author's reaction to a particular interpretation of elements of their work in a given context (for example, a critical defence of the work against a charge of subversion, or immorality, before a censorship board).

Broadly speaking, these activities can be categorized into two main types:

1 'Formal' analyses or critiques of a particular idea or theme.

2 More 'informal' approaches involving such things as in-role character monologues, and so on.

Students often think in terms of one or the other type, but this should not be the case. You could – and in fact should – try to vary your presentation, in part because generally speaking the more varied the content and approach, the more engaging the presentation will almost certainly be. In addition, varying the content will, in all likelihood, enable you to demonstrate independent understanding of the material you wish to cover.

Another thing you ought to consider is the relationship between the topic you eventually choose and the activity you select as a means to explore that topic. For instance, it might well be the case that a monologue from the point of view of a character other than the one in which a particular novel is written would be a good way to explore the importance of a key issue in the text, or the traits of a particular character – *but not necessarily*. Perhaps a more formal approach would be best. In other words, once you have selected the topic and asked your teacher for feedback on whether it is an appropriate one, *then* start thinking about the best way to explore that particular topic. Not the other way round.

Sometimes, for example, students who happen to be good at drama might opt from the outset to do something of a 'dramatic' nature on the grounds that it is their personal strength. While this may well be an admirable skill, it does not guarantee high marks. Likewise, not being particularly good at drama should not deter you from choosing something of a performance nature. You are not going to be assessed on your skills as a theatre practitioner because it is a *literary* course; marks will be awarded for the extent to which you demonstrate knowledge and understanding of the particular text(s) and your ability to offer interpretation of them.

Activity

To check your understanding of the individual oral presentation so far, here is a little test:

a Think of one text you are currently reading – or have just read, whether as part of your literature course, or elsewhere.

b Write down something about the text that interests you – an aspect of character or relationship, a theme or a feature of the work's language and style, perhaps an important motif or image, something to do with the development of action or the creation of tension. You choose.

c Next, break down the topic a little – what main ideas would need to be covered in a detailed exploration of it?

d Finally, decide on a presentation that might work as a means to demonstrate your understanding of the topic – you could use PowerPoint, drama, a for-and-against debate, incorporate artwork and/or music. How about your own writing? Think about *why* this particular presentation format would work best as a means to explore your ideas.

e Share your ideas with a partner and give each other some feedback.

Here are some specific examples of presentation topics that students have chosen to do in the past. Read them through and discuss what you like or dislike about them, as well as how straightforward or challenging they might be.

- An exploration of the way setting is used to represent the experience of isolation in *The Wind-Up Bird Chronicle*, by Haruki Murakami. The presentation was accompanied with contemporary photographs of urban Japan.

- Two monologues written from the point of view of the characters Estelle and Inez in Sartre's *No Exit*, followed by a rationale. The focus of the presentation was the concept of 'bad faith' and the way the characters are locked in their dependency on each other.

- A PowerPoint or Moviemaker 'film', with accompanying rationale, which used text, images and music as a means to explore the use of imagery in Slyvia Plath's poetry.

- A formal presentation that explored parallels between the film *Apocalypse Now* and the novel *Heart of Darkness* by Joseph Conrad, on which the film is based.

- A formal exploration of Keats' exploration of the relationship between sense experience and the imagination, accompanied by 'Romantic' art of the period.

- A presentation that used aspects of costume and various symbolic props in an analysis of the character of Okonkwo in *Things Fall Apart*. The focus was on the tension that arises from his threatened sense of identity as the novel develops.

- A description of a memory of a student's grandfather, as a pastiche of Michael Ondaatje's *Running in the Family*. The presentation concentrated on the impact of Ondaatje's use of sense imagery and elements of magical realism.

- Three posters with collages of text and images, which were designed to reflect the contrasting world views of the central characters, Joe, Jed and Clarissa in Ian McEwan's *Enduring Love*. The presentation looked at the shifting presentation of 'truth' in the novel as a result of these different paradigms.

- The use of imagery in the graphic novel *Persepolis*. How does Marjane Satrapi use the form of the graphic novel to represent things not said in the dialogue?

- An exploration of the extent to which Stevens, as an unreliable narrator in Kazuo Ishiguro's *The Remains of the Day*, is changed by his presentation in the Merchant Ivory film.

What should my presentation demonstrate?

The individual oral presentation is assessed through criteria that are very similar to other sections of the course. Fundamentally, you are aiming to demonstrate 'knowledge and understanding' of the work(s) you have chosen and an ability to talk about it in an appropriate language and register. You should not forget that, as literary works, some attention at least should be paid to their craft. The more sophisticated and detailed your analysis, the higher your mark.

Look at the official assessment criteria for an individual oral presentation at the end of this chapter on pages 125–6.

In addition, there is a band of criteria for the assessment task that focuses entirely on presentation skills. You are expected to demonstrate care with the choice and execution of your presentation and, perhaps most importantly, an ability to engage your audience. Of all people, perhaps, you as a student are in a very good position to know what counts for effective presentations. Every day of your school life you will see either teachers or students or both 'presenting' things, and you will know the kinds of strategies that work, as well as the ones that don't. You may well have a highly-interesting topic on a particular work, as well as a presentation written out in an appropriate register, with an intelligent command of language and detail, but if you stand at the front of the classroom and simply 'read it out' from cue cards, it is unlikely that you will be able to gain top marks.

Therefore, the assessment demands careful thinking, time to prepare and practice – all of which you are in a position to do. We will return later to the features of good practice in this part of the course on pages 120–1, but as we go through the next section, try to keep the importance of presentation in mind.

What kinds of texts are used in Part 4?

In the other components of the IB literature course, your teacher will select works to be studied from a list of possible titles provided by the IB. In Part 4, however, your teacher is given 'free choice' to select works from wherever they choose. Therefore, for Part 4, teachers might:

- choose texts that balance choices made elsewhere, for example so that enough places, periods and genres are being covered over the course as a whole
- choose texts that are appropriate to the region in which you are studying
- choose texts in which you or they have a particular interest, or which are relevant for a significant reason.

One thing that is often true, however, is that Part 4 can be used to embrace texts that are slightly less 'familiar' or canonical, and even present you with the possibility of using film as a point of reference. The following notes are designed to help you with a range of possible presentation topics and types, depending on the choices of work your teacher makes.

Prose other than fiction, incorporating student writing

One possibility is that your teacher elects to study one or more works of prose other than fiction. As covered in Chapters 13–15 of this book, this genre could include such texts as travel writing, autobiography, letters, essays and speeches. You would be expected to show 'knowledge and understanding' of an aspect of content and/or style – just as you would a work of fiction.

In terms of presentation topic, there will be a host of things to consider, ranging from the fairly traditional exploration of such things as character, relationship, narrative voice or theme to features that distinguish this genre a little more exclusively. For example:

- Setting or place is often an important feature of autobiographical or travel writing? How is setting represented through language and style? What role does setting play in your text:
  - As a means to create atmosphere and tension?
  - As a tool to reflect character development?
  - As both a literal and symbolic motif?

- What different kinds of 'voices' are created in letters and/or speeches?

- Does your autobiographical work have something to say about the relationship between reality and fiction? How do 'literary features' affect the representation of 'truth' in your chosen work?

- Is travel writing and/or autobiography more interested in emotional or factual truths?

- How important is imagery of the senses to your work of literary non-fiction?

- How does your work of non-fiction manage to create a sense of development? Through plot? Character? Setting? Relationship? Theme?

Incorporating student writing

As part of your presentation on non-fiction works, or indeed any of the works you study for Part 4, why not think about using some of your own writing as a means to help illuminate a particular idea or an aspect of style? As we saw in Chapter 3 on page 45, the writing of pastiches or the use of creative writing to engage further with such things as diction, tone and imagery can be immensely productive analytical exercises. Furthermore, prose other than fiction might well lend itself to this suggestion because, by its very nature, you will find yourself faced with points of personal connection. You will, for instance, have experiences of travel, of place and setting, of autobiography, that might provide you with the opportunity to show understanding of the original work in and through exploration of equivalent personal experiences.

The following extract is a piece of personal reflection, written by a student in response to Barbara Ehrenreich's *Nickel and Dimed*, a non-fiction journalistic account of the author's experience trying to make a living as an unskilled female worker in America, on a minimum wage.

It's interesting to step through the same doors that I've been through for at least ten times already and see everything in a new light. There I was, standing at the entrance of Walmart, with only two hours to spare before the bus returned to pick us up. Only this time, my role wasn't that of an ordinary customer, but an attentive observer, with a mission to scope out anything interesting happening around.

Donned in neat polo shirts and smart blue vests, lips fixed in a complacent smile, the Walmart employees seemed to be enjoying their time during their shifts, though their attitudes vary with the difference in age. The younger generation, the ones around their twenties or so, seem more intent on pleasing their customers, eagerly offering their services with what seemed like a genuine smile, like the one the young man behind the counter at the electronics section had, beaming at each customer, chirping greetings cheerfully as they passed by. The older generation is less passionate, speaking only when prompted with questions, stoic expressions etched on their faces, especially when answering simple questions such as, "Excuse me, could you tell me where I'd be able to find suntan lotion?"

…Obvious impatience and annoyance can be seen on the faces of those who are alone, lips downturned into a frown as they tap their feet, and "What? No, you can't go first even *though* you only have one item and I have fifty." But for the others, this wait is the time when they can catch up with each other, and if anything, the latest gossip. This group consists mainly of families, and it seems to me that Walmart is not just a shopping center for them, but a meeting point, a place for weekly, even monthly, social gatherings. Even the employees behind the cashier join in these friendly conversations of "Hey Kate, how's your mother doing? Is she feeling better?" and "Carol! I hear Thomas has been doing great in school. Good job!" It almost makes me feel like an outsider in a community that is so close-knit.

How could this student use the writing as the basis of a presentation? As a means to illuminate aspects of style? To engage with the original work's thematic content or presentation of character, place and time?

A presentation that looks at a particular non-fiction work, or a key feature of non-fiction as a genre, combined with your own writing – perhaps in the style of this work or genre characteristic, followed by a critique of what you have written – could represent a really interesting and engaging oral.

Another possibility that 'free choice' gives your teacher, is to take advantage of late 20th-century developments in 'alternative' kinds of novels. Graphic novels, hypertext narratives and fan fiction are narrative forms that have really taken off in recent years, and represent an exciting way of thinking again about the components of more traditional narrative forms.

You will probably know what a graphic novel looks like, even if the phrase simply makes you think of a Spiderman or Batman comic. The spread of graphic novels, however, through the latter half of the 20th century has reflected an increasing interest in the genre, arguably encouraging its reassessment as a serious and sophisticated form of literary art.

Persepolis: The Story of an Iranian Childhood, for example, is a graphic novel written by the French-Iranian writer Marjane Satrapi. It is an autobiographical story of the author's childhood in Iran up to and beyond the Islamic revolution. The book explores many different issues, not least the kind of life Iranian citizens experienced prior to and during the overthrow of the Shah and the ensuing war with Iraq. Dissatisfaction with increasing cultural and political repression leads to Satrapi's departure from Iran for a western education in Vienna and then, finally, after an ultimately unhappy spell back in her home country, including a failed marriage, she settles down in France. The novel is an engaging mix of political and cultural comment, intimate first-person reflection and an exploration of Satrapi's relationships with family and friends. Its narrative and tone move between moments that are deeply serious, sometimes quite disturbing and at other times very warm, even funny. It was recently turned into a successful film, which might lead to an interesting exploration of film adaptation, as covered later in this chapter on page 114.

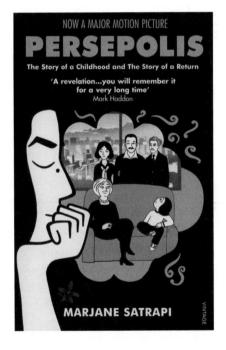

In an increasingly visual age, where information is communicated as much through visual as written text types, the way graphic novels play with the relationship between the written word and visual image is inherently relevant and, in many cases, deeply interesting. Any analysis of a particular aspect of the content of this type of text will inevitably open the door to an exploration of the visual means through which the text works.

Presentation ideas might include:

- the visual dimension: how does the visual composition of individual panels reflect one or more of the novel's key concerns – either in terms of character or theme?
- the role point of view plays in the graphic novel you have studied
- the importance of imagery and visual symbolism.

Hypertext narratives are stories created specifically for reading on the internet. Conventional, linear storylines give way to narratives that you 'construct' simply by clicking on a particular word or page link. In a sense, this is what you are doing every time you browse the internet – creating a story out of connecting ideas, themes or motifs – and hypertext narratives effectively turn this activity into a literary form. As an example of this, the 'novel' entitled *253* by Geoff Ryman takes as its premise the fact that on an average Bakerloo Line London underground train, there are 252 passenger seats and one driver. In the narrative, you can click on the links for each passenger and discover, and perhaps almost 'create', links and relationships between them. This type of novel has much to say about the reader's involvement in storytelling (as we looked at in Chapter 3 on page 29) and makes for a very interactive reading experience.

Visit www.ryman-novel.com to access the internet 'novel' *253* by Geoff Ryman.

Presentation idea: why not look at the way the reading experience of a traditional novel compares with one in hypertext? Perhaps you could write your own short hypertext novel and demonstrate how it works on screen – comparing the ways in which our 'encounter' with it differs from conventional linear narrative.

Fan fiction is so called because of its origins in 'fanzines', which were magazines devoted to amateur writing that had sprung from known or published science fiction works. In essence, it describes a type of fiction in which narratives are created in response to pre-existing works; they are written, as it were, by 'fans' of the original texts. The Star Trek phenomenon and its spin-off stories are examples of the kind of narratives that inspire these types of works, and with the potential of the internet, any amateur writer can contribute to an ever-growing series of narratives that stem *from* particular texts, or even infuse them by writing in the spaces of 'off-stage' events, extra chapters, unwritten scenes, etc.

Visit www.fanfiction.net for internet examples of fan fiction.

Presentation idea: argue the case! Why not write a speech, with supporting examples, in which you argue that fan fiction, or indeed any of the above, should be regarded as important works of literary fiction?

Can I bring film into my presentation?

You will undoubtedly spend a considerable amount of your time watching films, but how much critical attention do you effectively pay to them? In Part 4, your teacher may well refer to a film version of a work you happen to be studying – either an adaptation or a transformation. If not, you might be in a position to bring film into your presentation as a point of reference.

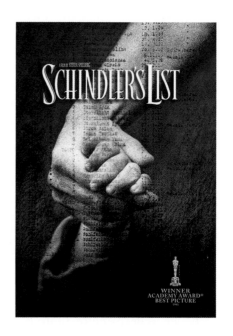

It might be that you look at complete films as adaptations of fictional or even non-fictional narratives, or perhaps you might look at extracts, even stills, that draw attention to key moments.

Some interesting presentation ideas could well emerge from the following questions:

● What is the relationship between types of camera shot and narrative points of view?

- Can film ever successfully represent interior monologue?

- How can a particular type of narrative voice be represented in film?

- What happens to novel or play adaptations when aspects of the original narrative are cut out or changed?

- When do films seek to 'update' more traditional narratives (for example Shakespeare/Charles Dickens), and what is the effect of this on the way we 'read' the text?

- What kinds of devices does film use that replicate or change the way written texts are structured?

- In what ways do written and visual texts make use of symbolism?

- In what ways are written texts changed by the introduction of elements such as sound and music in their filmic adaptations?

Any of the questions above represent potentially interesting starting points for a presentation topic.

In terms of texts, there will of course be as many options for your teacher as there are films made in response to literary works. As a few examples, you might find yourself looking at the following:

- Film adaptations of texts: there are probably hundreds of films that have been made of Shakespeare's plays or classic novels such as those of Dickens, the Brontës, Jane Austen or E. M. Forster. A few other successful examples of direct adaptation include:
  - *All Quiet on the Western Front* (1930).
  - *The Third Man* (1949).
  - *Death in Venice* (1971).
  - *Being There* (1979).
  - *Empire of the Sun* (1987).
  - *Schindler's List* (1994).
  - *L.A. Confidential* (1997).
  - *The Reader* (2008).

- More experimental works, with interests in interior lives, have perhaps proved more difficult to turn into film. Kazuo Ishiguro, Milan Kundera and Graham Swift are contemporary novelists who have all written novels that center on complex multi-layered narrators or narrative voices being made into films. The latter author's Booker prize winner, *Last Orders,* which tells its story through multiple points of view, in voices of characters who speak with a south London dialect, was made into a film by Fred Schepisi in 2001. Whether the film manages to realise this strength of the book might well prove an interesting angle for exploration. A more successful attempt, perhaps, at representing the interior life of a character in a novel was perhaps realized in the film *The Hours,* which is an adaptation of the novel *Mrs Dalloway* by Virginia Woolf.

While film arguably struggles with the narrative possibilities of literary fiction, structure is less of an issue. You might well know, for instance, of the movie *Memento,* which is based on a short story

Film still taken from *Last Orders*

called *Memento Mori* by Jonathan Nolan. The short story tells two narratives – one of a man in hospital who is suffering from amnesia after a brutal attack, the second told in the third person of his escape from the hospital and his revenge on the man who was responsible. In the film, the two narratives are changed into two stories being told simultaneously – one going forwards, the other in reverse. It is not until the end of the film that the two converge and the pieces all fit together.

● Interpretation in film might be an alternative route. One particularly well-known example of a movie that treats its source material as a source of inspiration rather than something to directly adapt, for instance, is *Apocalypse Now*. The movie takes Conrad's novel *Heart of Darkness* and translates it into the context of the Vietnam War. Similarly, *Blade Runner* is a science fiction film loosely based on the novel *Do Androids Dream of Electric Sheep?* by Philip K. Dick. Alternatively, consider *The French Lieutenant's Woman* by John Fowles, which was turned into a successful film in 1981. Perhaps not least because of the imagination of Harold Pinter as the film's screen writer, the novel's self-conscious narrator, who frequently comments on his own characters as fictional creations and the limitations of the society in which they live, is translated in the film to a story within a story. The novel's account of the Victorian love affair is treated as a film being made in the 20th century and the actors playing the roles become the equivalent of an ironic, distancing narrative technique. A similar approach was used in *A Cock and Bull Story*, which is a more recent film interpretation of *Tristram Shandy* by Laurence Sterne.

● Thematic connections between film and text could be interesting too; the gothic genre, for example, has inspired many works of fiction in literature and film. There are countless adaptations of *Dracula* and *Frankenstein*, and modern horror films like *Scream* inevitably have their ironic roots in the whole gothic tradition.

Dracula

The individual oral presentation in practice
Assimilating ideas: Raymond Carver and *Short Cuts*

The fundamental challenge of the Part 4 individual oral presentation is to come up with an interesting topic and an appropriate format. If you have access to Raymond Carver's short stories and the film *Short Cuts*, the following activity is something you could try, either on your own or with a partner. If you don't have access to the material, then you might at least be able to come up with some ideas that realize the different ways in which the presentation can be treated.

Raymond Carver was an American short story writer and poet (1938–88) who is known for writing that deals with the 'real lives' of ordinary, often working-class American people and their relationships. His narrative style is known for its sparseness and brevity, language being used in a very economic way, and has been described as a kind of 'minimalism'. Quoting two other very famous American writers, Carver said this of the short story as a genre:

Raymond Carver

> V. S. Pritchett's definition of a short story is "something glimpsed from the corner of the eye, in passing". First the glimpse. Then the glimpse given life, turned into something that will illuminate the moment and just maybe lock it indelibly into the reader's consciousness. Make it a part of the reader's own experience, as Hemingway so nicely put it.
>
> *Raymond Carver*

Robert Altman was an American film director who died in 2006. He made his breakthrough with the film *MASH* (which became a highly-successful television series) concerned with the lives of various American soldiers serving in the Korean War. Other well-known Altman films include *The Long Goodbye, McCabe & Mrs. Miller, Nashville, The Player* and, most recently, *Gosford Park*. In a way, Altman's interest in 'realism' more than plot – in characters and relationships explored with a strong sense of authenticity – places him in a similar vein to Carver.

In 1993, Altman wrote and directed a film called *Short Cuts*, which is, in fact, the title of one of Raymond Carver's short story collections. The film takes nine of the stories Carver wrote as well as one poem, and turns them into a film narrative in a way that develops connections between them. The short story titles are:

- *Neighbors*
- *They're Not Your Husband*
- *Vitamins*
- *Will you Please be Quiet, Please?*
- *So Much Water So Close to Home*
- *A Small, Good Thing*
- *Jerry and Molly and Sam*
- *Collectors*
- *Tell the Women We're Going*
- *Lemonade* (a poem).

Activity

1 If possible, try to get hold of copies of some, if not all, of Carver's short stories listed above and write some thoughts about them.

In exploring the relationship between the stories and the film *Short Cuts*, a number of fairly obvious issues might well come to your attention. For example:

- The way the film weaves a narrative in order to find connections between the stories: what is gained or lost in doing so?

- In what ways are one or more hallmarks of Carver's narrative style recreated or changed by the narrative of the film?

- Which particular themes and/or motifs of Carver's stories does Altman manage to communicate in his film?

- How are the features of film language (camera shot/editing/dialogue, etc.) used to portray one of the stories in particular?

2 Taking one of the questions listed in Activity 1, or another of your own, break it down into

a little more detail. Discuss with a partner possibilities for the format of an individual oral presentation. Would you consider, for instance, doing any of the following?

- Using PowerPoint (or equivalent) to make a formal presentation on a particular theme.

- Performing a dramatic monologue or some other kind of role play.

- Making a persuasive speech or a critical review.

- Performing an imagined interview with either the writer, or one or more characters.

What kind of content would you make use of?

- Quotations from the stories.

- Images, photographs or paintings.

- Clips from the film.

- Quotations from interviews with Altman and Carver about their work.

- Props or some other kind of visual aid.

How should I structure my presentation?

This is inevitably up to you, and will depend on the type of presentation you intend to deliver, as well as what you intend to say. If you are relying fairly heavily on PowerPoint, then it is likely that the slides will provide you with a fairly coherent sequencing of ideas. If you are varying your presentation more, for instance introducing an element of performance or some other kind of 'creative' ingredient, then your presentation might be broken into different sections. Whichever method you choose, it is important to organize your ideas carefully.

Let's have a look at a 'presentation proposal'. Read through the proposal on pages 119 and 120 and think carefully about it, both in terms of its content as well as the way the ideas have been organized.

This presentation is based on the graphic novel *Watchmen* by Alan Moore and Dave Gibbons. First published in 1986, the novel focuses on the interconnecting lives of five key characters, each with a 'superhero' past, from which they have been forcibly retired. The death of one of them, however, inspires a re-evaluation of their lives and relationships, resulting ultimately in them coming back as vigilante crime fighters. Similar to another acclaimed comic book graphic novel, *The Dark Knight Returns*, the characters each have significantly flawed personalities, often closer to the villains they claim to stand against than figures in conventional society. It is also a work with very obvious political overtones; set in a period of arms race paranoia, the novel plays with various events in American 20th-century history, including the Vietnam War and President Nixon. Superheroes have, for the most part, been subsumed into the 'reality' of cultural life and for much of the novel are frowned upon as remnants of a bygone era. In addition, the novel explores key 20th-century scientific concepts, including the world of quantum physics, as well as essential philosophical ideas associated with existentialism.

What removes *Watchmen* from its fairly conventional superhero origins is a strong element of self-consciousness. Through a variety of means, the novel draws attention to the conventions of superhero comics and re-works them. For instance, through the inter-connecting lives of the central characters is reference to another comic book story (called *Tales of the Black Freighter*) being sold on a news stand; characters talk about their costumes and the significance – or otherwise – of them; at the end of each chapter are excerpts in which the background of particular characters is filled in, there are extracts of character autobiography, even an essay on ornithology! Each of these serves to highlight the conventions of different kinds of texts and so, by association, those of the comic book genre also. The result is a kind of deconstruction of all the comics that have gone before and an attempt to use their characteristics in a highly-inventive, ironic and sometimes satirical way.

Multi-layered, complex and very much concerned with the formal structure of texts, the relationship between story and plot, as well as a host of thematic concerns, the graphic novel is a complex exploration of the fundamental relationship between art and life, hence this student's choice of topic for their presentation:

As noted earlier on page 107, making notes as you go through each of the Part 4 works on possible ideas for the content and the format of your presentation is a very good practice to adopt.

A student's individual oral presentation proposal

Individual oral presentation topic: the relationship between fantasy and reality in *Watchmen*	
Content	**Slides**
1 Brief introduction to the novel: • Background (author, dates, etc.) • Brief outline of story.	• Basic facts as bullets. • Picture of front cover.
2 'Fantasy' in *Watchmen:* its roots in superhero comic tradition: • Superhuman powers (Dr Manhattan). • Values of characters – standing for justice (as opposed to law). Mention Superman. • Use of costumes. • A 'real' setting is altered with such things as electric cars, Nite-Owl's airship, different kinds of buildings, Dr Manhattan's transportation to Mars, etc.	• Slide of Superman and Dr Manhattan side-by-side. • Slide of cityscape.

3 'Realism' in *Watchmen*:
• Setting – a recognizably American city setting – dirt, grime, and so on.
• Political backdrop – involvement of superheroes in the Vietnam War/Nixon.
   – Russia's invasion of Afghanistan following Dr Manhattan's exile to Mars.
• How the superhero tradition is deconstructed:
   – Most characters do not possess superhuman powers – mention Adrian Veidt (formerly superhero Ozymandias) who is now a businessman.
   – For much of the novel they are 'retired' – except for Dr Manhattan and The Comedian, who are sponsored by the government.
   – They are unpopular with police and public (hence introduction of legislation that makes them outlaws).
   – Absence of super villains – the characters here are forced to confront contemporary events and moral issues, as opposed to tangible individual enemies.
   – Characters are flawed – subject to petty jealousies and emotional weaknesses – and the presence of sexual desire (explain through triangular relationship between Dr Manhattan, Laurie Juspeczyk and Dan Dreiberg).
• Complexity of character development including relationships – e.g. 'facts' such as Juspeczyk's discovery that The Comedian was her biological father and Dr Manhattan's emotional development whilst on Mars – his journey from alienation to re-engagement with humanity while on Mars.
• Costume: something of which the characters are 'aware' – their exploration of its value and purpose, the sexual implications, etc.
	• Dialogue extract 1
	
	• Dialogue extract 2

● Exploration of moral and ethical complexities, largely in Adrian Veidt's plan to unite humanity through creating a fake alien invasion and the death of The Comedian, etc. – utilitarian values. (Compare with moral simplicity of traditional comic book characters – good versus evil.) ● Philosophical motifs, e.g. existentialism of Rorschach.	

4 What is the 'effect'?
● The novel is as much about 'real' human life as an escapist fantasy. Key themes:
 	
  – Power: human and superhuman worlds.
  – The novel as an attack on the faith people can place in icons of power – notably politicians.
  – How the deconstruction of the heroes in the novel adds to this.
 	
● Self-consciousness in the novel: it draws attention to the act of storytelling rather than the story itself. How?
 	
  – Through the things already mentioned, e.g. the deconstruction of traditional heroism and the comic book format.
  – Story within a story (*Tales of the Black Freighter*) which acts as a reflection of some characters and plot events in the 'real' story.
  – End of chapter narratives: autobiography, letters, newspaper articles, etc.
  – Structure: how the narrative plays with time in terms of chronology, overlaps past and present – as a means to reflect the nature of how we 'experience' reality, i.e. not as linear, but as something more complex.
  – Also – concept of multiple points of view, as a means to say something about perception, about 'seeing the world'.
	"Who watches the watchmen?"
	
	Moore quote: "*Watchmen* came to be about power. About power and the idea of the superman manifest within society."
	
	Moore quote: "It was about its own structure. It was about a certain way of viewing reality."
	
	Moore quote: "All the different characters in *Watchmen* have got a completely different view of the world. Dr Manhattan has this kind of dispassionate quantum view. Rorschach has got this fierce, morally-driven kind of psychotic view that is… something you could imagine people believing… Nite-Owl – he's got a largely romantic view of the world… none of them are presented as being more true than the others."

5 Conclusion: Summary of the reasons for this novel to be looked at as serious literary art: its interplay of fantasy and reality is used as a means to make thoughtful comment on cultural issues, as well as the role and function of art itself.	

What do you think of this proposal? Discuss with a partner the way it is structured. Did you notice how the presentation moves from general background, through to analytical exploration towards more interpretive comment? Once again, this should not establish itself as a formula, but at least provide some guidance as to how specific you ought to be, and the way in which your ideas can be organized and developed.

How can I make my presentation effective?

One of the strands of assessment criteria for Part 4 focuses on the presentation itself, and the degree to which you have incorporated strategies that engage the interest of your audience. Before reading the notes that follow, talk as a group about strategies that make presentations effective.

Using PowerPoint

Software such as PowerPoint has more or less become the standard means of presenting information, and you will probably have used the program many times already.

There are, however, good and bad ways to make use of PowerPoint. All too often, presenters fail to recognize that PowerPoint is essentially a visual tool, not something to be read. Excessive use of text is usually highly distracting. Here are a few tips:

Things to remember:

1   Do not attempt to write everything you are going to say on a slide. There is no point reading from a slide because your audience will quickly switch off. Your voice is far more interesting than lots of text on a screen.

2   When you incorporate bullet points, only use a few. Lots of bullets can be just as distracting as lots of text.

3   PowerPoint works extremely well with pictures and photographs as a means to reinforce your ideas.

4   Avoid making use of highly-contrasting colours, distracting templates and the more extreme features of text animation. They may be fun to play with but, again, in presentation terms, they will have the same effect as a firework display and detract from your talk.

5   Do not use lots of slides: a handful of well-chosen, well-designed slides are far more constructive than 50 slides with masses of text and pictures. The recommended number is about one or two slides per minute of your presentation.

6   Font: avoid a non-standard font (especially one that is hard to read) and avoid using any font that is smaller than 18 point.

In addition, whether or not you use PowerPoint, make a note of the following:

•   Prepare your talk well. You will not have to memorize it completely, but a few glances at your notes from time to time are all you should need.

•   Structure is very important: as we saw in the *Watchmen* example on pages 119 and 120, it is not a bad thing to have two or three main sections broken down into the equivalent of individual paragraphs. Think of it like a house – the two or three floors of which are the main ideas, and the rooms on each floor are the paragraphs. Individual items within the rooms are, of course, the details of your talk.

•   Variety is a key principle in terms of the way you organize the sections of your presentation, for instance a monologue placed in the centre of a formal talk to break it up, or even in terms of the way you use visual material – asking us to look perhaps at an image first, then a quotation, then an audio clip, etc.

•   Speak slowly and clearly.

•   Look at individuals in your audience as much as possible. Hiding behind sheets of paper or cue cards will very quickly bring about a loss of interest.

Finally, below is a transcript from a standard level student's individual oral presentation. It is based on the poem 'The Hollow Men', by T. S. Eliot. In his presentation, the student decided to focus on Eliot's use of imagery, and he has used photographs as a means to illuminate some important features of the poem's visual, sensual appeal. Read the presentation through and discuss what you think are its merits.

A standard level student's individual oral presentation

Eliot wrote 'The Hollow Men' in 1925, seven years after the end of the First World War. This was an interesting period in his life. His marriage to Vivienne Haigh-Wood was slowly deteriorating, and Eliot was becoming more and more religious, finally converting to Anglicism in 1927. Eliot lamented the decline of religion in Europe after the First World War, thinking that the war had left people spiritually damaged. He also believed that industrialization was causing society to deteriorate and lose moral values. Many of these aspects of his life and beliefs are reflected in the imagery he uses in 'The Hollow Men'.

The most prominent of these images is that of the hollow men themselves. Used both in the title and the first line, this idea of empty, scarecrow-like figures is central to the poem. The idea of the men being 'hollow' and 'stuffed' suggests some parody of life, the men have human form but little else about them is human. The hollow men here are a metaphor for human society, and through this image Eliot suggests that people's lives appear to be missing something – hence they are hollow. I have chosen to represent this image using this picture (below left) since the pumpkins represent a lifeless parody of human beings in the same way as Eliot's image of scarecrow-like figures. Similarly, the way in which their staring faces glow with red light mirrors the way the heads of Eliot's hollow men are 'stuffed with straw'. The image is that of human beings replaced by something lesser, which does not have any of the intrinsic values which make us human, and this represents what Eliot believed to be happening to society during this time.

Throughout the poem, Eliot reveals to us exactly what he believes to be making society 'hollow'. The first of these is the decline of religion. During this time, Eliot was becoming more and more religious, and two years after writing the poem he converted to Christianity. He believed that loss of religion was causing society to degenerate, and especially that after the horrors of the First World War, people were spiritually 'exhausted' as it were. This lack of spiritualism is one of the reasons why Eliot portrays society as empty, and evidence to this end is given in some of the images he uses in this poem.

One of these images is 'prayers to broken stone'. The idea of praying is obviously a deeply religious act, however in this case the prayers are not being offered to God, but to 'broken stone'. The image of broken stone is important because it represents idol worship.

Stone can neither listen to prayers nor respond to them; furthermore the idea of the stone being broken shows how worthless it is. The hollow men have turned away from religion to worship other less worthwhile things – mere 'broken stone'; through this image, Eliot is commenting on the way in which he believed that in turning away from religion, society was becoming itself less wholesome and fulfilling. I have represented this idea with this image (below left) firstly because it depicts a church, so links to the idea of religion in the poem. However, the church in the photograph only has one wall, so while it may look like a church from the front, it is in fact hollow and empty – worthless like the metaphorical 'stone images' that the hollow men have turned to. This church is neither substantial nor strong, and this represents the commentary that Eliot is making with this piece of imagery in the poem – that by turning away from religion and basing their lives, as it were, on the sand – they lack the strong moral foundations that people used to have and as such are lesser beings – they are hollow.

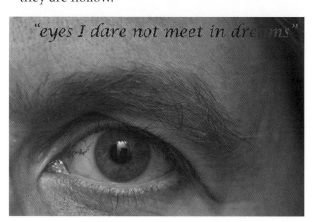

Another comment which Eliot makes about the hollow men is their inability to face reality. He does this primarily through the use of the image of eyes. Eyes in traditional culture are known as 'the mirror of the soul', with the idea that someone's thoughts can be gauged by reading their eyes. The idea of looking in someone's eyes also implies honesty and sincerity. The phrase 'eyes I dare not meet in dreams' then shows how the hollow men lack the sincerity and honesty that allows them to look in the eyes of another. Here the eyes can be seen to represent judgment, or the eyes of god. This image of averted eyes shows how the hollow men are trying to hide from truth and honesty and are unable to face up to reality. Use of the phrase 'dare not' suggests cowardice, showing the fundamental lack of integrity of the hollow men since they are unable to face up

to their own failings – they cannot confront the eyes of judgment. The picture that I have chosen to represent the image of the eyes (below left) also reflects these same ideas. The idea of eyes being the mirror of the soul is reflected in the way you can see through the pupil in the picture, and the eye in the picture represents the idea of the all-seeing eye of judgment or God which the hollow men are trying to hide from. In turn, through this image Eliot is making a commentary about the whole of society – that due to the loss of intrinsic moral quality – perhaps due in part to the decline of religion – people can no longer face up to the consequences of their actions. They can no longer, as it were, look reality in the eye. This inability to face up to reality is another of the reasons for the hollow men's seeming emptiness, since at heart they are nothing but cowards, unable to face up to the consequences of their actions, and so lack any moral integrity. Therefore it is as if they are living a lie instead of a real life, and it is this which makes their lives empty. This reflects Eliot's belief that due to industrialization, society in the years following the First World War was being split up and in his opinion was losing many of the moral and social values which it once held.

Eliot also portrays the hollow men as being lost, trapped in some terrible land. This is described using very dark imagery such as 'dead land', 'cactus land', and 'last of meeting places'. This imagery contains many connotations of death and through this Eliot is comparing the hollow men to people who have died, saying that their lives are no more fulfilling than death itself, since their world is a 'dead land'.

However, Eliot takes the metaphor of death even further than this. He describes the hollow men as 'gathered on this beach of the tumid river'. A beach is like a boundary between the land and the river, and in the poem it represents the boundary between life and death. It is as if the hollow men have died but are unable to completely let go of life and pass on in peace, so they remain trapped in a limbo-like place. This could be seen as a punishment for their failings and their inability to face up to these failings. This links in strongly with the idea in Christianity that if you confess to your sins you will be pardoned and go to heaven, however the hollow men do not have the courage needed to face up to their sins, so are punished. Through this image Eliot is condemning further the society in which he lives, since having previously described them as baseless and craven, he is now saying that they will be punished for it in the way the Christian teachings describe. This also reflects Eliot's stronger leaning towards religion at this time, just before his conversion to Christianity.

Reinforcing the idea that the hollow men are trapped in limbo as a punishment for their lives is the contrast Eliot draws between the hollow men and 'those who have crossed with direct eyes to death's other kingdom'. Describing these people as having 'direct eyes' shows that unlike the hollow men they have all the values associated with moral integrity – most importantly here the courage needed to face up to their lives and confess to their sins. Use of the word 'direct' implies honesty and sincerity – values which the hollow men themselves lack. The comment that Eliot is making here is that people who retain the old religious and moral values are superior to those who have turned away from them, and as such these people will not be punished.

Another comment which Eliot makes about society is that there no longer seems to be any purpose to life. He does this by describing the hollow men as 'lost, violent souls'. Describing them as lost shows how their life has no purpose, since they do not know where they are going. Use of the adjective 'violent' in conjunction with lost shows how they are troubled and disturbed, since they feel the need to be violent, but have nowhere to aim their violence.

"we grope together and avoid speech"

Another phrase which shows how the hollow men are lost is 'we grope together and avoid speech'. The word 'grope' evokes the image of people who are blind or lost, and so are feeling their way in the dark without knowing where they are going. This shows how the lives of the hollow men are hidden and they are feeling their way step by step. The phrase 'avoid speech' shows that not only are the hollow men lost, they are also cut off from everything, even each other. Even when they are 'gathered together' they are still unable to communicate. Through this idea Eliot is making a comment about the way in which people seemed to be cut off from one another. Eliot was very opposed to modernization and believed that the industrialization of Europe was causing society to change for the worse. It also reflects the situation in Eliot's own life at the time, especially his relationship with his wife, from who he was becoming more and more estranged.

"the valley of dying stars"

Eliot had a very grim view of life and society when he wrote this poem, and nothing portrays the lack of hope and life better than the phrase 'valley of dying stars'. Stars have always been seen as a symbol of hope, life and light, and this idea of the world being a valley in which the stars are dying is a metaphor for all the hope and light of life disappearing. This image reinforces all of the other ideas about what Eliot believed to be wrong with society, and his own life, and it also shows that he thought the moral and social decay that was happening was a permanent change for the worse, since there was no hope left in the world – the stars – a powerful symbol of hope – had died and there was no longer any light to light up his or anyone else's life. Of all the images Eliot uses in this poem, for me this one is the most evocative, as it seems to sum up all of Eliot's views on religion, morality and society, by saying that all that is good, is dying, and there is no hope of it coming back.

Internal assessment criteria: individual oral presentation (standard level)

Criterion A: knowledge and understanding of the work(s)

- How much knowledge and understanding does the student show of the work(s) used in the presentation?

Marks	Level descriptor
0	The work does not reach a standard described by the descriptors below.
1–2	There is very limited knowledge and virtually no understanding of the content of the work(s) presented.
3–4	There is some knowledge and superficial understanding of the content of the work(s) presented.
5–6	There is adequate knowledge and understanding of the content and some of the implications of the work(s) presented.
7–8	There is good knowledge and understanding of the content and many of the implications of the work(s) presented.
9–10	There is very good knowledge and understanding of the content and most of the implications of the work(s) presented.

Criterion B: presentation

- How much attention has been given to make the delivery effective and appropriate to the task?
- To what extent are strategies used to interest the audience (for example, audibility, eye contact, gesture, effective use of supporting material)?

Marks	Level descriptor
0	The work does not reach a standard described by the descriptors below.
1–2	Delivery of the presentation is inappropriate, with virtually no attempt to interest the audience.
3–4	Delivery of the presentation is sometimes appropriate, with some attempt to interest the audience.
5–6	Delivery of the presentation is generally appropriate and shows an intention to interest the audience.
7–8	Delivery of the presentation is consistently appropriate, with suitable strategies used to interest the audience.
9–10	Delivery of the presentation is effective, with very good strategies used to interest the audience.

Criterion C: language

- How clear and appropriate is the language?
- How well is the register and style suited to the choice of presentation? (Register refers, in this context, to the student's use of elements such as vocabulary, tone, sentence structure and terminology appropriate to the presentation.)

Marks	Level descriptor
0	The work does not reach a standard described by the descriptors below.
1–2	The language is inappropriate, with virtually no attempt to choose register and style suited to the choice of presentation.
3–4	The language is sometimes appropriate, but with little sense of register and style suited to the choice of presentation.
5–6	The language is mostly appropriate, with some attention paid to register and style suited to the choice of presentation.
7–8	The language is clear and appropriate, with register and style well suited to the choice of presentation.
9–10	The language is very clear and entirely appropriate, with register and style consistently effective and suited to the choice of presentation.

Internal assessment criteria: individual oral presentation (higher level)

Criterion A: knowledge and understanding of the work(s)
- How much knowledge and understanding does the student show of the work(s) used in the presentation?

Marks	Level descriptor
0	The work does not reach a standard described by the descriptors below.
1–2	There is little knowledge or understanding of the content of the work(s) presented.
3–4	There is some knowledge and superficial understanding of the content of the work(s) presented.
5–6	There is adequate knowledge and understanding of the content and some of the implications of the work(s) presented.
7–8	There is very good knowledge and understanding of the content and most of the implications of the work(s) presented.
9–10	There is excellent knowledge and understanding of the content and the implications of the work(s) presented.

Criterion B: presentation
- How much attention has been given to make the delivery effective and appropriate to the task?
- To what extent are strategies used to interest the audience (for example, audibility, eye contact, gesture, effective use of supporting material)?

Marks	Level descriptor
0	The work does not reach a standard described by the descriptors below.
1–2	Delivery of the presentation is seldom appropriate, with little attempt to interest the audience.
3–4	Delivery of the presentation is sometimes appropriate, with some attempt to interest the audience.
5–6	Delivery of the presentation is appropriate, with a clear intention to interest the audience.
7–8	Delivery of the presentation is effective, with suitable strategies used to interest the audience.
9–10	Delivery of the presentation is highly effective, with purposeful strategies used to interest the audience.

Criterion C: language
- How clear and appropriate is the language?
- How well is the register and style suited to the choice of presentation? (Register refers, in this context, to the student's use of elements such as vocabulary, tone, sentence structure and terminology appropriate to the presentation.)

Marks	Level descriptor
0	The work does not reach a standard described by the descriptors below.
1–2	The language is rarely appropriate, with a very limited attempt to suit register and style to the choice of presentation.
3–4	The language is sometimes appropriate, with some attempt to suit register and style to the choice of presentation.
5–6	The language is mostly clear and appropriate, with some attention paid to register and style that is suited to the choice of presentation.
7–8	The language is clear and appropriate, with register and style consistently suited to the choice of presentation.
9–10	The language is very clear and entirely appropriate, with register and style consistently effective and suited to the choice of presentation.

7 Literature in translation

Objectives

- to discern what attitudes are needed for literature in translation
- to understand fully the process of fulfilling the requirements of this component of your English course

A particular kind of reading

In this part of the IB literature course you will be reading some literary works that, unlike the work you have done in writing commentaries, involve texts that have not been originally written in English. You will certainly have noted by now that one of the special goals of the IB courses is to develop your sense of the world beyond where you live and where you may have grown up.

Recognizing that your sense of the world is likely to be quite a bit more global than that of your parents, and their parents given your access to the internet, to many other forms of media, and also your possibility of travelling on holiday or going to schools far beyond your community, the chefs of the IB are still committed to giving you a menu of reading that should provide some new perspectives.

Although you can travel in either virtual or physical reality to some very 'exotic' places, in a lifetime there are some limitations. Yet, there are few limitations to travel through the experiences of other people in other times and places. As you prepare for university, it's a good thing to have ventured into a larger world. Whether this expansion of your experience occurs physically or virtually, literature continues to be another way to immerse yourself in the worlds, the cultures, the values of other people.

Hikone Castle, Japan

Landwasser Viaduct, Switzerland

Some subtleties you'll have to come to terms with

We all tend to suffer, to a degree, from the habit of jumping into a book head first – after all, we are pretty familiar with the business of reading books. Having been 'in school' for as many years as you have at this point in your life, you may not always be enthusiastic about things you are asked to read. Still, embarking on the reading of works from other cultures that are somewhat or very different is not a task you want to take entirely lightly.

On the one hand, there's the 'you' that you bring to the book, with your particular linguistic background, class, racial and gender circumstances, the kind of 'soup' that your life 'swims' in. On the other hand, there's another kind of very or somewhat unfamiliar soup – the voices, events, conflicts and values that inhere in the text you are encountering. It's not easy to understand the other people, world, values and conventions that you will find in such a text, and it's also not easy to keep all that in mind as you become engaged with the play or the novel. Always, there is one set of readers reading the text within their own national context and another set, possibly very wide ranging, reading it within a whole variety of other places and times.

As David Damrosch says, "Every single work of world literature is the locus (the Latin for 'site' or 'place') of a negotiation between two cultures" (Damrosch 2003). Negotiating between the two cultures adds a new dimension to coming to grips with a piece of literature. In this part of your course, you will in most cases be dealing with works from another culture in terms of both time and place. Of course, you may be dealing with a work from your birth culture or that of your parents, which gives you quite an advantage in reading that work and makes you a resource for your classmates.

Damrosch also offers us some vivid images to keep us on our toes. We must juggle two things at all times: how we 'hear' the text from our own point of view, and how the work 'swims' constantly in its own soup.

Possibly you have an acquaintance with the *Doctor Doolittle* books, something you may have read long ago, or you might be familiar with the various *Doctor Doolittle* films. One of the interesting features of the original *Doctor Doolittle* books by Hugh Lofting is the two-headed pushmi-pullyu, since this creation itself has an appropriately multicultural genesis. It is, according to Lofting, a relative of "the Abyssinian gazelles and the Asiatic chamois". Another analogy Damrosch uses is the two-headed Janus who guarded the door in Roman times.

Whatever image we choose, it is essential that we look both ways, or keep two sets of cultures in our mind when we encounter these texts. We need to keep a kind of double vision in our head, which we hope will gradually coalesce, especially when we go on to talk or write about these works.

Activity

A kind of self-test of your grasp of these principles might be in order here, so your class will explore one or both of the following exercises in getting to terms with translated texts.

1 Find a copy of the story *The Privy Councillor* by the 19th-century Russian writer, Anton Chekhov. Your teacher may provide you with a hard copy or you can find it on the internet at: www.ibiblio.org or www.gutenberg.org.

Even in the first few paragraphs of the story, you will find sufficient 'hurdles' that will challenge you in moving from your own context to that of the story. Questions will arise:

- Where is the story set?
- Where are Marienbad and Kotchuevko – are they in the country or in the city?

- What *is* a 'privy councilor'?
- Is Petersburg the same as St Petersburg?
- Was it considered a good thing to be an 'actor' in 1870's Russia?
- How do we pronounce the names of the people; is there any class implication in them?
- Who is being spoken to by the mother: a male or a female?
- Do the features of the house indicate belonging to a certain class?
- What might all of this have to do with how we judge the story: is it a successful piece of writing?

2 This exercise involves a painting by the American painter of the 20th century, Edward Hopper, and a poem inspired by the painting by a poet from Catalonia, a region in Spain that includes Barcelona, where the poet lives. His name is Ernest Farrés, and the poem is called 'House by the Railroad, 1925'. Ernest Farrés has written a whole volume of poems entitled *Edward Hopper* (2006), which has been adapted to a stage production.

Work with the painting shown here and the poem that follows. The task requires you to take account of the time and place of the painting, as well as what the poem might be trying to say to you, both perhaps about the house in the painting and the ideas and feelings evoked by it.

"The single focus of the painting is a large gray house in an imported French style… Hopper… invented this house based on some he came across in New England and others he may have seen on Paris boulevards… The two themes of modern progress and historical continuity come together in the second man-made feature of the painting, a railroad track."

http://picturingamerica.neh.gov/

a What thoughts and feelings does the painting evoke for you?

b What seems to be the attitude of the painter to his subject?

c What might be the connection between the ideas of this Catalan poet and the painting that evokes this particular poetic exploration?

d What things are very clear to you about the poem and which references are puzzling?

House by the Railroad, 1925

I fantasize that luck is placed

Within my reach. Of course, there's different kinds.

Take that kind that turns up ad hoc, for instance,

And the kind that unfolds

backwards. There are deficits and surpluses

of luck. By the same token, we have good luck,

everyday luck, luck-you-don't remember,

and bad luck, a.k.a. misfortune.

Luck that puts us on easy street and luck

that's an asp, a scorpion fish, a wild boar, a starling.

I have a vision of train tracks half covered

with grass and rust, hurling themselves –

like a jagged line or a blade

with an iridescence that catches you by surprise –

against a tomorrow without an Achilles heel.

And I imagine who-knows-what plains

and mountains untouched by human hand

and still not weather-proofed

at the mercy of nor'easters, downpours and heat.

But the fantasies don't stop here.

Like the rip in a memory of a past life,

Another jolts my mind:

I recognize myself holding vigil

inside a huge Victorian house,

vacant, foreboding, phantasmagorical,

without going crazy for what I can't possess

yet cut off from the world, supreme example

of original innocence.

Ernest Farrés (translated by Lawrence Venuti)

There is no question that by offering both the painting and the poem, the travel across time, place and culture has become complex and subtle. In what aspects do you feel confident about your perceptions and conclusions and which make you feel somewhat uncertain?

What might be interesting is for your class as a group to establish a blog (or use the one already set up for your class) and ask people to enter their responses to all or some of the questions in the activity on page 129. Finding out more about Chekhov, Farrés or the paintings of Edward Hopper puts you into the mode of extending the range of your intercultural overview.

Reading towards assessment: stages in the process

In line with our earlier discussion on what's involved in following this IB literature course, we need to move on to the reading, discussion, recording and writing that will work towards completing the assessment for this part of the course, which is called 'literature in translation'. The required stages of this process are as follows:

1 Reading.

2 Research leading to the delivery of the interactive oral.

3 Reflective statement.

4 Supervised in-class writing.

5 Essay.

Stages 3–5 are addressed in Chapter 8.

Stage 1: reading

At a designated point in your course, you will be asked to read two or three works of literature in translation. Your teacher may decide that reading works from one region has advantages over reading works from two or three cultures. This is not an easy matter to decide.

In some cases, the works will be completely new to you; in others, you might be familiar with the author or title.

If you are following the course at higher level, you will be reading three works; if at standard level, you will read two.

Possible texts for study

In considering the reading of the syllabus, we are going to allude to three works written by authors with quite different backgrounds. The first is Haruki Murakami, a quite well-known Japanese writer of fiction and his novel *The Wind-Up Bird Chronicle,* which entails the strange adventures surrounding the present of the protagonist, Toru, and the past of Japan, particularly the Second World War. Toru finds himself abandoned by his wife, and subsequently encounters many people who help him find his identity. One of his crucial experiences is meditating at the bottom of a well, where he finds both time to reflect on his life and the entry to other surreal experiences.

The second novel, *Broken April,* is by an Albanian writer, Ismail Kadare, and deals with both a love story of a newly-married couple and a cultural phenomenon, the blood feud, that while foreign to many of us, is quite contemporary in its cultural backdrop as blood feuds continue to this day. The character Gyorg must pursue a revenge killing for his brother's death according to the laws of the blood feud (called the

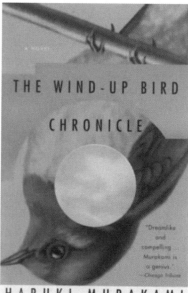

Kanun) and Bessian and Diana, the couple, encounter each other in the highlands of Albania with significant changes in all of their lives.

The third novel is a short but quite challenging work called *The Hour of the Star,* written by Clarice Lispector. This work deals with the fate of a young woman, Macabéa, who comes from the northeast of Brazil to the city of Rio de Janeiro. One of the most interesting features of this novel is the voice of Rodrigo, the narrator, who both tells his own story and that of Macabéa.

Obviously, we cannot do a probing study of these three works in this chapter, but we can show you what students have done with the actual stages of the required IB literature course in this part of the syllabus. You should understand that not only are novels available for study in Part 1: literature in translation, but plays, poetry and works of prose other than fiction may be studied here, and your study of works in translation may involve these rather than novels.

More on the process of reading in this part of the syllabus
At this point, it might be useful to think a little about taking on the task of reading the two or three texts and what difficulties you as an individual experience as you get into them.

Here are some suggestions:

- You might want to do some quick research about the author before you begin.
- You might want to set up a place on your computer or in your notebook to briefly summarize what happens in each chapter; this can save you a great deal of time later.
- Do not depend on what websites can deliver for a 'quick fix'; that is someone else's reading experience, not yours, and, though it might appear otherwise, it won't ultimately help you when it comes to writing your essay.
- Finally, you will want to bring your insights to the discussions of the text in your classes.

Stage 2: research leading to the delivery of the interactive oral
Research
In this stage, either early or later in your classroom discussions, your chief goal is to explore the **context** of the works you are reading. You will work together with some of your classmates to explore the background of the work, whether it is a novel, a set of poems or a play.

The features that you might research in terms of context could be some of the following:

- Relevant elements of the writer's biography.
- The historical aspects, political or social, of the work.
- The geographical backdrop against which the work is set.
- The sociological or anthropological situations of the characters.
- Cultural issues and practices having to do with economics, gender, class or race.

Here, a class wiki could be very useful, giving people a chance to pose questions or articulate reactions, with the opportunity for others to help clarify or even to confirm confusion or uncertainty. This feature could offer your teacher the chance to respond as well. Developing the wiki could produce a kind of companion document that would be both a reference and a prelude to the next stage of the process which involves:

- research
- delivery of the research during a presentation
- discussion.

There are a number of ways to accomplish the above, but all of them will lead to the next stage of the process.

The interactive oral

Having done your research with your group, you will need to plan how to present your findings to the whole class. There are several ways to do this interactive oral:

- You might assign, among yourselves, particular aspects for a brief presentation to the class, then open up to a whole-class question-and-answer discussion period.

- You may choose to present views within your research and have different members of a panel present various views of those ideas.

- You may offer some short presentations and then involve the whole group in some activities such as role playing, forum theatre and written reactions.

The essence of this activity is to explore and clarify the cultural situation that is the backdrop and texture of the work on which you are focused. You may also expect your teacher to participate in whichever form of interactive oral you choose.

You may choose some supplementary visual material to help, and you might also want the rest of the class to have at hand some printed or visual material that you have prepared.

The following is an outline prepared by a group of students working on the novel *Broken April*.

> **Take serious note of the following:**
>
> It is very important to be clear about one thing as you do this research: you are not at this stage finding a topic about which to write your essay. That essay will focus on some aspect of the author's choices about the imaginative representation of their thoughts and feelings, the stylistic choices that are made to deliver to us a piece of literature.

Context presentation on *Broken April* by Ismail Kadare:

1 The Communist regime of Enver Hoxha (1908–85).

  a Communism vs. religion and tradition in Albania.

  b Kadare's own relation to the Hoxha regime.

2 The role of the High Plateau in the novel.

3 The traditions of the *Kanun* and blood feuds.

  a Blood feuds in contemporary Albania and elsewhere. Are there similar traditional and equally disturbing customs in other countries?

Ismail Kadare

As you can see, these students looked at political, biographical and other cultural issues, and even connected the context to contemporary issues, given that blood feuds persist into the 21st century. They provided some short summaries under each heading to the whole class.

With this introduction to the context of this Albanian novel, students are more fully equipped to understand what they are reading, and to move on reliably to discuss the novel from a stylistic viewpoint.

Activity

a Taking one of the texts you are working with in Part 1, within your small group make a list of things you think are important to understand about the cultural context of the novel.

b Then 'divide and conquer': assign the elements within the groups and return to the next class with some research on that element.

c Work with your group to develop a plan for a presentation to give to the whole class. This will be your interactive oral, something your teacher will schedule and participate in.

8 Writing: completing the assessment

Objectives
- to assist you in completing your literature in translation written assignment

As Chapter 7 outlines, the IB has set out a clearly staged process for you to complete a successful essay, one that, first, takes into account where and when the materials are set. This process will help you to decide on a good literary title or topic – an important element of any good essay.

Having become familiar with the contexts of the works you are studying for literature in translation, you will be asked to do three different pieces of writing:

- The reflective statement (stage 3).
- Supervised in-class writing (stage 4).
- A completed essay on one of the works in this part of the syllabus (stage 5).

Stages 1 and 2 are addressed in Chapter 7.

Stage 3: reflective statement

In order to help students further deepen their sense of context, after each interactive oral this IB literature course asks each student to write a short reflection in response to the following question:

> How was your understanding of cultural and contextual considerations of the work developed through the interactive oral?

You will write your response in class and it should be 300–400 words in length.

Below is a sample of a reflective statement on the interactive oral outlined in Chapter 7 on page 132:

I thought it was interesting to challenge the biased lens through which I was viewing the Albanian blood feuds in Kadare's novel. It's very easy to jump on board with his apparent rhetorical agenda and label blood feuds as ridiculous, barbaric, archaic, exotic, etc. When people consider equally 'ridiculous' seeming laws or practices from other countries, however, I have to ask "Am I living within similar constructs" that are not labelled as negatively as blood feuds are?

This is not to say that I disagree with Kadare's rhetorical agenda – if the atrocities committed in Albania are similar to atrocities of class and race in the United States, well, they are still atrocities. I do think it's important for readers of *Broken April*, as it is for the characters of Bessian and Diana, to realize that an outsider cannot understand the functional extent of the blood feuds within the Albanian culture. *Do* the blood feuds primarily encourage unnecessary killing, or do they provide a structure (as in the *Kanun*) for people to manifest violence, which they are likely to do anyway?

Bessian's devotion to the culture of the High Plateau and Diana's resistance to it could, perhaps, indicate the dilemma that every reader faces with the beliefs and practices of the *Kanun*: should we romanticize such things (as Bessian does) or follow our instincts (as Diana does)? Should we find this all so different from people's devotion to their church or their political parties, for example?

As this reflective statement shows, this student is still working through questions about the context of the novel, which may or may not become part of their final essay. However, such thinking does help the student to be thoughtful and aware of both the context and the tendency to draw easy conclusions.

One thing you should know and remember is that your reflective statement will be sent to the examiner along with your final essay, and will be evaluated on the question you were asked to consider. The above example is a bit short, but it does show the angle desired in the reflective statement.

Activity

After each interactive oral, you will need to write a short reflective statement answering the question posed on page 134.

After each student has completed one reflective statement, in small groups read the statements aloud and discuss how your approaches to this exercise are different or similar. You should also make a list of what you think are the most desirable and effective features of these statements. Then a speaker from each group should report this list back to the whole class.

Stage 4: supervised in-class writing

Once you have completed the interactive orals and the reflective statements, you have one more stage before embarking on an essay on *one* of the two (standard level) or three (higher level) works in translation.

At this point, your teacher will provide you with several prompts on each of the works you have studied.

During a class session of 40 to 50 minutes, you will be asked to write a short essay conveying your initial ideas on *one* of the prompts appropriate to the works you've studied. This essay will be developed into a 1200–1500-word essay, which you will submit along with your reflective statement to an examiner for evaluation.

Summary of the process

To sum up, you will produce three pieces of writing, copies of which your teacher will have. These are:

1 Reflective statements for each of the two or three interactive orals on the individual works you've studied.

2 A piece of supervised writing on *one* of the works you have studied in response to a prompt provided by your teacher.

3 A 1200–1500-word essay, which you will submit for assessment amounting to 25 per cent of your final IB literature grade.

Sample prompts

Here is a sample of some prompts for the three novels mentioned in Chapter 7 on pages 130–1:

The Hour of the Star

- To what extent are the two primary characters affected by the backdrop against which Lispector places them?
- How far would you estimate the ending of the novel to be successful and on what grounds?

Broken April

- There is clearly emotional 'electricity' created by Kadare between Diana and Gyorg. How is this included in the **plot** and to what effect?
- The chapter on Mark Ukacierra, the steward of the *Kanun,* provides a number of points of interest and clarification in the novel. How do you see Mark's role in the novel?

The Wind-Up Bird Chronicle

- What single minor character do you judge to have a critical effect on the unfolding quest of the protagonist, Toru?
- Particular events in Japan's history are imported into the plot of the novel. Discuss Murakami's inclusion of one or two and their effectiveness.

The following are some essay titles that students have created for their essays:

The interactions between Diana and Gyorg and their effect on Bessian's character evolution

Lieutenant Mamiya's contributions to the plot of *The Wind-Up Bird Chronicle*

How Lispector's rhetorical purposes are served by the conclusion of *The Hour of the Star*

Murakami's use of the Manchukuo and the Nomonhan incidents in enriching his novel

As you can see, there are a number of possible directions that essays can take based on the prompts given for the supervised writing.

Activity

Taking just one of the works you have studied in translation, invent three or four prompts that you think might lead to interesting essays. The prompts should help you to consider how the writer has chosen and arranged elements of the work to a good outcome.

Stage 5: essay

Having worked through the four stages of preparation, you should now be well equipped to choose a topic that interests you and that will be suitable for an essay of 1200–1500 words.

You now need to:

- decide precisely on which topic you will pursue out of one of your pieces of supervised writing
- refer back to your text and decide whether you have a topic that is both true to the way the work is developed and for which you can gather enough evidence to support your argument
- consult with your teacher, in whatever way they recommend, about the topic you have chosen. At this stage, it would be useful to have a short outline of the way you plan to proceed.
- look carefully at the criteria that the examiner will use to evaluate your essay. They are as follows:
  - How much knowledge and understanding has the student shown of the work studied in relation to the assignment?
  - To what extent does the student appreciate how the writer's choices of form, structure, technique and style shape meaning?
  - How effectively have the ideas been organized and how well are references to the passage integrated into the development of the ideas?
  - How clear, varied and accurate is the language?

Finally, you are ready to write your first draft of the essay. Once this is completed, you need to submit it to your teacher to see if they have any recommendations.

- This first draft should be a clean copy without technical errors such as spelling and punctuation.
- The text used and its translation should be annotated.
- Any secondary sources used should be properly and faithfully cited.

You should understand that your teacher is *not* acting as your editor. At this stage, their role is simply to point out general or recurrent problems in organization, detail and presentation.

> Please do remember that the upper word limit is 1500 words. As with the extended essay, examiners will not read more than 1500 words.

Activity

Read the following piece of supervised writing and the essay that grows out of it. It should give you a sense of how an essay can evolve from a prompt through supervised writing to a final essay.

When you have finished, make a list of comments or questions you would like to raise in a class discussion.

Example of supervised writing and essay

Supervised in-class writing

How far would you estimate the ending of *The Hour of the Star* to be successful and on what grounds?

In Clarice Lispector's *The Hour of the Star*, the ending is extremely successful; perhaps even the most significant part of the book. In the final eight pages of the book, from the moment Macabéa steps into the street and is run over, to the final statement "Yes" (p86), the ending ties together all the themes and messages of the novel with one clarifying thread: the narrator's personal experience. Rodrigo presents the reader with his own experience of writing the ending, which makes the experience suspenseful as Rodrigo discovers the events of the plot at the same time as he presents them to the reader and reacts profoundly to each development. Through Rodrigo's reflections, the significance of the book's themes is clarified: it becomes clear that the book is entirely Rodrigo's story, and Macabéa and his readership both exist to serve his experience. The ending is at once suspenseful, as Rodrigo keeps Macabéa alive, saying "the hour has not yet come" (p82) and comfortingly resolving, as Macabéa "become[s] more and more transformed into Macabéa, as if she were arriving at herself" (p81). Rodrigo also brings the reader into the story very directly one last time, admonishing when Macabéa is dying, "Pray for her and interrupt whatever you're doing in order to breathe a little life into her" (p82).

Rodrigo's own experience in writing the book is also forcefully summed up in the ending, as he emphasizes his deep involvement in the plot. He speaks of this "great joy" when he finds that the "hour has not yet come for the film-star Macabéa to die" (p82), claiming that he "shall do everything possible to see that she doesn't die" (p80). And yet she does die, and his reaction is chaotic, as he seemingly goes mad, saying, "I am innocent! Do not devour me! I am not negotiable!" and bemoaning that "all is lost", he "cannot laugh", and finally says, "Macabéa has murdered me" (p85).

These aspects are only a few of the many that Rodrigo brings together in his ending, skilfully bringing together the story into one scene of great impact.

Essay

The following is the essay that the student developed from their supervised writing:

Effectiveness of the ending in Clarice Lispector's *The Hour of the Star*

In the ending of *The Hour of the Star*, Clarice Lispector brings the plot to a powerful close in one climactic scene of Macabéa's death. The scene is at once suspenseful, as Rodrigo keeps Macabéa alive when she is dying, saying "the hour has not yet come" (p82), and comfortingly resolving, as Macabéa "become[s] more and more transformed into Macabéa, as if she were arriving at herself" (p81). Lispector uses this scene to skilfully tie together all the book's themes, from the theme of words being similar to music to the theme of life and death, thus leaving the reader with a clearer image of what Lispector intended to convey. In this scene, Lispector also brings the narrator, Rodrigo, closer to his readers, and clarifies Rodrigo's role in Macabéa's story, which helps to resolve the confusing relationship between Macabéa's plotline and Rodrigo's.

The first important effect in the end scene is the clear merging of Macabéa and Rodrigo's stories. This scene emphasizes that *The Hour of the Star* is more Rodrigo's story than Macabéa's. This is conveyed when the climactic event of Macabéa's death is overshadowed by Rodrigo's personal reactions, as he bemoans that "all is lost, and the greatest guilt appears to be mine", and even claims, "Macabéa has murdered me" (p85). His reaction to her death is so strong that he seems to go crazy, saying, "I have been to the land of the dead and after the most gruesome horrors I have come back redeemed. I am innocent! Do not devour me! I am not negotiable!" (p85). This focus on Rodrigo at a moment that is so important to Macabéa's story reminds the reader of Rodrigo's statement at the beginning of the book, when he said, "obviously I am one of the more important [characters]" (p12). Clearly, not only is Rodrigo one of the most important characters, as he may have appeared throughout the book, but he ends up being the most important character. This makes explicit the message that is present throughout the book: that Macabéa's story is significant only in the context of Rodrigo's experience. This clarification is helpful because previously in the book, although Rodrigo is highly involved in the narration, it is unclear whether he still intends for Macabéa's story to be a story on its own or simply to be part of his own story. When this scene completely merges Rodrigo's story with Macabéa's, it helps the reader to better understand the rest of the book as each scene fits into the context of Rodrigo's experience and no longer needs to fully make sense from the perspective of Macabéa's experience.

Besides providing clarity and closure, Rodrigo's direct involvement in the final scene also creates suspense, as he speaks of his "great joy" when he finds that the "hour has not yet come for the film-star Macabéa to die" (p82), and then claims that he "shall do everything possible to see that she doesn't die" (p80). His continual comments that create suspense, such as "I don't believe that she is going to die, for she has so much will to live" (p83), increase the effectiveness of the resolution when Macabéa does die and "is finally free" (p85).

The second important effect in the end scene is the way Rodrigo brings the reader so directly into the story. Although Rodrigo addresses his readers directly in many parts of the book, the final scene involves the reader to an exaggerated degree, to the point where it almost seems as though the reader is one of the characters in the story. Towards the beginning of the closing scene, soon after Macabéa is hit by the car, Rodrigo admonishes his readers, "Pray for her and interrupt whatever you're doing in order to breathe a little life into her" (p82). A few sentences later, he brings the reader into his statement that "life is a punch in the stomach" by preceding it with, "Let my reader take a punch in the stomach and see how they enjoy it" (pp82–3).

This reader engagement is powerfully emotive because it keeps readers from reading the scene from a detached perspective, and instead makes them feel as if they are directly involved in Rodrigo's creation of the plot and therefore gives them a feeling of responsibility. Rodrigo even seems to seek the reader's approval of the plot, saying, "I have just died with the girl. Forgive my dying. It was unavoidable" (p85). In the context of this scene, the particularly strong reader involvement increases the emotional impact of the scene as the reader is presented with Macabéa's death after having been asked to "pray for her", and becomes directly involved with Rodrigo's despair as he pleads, "forgive my dying" and "Do not devour me!" (p85). In the context of the whole book, Rodrigo's direct words to the reader bring closure to the whole plot, as he ends the book by first closing Macabéa's story in her death, then his own story by saying "now it only remains for me to light a cigarette and go home" (p86), and finally leaves the reader alone to think of a broad and somewhat unrelated issue, "the season for strawberries" (p86).

The third and final aspect of the closing scene that I find particularly effective is the way it brings together the important themes in the book. Rodrigo does this particularly effectively by using one theme that runs through the book – that of music and silence – to weave through the entire final scene and to bring up references to other themes in the book. Each statement that involves music in the final scene is powerful and simple. Firstly, Rodrigo uses music to clarify for the reader his own perception of death, saying, "I know that when I die, I shall hear him playing and I shall crave for music, music, music" (p82). Secondly, he uses music to conclude Macabéa's story, saying, "I now understand this story. She is the imminence in those bells, pealing so softly" (p85), and then defines Macabéa with a musical metaphor: "At heart, Macabéa was little better than a music box sadly out of tune" (p86). This is a powerful way for Rodrigo to conclude Macabéa's story because the aural imagery of bells "pealing" and a "music box sadly out of tune" is very clear and emotive. The third way Rodrigo uses references to music and silence is in connecting back to the beginning of the book. For example, his statement in the final scene, "I hear the ancient music of words upon words" (p84) ties back to the connection he makes at the beginning between writing with making music, saying, "Those words are sounds transfused with shadows" (p16). In another part of the final scene, Rodrigo's statement, "Silence. Should God descend on earth one day there would be great silence" (p85) seems to use silence to bring Rodrigo to the conclusion of his desire to discover the world and its God (p18). There is also specific aural imagery created with silence, so that the reader can visualize "Macabéa [struggling] in silence" (p82) and can feel the "silence... such that thought no longer thinks" (p85).

Clearly, by referring to music and silence in the final scene, Rodrigo effectively brings together many themes, creates emotive aural imagery, and provides a clear and emotionally impactful conclusion to Macabéa's life and to his own reflections on death.

In conclusion, the ending of *The Hour of the Star* is very effective for many reasons. It is very climactic, providing clarity and resolution for the reader by concluding Macabéa's plotline, which ends in her agonized death, in the context of Rodrigo's experience. The climactic effect is enhanced by Rodrigo's references to music and silence, which in themselves are themes that run through the book, and are also used to tie together other important themes and therefore provide resolution and closure to the complex story. The clear aural imagery created by the references to music and Rodrigo's particularly direct involvement of the reader also adds to the emotional impact of the scene, strengthening the conclusive messages that Rodrigo conveys.

(1352 words)

Works cited:

Lispector, C. 1992. *The Hour of the Star*. Trans. Giovanni Pontiero. New York. New Directions Paperbook.

Felstiner, J. 1980. *Translating Neruda: The Way to Macchu Pichu*. Chicago. Stanford University Press.

Examiner's comments

The supervised writing begins some lines of discussion that will develop in the essay, such as the portrayal of the voice of Rodrigo through his expression of his attitudes toward Macabéa and the suspense the candidate sees emerging. The question of where Lispector has placed her focus – Rodrigo? Macabéa? – is also raised.

In the essay, the candidate elaborates on some of these points and adds another, the relation of words to music in the novel. Life and death, words, silence and their relation to music are considered, as is Rodrigo's relation to Macabéa as the teller of her tale.

In terms of the four descriptors for the essay, the essay delivers a strong sense that the candidate has detailed knowledge of the text and a good deal of perceptive insight into the characters and their construction. However, the candidate could have provided a more ample demonstration of the merging of the two characters. In 1352 words, the candidate would have had an opportunity to explore this strand of the argument.

The candidate provides sufficient evidence of knowing how to express an appreciation of the author's choices, using the appropriate terminology (climactic event, suspense, metaphor, aural imagery, for example) and showing in particular the choices governing structure and their effect.

Ideas are persuasively organized, although there is some sense that a tight structure has excluded some further textual evidence and development of the argument. One almost has the sense that a rigid structure has taken precedence over considerations of delivering full treatment of the materials to the reader.

Language is accurate throughout as well as effective.

Theory of knowledge connections

A theory of knowledge consideration for literature in translation

One of the interesting knowledge questions that almost always arises in the process of reading literature in translation is what we think about the quality of our knowledge of the texts, given that we are reading them in translation from their original language. There's bound to be a voice in our head that asks, "What kind of version of the author's original ideas and words are we receiving?"

The very common and conventional way of expressing these doubts is to refer to what is 'lost in translation'. The question has almost passed into English as an idiom. It has been used as the title of a film produced in 2006, and there is also a novel by Nicole Mones of the same name, as well as other places where the phrase appears. If you have internet access, you can visit www.babelfish.com and test for yourself a few phrases. Try something like: "I have doubts about this computer software" and then something like "I was under the weather yesterday, but today I am simply over the moon". The results, as you will see, vary (sometimes quite entertainingly) with how literal your utterance is, or how metaphorical or idiomatic it is. The exercise will probably confirm your faith in the idea of things being 'lost in translation', especially given that much of what we consider to be 'literature' is full of metaphorical expressions.

However, some literary scholars and professional translators can take a rather different view of what happens in translation. David Damrosch, who is mentioned in Chapter 7 on page 128, takes the opposite view. He proposes that, "World literature is writing that gains in translation" (Damrosch 2003). He sees that, while some works may indeed be bound to their national circumstances, we need to acknowledge that "literary meaning exists on many levels". We only need to think of literary works 'translated' successfully into film (some are, some aren't) to understand that while some things disappear, others are heightened. "To use translations," Damrosch says, "means to accept the reality that texts come to us mediated by existing frameworks of reception and interpretation."

Without accessing the world through translations of what people of other cultures and other nations offer as perceptions of human life and ideas leaves us to the fate, George Steiner would say, of becoming "arrogant parishes bordered by silence" (Steiner, quoted in Felstiner, 1980).

Here is another reflection on the issues of knowledge and translation by a professional translator, Dorota Ratusinska, a former IB student from Poland:

"My thoughts on what is 'lost in translation' are subjective. They are subjective, as I make a living by taking a text in one language and transforming it into another. I say 'transforming' because the original text, also known as the source text, changes its form as it becomes the target text. I have observed that when a translation is done well, or very well, then what is lost in the process amounts to two items:

1   The original clustering of letters (or sounds), which created text in language A.

2   The darkness that concealed the meaning and form of text in language A from anyone who does not understand or know language A.

A good translation of literature will preserve all the meaning and often the artistic form after the transformation. Shakespeare's plays would be concealed from the world of non-English speakers were it not for some magnificent translations of his work. Because of this work, darkness is lifted from Hamlet's tragedy, the magic of Prospero and from the quick wit of Portia in *The Merchant of Venice*.

One can think of translation as analogous to the number 10 composed of various sets of elements: 5+5, 4+6, 2+2+2+2+2. The components differ but the result is the same. The author of the most authoritative translation of Shakespeare's plays into Polish, Stanisław Barańczak, did such a magnificent job (as this was the fruit of his lifelong labour) that it seems pointless for anyone else to try and tackle it again. I do believe that some day, someone will do it again, with great results to boot. When I read his text side-by-side with Shakespeare's original, my head shakes in amazement as each line is so precisely aligned with the corresponding translation, the emotional load is so identical, not to mention the precise rhyming and the meter. A miracle of the human mind indeed."

'A speaker deftly juggles a host of images before his audience'

'Two women speak to each other with florid and rapid phrases'

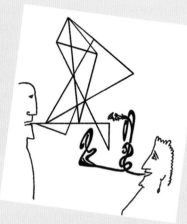

'A man speaks angularly while a woman replies with warm fluidity'

- Where do you stand on the reliability of the knowledge and understanding involved in reading translated texts?

- How do the three cartoons by Saul Steinberg above speak to the issues of knowing where we stand when we read translated texts?

Conventions and genre

> **Objectives**
> - to understand the nature of literary conventions
> - to understand the concept of genre

At this point, we're going to move into exploring some labels that people use when they talk about literature. You have already encountered some of them under other labels appropriate to your earlier years of studying literature. You will likely have called them 'literary features' or even 'literary terms'. Now it's time to explore them more precisely and *apply* them to some things you'll need to be familiar with in order to complete this part of your IB literature course.

The term 'convention'

Conventions have been with you since birth. In many cultures, there are rituals that welcome a new baby into the world: baptisms, a *bris*, (religious ceremony held on the eighth day of life for male Jewish infants) throwing a silver coin into the baby's first bath water. You might have called these 'rituals' and, in fact, there is a good deal of similarity between rituals and conventions. We are primarily concerned with the way repeated formulas or techniques or 'conventions' are associated with the way literary works are written.

Literary conventions

Whether it was beginning a story with "Once upon a time," or "A story, a story, let it come, let it go!" or teaching you some of the simple rhyming poems of your culture, these were conventions you easily and 'naturally' assimilated. When you learned to read, you were taught either to read from left to right, or right to left. Not knowing or observing this convention is a real obstacle to understanding what is on the page.

Social conventions

It is important to remember that conventions sometimes feel 'natural', but they are really cultural inventions. Before the Second World War, in North America, pink clothes were thought to be especially appropriate for boys, as pink was thought a 'stronger' colour than blue. Inexplicably, the notion was gradually reversed and the convention changed. Such conventions, however, become deeply embedded in particular cultures.

Activity

Make a short list of social conventions about behaviour that you take for granted. Choose one of these conventions and carry out a little research to establish where it has come from. You may encounter some surprises and start to think more radically about the presence of conventions in our lives.

You are certainly familiar with conventions connected to your computer and mobile phone use: netiquette, emoticons, acronyms, for instance. With these, we are getting closer to the territory of 'literary conventions'. You may not be constantly conscious of how much writing you are doing on your computer or mobile phone, but you certainly can recognize that you have internalized certain conventions connected to all of these uses. Literary conventions have to do with the way things are delivered in both written and oral speech.

Emoticons, too, are hardly new. In 1912, Ambrose Bierce, in his essay, 'For Brevity and Clarity' wrote: "I crave leave to introduce an improvement in punctuation – the snigger point… It is written thus ‿ and represents, as nearly as may be, a smiling mouth. It is to be appended with every full stop, to every jocular or ironical sentence, thus: 'Mr. Edward Bok is the noblest work of God ‿'" Even medieval monks inserted faces in manuscripts to cue emotional responses (*Wired*, 19 September 2010).

Most of you will be familiar with, or often use in your texts and emails, such emoticons as shown below.

:)	Happy	: D	Laughing	: |	Straight face
: (	Sad	:-o	Surprise	: /	Skeptical
:' (	Crying	B)	Shades	`_	Mad
; -)	Wink	: {	Frown		

> Did you know that texting acronyms have actually been around for a long time – Leonardo da Vinci used them? These sorts of acronyms were and are called 'rebuses'. Here's a famous one for you to decode: YY UR YY UB IC UR YY 4 ME. You might be interested in checking on the conventions associated with rebuses.

As far as **conventions connected with literary art** are concerned, you actually already know quite a few of them:

- If you open a book at random in a bookstore, how do you know you're looking at what is probably called a poem?
- What does it mean when you're at the theatre and the curtains open, the lights dim or when the audience applauds?
- When you open a novel, do you expect it to contain a single continuous piece of writing?
- In a graphic novel, what are those 'balloons' around the characters?

For Paper 2 of the exam, one of the things you'll be asked to think, discuss and write about are 'conventions'.

In the past, these conventions may have been described to you as 'literary features' or 'literary devices'. Such things as stanzas, soliloquies or symbols are some of these. Your sense of how writers use these and the effects these have on the quality of their writing are things you will be called upon to use throughout the course. In preparing for Paper 2, you will need to:

- become familiar with the names of the conventions (and their correct spelling)
- practise using conventions when you talk about the works you have studied.

Activity

What literary language or conventions would you list under the following categories? See how many of the following blanks you can complete.

Poetry

S _ _ _ _ a

Rh _ _ _

A _ _ _ _ _ _ _ _ _ _ n

Me _ _ _

E _ _ _ m _ _ _ _ _

Novel

C _ _ _ t _ _

O _ _ _ s _ _ _ _ _ _

N _ _ _ _ _ o _

P _ _ _

E _ i _ _ _ _ _

Drama

A _ _ _ e

E _ _ t

M _ n _ _ _ g _ _

S _ _ _ _ D _ _ _ c _ _ _ _ _

P r _ t _ g _ _ _ _ _

Answers on page 149.

You may ask, "Where are metaphor, imagery, climax, flashback and some of the other terms we've worked hard to learn?" Those offered in the activity above are very specifically connected to a particular form of literature. The answer to your question is that some of the terms for conventions are found in more than one of the **genres**. Therefore, you will find them referred to in relation to several forms of literary art in Chapters 10–15. A basic understanding of the term 'genre' itself will be one of the tools you will need to complete this IB literature course successfully. At this point, we need to look at some of the issues connected to genre.

Genre

'Genre' is perhaps both a familiar and yet problematic term that we need to examine. Trying to get a firm handle on this term as it is used in the study of literature is like trying to handle quicksilver. Use Google to find two or three websites that appear ready to define or to deliver some clarity about this term and you will see how hard it is to tie down a specific meaning.

One of the better explanations can be found in Chris Baldrick's *Oxford Concise Dictionary of Literary Terms* (OUP, 1990). You may actually have

"In all the edifice of thought, I have found no category on which to rest my head…"
E. M. Cioran

one of these in your classroom or you can find it online. What's helpful about this entry on genre is that it is in fact 'concise'.

What are the significant elements in you gaining an initial understanding of the term 'genre'?

1 The first aspect of this entry in the *Oxford Concise Dictionary of Literary Terms* is the sentence: "A literary genre is a recognizable and established category of written work employing such common *conventions* as will prevent reader or audiences from mistaking it from another kind." So if something is printed in acts and scenes, for example, you will most likely be encountering a play. However, in the expanded 'genre-world' in which we live, you can't always count on that.

2 A second aspect to address is pronunciation. The term comes from the French and is in fact a French word adopted and used in English. It is not an easy word for English speakers to pronounce and many turn it into a two-syllable word, which is a questionable course of action. You can find a good deal of advice about how to pronounce it from *'sean-ra'* to *'ZHAN-r'* to *'jon-re'*. If you can manage it, the best course of action may be to simply say it like the French, as a one-syllable word.

3 The third aspect of the entry notes that there is much 'confusion' surrounding the term. You have probably already discovered this in your Google search earlier. Here lies the most difficult aspect of the term 'genre' – something that tends to happen with many elements of literary terminology.

As Chris Baldrick points out, literary terms are often 'hard words', often because terms we use in non-literary conversation and writing, like 'mood', 'feminine' or 'alienation' often become terms used to talk about literature. 'Genre' is no exception and it is used today to talk about film, visual art, music and video games. That's because the definition of 'genre' (kind, class, species) is suitable for many purposes.

In talking about literature in English, the term 'genre' is used in a variety of ways. One broad way is to look at works of literature in large generic terms. Here, all the traditional works are divided into lyric, narrative (or epic) and dramatic categories. The literary critic, M. H. Abrams, sees the "total literary domain" as traditionally divided into "the poetic or lyric (uttered throughout in the first person); epic or narrative (in which the narrator speaks… then lets his characters speak for themselves); and drama (in which the characters do all the talking)." This is a framework that is often used and, though not always workable, can sometimes be employed to distinguish different forms of literature (Abrams 1981).

> Draw up a quick list of literary works categorizing them as 'lyric', 'narrative' or 'dramatic'. Compare your list with a partner's.

Here are some alternative categories and labels related to genre:

● Prose or poetry.

● Genre can also be used to describe particular forms of prose or poetry, such as prose that is fiction, prose other than fiction, or narrative or dramatic poetry.

● Sometimes literary works are grouped into 'sub-genres' such as the picaresque novel or the personal essay for prose, or elegy, ode or sonnet for poetry. More recent types like 'fan fiction' or 'slipstream' works stretch the boundaries even further. In fact, slipstream fiction (the blending of fantasy and science fiction) is one of the contemporary indicators of the problems inherent in firm genre distinctions. We will encounter more of this crossing of genre boundaries as we look further into different genres.

Therefore, there is a singular lack of agreement on the issue of 'genre'. Additionally, genres change over the course of history; some disappear and others emerge. They operate in specific economic and social contexts. George Steiner, another writer about language and literature, in discussing genre, points out that the novel, for example, in its focus, production and the reading habits demanded of its audience, matches the evolution of the industrial, mercantile bourgeoisie of the early 19th century into the early 20th century. This is one point of view that ties literary production to social and economic situations, something we will find in variations of approaches like Marxist criticism.

Having read the *Iliad* and the *Odyssey*, the great Homeric epic poems, we would perhaps be startled to find a contemporary poem that is similar in length and style. Some works are hard to identify by genre and others strive to spring out of the bounds of any genre. Steiner describes the metrical poetry of William Blake, the 18th-century British poet, as a body of work that includes epic verse that is "so hurtling and uncertainly stressed" it seems like free verse, and whose poems are inseparable from the art created in conjunction with them (Steiner 1967).

The mind, of course, seeks control over the vast phenomenon of both the natural world and the products of the human mind, both material and immaterial. The scientific view of the natural world leads to the creation of categories like tables and systems of classes, as well as further specifications of genus and species. Philosophy seeks to divide its objects of study into fields according to the objects of study: ethics, knowing, being.

One of the most active discussions going on in literary criticism is how to determine the nature of any of the genres, how to handle works that seem to blend features of various traditional genres, and whether 'genre' is a useful tool at all. It's not surprising, then, given the varieties of ways of constructing literary works, that the human impulse to categorize and organize should spring up in the field of literature. Some modern and influential critics like Tzvetan Todorov seek to ask first what literature itself is (not an easy question) and then to interrogate 'genre' as a system of categories.

History has a significant role to play in such questions, and critical writing about such distinctions as lyric, epic and dramatic is vast and abundant and often contradictory. However, as writing has developed into a whole body of literature, the particular features of texts have generated more and more classifications. Some writers like Maurice Blanchot will go so far as to negate the usefulness of genre at all.

Nevertheless, genre is a traditional element of talk about literature and the question arises about what can happen when writers 'play' with or subvert the conventional boundaries of particular genres. Some writers believe that only by seeing how pieces of writing do or do not fit within the norms that seem to govern as specific a genre as 'drama' or 'play', can we see a writer operating in innovative ways. Todorov in his article

"Every book arises from literature alone."
Maurice Blanchot

147

'The Origins of Genre' proposes that "transgression" requires a "law". He also proposes that the transgressions question and illuminate the laws (Todorov 1976). In other words, unless there seem to be rules that define a particular genre, it's difficult to see how writers are creatively working to write 'new' kinds of works.

Here's a rather personal response from someone on the internet who calls himself 'Professor beej' to the issue of expectations placed on genres and how a reader might respond to both them and their changes:

> So given my mode of thinking now, a novel written with me (or someone like me) as the intended reader must, in some form or fashion, exist outside the predescribed boundaries of genre while holding faithful to what makes those genres worth reading in the first place. I also think that any work which holds someone like me as the intended reader must incorporate many conventions that are normally found in only one genre in order to remain interesting. And I think the latter is more important. I feel more at home reading a book or seeing a movie that blends two well-loved genres over something that tries to re-establish or reinvent something I already hold dear and fails (*Twilight*, I'm looking in your direction). The best made works are those which can stay faithful to tradition while still being original in some way.

www. professorbeej.com

Another thinker on this issue, Hans Robert Jauss, is known for his notion that a 'horizon of expectation' on the part of the reader is based, among other aspects, on what the reader expects a genre 'to do' or deliver. His work in reader reception theory foregrounds the reader as one who, in a sense, completes the written work by reading it. Therefore, if you have an idea, for example, of what a short story usually looks like, your reading will be affected by that experience and that expectation will enter into your response to the story as a good or bad one, as something new and interesting, or so familiar as to lack interest or be difficult to understand.

So far, we have covered fairly simplified descriptions of some thinking about genre. What is important for you to keep in mind is that clear lines or 'boundaries' that *generally* separate one class or kind of literature from another are not as easily defined today as perhaps they once were, or as they are in other disciplines. An example of 'Class crustacean' may sometimes look like 'Class insect', but you will not succeed in zoology if you cannot keep them distinct.

The blurring of boundaries between one genre and another can create all sorts of intellectual havoc, but all the refinements and arguments are more than you need to grapple with in a more than basic way at this level of your study of literature; you are hardly expected to resolve the issue, but you do need to know that scientific certitude and precision are not likely to be found in definitions of literary genres.

Fortunately, the IB literature course reduces the complexity of these issues for you in a sense, because it designates five genres for study and two of these are combined to reduce the big picture to four. These are fairly traditional genres and have some clearly-established conventions.

Two species of insect that look very similar but are, in fact, very different

You will likely touch on all of the following genres in your IB literature course:

- Drama.
- Poetry.
- The novel and short story.
- Prose other than fiction (which includes autobiographies, travel narratives and essays).

Even here you will see that there may be some reason to quarrel with these labels, and this could lead to an interesting class discussion. Why, for example, is the label 'prose other than fiction' chosen rather than 'non-fiction'?

In Part 3 of your syllabus, you will focus on one of these genres, reading several works of that form, and you will be expected to work with the conventions of that particular genre.

As you continue through this unit, you may wish only to attend to the genre you are studying for Part 3, although you will find that you will, in fact, be expected to know about the other genres to some degree for other parts of your course. For this reason, Chapters 10–15 will be good reference guides.

Activity

a Skim through Chapters 10–15 on the various genres and choose one genre that particularly interests you, and perhaps the one you most commonly choose to read.

b Make a list of what you consider to be the conventional or usual features of this form.

c Check your list against the list of conventions at the end of the relevant chapter. What do you discover?

As you work with the three (standard level) or four (higher level) works of Part 3, you will become more in tune with these ideas of genre and convention. As you practise essays in response to the kinds of questions that will be posed in Paper 2, you will become more able to talk about literature in these terms. You may even find that you are more able to think and talk about visual art, film or music, for example, with a more confident sense of the way artists in these media are working.

Answers to activity on page 145.

Poetry: stanza, rhyme, alliteration, meter, enjambment.

Novel: chapter, omniscience, narrator, plot, epilogue.

Drama: aside, exit, monologue, stage directions, protagonist.

10 Drama

Objectives

- to look carefully at the genre called drama
- to understand the major types of the form in English
- to survey the history of drama in English
- to understand the conventions of plays

What is drama?

Drama is a form, like poetry, with a lengthy and diverse history. It has arisen as a form of human expression in many cultural traditions, often with its roots in dance, music and poetry. The Greek dramatist, Aeschylus, is responsible for a play called *The Persians,* which dates from 427 BCE. The *Natya Shastra* is the work of Bharata, and it is a guide to the theatrical arts, written in Sanskrit around 200 BCE, or somewhat later. The Chinese drama *Top Scholar Zhang Xie* was written during the Song Dynasty (960–1279 CE). Many tribal rites and indigenous practices include music, recitation or chants and dance, which can surely be called forms of dramatic presentation.

What is meant by the term 'drama' for your study in this course?

Drama or plays almost always include:

- words in some form – prose or poetry
- action embodied in performance
- a receiver – an audience, a viewer, or sometimes a reader or listener.

In his study of the art of drama, *The Idea of a Theater,* Francis Fergusson talks about our "perennial need for a direct and significant imitation of human life and action which can be played as music is played" (Fergusson 1949).

Of course, many familiar with Aristotle's *Poetics*, often regarded as the well-spring of western thinking about drama, describe tragedy as the "imitation of an action", a description that can also be extended to most other forms of drama.

Fergusson's reference to "played" is a useful one, as besides referring to the repetition of the same or a similar imitation, it reminds us of a fairly essential difference between drama and other genres. Although poetry is often best understood and appreciated as a spoken form, and works in other genres can be 'transformed' into performance, drama is essentially meant to be performed. Therefore, although you may be reading plays in your IB literature course, studying them with performance always in mind is the most desirable strategy.

While you may be holding the 'play' in your hands, it is essential to remember that it is, in a way, an incomplete work of art until it is performed. You will need to make some imaginative leaps and conjectures about the script if you are to gain a reliable sense of the play, especially if you have little or no access to the performance of plays where you go to school.

Some activities

Your teachers will be conscious of the need to keep the performance of plays in mind, and they will have collected a variety of activities that encourage this. You may be able to attend some productions of plays done by professional actors or presented by theatre groups within your school.

You are likely to have access to films and videos. Some of the plays we will be including later in this chapter can be found as short clips on YouTube. Also, within your class you will have the opportunity to read, perform or film your own ways of moving beyond the script. The more ways you find to embody the ideas, the feelings and the words of the play, the better sense you will have of it as theatre and the better you will be able to write about it.

The more you 'play' with plays, working out the immense possibilities for "direct and significant imitation of human life" the better 'knower' you will be of this form of art.

Activity

The way a dramatist opens a play is extremely important. They are inviting you into the ideas and actions, and there are many techniques for providing the **exposition** – of situating you in the world of the play.

Older plays often provide formal and separate speeches for the audience, both at the beginning of the play (**prologues**) or at the end (**epilogues**). In many ways, these speeches are in a form similar to the performance of a long poem, as they have a single speaker, but they are very closely tied to the ensuing theatrical expansion beyond just one actor.

Newer plays have their own methods of providing the audience an entrance into the world on stage.

Read the two play openings that follow below and on pages 152–6. In groups of three, discuss the openings and take turns to perform each of them individually.

a   The first comes from a play by Peter Shaffer, *Equus*, which tells the story of a psychiatrist attempting to help a young man, Alan, through a traumatic period of his life, when he has blinded six horses with an iron spike. Shaffer chooses to open the play with a reflection by Dysart, the psychiatrist.

Equus

Act I

Darkness.

Silence.

Dim light up on the square. In a spotlight stands ALAN STRANG, *a lean boy of seventeen, in sweater and jeans. In front of him, the horse* NUGGET. ALAN's *pose represents a contour of*

---

great tenderness: his head is pressed against the shoulder of the horse, his hands stretching up to fondle its head. The horse in turn nuzzles his neck.

The flame of a cigarette lighter jumps in the dark. Lights come up slowly on the circle. On the left bench, downstage, MARTIN DYSART, *smoking. A man in his mid-forties.*

DYSART: With one particular horse, called Nugget, he embraces. The animal digs its sweaty brow into his cheek, and they stand in the dark for an hour – like a necking couple. And of all nonsensical things – I keep thinking about the *horse*! Not the boy: the horse, and what it may be trying to do. I keep seeing that huge head kissing him with its chained mouth. Nudging through the metal some desire absolutely irrelevant to filling its belly or propagating its own kind. What desire could that be? Not to stay a horse any longer? Not to remain reined up for ever in those particular genetic strings? It is possible, at certain moments we cannot imagine, a horse can add its sufferings together – the non-stop jerks and jabs that are its daily life – and turn them into grief? What use is grief to a horse?

[ALAN *leads* NUGGET *out of the square and they disappear together up the tunnel, the horse's hooves scraping delicately on the wood.*

DYSART *rises, and addresses both the large audience in the theatre and the smaller one on stage.*]

You see, I'm lost. What use, I should be asking, are questions like these to an overworked psychiatrist in a provincial hospital? They're worse than useless; they are, in fact, subversive.

[*He enters the square. The light grows brighter.*]

The thing is, I'm desperate. You see, I'm wearing that horse's head myself. That's the feeling. All reined up in old language and old assumptions, straining to jump clean-hoofed on to a whole new track of being I only suspect is there. I can't see it, because my educated, average head is being held at the wrong angle. I can't jump because the bit forbids it, and my own basic force – my horse-power, if you like – is too little. The only thing I know for sure is this: a horse's head is finally unknowable to me. Yet I handle children's heads – which I must presume to be more complicated, at least in the area of my chief concern… In a way, it has nothing to do with this boy. The doubts have been there for years, piling up steadily in this dreary place. It's only the extremity of this case that's made them active. I know that. The *extremity* is the point! All the same, whatever the reason, they are now, these doubts, not just vaguely worrying – but intolerable… I'm sorry. I'm not making much sense. Let me start properly; in order. It began one Monday last month, with Hesther's visit.

[*The light gets warmer.*

He sits. NURSE *enters the square.*]

NURSE: Mrs Salomon to see you, Doctor.

DYSART: Show her in, please.

[NURSE *leaves and crosses to where* HESTHER *sits.*]

Some days I blame Hesther. She brought him to me. But of course that's nonsense. What is he but a last straw? a last symbol? If it hadn't been him, it would have been the next patient, or the next. At least, I suppose so.

[HESTHER *enters the square: a woman in her mid-forties.*]

HESTHER: Hallo, Martin.

[DYSART *rises and kisses her on the cheek.*]

DYSART: Madam Chairman! Welcome to the torture chamber!

HESTHER: It's good of you to see me right away.

DYSART: You're a welcome relief. Take a couch.

HESTHER: It's been a day?

DYSART: No – just a fifteen-year-old schizophrenic, and a girl of eight thrashed into catatonia by her father. Normal, really… You're in a state.

HESTHER: Martin, this is the most shocking case I ever tried.

DYSART: So you said on the phone.

HESTHER: I mean it. My bench wanted to send the boy to prison. For life, if they could manage it. It took me two hours solid arguing to get him sent to you instead.

DYSART: Me?

HESTHER: I mean, to hospital.

DYSART: Now look, Hesther. Before you say anything else, I can take no more patients at the moment. I can't even cope with the ones I have.

HESTHER: You must.

DYSART: Why?

HESTHER: Because most people are going to be disgusted by the whole thing. Including doctors.

DYSART: May I remind you I share this room with two highly competent psychiatrists?

HESTHER: Bennett and Thoroughgood. They'll be as shocked as the public.

DYSART: That's an absolutely unwarrantable statement.

HESTHER: Oh, they'll be cool and exact. And underneath they'll be revolted, and immovably English. Just like my bench.

DYSART: Well, what am I? Polynesian?

Peter Shaffer

The play so far has set up two essential relationships: Dysart to Hesther, the solicitor, who wants to refer Alan, the young man, to Dysart; and the relationship of Dysart to Alan, the focus of the play. The mix of monologue and dialogue has made for an efficient foregrounding of the issues and the people.

b In a somewhat similar way, using a single speech in a context very different from the British setting of *Equus,* the Ghanaian playwright Ama Ata Aidoo opens a play about a young local man, Ato Yawson, who, when he returns from studying in North America, returns with Eulalie, also educated and African American. The play explores the interesting and sometimes intense cultural clashes that take place in the process of Ato's return to his native environment. This speech opens a section called 'Prelude', setting the Ghanaian context which then immediately flows into an argument between Ato and Eulalie, foregrounding their different values, some of the essential material of conflict in the play.

The Dilemma of a Ghost Prelude

I am the Bird of the Wayside –

The sudden scampering in the undergrowth,

Or the trunkless head

Of the shadow in the corner.

I am an asthmatic old hag

Eternally breaking the nuts

Whose soup, alas,

Nourished a bundle of whitened bones –

Or a pair of women, your neighbours

Chattering their lives away.

I can furnish you with reasons why

This and that and other things

Happened. But stranger,

What would you have me say

About the Odumna Clan?...

Look around you,

For the mouth must not tell everything.

Sometimes the eye can see

And the ear should hear.

Yonder house is larger than

Any in the town –

Old as the names

Oburumankuma, Odapadjan, Osun.

They multiply faster than fowls

And they acquire gold

As if it were corn grains –

But if in the making of

One Scholar

Much is gone

You stranger do not know.

Just you listen to their horn-blower:

    'We came from left

    We came from right

    We came from left

    We came from right

    The twig shall not pierce our eyes

    Nor the rivers prevail o'er us.

    We are of the vanguard

    We are running forward, forward, forward…'

Thus, it is only to be expected that they should reserve the new addition to the house for the exclusive use of the One Scholar. Not that they expect him to make his home there. No… he will certainly have to live and work in the city when he arrives from the white man's land.

But they all expect him to come down, now and then, at the weekend and on festive occasions like Christmas. And certainly, he must come home for blessings when the new yam has been harvested and the Stools are sprinkled. The ghosts of the dead ancestors are invoked and there is no discord, only harmony and a restoration of that which needs to be restored. But the Day of Planning is different from the Day of Battle. And when the One Scholar came… I cannot tell you what happened. You shall see that anon. But it all began on a University Campus; never mind where. The evening was cool as evenings are. Darkness was approaching when I heard the voices of a man and woman speaking…

EU: Graduation! Ah well, that too isn't bad. But who's a graduate? What sort of creature is it? Why should I have supposed that mere graduation is a passport to happiness?

ATO: [*Harshly*] If you must know, woman, I think you do get on my nerves. Since you do not think much of a degree, why for heaven's sake did you go in for it?

EU: Don't shout at me, if you please.

ATO: Do keep your mouth shut, if you please.

EU: I suppose African women don't talk?

ATO: How often do you want to drag in about African women? Leave them alone, will you… Ah yes they talk. But Christ, they don't run on in this way. This running-tap drawl gets on my nerves.

EU: What do you mean?

ATO: I mean exactly what I said.

EU: Look here, I don't think that I'll stand by and have you say I am not as good as your folks.

ATO: But what have I said, for goodness sake?

EU: Well, what did you mean by running-tap drawl? I only speak like I was born to speak – like an American!

ATO: [*Contrite*] Nonsense, darling… But Sweetie Pie, can't we ever talk, but we must drag in the differences between your people and mine? Darling, we'll be happy, won't we?

EU: [*Relaxing*] I'm optimistic, Native Boy. To belong to somewhere again… Sure, this must be bliss.

ATO: Poor Sweetie Pie.

EU: But I will not be poor again, will I? I'll just be 'Sweetie Pie'. Waw! The palm trees, the azure sea, the sun and golden beaches…

ATO: Steady, woman. Where did you get hold of a tourist brochure? There are no palms where we will live. There are coconut trees… coconut palms, though. Unless of course if I take you to see my folks at home. There are real palm trees there.

EU: Ah well, I don't know the difference, and I don't care either. Coconut palms, palm-palms, aren't they all the same? And anyway, why should I not go and see your folks?

ATO: You may not be impressed.

EU: Silly darling. Who wants to be impressed? Fine folks Eulalie Rush has herself, eh? Could I even point to you a beggar in the streets as my father or mother? Ato, can't your Ma be sort of my Ma too?

ATO: [*Slowly and uncertainly*] Sure she can.

EU: And your Pa mine?

ATO: Sure.

[*Following lines solemn, like a prayer*]

And all my people your people…

EU: And your gods my gods?

ATO: Yes.

EU: Shall I die where you will die?

Ama Ata Aidoo

The tension between a returning Ghanaian and the African-American woman who accompanies him provides some interesting comparison to the tensions set up in the opening of *Equus*. Look again at both of these openings and think about:

- their similarities and differences
- the way context is conveyed
- the likely effect on audiences in terms of involving them in the play... or not.

Kinds of drama/plays

In studying drama in the IB literature course in English, there are three main types of plays you are likely to encounter as part of your syllabus. They are:

- tragedy
- comedy
- tragicomedy.

Plays classified as "theatre of the absurd", melodrama, farce and epic theatre are also likely to be included, though some of these are often likely to appear in your works in translation.

Comedy / Tragedy

A short review of these three main types is in order, especially for plays originally written in English. In class, you will explore these descriptions in more detail in relation to particular plays, but it is important to remember that the individual work will never be a perfect representation of a definition of the form. In your reading, definitions of the form can provide a frame within which you will consider and explore the individual play, but no work of art is usefully reduced to its class or definition. With a play, in its dual nature as both words on a page and its performance, there are even more variables to take into account in your reflections and writing.

Tragedy

Tragedy is best understood as a term in relation to the time in which a particular play was written. Much theory and terminology about tragedy can be traced back to Aristotle's *Poetics*, a document that is variably understood and applied today and best used with great care. There is a considerable difference between the contexts (values, the structure of society, the political structure and the actual geographical places) that produce Sophocles' *Oedipus Rex* and Arthur Miller's *Death of a Salesman*, often identified as examples of classical tragedy and modern tragedy.

However, it is quite legitimate to make some assertions about what we mean when we call a play a 'tragedy'. The description that you may have learned in your earlier years is not entirely inappropriate: A tragedy is a play with an unhappy ending. Often, the **protagonist**, or leading character in a tragedy, faces both a kind of defeat and a kind of enlightenment or transcendence: a surpassing of weaknesses to arrive at understanding, often of limitations.

Early in the play, the protagonist faces a tragic dilemma, where they have a choice in which neither of the outcomes is 'good'. Still, the situation demands a choice with its attendant consequences.

We see the consequences of such dilemmas towards the end of *Equus*. After Alan has been through a kind of 'cure', Dysart, the psychiatrist, who has struggled deeply with his own profession, speaks to Hesther, the person who has encouraged him to treat Alan:

Equus

Act 2, Scene 35

All right! I'll take it away! He'll be delivered from madness. *What then?* He'll feel himself acceptable! *What then?* Do you think feelings like that can simply be re-attached, like plasters? Stuck on other objects we select? *Look at him…* My desire might be to make this boy an ardent husband – a caring citizen – a worshipper of abstract and unifying God. My achievement, however, is more likely to make him a ghost!… Let me tell you exactly what I'm going to do to him!

[*He steps out of the square and walks round the upstage end of it, storming at the audience.*]

I'll heal the rash on his body. I'll erase the welts cut into his mind by flying manes. When that's done, I'll set him on a nice mini-scooter and send him puttering off into the Normal world where animals are treated *properly:* made extinct or put into servitude, or tethered all their lives in dim light, just to feed it!

Peter Shaffer

An equally powerful moment occurs in the Canadian playwright Sharon Pollock's play, about the travel of the famous Native American figure Sitting Bull and his son into Canadian territory after the Montana massacre at Little Big Horn. Superintendent Walsh, of the Canadian Northwest Mounted Police, believes in the integrity of his government and has forged a relationship with Sitting Bull, but finally finds he must betray the trust he has built between himself and Sitting Bull and rejects the Sioux leader's plea.

Walsh

SITTING BULL:	White Sioux…
WALSH:	*without turning* Yes.
SITTING BULL:	I wish to speak with you.

WALSH *turns and looks at him.*

WALSH:	I'm listening.
SITTING BULL:	Have you had news from the Great White Mother?
WALSH:	My news is always the same… No reservations, no food, no clothing, no supplies.
SITTING BULL:	I wish you to send the Great White Mother a special message from Sitting Bull.
WALSH:	What is it?

SITTING BULL: Tell her… once I was strong and brave. My people had hearts of iron… But now, my women are sick, my children are freezing and I have thrown my war paint to the wind. The suffering of my people has made my heart weak and I have placed nothing in the way of those who wish to return across the line. Many have done so. We who remain desire a home. For three years, we have been in the White Mother's land. We have obeyed her laws and we have kept her peace… I beg the White Mother to… to…

WALSH: Go on.

SITTING BULL: …to have… pity… on us.

WALSH: Right!… Well then… I'll see that this goes off…

SITTING BULL *makes no move to leave.*

      Is there anything else?

SITTING BULL: *gazing at Walsh* White Sioux…

WALSH: Yes?

SITTING BULL: *speaking slowly and with effort* …I find it necessary… to make a request…

WALSH *stares at him.*

      …a request… for… provisions for my people. We have nothing.

WALSH: *brusquely* Your provisions wait for you across the line. If you want provisions, go there for them.

SITTING BULL: We hear you have a quantity of flour and I have come to ask you for it.

WALSH: If you wish to do business, you do it at the trading post.

SITTING BULL *takes off his ragged blanket. He holds out the blanket to* WALSH. WALSH *begins to breathe heavily as he struggles to retain control of himself.*

      I have appealed to the Great White Mother and the Great White Mother says no.

SITTING BULL: I ask for only a little.

WALSH: *exploding* And I can give you nothing! God knows, I've done my damndest and nothing's changed. Do you hear that? Nothing's changed! Cross the line if you're so hungry, but don't, for Christ's sake, come begging food from me!

Sharon Pollock

Tragedy is almost always complex and challenging for the audience and painful both for the audience and for the characters in the play. Walsh, who has tried his best to be fair to Sitting Bull, is ultimately 'bested' by his own government.

Comedy

Comedy, on the other hand, is even more difficult to define, and no one has really done so convincingly. We almost wish Aristotle had written another complete treatise discussing comedy.

We certainly know what makes us laugh when we laugh, but the great range of causes for this response appears more difficult to sort out than the causes for our responses to tragedy.

Writers and critics have given various labels to what is 'comic', but no clear lines or distinctions have emerged in the same way that discussions and definitions associated with tragedy have led to some common notions.

Labels such as 'romantic' versus 'scornful' comedy, or 'laughing' as opposed to 'smiling' comedy are caught in a web of connotations. Again, we often embark on a long journey to sort out the variations in intention and effect only to arrive at the more simple conclusion that a comedy has a 'happy ending', which is not the case with most if not all tragedies. Also, comedy often aims – when it has a rhetorical agenda – to correct or re-direct human manners and habits.

A play many students know, and one which is often used in the IB literature syllabus to represent comedy, is Oscar Wilde's *The Importance of Being Earnest*. Pretensions, deception, contradictory words and behaviours are all treated in a way we regard as amusing or satirical in this play.

Activity

Tom Stoppard has produced an interesting version of a play *Indian Ink*, in which two time frames are intermingled against a background in India. The major character, Flora Crewe, arrives in a small Indian town in the 1930s and then Stoppard advances the play 50 years when an American academic tries to unravel the 'real' story of a nude painting of Flora.

In the scene below, Das (the Indian who may have painted the picture) and Flora are engaged in both words and actions that depend on various elements of comedy to produce a fast-moving and entertaining scene.

Identify several humorous elements and explain why such elements contribute to comedy in this scene.

Indian Ink

DAS: You still have said nothing about the painting.

FLORA: I know.

DAS: I cannot continue today.

FLORA: I understand. Will we try again tomorrow?

DAS: Tomorrow is Sunday.

FLORA: The next day.

DAS: Perhaps I cannot continue at all.

FLORA: Oh. And all because I said nothing. Are you at the mercy of every breeze that blows? Are you an artist at all?

DAS: Perhaps not! A mere sketcher – a hack painter who should be working in the bazaar!

          (*He snatches up the 'pencil sketch' from under* FLORA's *hand.*)

FLORA: (*Realizing his intention*) Stop it!

          (DAS *tears the paper in half.*)

DAS: Or in chalks on the ghat!

FLORA: Stop!

          (*But* DAS *tears the paper again, and again and again, until it is in small pieces.*)

          I'm ashamed of you!

DAS: Excuse me, please! I wish to leave. I will take the canvas –

FLORA: You will not!

          (*It becomes a physical tussle. A struggle. She begins to gasp.*)

DAS: You need not see it again!

FLORA: You will not take anything! We will continue!

DAS: I do not want to continue, Miss Crewe. Please let go!

FLORA: I *won't* let you give up!

DAS: Let go, damn you, someone will see us.

FLORA: – and stop crying! You're not a baby!

DAS: (*Fighting her*) I will cry if I wish!

FLORA: Cry, then, but you will finish what you started! How else will you ever … Oh!

          (*And suddenly* FLORA *is helpless, gasping for breath.*)

DAS: Oh… oh, Miss Crewe – oh my God – let me help you. I'm sorry. Please. Here, sit down –

          (*She has an attack of breathlessness. He helps her to a chair.* FLORA *speaks with difficulty.*)

FLORA: Really, I'm all right.

          (*Pause. She takes careful breaths.*) There.

DAS: What happened?

FLORA: I'm not allowed to wrestle with people. It's a considerable nuisance. My lungs are bad, you see.

DAS: Let me move the cushion.

FLORA: It's all right. I'm back now. Panic over. I'm here for my health, you see. Well, not *here*… I'll stay longer in the Hills.

DAS: Yes, that will be better. You must go high.

FLORA: Yes. In a day or two.

DAS: What is the matter with you?

FLORA: Oh, sloshing about inside. Can't breathe under water. I'm sorry if I frightened you.

DAS: You did frighten me.

FLORA: I'm soaking.

DAS: You must change your clothes.

FLORA: Yes. I'll go in now. I've got a shiver. Pull me up. Thank you. Ugh. I need to be rubbed down like a horse.

DAS: Perhaps some tea… I'll go to the kitchen and tell –

FLORA: Yes. Would you? I'll have a shower and get into my Wendy house.

DAS: Your…?

FLORA: My big towel is on the kitchen verandah – would you ask Nazrul to put it in the bedroom?

(DAS *runs towards the kitchen verandah, shouting for Nazrul.* FLORA *goes into the interior, into the bathroom, undressing as she goes, dropping the blue dress on the floor, and enters the bathroom in her underwear.*

DAS *returns, hurrying, with a white towel. He enters the interior cautiously, calling 'Miss Crewe…' He enters the bedroom and finds it empty. From the bathroom there is the sound of the water pipes thumping, but no sound of water.*)

FLORA: (*Off stage*) Oh, damn, come on!

DAS: Miss Crewe…

(*The thumping in the pipes continues.* DAS *approaches the bathroom door.*)

DAS: (*Louder*) Miss Crewe! I'm sorry, there's no –

FLORA: (*Off stage, shouts*) There's no water!

(*The thumping noise continues.*)

DAS: Miss Crewe! I'm sorry, the electricity –

(*The thumping noise suddenly stops.*)

(*In mid-shout*) The electric pump –

FLORA: (*Entering naked*) I have to lie down.

DAS: Oh! (*Thrusting the towel at her*) Oh, I'm so sorry!

(*Relieved of the towel,* DAS *is frozen with horror.*)

FLORA: I'm sorry, Mr Das, but really I feel too peculiar to mind at the moment.

DAS: (*Turning to leave hurriedly*) Please forgive me!

FLORA: No, please, there's water in the jug on the wash-stand.

(*She stands shivering, hugging the towel.*)

Do be quick.

DAS: *(Getting the water)* It's the electricity for the pump.

FLORA: Is there any water?

DAS: Yes, it's full… Here –

(He gives her the jug, and turns away.)

FLORA: Thank you. No, you do it. Over my head, and my back, please.

(DAS pours the water over her, carefully.)

Oh heaven… Oh, thank you… I'm terribly sorry about this. Oh, that's good. Tip the last bit on the towel.

DAS: There…

(She wipes her face with the wet corner of the towel…)

FLORA: I feel as weak as a kitten.

DAS: I'm afraid that's all.

FLORA: Thank you.

(She wraps the towel around herself.) Could you do the net for me?

(DAS lifts one side of the mosquito net and FLORA climbs onto the bed.)

I'll be all right now.

DAS: *(Misunderstanding; leaving)* Yes, of course.

Tom Stoppard

Tragicomedy

Much modern drama has combined elements of what we associate with both tragedy and comedy and given rise to what is now called 'tragicomedy', in an attempt to account for the serious and comic elements which are found there.

However, tragicomedy really has some much older counterparts and various other labels are given to the same plays; Renaissance plays also represent the dramatic impulse to represent both the tragic and the comic in the lives and fortunes of their characters. The inclusion by Shakespeare of comic scenes and characters provides what some call **comic relief**, but tragicomedy might be seen as a more integral blend of the tragic and the comic.

In the 18th century, Samuel Johnson, an important writer and critic of his time, praised tragicomedy and its effects on the audience. He wrote in Rambler: "…no plays have oftner filled the eyes with tears… than those variegated with interludes of mirth".

One useful approach to the nature of tragicomedy can be found in a study of this form by Verna A. Foster, who includes the words of Doctor Johnson just cited. This writer offers a helpful distinction of the way tragicomedy works in the two different periods.

In Renaissance tragicomedies, Foster says, "the protagonists are usually potentially tragic figures in an ultimately comic universe". Foster would consider Prospero in Shakespeare's *The Tempest* an example of this combination.

However, "in modern tragicomedy, the individual is more often a comic figure in a universe probably tragic or at best uncertain" (Foster 2004). Vladimir and Estragon in Beckett's *Waiting for Godot* are characters most of us would see as fitting this second context.

While this set of distinctions may be a little reductive, it is a useful guide to the label, 'tragicomedy'. If you are studying modern drama in Part 3 of your syllabus, you may find, along with Beckett, that such playwrights as Harold Pinter, Tom Stoppard, Wole Soyinka and Caryl Churchill will ask you to think about 'tragicomedy' as an appropriate description of their plays.

Other 'labels' for plays

Both **melodrama** and **farce** are forms of drama that inevitably appear in surveys of the genre called 'drama'. Melodrama is certainly something with which we are all familiar in this era, where TV has had such a great influence, and farce, too, has its place in weekly programming.

Melodrama

TV soap operas are perhaps the form of melodrama that you are most likely to encounter in contemporary experience. The melodrama tends to oversimplify serious matters, to heighten black and white contrasts. Characterization leans towards stereotyping. While we may be amused, fascinated or engaged in this form of melodrama, we may not be deeply moved. While there may be moments in plays that you read in your IB study that strike you as a little 'melodramatic', you may not actually find melodrama included in your set of plays. Plays such as Shaffer's *Sleuth* may be considered melodrama.

Farce

Farce is another form we also recognize from TV and films. The intent here is perhaps clearer than in other forms; Lawrence Perrine and others describe the effect desired from the audience of farce as "explosive laughter" (Perrine 1978). Whether from current favourites in the form of film such as *The Pink Panther* or *Lock, Stock and Two Smoking Barrels*, or in the situation comedies of TV, farce is characterized by physical comedy, ludicrous action, word gags, and absurd events and outcomes. While a whole play you study may not be categorized as 'farce', farcical elements appear throughout the history of drama.

Modern plays by Joe Orton and some plays by John Guare are often categorized as farce; Michael Frayn's *Noises Off* is a frequently performed contemporary example of farce.

Beyond these categories, you will find other types of drama such as epic theatre, comedy of manners, the theatre of the absurd, the theatre of cruelty, and feminist theatres. While there is not space to explore these here, you will find that some plays in your study will be connected both to one of the major forms discussed previously, as well as to more particular drama categories.

A brief history of drama written in English

Like the other short histories of genres included in this book, it would be impossible to pretend to cover the history of such complicated matters in a few pages. However, in order to introduce you to, or to review, some aspects of this history, the material relevant to the development of drama in English has been divided into three large sections:

- Medieval or pre-Renaissance drama.
- Renaissance drama.
- Modern drama.

The latter two sections cover the time periods in which drama has especially flourished. The first section suggests some of the roots for the development of drama, which at that time was occurring in Great Britain.

Medieval drama (*c.*12th–15th century)

Because of the interest in the middle ages in recent years, you may have encountered some versions of medieval drama at fairs where there is an attempt to replicate this period in British culture. You can find short clips of the performance of medieval stage performance on the Internet.

There were really two essential phases in dramatic performance in these centuries. In the earlier phase, the Catholic Church used dramatic representation to assist a non-literate population in learning materials relevant to the faith. The enactment of the Catholic Mass has itself many dramatic elements and one in particular – a kind of antiphonal trope, a chanted dialogue – was often incorporated into the liturgy of the Eucharist. Eventually, stories from the Bible were incorporated into the liturgical events connected to this ceremony.

Townspeople themselves then began to develop the stories into more elaborate dramatic representations, forming guilds or managing groups with particular biblical stories connected to particular groups. Eventually the productions moved out of the church and on to what were called 'pageant wagons' – portable stages that could be moved from town to town for performance. The stories were often grouped into 'cycles'. Soon, the public was able to view various versions of Bible stories in performances that were designed to both educate and entertain. Melodramatic versions of Herod and the massacre of the Holy Innocents or Noah quarrelling with his wife became popular features of these plays.

In addition to these biblical plays, often called the 'mystery' plays, were 'morality' plays with more explicitly didactic and serious aims, such as *Everyman*, and the less serious, often highly-comic work that was produced in the medieval university.

A significant role of the medieval theatre was to create an expectation and a practice of drama that was to lead to the exceptional vitality of play writing and performance from the 16th century to the middle of the 17th century in England, the period of such influential figures as Shakespeare, Christopher Marlowe, Ben Jonson and others.

Renaissance drama (16th–17th century)

One of the major developments in drama during this period was the actual construction of theatres, where people of all classes could attend much more developed plays which went far beyond the biblical subject matter of the medieval plays.

If you study Shakespeare in the IB literature course, you will become acquainted with many features of the theatre in this period: the actual design of theatres like the Globe; the importance of words far beyond the role of staging and costume and other theatrical effects; and the absence of women from any acting roles.

Shakespeare's Globe Theatre, London

Drama in this period became a major force in the development of the English language and the poetry of the stage. Shakespeare's overriding achievement in drama spurred inspiration, competition and imitation. The development of acting companies meant an expansion of plays available to the public. The interest and patronage of Queen Elizabeth and her court were a further element of the vigorous development of drama during this period.

Perhaps one of the most revealing examples of what the theatre and acting meant to its most well-known practitioner, William Shakespeare, can be found in his play *Hamlet*.

In this play, Prince Hamlet is given the role of the revenger of his father's murderer, who happens to be the current king, his uncle Claudius. Shakespeare not only introduces a play-within-a-play to help Hamlet out in the discovery of King Claudius's guilt, but also includes lines which tell us something now about the place of actors both in Shakespeare's estimation and for the period of Renaissance drama. Hamlet lets the audience know that his plan is hatched: "The play's the thing / Wherein I'll catch the conscience of the King" (Act 2, Scene 2, lines 614–5).

Hamlet is inspired by the arrival of a group of travelling players to come up with a further step in his plan to revenge his father's death, but this presence also gives Shakespeare the opportunity to celebrate acting itself. When Polonius, the Lord Chamberlain, suggests he will look after the players according to what he thinks people of their class deserve, Hamlet scolds him, saying, "God's bodkin, man, much better!" (Act 2, Scene 2, line 340). He speaks of them as the true recorders of the times in which the court is living: "the abstract and brief chronicles of the time" (Act 2, Scene 2, line 535).

Modern drama (19th–20th century)

Although the period between Renaissance drama and the advent of what is generally considered the 'modern' period in English drama contains some work in theatre that is both interesting and important – the works of William Congreve and William Wycherley, for example, who produced entertaining examples of the **comedy of manners** – the more likely emphasis in your IB syllabus will be modern plays, dating from the late 19th century into the 20th century.

As you study modern drama in English, you will find that other aspects of the development of drama will come into play. **Realism** and **naturalism** are two of these terms. Study of these terms can become quite extensive and you may well have encountered them in your study of novels.

Some rather simple definitions for these two terms can be a starting point, but as you look at particular plays your understanding of both labels will evolve. As noted earlier, it's always best to consider such labels as helpful to frame ideas, not as envelopes into which every related play must be tightly fitted.

Realism

Often defined as the attempt to show "life as it is really lived", realism presents problems both for the playwright and for the audience. "A willing suspension of disbelief", in the widest sense, is required in order for us to see on the stage or read in the script things that are not somehow selected, contrived and arranged in a way that life can never be. Still, moments, actions, conversations can certainly be presented in a play as replications of everyday human events and behaviour. Certainly, early practitioners of realistic drama were eager to move away from what they saw as the 'romanticism' of earlier works in the 19th century, often written on the continent of Europe. If we look at plays like Edward Albee's *Who's Afraid of Virginia Woolf?* we can certainly sense a drive to present life as it 'is really lived' in a particular context. Arthur Miller and Sam Shepard do not draw back from such realism as you will see in studying their plays.

Naturalism

In some ways, naturalism in drama may be even more problematic. As a product of the thinking and practice of Emile Zola, the French novelist, the goal here is to look clinically at the effects of birth and background on human behaviour. Often the force of society on characters is material for exploration in naturalistic drama and often, too, both the context and the choices of the characters are tinged with pessimism.

However, it is often difficult to draw any clear lines between what is 'realistic' and what is 'naturalistic' in any drama. A whole range of approaches is possible, from the social satire of George Bernard Shaw in a play like *Arms and the Man* to the dark and violent version of Shakespeare's *King Lear* by Edward Bond.

Although there are exceptions, it can certainly be said that modern drama has been much affected by the trends mentioned above. Whether we are reading or seeing the plays of Tennessee Williams, Sarah Kane or Louis Nowra, we are likely to encounter more of the tragic side of life than the comic or the farcical. That is not to say that comedy has disappeared in modern drama, just that seriousness tempered sometimes by humour, farce, gentle or biting satire is likely to be the more prevalent focus of plays you will read from the 20th and 21st centuries.

'Audience' versus 'reader': which should we use?

In many cases where students are working with drama in Part 3 of their Language A literature syllabus, access to the theatre and professional performances of particular plays may not be possible. Hence, your experience of the play will be limited to reading scripts or watching film versions, or classroom readings and performances. Possibly, your school or your theatre students may be staging a production.

Reading, as we know, is one way in which people can come to know plays. A fuller experience will be derived from seeing that 'script' enacted in performance. While you are studying plays in this IB literature course, both reading and seeing the plays in performance are regarded as legitimate experiences of the plays, but there will always be an expectation of close study of the text of the play, the script.

Which audience?

There are many complicated considerations in determining the effect on an audience. Who do we mean by 'the audience'? Playwrights produce their work in time and space. Historical and cultural context will affect the way the play is received.

For the purposes of your IB literature course, the only audience you really can know is a contemporary one, people of your own time, although research and your teacher's knowledge can give you some information about, say, the Shakespearean audience. Attending a performance of a play can give you a sense of your own reactions as well as those of people who are sharing that experience. Therefore, you need to exercise great care when you are writing about a play's effect on 'the audience'. This term may describe both a reader (you), a group of readers, or it may describe a theatre audience.

What *is* important is that you always keep in mind the likely or possible effects of the words, the movements and gestures either included by the playwright or implied, and the limitations and possibilities of different types of theatres. This consciousness is not always easy to maintain. Even with the help of films or videos, your experience of a play is not quite that of the theatre. If your experience is entirely limited to reading the plays, you will have to practise a larger sense of the work than if you were reading a novel.

So, how will you handle writing a Paper 2 essay about plays you have studied? While references to 'the reader' are in some cases acceptable, generally the IB examiner will expect you to both possess and communicate that you are well aware that you are discussing plays whose completion lies in performance. You can convey this awareness by referring to such matters as stage directions, to entrances and exits and to groupings of people on the stage; in fact, many of the conventions that follow in the next section of this chapter will provide you with ideas about addressing the plays as plays, and not just as texts.

The conventions of drama

Before we survey the conventions of the genre, it is important to note that what follows focuses chiefly on the conventions that have to do with the text of the play. There are many conventions that have more to do with acting than they do with the script of the play, such as blocking or pitch and tone. Sometimes the two sets of conventions are very close and overlap; some are very precisely connected to such matters as the words, the plot, characters and setting of the play, and are more likely to be found in the list that follows. Others have to do with techniques of performance and are generally not included in the list.

Conventions are also connected to particular historical periods; the conventions of Greek theatre are not precisely the same as those of Elizabethan or modern theatre. What follows does not attempt to be a comprehensive list of theatre or theatrical conventions; the terms found here are those most likely to be included in Paper 2 questions, in which genre and its conventions play a part.

Conventions associated with the words written and spoken

Dialogue includes all the words from the play designed to be spoken by actors, comprising the bulk of the script. **Monologues**, on the other hand, are long speeches spoken by a single character. When a monologue is spoken by a player alone on the stage it is called a soliloquy.

Verbal irony is a frequent feature of plays. It usually involves saying one thing and intending or implying another or additional meaning. It is sometimes referred to as **double entendre**.

The **aside** (usually designated in the script) gives the actors an opportunity to add something 'under their breath', for the benefit of other characters and also, or especially for, the audience.

Conventions associated with character portrayal

The protagonist of a play is usually the chief character who faces up to the problem or dilemma that the play addresses. A rival to this protagonist is called the antagonist. An anti-hero is a protagonist whose character includes some features that are the opposite of what is expected of a hero or heroine in a play.

Just as in novels, for example, there are likely to be secondary or minor characters in most plays. These characters have roles of varying importance. Sometimes they will be stereotypes, such as the fool, the villain, the confidante, and are often called **stock characters**. An **eponymous** character is one who gives the name to the play, as in *Hamlet*, for example.

Most of what needs to be known about characters will be revealed in the course of the play; sometimes, however, the material is called their back story. At times, these stories will be delivered by actually performing incidents from the past in **flashbacks**. Events that occur in the future are called **flash forwards**. Synonyms for these two terms are **analepsis** and **prolepsis**, respectively.

Playwrights often help to build impressions of characters by deliberately constructed entrances and exits. Delaying the entrance of a main character can help to build suspense; abrupt exits can convey a certain temperamental aspect of a character. Gestures and repetitive actions are also used to delineate characters and create expectations about them.

Finally, the substitution of actions and gestures for words through mime or pantomime is a technique quite opposite to the importance of words: the absence of words to convey meaning.

Conventions associated with the action or plot of the play

Freytag's triangle or pyramid is one of the commonly–used ways to map the action of plays. This approach was devised by the German playwright Gustav Freytag in the 19th century. It offers a way of understanding the structure of many plays, but it should be used as a general frame, not a representation of the exact structure of all plays. Perhaps it best serves as a useful measure of congruence and deviation. At the top of page 170 is a version by Barbara McManus. It is helpful to use the terminology of this triangle to refer to certain parts of a play.

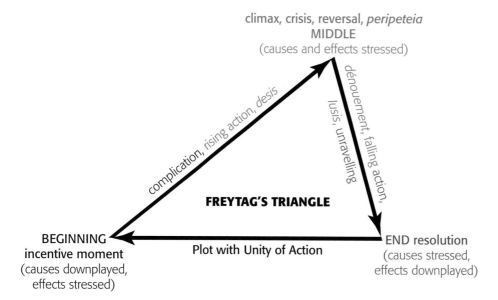

Freytag's triangle

The **exposition** of the play usually occurs in the first scenes or pages of the script, and answers at least some of the following questions: Who? What? When? Where? Why?

The **rising action** introduces most of the essential material and shows how the characters are involved in the action, the conflict or the issue on which the play focuses. It usually arises from some impulse introduced early in the play and is sometimes called the **exciting force** which sets off the **complication**.

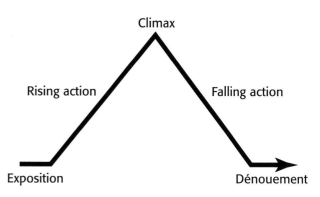

Most students are familiar with the high point of action in novels and films, called the **climax**, and this feature will likely be found somewhere along the line of action, sometimes in the middle, but sometimes unexpectedly early or late. Often, it is the point of greatest interest and sometimes of emotional response on the part of the audience.

Certain things in the action of the play are often seriously altered by the climax of the play and give rise to the **falling action**, which, in turn, leads on to what is invariably called the dénouement (the 'unknotting' of the threads of the plot) or the **resolution**. There are in fact so many ways in which plays can conclude that it is important to remain flexible when applying labels.

The action of the play may fall into such divisions as acts (often a larger unit) and scenes (either subdivisions of acts or units of their own). Acts and scenes (whether explicitly identified or not) are carefully decided by the playwright to deliver the action with an appropriate conceptual and emotional rhythm. Even intermissions designated by the playwright can affect the way the audience reacts to the play.

A **prologue** or an **epilogue** (often a speech by one voice) occurring respectively before the play begins or after it ends, can also be used in various ways to deliver information or reflections. **Curtain lines**, lines delivered at the end of an act or a scene, may also be used quite effectively by playwrights.

Other elements related to the unfolding of the action of the play, but not necessarily related to each other, are as follows:

- **Dramatic irony**, which adds another layer to the experience of the reader or audience. In this feature, the audience is provided with information that characters on the stage do not possess. The character may act in a way that only the audience knows to be disastrous, for example. Dramatic irony is also used to refer to outcomes that are the reversal of expectation. This feature can easily cross over into the territory of verbal irony, where the character's words carry a meaning unknown to the character but not to the audience.

- **Comic relief** is sometimes included in plays that are primarily serious or tragic. Words, actions or characters may be introduced to provide a lightening of the mood or circumstances, as the Fool does in Shakespeare's *King Lear*.

- *Deus ex machina*, a Latin term stemming from classical drama, is sometimes a useful one for explaining the introduction of an unexpected or improbable event (or person) that leads to a solution of some dramatic problem. The gods in Greek drama were sometimes lowered on to the stage to solve a tricky situation; hence the term 'god from a machine'.

Some conventions related to staging and performance

The performance of the play must take place in some physical setting. The **set** of the play is the arrangement of the stage to represent the setting of the action. It can include a backdrop as well as theatrical properties or props, which include furnishings and objects needed by the actors. **Lighting** and **sound** are often important atmospheric elements of plays. Music, of course, may play a major role here as well.

Stage business is another convention of theatre that is sometimes relevant to discussing plays; it refers to actions that are incidental to the immediate action, such as an actor playing with some article of clothing or the use of other props. Such actions can be used to develop a character or suggest some concern that is an alternative to the focus of the moment.

Two other features that may also be used to good effect and be most vivid in performance are the **freeze frame** and the **breaking of the fourth wall**. In the first feature, the action is stopped, the actors freeze and meaning is conveyed through this moment of silence and stasis. The second feature refers to the imaginary 'fourth wall' that is characteristic of the conventional proscenium stage, which often includes a curtain. The curtain functions as a 'fourth wall' which, when opened, allows the audience to view the set and the actors; in the absence of a curtain, there is still an imagined 'fourth wall' between the stage and the audience. While many modern productions of plays work well outside this conventional stage, the term continues to refer to actors acknowledging or speaking to the audience.

1 Choose a play that is part of your study of Part 3. In small groups, assemble a list of as many of the conventions listed earlier that you can find in that play and compose a chart which has the following three features:

   a The name of the convention.

   b A brief definition of the convention.

   c The exact location of the convention in the play, using act and/or scene, if possible. (Your grasp of the convention will be strengthened if you use more than one example.)

2 Choose one of the charts developed by the class (your own or one from another group). Working alone, write a short paragraph on the effect of one convention on its immediate context and/or the whole play.

Conclusion

You will discover that there is a lot to know and a lot to apply if you are going to study and write well about drama in Part 3 of your syllabus.

You need to understand that the more you read and see plays, the more you will understand about the intentions and the experience playwrights aim to provide. Lest you become overwhelmed by the breadth of what you must know and the difficulties to overcome, especially if your opportunities to enjoy theatre in its fullest are limited, you may enjoy what Christopher Durang's 'Mrs. Sorken' has to offer you in her view of theatre. Be wary of taking her ideas as factual!

Below are sections of her monologue designed to 'enlighten' you.

Mrs. Sorken

Enter Mrs. Sorken to address the audience. She is a charming woman, well dressed and gracious, though a little scattered. She is happy to be there.

MRS. SORKEN: Dear theatregoers, welcome, and how lovely to see you. I've come here to talk to you about theatre, and why we all leave our homes to come see it, assuming we have. But you have left your homes, and you're here. So, welcome!

Now I have just written down some comments about theatre for you, if I can just find them. *(Searches through her purse.)*

Isn't it refreshing to see someone with a purse? *(Looks some more through the purse.)*

Well, I can't find my notes, so I'll have to make my comments from memory.

(From here on, she is genuinely winging it – some of it may be thoughts she's prepared, much of it are thoughts that pop into her head as she is speaking. She is not nervous, though. She loves talking to the audience.)

Drama. Let's begin with etymology, shall we? …etymology, which is the history of the word.

The word "drama" comes from the Greek work "dran," which means to do, and which connects with the English word "drain," meaning to exhaust one totally, and with the modern pharmaceutical sedating tablet, Dramamine, which is the tradename of a drug used to relieve airsickness and seasickness and a general sense of nausea, or "nausée" as Jean Paul Sartre might say, perhaps over a cup of espresso at a Paris bistro. How I love Paris in the spring, or would, if I had ever been there; but Mr. Sorken and I haven't done much travelling. Maybe after he dies I'll go somewhere…

Secondly… we have the word "theatre," which is derived from the Greek word "theasthai," which means to view.

And nowadays we have the word "reastat," a device by which we can dim the lights in one's house slowly, rather than just snapping them off with a simple switch.

And thirdly, we have the Greek god "Dionysus," the last syllable of which is spelled "s-u-s" in English, but "s-o-s" in Greek, the letters which in Morse code spell *help* – "Dionysos" is the god of wine and revelry, but also the father of modern drama as we know it.

The Greeks went to the theatre in the open air, just like the late and wonderful Joseph Papp used to make us see Shakespeare. Shakespeare's language is terribly difficult to understand for us of the modern age, but how much easier it is when there's a cool breeze and it's for free. If it's hot and I have to pay, well, then I don't much like Shakespeare. I'm sorry, I shouldn't say that. He's a brilliant writer, and I look forward to seeing all 750 of his plays. Although perhaps not in this lifetime.

But back to the Greeks. They went to the open-air theatre expecting the drama they saw to evoke terror and pity.

Nowadays we have enough terror and pity in our own lives, and so rather than going to the theatre looking for terror, we go looking for slight irritation. And rather than looking for the theatre to evoke pity, we look merely for a generalized sense of identification as in "Evita was a woman, I am a woman." Or "Sweeney Todd was a barber, I go to the hairdresser." Or "Fosca in *Passion* should have her moles removed, I know a good dermatologist." That sort of thing.

But did the Greeks really experience terror and pity? And if so, what was it in all that matricide-patricide that so affected them?

I know that seeing Greek drama nowadays, even with Diana Rigg in it, really rather baffles me, it is so very different from my own life. My life with Mr. Sorken is not something that Diana Rigg would wish to star in, even on PBS. My life, I'm sorry to say, is not all that interesting.

Indeed, addressing you at this moment, I'm sorry to say, is the high point of my life to date.

Could I have lived my life differently? Women of my generation were encouraged to marry and to play the piano, and I have done both those things. Is there a piano here? I don't see one. I might have played a sonata for you, or a polonaise.

But back to my theme – Drama, from the Greek word "dran."

When we leave the drama, we return to our homes feeling "drained." And if it's been a good night in the theatre, we leave feeling slightly irritated; and feeling identification with Evita or Fosca or that poor Mormon woman in *Angels in America*.

And so, drained, we get into our nightgowns, we adjust our reastats from light to darkness, we climb into bed next to Mr. Sorken, we fall into a deep REM sleep, dreaming God knows what mysterious messages from our teeming unconscious; and then in the morning we open our eyes to the light of the new day, of the burgeoning possibilities.

Christopher Durang

Poetry

What is poetry?

The quotations opposite, from Stevens and Poe, are only two attempts to define poetry and you will see others in the margin as we move through this chapter. The reality is that no one definition of poetry will satisfy everyone's sense of what it is.

These two definitions have been selected because the first emphasizes the elusive reasons why many people find poetry so compelling, and the second helps to emphasize one aspect of poetry that students often struggle with and reduce to strategies of spotting and naming: the aspect of sound and music in poetry. One description is analogical or metaphorical, the other is more literal. But, essentially, poetry is like language itself: a construct of sound and meaning.

The ideas of the second definition are ones you have likely been familiar with since you were a young child, whether in rhymes you were taught or invented. One writer about the sound of poetry, Alfred Corn, calls his book *The Poem's Heartbeat*. Very often, when people talk about the less cognitive aspects of poetry – its sound – they will begin to talk about the pleasure listeners take in rhythm and regularity, and this is indeed part of your everyday experience: listening to your favorite music – and sometimes to the words that accompany that music. However, it may be that you do not see the connection between this familiar activity and the poems you are asked to read or 'study' in your English class. So, contrary perhaps to the approach often taken in your classes, this chapter is going to take a circular path.

In reviewing and extending your experience with poetry, this chapter will begin with sound, move to meaning and end with an exercise aimed to bring the two together in a way that may help you. If you do not already find some interest, pleasure and confidence in reading poetry, perhaps this chapter will open a new avenue to those things, as well as provide you with the knowledge you will need to write about poetry for your exam.

Prose? Poetry?

To begin with, it's a good idea to try to clear away any confusion in the way the terms 'prose' and 'poetry' are used in this book. When poetry is addressed, the genre discussed will be characterized by either some regular (or metrical) rhythm or the shaping of lines with some

"Poetry is a pheasant disappearing in the brush."
Wallace Stevens

"I would define… the Poetry of words as the rhythmical creation of beauty."
Edgar Allan Poe

other form of rhythm: repetition of line length, line beginnings or patterns of words.

In John Keats' poem 'When I Have Fears', we have **metrical verse** (or poetry):

> When I have fears that I may cease to be
> Before my pen has gleaned my teeming brain…

Can you hear the alternation of heavy and light emphasis (**stress**) here?

In Walt Whitman's poem 'Cavalry Crossing a Ford', we have **free verse** (or poetry):

> Behold the silvery river, in it the splashing horses loitering stop to drink,
>
> Behold the brown-faced men, each group, each person a picture, the negligent rest on saddles…

You will note that here it is not possible to hear that regular alternation of stress and unstress, or heavy and light emphasis. The poet has, in a sense, 'freed' himself of the regularity of metrical verse. You might, however, notice that Whitman has given some rhythm to the lines by other means.

You will also notice that the lines as you see them on the page have some different features by which you conventionally recognize them as poetry and not prose.

For example, looking at some lines of what in literary study is called prose, note the difference in the way the lines appear on the page:

> The car was going a wild forty-five miles an hour across the open and as Macomber watched, the buffalo got bigger and bigger until he could see the gray, hairless, scabby look of one huge bull and how his neck was a part of his shoulders and the shiny black of his horns as he galloped a little behind the others that were strung out in that steady plunging gait…
>
> *Ernest Hemingway*

You would almost certainly recognize this not as poetry but as what is probably part of a story, perhaps a novel or even part of an essay.

However, you might also be quick to notice that some rhythm is present here and it's useful to think about what causes this. So, as you can see, our decision about prose and poetry is somewhat dependent on what we see on the page. If you were to only hear these pieces by Whitman and Hemingway, it would be hard to say one is free verse and one is prose.

In relation to using visual cues, what can we say about the following published poem in *The New Yorker*? It's listed under the 'poetry' heading in the table of contents of the journal. It offers another version of poetry called the **prose poem**. Hearing it would be very much like hearing the Hemingway extract on the previous page.

The Straightforward Mermaid

The straightforward mermaid starts every sentence with "Look…" This comes from being raised in a sea full of hooks. She wants to get points 1, 2, and 3 across, doesn't want to disappear like a river into the ocean. When she's feeling despairing, she goes to eddies at the mouth of the river and tries to comb the water apart with her fingers. The straightforward mermaid has already said to five sailors, "Look, I don't think this is going to work," before sinking like a sullen stone. She's supposed to teach Rock Impersonation to the younger mermaids, but every beach field trip devolves into them trying to find shells to match their tail scales. They really love braiding. "Look," says the straightforward mermaid. "Your high ponytails make you look like fountains, not rocks." Sometimes she feels like a third gender – preferring primary colors to pastels, the radio to singing. At least she's all mermaid: never gets tired of swimming, hates the thought of socks.

Harvey, M. *The New Yorker*. 16 August 2010.

These may be dilemmas you have encountered before, and there is no simple solution to the distinguishing of prose and poetry. However, before we leave you sitting on the 'horns of this dilemma', let us just look at some attempts to define prose in the margin opposite. These may or may not help you, but you will at least see that 'experts' who write about these issues also have trouble being precise.

You will note that the absence of *regular* stress and unstress ('formal patterns of verse' and 'a regular metrical principle') is important to these attempts to distinguish prose from poetry.

When it comes to defining poetry, the issue is often even more complicated, so we are going to create a working definition for this chapter, which may help you to have a baseline from which to work. When some poets define poetry, they often depend on poetry (or **metaphor**) itself in shaping their definition, as in the "pheasant disappearing in the brush" at the beginning of this chapter. Others manage to be more direct. Others define it by its effect.

What is poetry as it is treated in this chapter and in this book?

Poetry is:

- language selected and compressed for maximum effect
- language that consciously uses rhythmic effects such as regular stress and unstress, or repetition of some kind

"Prose is… the form of language that is not organized according to the formal patterns of 'verse', although it will have some sort of rhythm… the significant unit being the sentence rather than the line."
Chris Baldrick

"Prose is… a type of language not organized according to a regular metrical principle or pattern, as is poetry."
Edward Quinn

"If I feel physically as if the top of my head were taken off, I know that is poetry."
Emily Dickinson

"Poetry is simply the most beautiful, impressive and wisely efficient way of saying things."
Matthew Arnold

"The refinement of the poem, its subtlety, is not to be known by the elevation of the words, but – the words don't matter so much – by the resources of the music."
Robert Frost

● language that is strikingly arranged, as in 'lines' on the page or in some format that differentiates it from the prose of expository or fictional writing.

You will note that even the mermaid prose poem on page 177 has a particular visual quality that may distinguish it from prose.

As you can see, just like the boundaries between the genres (or the difficulties of drawing them), the definitions of prose and poetry present us with some problems.

The "usual aim [of prose] is to move the reader along without calling attention to itself."
Northrop Frye

"We need… a burst of air in at the window of our prose."
William Carlos Williams
(speaking of poetry)

Activity

Either:

a Using your knowledge of poems you have read in the past and the lyrics of music that you like, construct in very literal, analogical or metaphorical terms a definition of poetry. Add some examples to support your view. Your definition can be as short as one paragraph or as long as an essay.

Or:

b Read the two extracts about hummingbirds below and on pages 179–80 – one in poetry and one in prose – both written by Diane Ackerman. Discuss with your group what you see as the differences of delivering one version in poetry and one in prose. Which do you think captures the essence of hummingbirds more effectively, more vividly? What does the prose version offer that the poetry does not?

The Dark Night of the Hummingbird

A lot of hummingbirds die in their sleep,
dreaming of nectar-sweet funnels they sipped.
Moth-light, they swiveled at succulent
blooms, all flash and ripple – like sunset,
but delicate, probing, excitable,
their wings a soft fury of iridescence,
their hearts beating like a tiny drumroll
fourteen hundred times a minute,
their W-shaped tongues, drawing nectar
down each groove, whispering: *wheels
    within wheels*,
By day, hovering hard, they fly nowhere
at speed, swilling energy. But to refuel,
they must eat, and to eat they must hover,
burning more air than a sprinting impala.

So, in the dark night of the hummingbird,
while lilies lather sweetly in the rain,

the hummingbird rests near collapse,
its quick pulse halved, its rugged breath
    shallow,
its W-shaped tongue, & bright as Cassiopeia,
now mumbling words like *wistful* and *wan*.
The world at once drug, anthem, bright lagoon,
where its heart knew all the Morse codes
for rapture, pales into a senseless twilight.
It can't store enough fuel to last the night
and hoist it from its well of dreams
to first light trembling on wet fuchsia,
nor break the hard promise life always keeps.
A lot of hummingbirds die in their sleep.

Diane Ackerman

Mute Dancers: How to Watch a Hummingbird

A LOT OF HUMMINGBIRDS DIE in their sleep. Like a small fury of iridescence, a hummingbird spends the day at high speed, darting and swiveling among thousands of nectar-rich blossoms. Hummingbirds have huge hearts and need colossal amounts of energy to fuel their flights, so they live in a perpetual mania to find food. They tend to prefer red, trumpet-shaped flowers, in which nectar thickly oozes, and eat every 15 minutes or so. A hummingbird drinks with a W-shape tongue, licking nectar up as a cat might (but faster). Like a tiny drum roll, its heart beats at 500 times a minute. Frighten a hummingbird and its heart can race to over 1,200 times a minute. Feasting and flying, courting and dueling, hummingbirds consume life at a fever pitch. No warm-blooded animal on earth uses more energy, for its size. But that puts them at great peril. By day's end, wrung-out and exhausted, a hummingbird rests near collapse.

In the dark night of the hummingbird, it can sink into a zombielike state of torpor; its breathing grows shallow and its wild heart slows to only 36 beats a minute. When dawn breaks on the fuchsia and columbine, hummingbirds must jump-start their hearts and fire up their flight muscles to raise their body temperature for another all-or-nothing day. That demands a colossal effort, which some can't manage. So a lot of hummingbirds die in their sleep.

But most do bestir themselves. This is why, in American Indian myths and legends, hummingbirds are often depicted as resurrection birds, which seem to die and be reborn on another day or in another season. The Aztec god of war was named Huitzilopochtli, a compound word meaning "shining one with weapon like cactus thorn," and "sorcerer that spits fire." Aztec warriors fought, knowing that if they fell in battle they would be reincarnated as glittery, thug like hummingbirds. The male birds were lionized for their ferocity in battle. And their feathers flashed in the sun like jewel-encrusted shields. Aztec rulers donned ceremonial robes of hummingbird feathers. As they walked, colors danced across their shoulders and bathed them in a supernatural light show.

While most birds are busy singing a small operetta of who and what and where, hummingbirds are virtually mute. Such small voices don't carry far, so they don't bother much with song. But if they can't serenade a mate, or yell war cries at a rival, how can they perform the essential dramas of their lives? They dance. Using body language, they spell out their intentions and moods, just as bees, fireflies or hula dancers do. That means elaborate aerial ballets in which males twirl, joust, sideswipe and somersault. Brazen and fierce, they will take on large adversaries—even cats, dogs or humans.

My neighbor Persis once told me how she'd been needled by hummingbirds. When Persis lived in San Francisco, hummingbirds often attacked her outside her apartment building. From their perspective she was on *their* property, not the other way round, and they flew circles around her to vex her away. My encounters with hummingbirds have been altogether more benign. Whenever I've walked through South American rain forests, with my hair braided and secured by a waterproof red ribbon, hummingbirds have assumed my ribbon to be a succulent flower and have probed my hair repeatedly, searching for nectar. Their touch was as delicate as a sweat bee's. But it was their purring by my ear that made me twitch. In time, they would leave unfed, but for a while I felt like a character in a Li'l Abner cartoon who could be named something like "Hummer." In Portuguese, the word for hummingbird (*Beija flor*) means "flower kisser." It was the American colonists who first imagined the birds humming as they went about their chores.

Last summer, the historical novelist Jeanne Mackin winced to see her cat, Beltane, drag in voles, birds and even baby rabbits. Few things can compete with the blood lust of a tabby cat. But one day Beltane dragged in something rare and shimmery—a struggling hummingbird. The feathers were ruffled and there was a bit of blood on the breast, but the bird still looked perky and alive. So Jeanne fashioned a nest for it out of a small wire basket lined in gauze, and fed it sugar water from an eye dropper. To her amazement, as she watched, "it miscarried a little pearl." Hummingbird eggs are the size of coffee beans, and females usually carry two. So Jeanne knew one might still be safe inside. After a quiet night, the hummingbird seemed stronger, and when she set the basket outside at dawn, the tiny assault victim flew away.

It was a ruby-throated hummingbird that she nursed, the only one native to the East Coast. In the winter they migrate thousands of miles over mountains and open water to Mexico and South America. She may well have been visited by a species known to the Aztecs. Altogether, there are 16 species of hummingbirds in North America, and many dozens in South America, especially near the equator, where they can feed on a buffet of blossoms. The tiniest—the Cuban bee hummingbird—is the smallest warm-blooded animal in the world. About two and one-eighth inches long from beak to tail, it is smaller than the toe of an eagle, and its eggs are like seeds.

Hummingbirds are a New World phenomenon. So, too, is vanilla, and their stories are linked. When the early explorers returned home with the riches of the West, they found it impossible, to their deep frustration, to grow vanilla beans. It took ages before they discovered why—that hummingbirds were a key pollinator of vanilla orchids—and devised beaklike splinters of bamboo to do the work of birds.

Now that summer has come at last, lucky days may be spent watching the antics of hummingbirds. The best way to behold them is to stand with the light behind you, so that the bird faces the sun. Most of the trembling colors aren't true pigments, but the result of light staggering through clear cells that act as prisms. Hummingbirds are iridescent for the same reason soap bubbles are. Each feather contains tiny air bubbles separated by dark spaces. Light bounces off the air bubbles at different angles, and that makes blazing colors seem to swarm and leap. All is vanity in the end. The male's shimmer draws a female to mate. But that doesn't matter much to gardeners, watching hummingbirds patrol the impatiens as if the northern lights had suddenly fallen to earth.

Ackerman, D. 'Mute Dancers – How to Watch a Hummingbird.' *The New York Times Magazine*. 29 May 1994.

Classes of poetry

Although there is a great deal of discussion about how to distinguish among different forms of poetry, for our purposes we are going to keep it rather simple and follow most thinking about these categories. We could call these distinctions either the **divisions** of poetry or we can simply call them **forms** of poetry, although we know that there are even more specific forms of poetry.

Lyric poetry

Lyric poetry is generally spoken by a single voice, perhaps the poet or another person called the **voice** or the **speaker**, expressing ideas and emotions. Emotion is most frequently the material of lyric poetry. It's easy enough to see the link between these usually first-person expressions and the lyrics of songs.

Narrative poetry

Narrative poetry is a somewhat less popular form of poetry in our own time, but it has an important history, which includes the great **epic poetry** of the past, from Homer's *Iliad* and *Odyssey* to Milton's *Paradise Lost*. Narrative poetry is usually understood to include a **narrator** and a **narrative** or **story**. Students will sometimes observe that lyric poems often contain a narrative or a story, that of a loss or a discovery, for example, and will want to include a narrator as the speaker. This is possible, but it's easier to keep things clear if you keep in mind the primacy of the role of emotion in lyric poetry, where a 'story' is usually secondary. Calling the voice in a poem just that, 'voice', is another helpful strategy.

Dramatic poetry

This is usually considered the third form or category of poetry. Modern poets sometimes write poetry in which they create a clearly invented speaker who voices their ideas and sentiments. This form is known as dramatic monologue.

It's important to remember that, while not always emphasized, the poetry of Shakespeare's plays is **dramatic poetry**. It partakes in all the auditory and visual pleasures that we can enjoy in poetry, adding the other dimension of theatrical delivery. In fact, in Shakespeare's own time, one of the primary pleasures for his contemporaries was to hear talented actors perform what Coleridge said of poetry: "The best words in their best order."

In addition to these main classes of poems, there are a number of specific forms that you may encounter and study, such as **ballad**, **sonnet**, ode or elegy. As you study these in class, you will also need to explore the specific conventions that govern them.

Getting to like poetry for what it is

Two thoughtful writers, Hugh Kenner who writes about poets and Ed Hirsch who both writes about poets and is one himself, have both expressed strong sentiments about how essential 'what is heard' is to the nature of poetry and its appreciation as well as 'what is seen' on the page. Robert Frost expresses the same view on page 177.

Hugh Kenner, in an essay called 'Ear Culture', tells of a past student whose father regularly recited poetry and what she had internalized about poetry by likewise memorizing poems. Kenner comments on what she had learned from that experience – a kind of internal sense of what poetry is really about… the engagement of "sound" in poetry, "a power to possess the body" (Kenner 1989). What concerns Kenner as he talks of his students today is that, missing out on the physicality, the 'heartbeat of poetry', they see reading poetry as simply a 'decoding' exercise: "this must mean this", "that must mean that", and so on. This is sometimes the way poetry is handled in schools.

> *"And then, what unexpressed thought might we come to after a great deal of this kind of 'digging'? Is it simply that 'poets just can't talk straight'?"*
> Hugh Kenner

Activity

Discuss with a partner any lines of poetry or lyrics of songs you might particularly remember. Can you say exactly *why* you like these or remember them? Is it all about what they mean, or is the sound of the words so linked to the way you hear them that you can't forget them?

Ed Hirsch, in his book *How to Read a Poem*, also puts considerable emphasis on the importance of the appeal to both the eye and the ear in talking about lyric poetry. Using the French poet Paul Celan's notion of the poem as 'a message in a bottle', Hirsch offers a number of assertions about poetry. One of his most passionate ones is the appeal that poetry has for the ear. Hirsch points out that until printing came along, the separation between the lyric and musical performance was not often present. At the time when poems appeared in print and became widely available, the visual aspect of poems became important. So, in poetry today, the best combination may be:

- hearing with the ear
- seeing with the eyes the way the poem looks on the page
- grasping the poem with both the heart and the head (and remembering that we may not be able to reduce the lyrics to an alternate version of words, sometimes called **paraphrasing**).

Both Kenner and Hirsch have much more to say about ear and eye, and you may want to explore their writing. What is important here is to remind you that the reading of poetry is not primarily an exercise of 'decoding' or 'paraphrasing', but something created out of the body, the voice, the hands, something 'muscular' as both Kenner and Hirsch propose. If poetry becomes for you, as students often say, the 'dissecting' or 'picking apart' of what this writer can't seem to say clearly, it will be hard for you to connect with it. If you only go looking for a 'message' to change your behaviour or improve your morals, you are also likely to be disappointed or tire of the search.

A new appreciation of what poetry has in its very roots, this em-body-ment, may account for such contemporary events as 'poetry slams' and other performance art involving poetry. It accounts for rope-skipping rhymes, choral readings and perhaps theatre itself.

Either:

a Visit www.poetryfoundation.org and select some poetry to listen to. Write a short response, focusing on the experience of listening to poems you have never seen on the page.

Or:

b Research online for one of the following poets reading in connection with music:

- Roy Nathanson, 'By the Page'.
- Joy Harjo, 'My House is the Red Earth'.
- Sonia Sanchez, 'I Have Walked a Long Time'.

Comment on your reaction to the combination.

A brief history of the evolution of English poetry

You will very likely have been exposed to the history of English poetry in your school experience, if not sequentially, at least by reading individual poems and poets who have been important since the very early days of composition.

There are really five 'large' phases that could help you insert individual poems into particular points of this history.

Medieval poetry

Probably the most significant figure for the 'common reader' of poetry is Geoffrey Chaucer, who was writing in the late 14th century and created *The Canterbury Tales*, a framed **narrative sequence** of tales told by travellers on pilgrimage to Canterbury. These poems are written in an older form of English, one which is accessible even to modern readers with a good, annotated text and some perseverance.

Here is an extract of one of the liveliest tales told by the priest accompanying one of the nuns. It tells the tale of a rooster who has been captured by a fox and then tricks the fox:

The Nun's Priest's Tale

This cok that lay upon the foxes bak,
In all his drede unto the fox he spak,
And saide, "Sire, if that I were as yet,
Yit sholde I sayn, as wis God helpe me,
'Turneth ayain, ye proude cherles alle!
A verray pestilence upon you falle!
Now am I come unto this wodes side,
Maugree your heed, the cok shal here abide,
I wol him ete, in faith, an that aoon.'"
The fox answrede ,"In faith, it shal be doon."
And as he spak that word, al sodeinly,

The cok brak from his mouth deliverly,
And heigh upon a tree he fleith anoon.

Geoffrey Chaucer

The plot here is fairly predictable. Can you 'translate' this Middle English into understandable modern English?

There is, however, an even older form of English found in an earlier work, *Beowulf*, written before the 10th century in a far less accessible form. This **epic** is a wonderful narrative tale of battle and monsters, but for modern readers it really needs to be read in translation.

Other various kinds of poetry were written up until the 15th century, but nothing to match the expansion of writing in English that characterized the next period in English literature, of which such figures as Shakespeare and Milton were a significant part.

Renaissance poetry

In this period, mainly the 16th century, the handwritten and copied texts of the medieval period were able to be much more widely disseminated, thanks to the invention of the printing press. Still, hearing poetry continued to be important, as literacy was still limited. One of the significant forms of lyric poetry of this period was the **sonnet**, popular with many of the poets at the court and, of course, Shakespeare. You will find the wording of Renaissance English much more accessible than that of Chaucer's poetry. You will probably notice, however, that attending a Shakespeare play is much easier to understand than reading the text, again a point about hearing as opposed to reading poetry. Writers other than Shakespeare were very taken by the possibilities of this lyric form. Below, is one of the sonnets of a major contemporary of Shakespeare, Edmond Spenser; it's interesting to observe the development of language.

If you like, you can listen to this sonnet on YouTube, before or after reading it here.

Sonnet 75

One day I wrote her name upon the strand,
But came the waves and washed it away;
Againe I wrote it with a second hand,
But came the tyde and made my paynes his pray.
"Vaine man," sayde she, "that does in vaine assay,
A mortall thing so to immortalize,
For I my selve shall lyke to this decay,
And eek my name bee wiped out lykewize."
"Not so," quod I, "let baser things devize
To dy in dust, but you shall live by fame:
My verse your vertues rate shall eternize,
And in the heavens wryte your glorious name.
Where whenas death shall all the world subdew,
Our love shall live and later life renew."

Edmond Spenser

Note here both the evolution of English as well as the very strict structure and rhythmic pattern of stressed and unstressed syllables. Note, also, that words are spelled differently from today. Spelling in English did not really become regularized until about the 18th century.

The Renaissance period gave us poetry in all of the three major forms: lyric, narrative and dramatic. In the next two centuries, however, lyric poems were a particularly dominant form of poetry.

The 18th century and the precursors of the English Romantic movement

In conjunction with the movement toward rationalism spurred on by the Enlightenment, English poetry in the 18th century tended to be quite intellectual and often satirical. It set the stage for the reaction of romanticism, which offered a counter-balance to its predecessors who wrote such intellectual poetry in the 18th century. Compare extracts from the following two poems to get a sense of the contrast.

An Essay on Criticism

A little learning is a dangerous thing;
Drink deep, or taste not the Pierian spring.
There shall shallow draughts intoxicate the brain,
And drinking largely sobers us again.
Fired at first sight with what the Muse imparts,
In fearless youth we tempt the heights of arts,
While from the bounded level of our mind
Short views we take, nor see the lengths behind.

Alexander Pope

The Lotos-Eaters

Why are we weighed upon with heaviness,
And utterly consumed with sharp distress,
While all things else have rest from weariness?
We only toil who are the first of things,
And make perpetual moan,
Still from one sorrow to another thrown;
Nor ever fold our wings,
And cease from wanderings,
Nor steep our brows in slumber's holy balm;
Nor hearken what the inner spirit sings
"There is no joy but calm!" –
Why should we only toil, the roof and crown of things?

Alfred Lord Tennyson

Both of these extracts are from longer poems, so these give you only a brief sample of the poets' ideas and feelings, but there are some inferences that can be drawn in the changing focus of some of the poetry of the 18th and 19th centuries.

After the strong emphasis on intellectual reasoning in 18th-century poetry, the Romantic movement in the middle to end of the 19th century tended to value both the imagination and the expression of the self, and these appear in many of the lyric poems. Both narrative and dramatic poetry continued to be written, but with much less popularity and prevalence than in earlier periods.

Activity

Read the extracts written by Pope and Tennyson and see what similarities and differences they have.

a What is your sense of the voice and attitude of the speaker?

b How alike or different is each verse, its rhythm and pace?

c What values seem to be foregrounded and praised in each extract?

The 19th and 20th centuries

Again, the dominance of lyric poetry is sustained into these two centuries. Dramatic poetry still can be found, narrative poetry as well, but one strong interest in poetry tended to be its connection with certain movements in the visual arts such as surrealism and symbolism. Stories tended to be more often found in the novel and short story than in poetry. Drama had its own development as well, but the poetic demands of the 16th century had disappeared; the blank verse practised by Shakespeare and his contemporaries had largely disappeared from the theatre.

One of the interesting features of the developments in poetry in the 19th and 20th centuries, especially from the angle of the auditory and the visual, was the experimentation with different formal aspects of poetry such as how the poem would appear on the page, and how sound features would be handled in poetry.

Experimenters such as Walt Whitman (1819–92) and Gerard Manley Hopkins (1844–89) were looking into other ways than the regularity of metrical poetry, than regular alternation of stress and unstress, to form poetic lines. With these poets and others, the evolution of free verse began to take shape and has influenced modern poetry to the degree that it has become a dominant form. Still, poets were looking for that connection to the whole person, the ear, the eye, the mind.

Reaching this point in our discussion of poetry makes a convenient transitional moment to turn to our final section of this chapter, the conventions of poetry. Here, we will reverse the pattern of our attention and look first at the conventions that have to do with putting the words together, the **conventions of meaning** in poetry. These are the ways of making meaning in this particular genre. (Keep in mind that many of the conventions listed below are also shared to some degree by other genres.) Then we will return to what makes the poem resonate in the ear, the **conventions of sound**.

Conventions of meaning in poetry

There is no question that we are looking at very carefully selected words when we are looking at poetry. We are also looking at a very deliberate choice of **voice** or **speaker** who will speak those words and, whether or not we are conscious of it, much of our response to a given poem will be shaped by that voice. The voice **frames** the words. Everything that happens inside the poem happens within that framing voice.

"Poetry is the spontaneous overflow of powerful feelings; it takes its origin from emotion recollected in tranquility…"
William Wordsworth

"A Poet is a nightingale, who sits in darkness and sings to cheer its own solitude with sweet sounds… Poetry is the record of the best and happiest moments of the best and happiest minds…"
Percy Bysshe Shelley

"As heightened speech in a receptive ear, poetry… can be a kind of action. It enters the listening body to change its habits of feeling and perception… Speaking for myself, I've never read with such emotional urgency as I did in my early twenties. In those days poetry and erotic passion were different facets of the same desire to be otherwise than I felt myself to be. With the same bewildering helplessness, I fell for poems and poets the way I fell for women, seeing in both the promise of a heightened life, a better life, the more remote, the better."
Alan Shapiro

"Poetry is not talk. It sounds like talk… but poetry is talk altered into art… Words are to poems as stone is to a stone sculptor."
Donald Hall

Therefore, identifying that frame, that **tone**, has a great deal to do with hearing the poem reliably. Tone, of course, is a word we use in everyday speech; you should be, and probably often are, particularly sensitive about your management of tone in your interactions with others.

In literature, and particularly in poetry, we are talking about the **attitude** of the voice or the speaker to their material, or sometimes even to an audience. Tone is normally described with emotional words such as: "admiring", "incredulous", "mocking", "devastated". If we make clumsy determinations about tone, we are likely to misread what the author is trying to deliver. This misstep frequently occurs when we are reading or hearing a poem with an ironic tone.

Activity

Look closely at the following samples and see if you can find some satisfactory words to describe the tone you hear.

Neutral Tones

The smile on your mouth was the deadest thing
Alive enough to have strength to die;
And a grin of bitterness swept thereby
Like an ominous bird a-wing…

Thomas Hardy

Pike

Pike, three inches long, perfect
Pike in all parts, green tigering the gold.

Ted Hughes

E. S. L.

Tonight my students must

Agree or disagree:
America is still a land of opportunity:
The answer is always uniformly, Yes – even though
"It has no doubt that here were too much free,"
As Miss Torrico will insist,
She and I both know

That language binds us fast,
And those of us without
Are bound and gagged by those within. Each fledgling
Polyglot must shake old habits: tapping her sneakered feet,
Miss Choi exorcises incensed ancestors, flouting
the ghosts of her Chinese past.

Charles Martin

Tone is not always easy to identify. Tone can also shift within a poem, moving, for example, from admiring to disillusioned. Naturally, the choice of words has an essential effect on how tone is created, and they will be one of your chief signals about tone.

If you look at the three examples on page 187, you will see how particular words shape and define the tone. The interactive relationship between word choice or diction and the attitude or tone that you will hear in a poem is a combination that provides a good starting place for the appreciation of meaning in a poem. These are two critical conventions which you will need to practise in order to be able to write well about poetry in Paper 2.

In discussing the choice of words in poems, there are a great many terms that can be used by a writer like yourself to describe, first, the kinds of words a poet will choose to use, and, second, the effect those particular word choices have on their immediate 'environment' (the words close to that word, the whole line or the whole poem, and the tone in which it is delivered). Students sometimes forget that just identifying important words or patterns of words (or any other feature of the poem, for that matter) is not really enough when trying to talk appreciatively or critically about a poem. Readers will want to hear what you think that choice does to the poem or to the reader.

- What are some of the terms that are useful in discussing **word choice** in a poem?
- What's the **literal** or **denotative** meaning of the word? What **connotations** has the word acquired or been assigned by the poet?
- Do the words indicate the poet is working in a **formal** or an **informal register**?
- Does the poet use **archaisms** (older words not usually used today) or **neologisms** (words invented or made up)?
- How often does the poet use **concrete** or **abstract** words?

You will find that your instructors will want to add other distinctions to this short list. These are descriptive words, all of them, that will help you in articulating your critical response to the way words are used in poems.

Figurative language or imagery

People tend to use these two terms in different ways. 'Figurative language' works well as a term to cover almost every attempt that a poet can make to heighten and intensify language to make it sing in the human ear and appeal to the human eye. It works well because it covers the kind of **analogies** (comparisons) that people who work to turn 'talk' into art like to employ. It is sometimes helpful to simply think of poetry as a kind of writing that is often thinking of how to represent one thing by means of another. In a sense, and some critics take this view, poets do their work through the language of **metaphor**, to 'figure' or suggest one thing by another.

These figures of speech can take many forms. One thing can generally be expected of students: almost everyone can spot a **simile** or a **personification**. Comparisons using 'as' or 'like', or assigning human attributes to entities which are not human is a 'poetic' technique familiar to almost every student who has studied poetry before the IB literature course.

Notice that these figures of speech work through analogies or the language of metaphor to produce images for the reader. Very often, they employ reference to one of the five senses to do so; hence the term **sensory imagery**. Poets frequently depend on sensory imagery to convey both their meaning and their attitudes.

So, for purposes of your work in critical analysis, it's convenient to separate the heightening of language into:

- **imagery** – whereby the poet dips into the rich resources of the senses to convey thoughts and feelings
- **figurative language** or figures of speech – whereby things are compared or analogized to make ideas and feelings clearer or more intense.

In order to deal with imagery, you will need to review the five terms for the senses: visual, auditory, tactile, gustatory and olfactory.

Along with simile and personification mentioned earlier, you may find it convenient to stay with a very limited definition of metaphor, which you may have learned to identify as an implied comparison, without the indicators of 'as' or 'like'. Another interesting form of metaphor is called the conceit, whereby the poet takes very different things and 'yokes' them together in startling ways.

Activity

Think of other ways in which a poet may play with and intensify meaning. Thinking of them in pairs can be very helpful. Try to create your own examples of these kinds of 'figuration' (using one thing to provide a 'figure' of another).

Here are some interesting pairs:

- **Overstatement** (hyperbole) and **understatement** (sometimes for ironic or humorous effect.
- **Paradox** (a contradictory statement or sentiment which is surprising but also possibly true) and oxymoron (usually a smaller unit of contradiction, perhaps only two words).
- **Metonymy** (a very close association of one word or thing with another, so close that one can stand in for the other) and **synecdoche** (using a part to represent a whole).

In addition to systems of Greek and Latin poetry, as well as medieval ideas of poetry and rhetoric, there are many other ways in which poets have used very precise and even devious means and devices to heighten the effects of their poems. Some have to do with enriching meaning and some have to do with the way lines of poetry or units (**stanzas**) are constructed. Many of them have interesting names adopted from other languages, especially Greek: 'anaphora', 'chiasmus', 'antithesis', 'apostrophe' and 'zeugma'. Your class may or may not choose to investigate these terms.

Several of these are terms which relate to the way a poem is given a structure. Structure is the next feature that we will discuss here in terms of conventions.

Structure in poetry

We have noted that poetry is often presented on the page in a way which makes it fairly easy to differentiate from prose, although given the evolution of the prose poem as with Harvey's representation of the mermaid on page 177, you might at first be puzzled.

Poets are very conscious, given the usually limited span of their compositions, of getting things arranged in the most compressed and powerful way. This can come down to the very particular question of "Is this word better before or after that one?" It is true, however, that poets before the 20th century were more governed by the conventions of such forms as the sonnet or the ballad, for example, which are written in particular meters or stanzaic forms (stanzas). Conventional structures are, in one way, a help to poets and they are also a reason to resist. The development of free verse represents, in part, one form of resistance.

Word order is an important feature of structure. The **syntax** of a line can alter its intended meaning. Inversions of syntax (putting the verb before the subject, for example) can convey both feelings and ideas. **Spacing** of words and stanzas, **indentations** and **punctuation** can also be used for suggesting such feelings as uncertainty, enthusiasm or despair. **Line breaks** and **enjambment** are other structural tools poets can use to extend effects beyond even the literal or connotative meanings that come through the words. A parallel structure or an opposition as in **antithesis** and the repetition of a beginning word or phrase (**anaphora**) are other tools poets use as structural devices.

What we have pointed out here in terms of structure are only some of the tools the poet can use as conventions for organizing and arranging their words and sounds. In poetry, both meaning and sound are structured, laboured over with great care and consciousness of effect.

Sound in poetry

Before completing the circle of reading/hearing, studying, and then putting all of that thought into a second reception of the poem through reading/hearing, it's useful for critical analysis to try to see how the poet has used the structuring of sound to make an artful piece of writing. In critical reading, we temporarily separate these elements in order to go back to the poem with a deepened appreciation of it.

We have already talked a bit about metrical poetry and free verse. One seemingly troublesome distinction for students is the naming and nature of **rhythm** and **rhyme**. These are important aspects of how the poet handles sound.

Rhythm is a convention that is always involved in both metrical poetry and free verse; in fact, it is present in almost every human utterance. The differentiating factor of metrical poetry is that the rhythm occurs regularly, from a regular alternation of stress and unstress.

Rhyme is very often a convention of metrical poetry and sometimes of free verse.

"The body is poetry's door; the sound of words – throbbing in legs and arms; rich in the mouth – let us into the house."
Donald Hall

What is a workable definition of rhythm in poetry?

Rhythm is a pattern emerging in the sound of the poem that usually involves some recurrence of what we might call a 'beat', or a variation in emphasis on syllables between 'heavy' and 'light'. With regular rhythm, the lines of poetry begin to move towards music.

What is a workable definition of rhyme in poetry?

Rhyme involves the same sound of two or more words or syllables, often at the end of a line of poetry but sometimes in the middle of a line.

Here's an example of metrical poetry in one of Robert Browning's poems:

How They Brought the Good News from Ghent to Aix

I sprang to the stirrup, and Joris, and he;
I galloped, Dirck galloped, we galloped all three;
"Good speed!" cried the watch, as the gate-bolts undrew;
"Speed!" echoed the wall to us galloping through;
Behind shut the postern, the lights sank to rest,
And into the midnight we galloped abreast.

Robert Browning

Defining rhythm and rhyme is a lot more difficult than seeing it in a poem. Look closely at the lines of poetry above and point out what you would call rhyme and see if you can mark the heavy and the light emphases (stressed and unstressed syllables) in the lines. Can you see any lines where there is a perfectly regular distribution of stress and unstress?

You might also notice that, after reading two or three lines of this extract, you begin to anticipate the rhythm and the rhyme; this phenomenon is called **expectation**, another convention of metrical poetry that can enhance both the pleasurable and memorable qualities of a poem.

Finally, it's worth noting that you will find some **variation** from the galloping rhythm in some of the lines, and a very regular 'beat' in others. In many ways, variation constitutes the real artistry of metrical poetry. If you try your hand at it, you will discover it's actually quite easy to write nonsense lines in metrical verse. Playing regularity against variation is where the skill lies in this kind of poetry; it is what Browning does in his extract. You might want to see if you can determine the effects he achieves on the meaning by practising variation.

Rhythm also finds a place in free verse, and occasionally rhyme does too. However, regularity is usually absent in the rhythm, and rhyme tends to be unpatterned or incidental. Poets writing in free verse often use such sound features as **alliteration**, **assonance** and consonance to create faint echoes of the rhyming of metrical verse.

In the following poem, see if you can select some elements of rhythm and rhyme.

Those Winter Sundays

Sundays too my father got up early
and put on his clothes in the blueblack cold,
then with cracked hands that ached
from labor in the weekday weather made
banked fires blaze. No one ever thanked him.

I'd wake and hear the cold splintering, breaking.
When the rooms were warm, he'd call,
and slowly I would rise and dress,
fearing the chronic angers of that house.

Speaking indifferently to him,
who had driven out the cold
and polished my good shoes as well.
What did I know, what did I know
of love's austere and tender offices.

Robert Hayden

After reading the poem aloud, you will notice, perhaps, that there is in fact a kind of rhythm to the utterance of this poem celebrating the poet's father. The lines are of similar lengths and there is also a kind of **declamatory** or **incantatory** quality, both to the list of the father's actions, as well as the son's. The repetition in the penultimate (second to last line) prepares for the very emotional and nostalgic closing. You will see that an old familiar favourite of students, **onomatopoeia**, makes its appearance, along with alliteration, assonance and consonance.

There are many more specific conventions of poetry you will already have learned in your study of this genre, and some you will discover. They are best examined as you study them in individual poems. Memorizing long lists of literary devices may be of some help, at least to get a sense of the range of tools available to poets, but without a firm connection to actual poems, and seeing them in various contexts, they are difficult to remember in a meaningful way. You can read Chapter 3 for further exploration and practice.

Activity

Returning to the aspect of sound in poetry, here is a small project that involves reading, listening and creating.

1 Choose a poem that you like from any source. Select a poem that is not much longer than a sonnet, around 14 to 16 lines. You might find it easier to work with a metrical poem.

2 Spend some time reading and re-reading the poem, maybe finding out something about the writer, even creating some visual or graphic representation, becoming truly familiar with the poem.

3 Using original music, or favourite musical works of whatever kind you believe suits the mood, rhythm and words of the poem, create a performance piece that you could either present yourself or with the help of others.

4 Write a short critical introduction or afterword in which you discuss the poem itself, some of your creative choices and their rationales. (In some cases, you may want to provide a little help with how you heard the meaning of the poem.)

5 Embody the poem in a performance.

Theory of knowledge connections

As a way of bringing together the emphasis of this chapter on the importance of seeing poetry as a meaningful and pleasurable facet of artistic expression, we will explore the connections of poetry to your theory of knowledge course by posing the question:

What kinds of truth can poetry convey and how is a truth delivered and experienced through this form of art?

What you need to do:

1 Read through the four short poems on pages 194–5 by yourself.

2 Organize yourselves into groups of four:

　a　Re-read the poems silently.

　b　Ask each member of the group to read aloud one of the poems.

　c　Ask each member of the group to say a sentence that essentializes a 'truth' that has been heard in one of the poems.

　d　Draw up a list of the poems and the 'truths' perceived by group members.

　e　Each member then reads each poem aloud again.

　f　In turn, each member chooses and talks about a 'truth' someone else has experienced from a particular poem, trying to understand how that 'truth' was derived from the poem.

3 The exercise should finish with a discussion of these questions:

　a　Was there a sense that everyone 'heard' the truths of these poems similarly?

　b　What was the role of hearing the poems and the way they sounded in discerning a truth?

　c　Are the truths derived from poetry believed to be as reliable, compelling or valid as truths derived from other ways of knowing?

Frogs

The storm broke, and it rained,
And water rose in the pool,
And frogs hopped into the gutter,

With their skins of yellow and green,
And just their eyes shining above the surface
Of the warm solution of slime.

At night, when fireflies trace
Light-lines between the trees and flowers
Exhaling perfume

The frogs speak to each other
In rhythm. The sound is monstrous,
But their voices are filled with satisfaction.

In the city, I pine for the country;
In the country I long for conversation –
Our happy croaking.

Louis Simpson

In Mind

There's in my mind a woman
of innocence, unadorned but

fair-featured and smelling of
apples or grass. She wears

a utopian smock or shift, her hair
is light brown and smooth, and she

is kind and very clean without
ostentation –

but she has
no imagination.

And there's a
turbulent moon-ridden girl

or old woman, or both,
dressed in opals and rags, feathers

and torn taffeta,
who knows strange songs –

but she is not kind.

Denise Levertov

The Sick Rose

William Blake

Question

Body my house
my horse my hound
what will I do
when you are fallen

Where will I sleep
How will I ride
What will I hunt

Where can I go
without my mount
all eager and quick
How will I know
in thicket ahead
is danger or treasure
when Body my good
bright dog is dead

How will it be
to lie in the sky
without roof or door
and wind for an eye

without cloud for shift
how will I hide.

May Swenson

May Swenson, 1913–89

The novel and short story

Objectives

- to come to terms with some of the terminology connected to novels and short stories
- to explore the shared features of novels and short stories
- to understand the conventions of these two genres

The broader terms

Before we can talk knowledgeably about specific conventions of the novel and short story, there are broader terms that we at least need to acknowledge, even if there are many discrepancies and disagreements about them. As we read and talk about this genre, we would do well to remember that these are terms, conventions and practices that we use, encounter and talk about in relation to films and short videos on the internet, and regularly employ to make our conversations more vivid and interesting. Although there may be some distinctive conventions we may later want to offer as distinguishing novels from short stories, there are many more features that are generally shared by both of these genres.

We can begin our investigation by trying to make sense of such terms as:

- fiction and non-fiction
- story and plot
- narrative.

Fiction and non-fiction (prose other than fiction)

Fiction is certainly not a new term for you. Simplistically, fiction is opposed to fact. Fiction is often described in terms of 'the imaginary or the imagined', what is not *real* or *true*. From your study of the theory of knowledge course, you will know how vexed (a common term used to indicate 'complicated' or 'arguable') all of these foregoing terms can be.

Nevertheless, we do use the term 'fiction' to indicate certain kinds of writing we take to be invented, and sometimes as a genre itself, which has sub-groups: science fiction or detective fiction. Novels and short stories are often, quite simply, called 'fiction'.

By contrast, then, 'non-fictional' forms should deal in fact, but we all know how questionable it is to regard newspaper articles, autobiographies and even history as pure fact. In addition, some works, such as historical novels, are a definitive blend of fact and fiction.

Particularly in recent times, it has become common to make such blends of fiction and fact, so that readers are sometimes unsure which one is in play. Often the first novel of a writer will be based on autobiographical experience, as in James Joyce's *Portrait of the Artist as a Young Man* or Dorothy Allison's *Bastard Out of Carolina*. So we can comfortably use these broader terms to describe two classes of writing that are recognizable. They come up most often in daily life when people are describing their preferences for one or the other. Looked at very closely, as they are in literary study, they do not always hold up as precise labels.

Story and plot

Story and plot are also what many would call 'vexed' terms. Many would define a story as simply a series or sequence of events, whereas plot involves causality, or effects on characters. Something developed less (story) and more (plot) complexly often characterizes views of the difference between these two.

A story can be told by even a young child, often characterized by a series of 'ands' as in:

> I went into the garden and I saw this animal and I got down on the ground to pet it and it bit me and…

A plot version of the same might include:

> Because no one else was awake, I went into the garden and now my finger is bleeding because when I got down to pet this animal, which I thought was like one of our kittens, it bit me and made my finger bleed.

In the plot version, we have a slightly better sense of the character of the child and the situation of her story. This latter approach to storytelling is what we have come to expect from a good novel or short story.

For H. Porter Abbott, story is defined as "a sequence of events involving entities" (Abbott 2002). You will notice he uses the word "entities" because, as you know, not all who act in stories are human beings: *Watership Down* by Richard Adams is an epic story whose characters are rabbits seeking to establish a new home; the *I, Robot* stories of Isaac Asimov includes both humans and robots.

"Sequence" is a term that can include either acts or happenings. There might be a sequence in a story, but you will have no guarantee that it will appear in the linear way we like to think things happen.

Stories exist everywhere in our lives and about our lives; some are long, some are no longer than what happened at last night's concert. They certainly include acts (which we could define as 'something done by someone') as well as happenings (things 'experienced by someone or some entity').

Narrative

In terms of getting ready to look at the conventions of novels and short stories, Abbott's term 'narrative' is perhaps helpful to us. He defines narrative as the "representation of a story" (Abbott 2002). Why does he add in "representation"? Well, particularly here where we are talking about novels and short stories, someone has chosen to represent a 'story' in a particular way, long or short, involving many characters or few, and all the other features that distinguish the 'representation' of a story. Gossip and rumour, which we all probably engage in, are the best evidence of how many ways a story can be 'represented'.

Sometimes people say that you can't have a narrative without a narrator, but we all know that almost always drama and films have stories, but not necessarily a narrator. Your study of history is often done through narrative accounts. There are stories in visual art and there are stories in poems, even those we most often call 'lyric poems'. And, of course, they exist in such narrative poems as A. E. Housman's 'The Grizzly Bear':

The Grizzly Bear

The Grizzly Bear is huge and wild;

He has devoured the infant child.

The infant child is not aware

He has been eaten by the bear.

A. E. Housman

"If poetry did not exist, would you have had the wit to invent it?"
Howard Nemerov

Activity

a Examine the painting below and make some inferences or conjectures about what appears to be happening. Is there perhaps a 'story'?

'A Beating' by Sidney Goodman

b Read the poem 'Artichoke' below. Does it, too, suggest that there is, among other things, a story or stories in the poem? Use your insights either to write or to discuss with others in your class how we infer stories from other forms of art.

Artichoke by Guilherme Lambert Gomes Ferraz (UWC-USA, 2010)

Artichoke

He had studied in private years ago

The way to eat these things, and was prepared

When she set the clipped green globe before him.

He only wondered (as he always did

When he plucked from the base the first thick leaf,

dipped it into the sauce and caught her eye

as he deftly set the velvet curve against

the inside edges of his lower teeth

and drew the tender pulp toward his tongue

while she made some predictable remark

about the sensuality of this act

then sheared away the spines and ate the heart)

what mind, what hunger, first saw this as food.

Henry Taylor

Narrative as a particular study

In the 20th century, a whole discipline emerged called **narratology**. Essentially, it is the theory and study of how narratives work in both fictional and non-fictional forms. Many scholars have explored, and still are exploring, such questions as:

- what is the nature of narrative and narratives
- what role does narrative play in human culture
- what is the relation of narrative to such terms as 'story' and 'plot'?

We will explore 'narrative' a little more fully below.

Narrative is a wide-ranging category in daily life as it is in many other disciplines or subjects, such as sociology, art, anthropology, history, theatre and even the daily news. However, in order to help you acquire a firm grounding in what you will need to know and apply in reading your works for this course and applying what you know to assessments, we will look at some essential aspects of how novels and short stories are constructed and received by readers.

Some of the basic questions related to these forms are as follows:

- What is the content of the story that is narrated?
- Who is narrating it?
- Who are the 'entities' (or characters) who act (thinking will be considered an 'action' for our purposes) and to whom things happen?
- Where does all this occur?
- How will this narrative be told in terms of time?
- Do there appear to be reasons why it is being told?

Activity

Read through the following narrative and see how many of the above questions you can answer at this point in our discussion. Don't be too concerned if some are difficult to answer; working through the following material should help.

The Kiss

The winters in Central Asia are piercing and bleak, while the sweating, foetid summers bring cholera, dysentery and mosquitoes, but, in April, the air caresses like the touch of the inner skin of the thigh and the scent of all the flowering trees douses this city's throat-catching whiff of cesspits.

Every city has its own internal logic. Imagine a city drawn in straightforward, geometric shapes with crayons from a child's colouring box, in ochre, in white, in pale terracotta. Low, blonde terraces of houses seem to rise out of the whitish, pinkish earth as if born from it, not built out of it. There is a faint, gritty dust over everything, like the dust those pastel crayons leave on your fingers.

Against these bleached pallors, the iridescent crusts of ceramic tiles that cover the ancient mausoleums ensorcellate the eye. The throbbing blue of Islam transforms itself to green while you look at it. Beneath a bulbous dome alternately lapis lazuli and veridian, the bones of Tamburlaine, the scourge of Asia, lie in a jade tomb. We are visiting an authentically fabulous city. We are in Samarkand.

The Revolution promised the Uzbek peasant women clothes of silk and on this promise, at least, did not welch. They wear tunics of flimsy satin, pink and yellow, red and white, black and white, red, green and white, in blotched stripes of brilliant colours that dazzle like an optical illusion, and they bedeck themselves with much jewellery made of red glass.

They always seem to be frowning because they paint a thick, black line straight across their foreheads that takes their eyebrows from one side of the faces to the other without a break.

They rim their eyes with kohl. They look startling. They fasten their long hair in two or three dozen whirling plaits. Young girls wear little velvet caps embroidered with metallic thread and beadwork. Older women cover their heads with a couple of scarves of flower-printed wool, one bound tight over the forehead, the other hanging loosely on to the shoulders. Nobody has worn a veil for sixty years.

They walk as purposefully as if they did not live in an imaginary city. They do not know that they themselves and their turbanned, sheepskin jacketed, booted menfolk are creatures as extraordinary to the foreign eye as a unicorn. They exist, in all their glittering and innocent exoticism, in direct contradiction to history. They do not know what I know about them. They do not know that this city is not the entire world. All they know of the world is this city, beautiful as an illusion, where irises grow in the gutters. In the tea-house a green parrot nudges the bars of its wicker cage.

The market has a sharp, green smell. A girl with black-barred brows sprinkles water from a glass over radishes. In this early part of the year, you can buy only last summer's dried fruit – apricots, peaches, raisins – except for a few, precious, wrinkled pomegranates, stored in sawdust through the winter and now split open on the stall to show how a wet nest of garnets remains within. A local speciality of Samarkand is salted apricot kernels, more delicious, even than pistachios.

An old woman sells arum lilies. This morning, she came from the mountains, where wild tulips have put out flowers like blown bubbles of blood, and the wheedling turtle-doves are nesting among the rocks. This old woman dips bread into a cup of buttermilk for her lunch and eats slowly. When she has sold her lilies, she will go back to the place where they are growing.

She scarcely seems to inhabit time. Or, it is as if she were waiting for Scheherezahde to perceive a final dawn had come and, the last tale of all concluded, fall silent. Then, the lily-seller might vanish.

A goat is nibbling wild jasmine among the ruins of the mosque that was built by the beautiful wife of Tamburlaine.

Tamburlaine's wife started to build this mosque for him as a surprise, while he was away at the wars, but when she got word of his imminent return, one arch still remained unfinished. She went directly to the architect and begged him to hurry but the architect told her that he would complete the work in time only if she gave him a kiss. One kiss, one single kiss.

Tamburlaine's wife was not only very beautiful and very virtuous but also very clever. She went to the market, bought a basket of eggs, boiled them hard and stained them a dozen different colours. She called the architect to the palace, showed him the basket and told him to choose any egg he liked and eat it. He took a red egg. What does it taste like? Like an egg. Eat another.

He took a green egg.

What does *that* taste like? Like the red egg. Try again.

He ate a purple egg.

One egg tastes just the same as any other egg, if they are fresh, he said.

There you are! she said. Each of these eggs looks different to the rest but they all taste the same. So you may kiss any one of my serving women that you like but you must leave me alone.

Very well, said the architect. But soon he came back to her and this time he was carrying a tray with three bowls on it, and you would have thought the bowls were all full of water.

Drink from each of these bowls, he said.

She took a drink from the first bowl, then from the second; but how she coughed and spluttered when she took a mouthful from the third bowl, because it contained, not water, but vodka.

This vodka and that water both look alike but each tastes quite different, he said. And it is the same with love.

Then Tamburlaine's wife kissed the architect on the mouth. He went back to the mosque and finished the arch the same day that victorious Tamburlaine rode into Samarkand with his army and banners and his cages full of captive kings. But when Tamburlaine went to visit his wife, she turned away from him because no woman will return to the harem after she has tasted vodka. Tamburlaine beat her with a knout until she told him she had kissed the architect and then he sent his executioners hotfoot to the mosque.

The executioners saw the architect standing on top of the arch and ran up the stairs with their knives drawn but when he heard them coming he grew wings and flew away to Persia.

This is a story in simple, geometric shapes and the bold colours of a child's box of crayons. This Tamburlaine's wife of the story would have painted a black stripe laterally across her forehead and done up her hair in a dozen, dozen tiny plaits, like any other Uzbek woman. She would have bought red and white radishes from the market for her husband's dinner. After she ran away from him perhaps she made her living in the market. Perhaps she sold lilies there.

Angela Carter

Looking at other features of novels and short stories
What do people write novels and short stories about?

The short answer is everything and anything. This does not mean that everything is suitable for every age, every culture, every audience, or even comprehensible to everyone. Not everyone is going to finish the following sentence in the same way: "This narrative is about…" We are all individual readers who bring a life of experiences to our reading. You might say that *The Kiss* is essentially about Tamburlaine, and I might say that it's about a woman who has a feminist agenda and encloses an old story in her own travel narrative. Whatever each of us decides will affect our answers to later questions.

Who is the teller of stories or narratives, and how many different ways can a writer do this telling?

Here is a question that has a much longer answer and so we will need to explore the varieties of this convention – the 'voice' in a story – to equip you to talk competently, in terms of this literary discipline, about different points of view, the angle of vision from which a narrative is told. Another term for the teller is '**narrator**', which clearly links with narrative, and 'voice'. Voice rather than narrator is a term that works best with poetry.

"The house of fiction has many windows but only two or three doors… In reality we are stuck with first- and third-person narration."
James Wood

The first-person narrator
One kind of narrative voice (or narrator) that we immediately recognize is the first person, or 'I narrator'.

V. S. Naipaul's story tells of a man from Bombay who travels as a servant to Washington, D.C., marries, and comes to terms with what seems to be his destiny:

One Out of Many

I am a simple man who decided to act and see for himself, and it is as though I have had several lives. Sometimes I walk to the circle with the fountain. I see the dancers but they are separated from me as by glass. Once when there were rumors of new burnings, someone scrawled in white paint on the pavement outside my house: *Soul Brother.* I understand the words; but I feel brother to what or to whom? I was once part of the flow, never thinking of myself as a presence. Then I looked in the mirror and decided to be free. All that my freedom has brought me is the knowledge that I have a face and I have a body, that I must feed this body and clothe this body for a certain number of years. Then it will be over.

Vidiadhar Surajprasad Naipaul

With this excerpt, we are certainly aware of an entity, as well as the end of a sequence of events (which includes both acts and happenings), the ingredients Abbott defines as a narrative (see page 198). We are reading the "representation of a [man's] story".

What we notice especially is that we are seeing the events through the eyes of someone telling us about them. He is the center, the focus of the story, and we have to rely on his perceptions. He might not be worthy of our trust, but he is all we have.

Another kind of first-person narrator

Sometimes a narrative can be told by 'we' (a first-person plural narrator), which is becoming a little more popular in the 21st century and it will be interesting to see how well readers like it.

In the story *Baked Mud* by Juan José Saer, an Argentinian writer (translated by Sergio Waisman), we have the story of a feud between a father and a son. The events are narrated by a pair of men in the town who watch the events being played out, but never give much detail about themselves, the observers. The closing of the story arrives without our knowing the names or identities of the observers, only that they have witnessed the events:

Baked Mud

The next day the yellow station wagon had disappeared. The only things left were the open door of the motel, the circle of chinaberry trees, the dry January sun. And in between Sebastien's dark stories about other floods and droughts, we also had our silence, our solitude and our fear.

Juan José Saer

It might be interesting to think through what differences there are in using 'I' or 'we' to deliver the story to the reader. Again, we are likely to raise issues of credibility or reliability when we compare these, something we will discuss once we have come to terms with the other major category of narrators, the third-person narrator.

The third-person narrator

Very often, the third-person narrator is called an 'omniscient' narrator. This label is then broken down into smaller sub-groups. In recent years, writers about narrative have extensively questioned the notion of omniscience, therefore, it is probably better to work with the label of third-person narration, given how many varieties of 'all-knowingness' (or not) can exist in novels and short stories. Once established societal roles and rules are broken and dispersed, as they perhaps were not in the time of Dickens or Jane Austen, it may be that, as James Wood suggests, "Authorial omniscience… has had its day" (Wood 2008). H. Porter Abbott, too, remarks that, "All narration is riddled with blind spots…" (Abbott 2002).

So how do we handle this other major form of narration? We will need to recognize that whoever tells the story is a voice constructed in a certain way by the author. The author creates a narrator or a voice for the telling of a particular tale. Whether that person is a criminal, a sensitive lover of earth and humankind, a drunkard, a coward or someone we are unable to imagine in any detail is not always easy to determine. We do know that narrators will generally talk about the entities or characters as we ourselves talk about others, using their names or pronouns such as 'he' or 'she'. However, in many cases, we will hardly notice this third-person narrator is present.

Reliable and unreliable narrators

There are a few more aspects that we should consider before we move beyond the telling of the tale. Whether or not we should trust the narrator is another of those 'vexed' questions. Some thinkers about fiction are absolutely sure we should never trust a first-person narrator. Others are far from sure that is so certain: James Wood takes the position that "first-person narration is generally more reliable than unreliable; and third-person 'omniscient' narration is generally more partial than omniscient" (Wood 2008). You may recall what Abbott said earlier about "blind spots" in third-person narration.

So, you will ask, how do I handle these terms, trying to talk about narration when I'm writing an essay for the IB literature course? You will have to make some decisions in relation to the particular work you are reading and you may want to come to that decision in company with your teachers and your fellow students. Keep in mind, though, that in future you're likely to be reading novels and short stories without their company, so you will need to have the know-how to answer the following questions yourself:

- Who's telling the story?
- How far do I trust the narrator?
- How much does trust matter to my reading?

Free indirect style

Another aspect of third-person narration, which provides some usually subtle effects, is something called 'free indirect style'. The work most often mentioned in conjunction with this way of telling is *Madame Bovary*, a 19th-century work by the French writer, Gustave Flaubert, who is regarded by many as an early master of the narrative.

We are all familiar with the ways through which narrators let the reader know what a character is thinking or feeling; the first of these is by describing:

> **Lady into Fox**
>
> With this spell of weather it was but natural that Mr Tebrick should think of taking his vixen out of doors. This was something he had not yet done, both because of the damp weather up till then and because the mere notion of taking her out filled him with alarm.
>
> *David Garnett*

A second way, of course, is through dialogue:

> **In the Eye of the Sun**
>
> "Mario!" she had cried. "Tiger-lilies! Where on earth did you get them, up here, in December?" and reached up to kiss him, her arms full of flowers, her hair piled on top of her head in a loose chignon.

"Here's the Law of Narrative Unreliability: Stop believing the narrator when you see the word 'I'."
Thomas C. Foster

"For you – Mrs. Madi" – he had shrugged – "all things are possible."

Now Olympia looks fearfully around her. She starts to lift the corner of the tablecloth. "You think maybe he is –"

"Relax, Olympia." Saif laughs. "He's hiding next door, terrified at all the noise."

Ahdaf Soueif

In both of these cases we find out what the characters involved are thinking or feeling. In the second case, as with much modern writing, such indicators as "She said" or "He interjected" are omitted, but you are very likely familiar with that convention of dialogue. In many ways, we are so familiar with dialogue we hardly notice how we have internalized that convention.

There is yet another somewhat more subtle way to operate with both the narrator's voice and a character's voice in play in an intermingled and simultaneous way, and that is called 'free indirect style'.

Free indirect style has been described by Abbott as "a kind of ventriloquism". Here, we will hear the narrator directly quoting what his character is thinking. Free of quotation marks, or the usual "She thought" or even the dashes sometimes used to indicate alternating speakers, the "author simply allows the character's voice momentarily to take over the narrative voice" (Abbott 2002).

Below is an example of free indirect style from a well-known story by Katherine Mansfield, 'Miss Brill', written in the early 20th century:

Miss Brill

Dear little thing! It was nice to feel it again. She had taken it out of its box that afternoon, shaken out the moth-powder, given it a good brush, and rubbed the life back into the dim little eyes. "What has been happening to me?" said the sad little eyes. Oh, how sweet it was to see them snap at her again from the red eiderdown!… But the nose, which was of some black composition, wasn't at all firm. It must have had a knock, somehow. Never mind – a little dab of black sealing-wax when the time came – when it was absolutely necessary… Little rogue! Yes, she really felt like that about it. Little rogue biting its tail just by her left ear. She could have taken it off and laid it on her lap and stroked it.

Katherine Mansfield

You may be a bit puzzled by this free indirect style of writing: what *is* this?! If you have ever read the story, you know that Miss Brill has gone out to sit in the park and she recalls assembling her 'outfit'. We hear her talking about her fox collar, something which, in the time of the story, would have been a decorative accessory. Notice, however, the melding of the third person 'she' with a representation of her own thoughts.

On the next page is another example of free indirect style from a novel by Olivia Manning set in Cairo during the Second World War, *The Levant Trilogy*.

You will perhaps see why James Wood calls free indirect style a way of inhabiting "omniscience and partiality at the same time". We see Simon acting and thinking, but we also hear 'exactly' (this is a fictional construct, after all) what he is thinking and the way he is thinking about it.

The Levant Trilogy

Simon, sun-parched, sweat-soaked, unshaven, sand in hair and eyes, needed a bath though he was too deep in grief to feel the want of anything. He was taken upstairs to a small room with a bathroom so narrow, the bath fitted into it like a foot into a shoe. Filling the bath, he lay comatose in luke-warm water until he heard the hotel waking up.

He could see through his bedroom window that the dusty saffron colour of the afternoon had deepened into the ochre of early evening. Time had extended itself in his desolation, yet it was still the day on which Hugo had died. At this pace, how was he to endure the rest of his life? How, as a mere beginning, was he to get through the week ahead?

He looked at himself in his shaving mirror, expecting to see himself ravaged by his emotion but the face that looked back at him was still a very young face, burnt by the sun, a little dried by the desert wind, but untouched by the sorrow of that day.

He was twenty years of age. Hugo had been his senior by a year and they were as alike as twins. Imagining Hugo's body disintegrating in the sand, he felt a spasm of raging indignation against this early death, and then he thought of those who must suffer with him: his parents, his relatives and the girl Edwina whom he thought of as Hugo's girl. He had seen Edwina when he first came to Cairo and he realized, with a slight lift of spirit, that he now had good reason to see her again.

Olivia Manning

At this point, you may be thinking that these examples are like other narrative conventions, and free indirect style seems to resemble both **interior monologue** and stream of consciousness, two other features of narratives.

This is, in fact, true and various writers distinguish or blend these terms. However, it's also useful to save the first term for what we usually call 'monologues' (a single speech) rather than a representation of intermittent reflections, feelings and sense-perceptions.

As for 'stream of consciousness' (often used by students to describe any extended presentations of thoughts by characters), this is a specific technique developed in the early 20th century by such writers as Virginia Woolf, James Joyce and William Faulkner.

What passages of stream of consciousness aim to do is to represent on the page of the narrative the flow of the mind. You know your own mental processes; to attempt to put them precisely on paper is no small challenge, both for the writer and the reader. Such an attempt often overrides the conventions of spelling, punctuation and syntax as it tries to present sense-perceptions, feelings, as well as thoughts as they occur in the human consciousness.

On the next page is an example of the movement towards representing the running thoughts of a character; James Joyce in *Ulysses* will go even further than this extract from William Faulkner, and will remove all punctuation marks.

The Wild Palms

"They are going to keep me on until summer at the store."

He heard this time; he went through the same experience as when he had recognized the number on the calendar he had made, now he knew what the trouble had been all the time, why he would lie rigidly and carefully beside her in the dawn, believing the reason he could not sleep was that he was waiting for the smell of his moron pandering to fade, why he would sit before an unfinished page in the typewriter, believing he was thinking of nothing, believing he was thinking of only the money, how each time they always had the wrong amount of it and that they were about money like some unlucky people were about alcohol; either none or too much.

William Faulkner

Are there any other kinds of narrators?

Aside from breaking first-person narrators into various categories such as 'first-person central' and 'first-person secondary', and third-person narrators into 'third-person omniscient' and 'third-person objective' as Foster does (2008), there is one other rare possibility about which people tend to have rather large arguments.

You may have been thinking, "Well, what happened to second-person narration?" Not a great deal, actually, but there is a way for it to exist. Many people would say that if 'you' appears in the work, we have second-person narration. Actually, it is usually the address of the second person as in "Dear reader, you may have been wondering why our hero seems to have disappeared…"

Nevertheless, there are people like Lorrie Moore, Jay McInerney and other modern writers who do offer something that can be called second-person narration. In Jack Hodgins' *A Passion for Narrative*, this sort of narration is described, helpfully perhaps, as the writer "talking to an earlier self" (1993).

Here's an example; see if you're convinced that 'second-person narration' is another form of narration.

Decide that you like college life

In your dorm you meet many nice people. Some are smarter than you. And some, you notice, are dumber than you. You will continue, unfortunately, to view the world in exactly these terms for the rest of your life.

The assignment this week in creative writing is to narrate a violent happening. Turn in a story about driving with your Uncle Gordon and another one about two old people who are accidentally electrocuted when they go to turn on a badly wired desk lamp. The teacher will hand them back to you with comments: "Much of your writing is smooth and energetic. You have, however, a ludicrous notion of plot."

Moore, L. M. 1985. 'How to Become a Writer' taken from *Self-Help*. USA. Warner.

One last issue about the teller of the tale that students sometimes find troubling is **tone**. In narration, tone occurs in two different ways: the attitude that the narrator takes to the material he writes about (the characters, the place where events and happenings occur) and a general attitude about the human condition, about human nature.

However, there are also the many tones that occur in descriptions made by characters, in interior monologues, and particularly in dialogue between characters. Much more about tone can be found in the discussion of another genre, poetry, in Chapter 11.

Other conventions involved in telling a story

Having come to terms with who tells the story, it is important to look at how the story is told. This involves looking at elements such as the 'entities' (**characters**) as well as where the story is **set**. There are also other conventions that are associated with fiction such as the handling of **time** and **space** in a narrative. Related to these are such features as the **structuring** of the novel, which can include chapters as well as suspense and coincidence. The choices in **language**, literal and figurative, are also something to consider in the novel and short story.

Beginning with the familiar: characters and characterization

Characters are all-important to writers of such narratives as novels and short stories. What do they say about characters?

> "*Characters are those primary substances to which everything else is attached.*"
> William Gass

You are certainly well aware that most narratives are inhabited by fictional constructs known as 'the characters' of the fictions. Who they are, how we connect with them and what they mean can provide us with much material for thought and conversation. When you are asked to talk about them in an IB literature essay, the emphasis expected is on how these characters are constructed and how they are used by the writers to achieve certain effects: their interest of the reader, the movement of the plot, their contribution to what might be the 'larger purpose' of the narrative. In earlier years, you may have been asked to write *your* version of the characters, what you liked or disliked or how you connected to them (or didn't).

However, when writing about characters for this IB literature course you will be especially asked to focus on two aspects:

- The construction of the characters by the writer – the art of characterization and all the techniques by which a character comes to life on the page.
- The way that character constructs are operating in the larger picture: the novel or short story.

First, let us look at the conventions through which a writer can construct and deliver a character to a reading audience.

Sometimes, the first introduction of a character will be with a **description**, offering some physical details. Older novels, when the genre was in its early stages, practised this convention frequently. These presentations of character often give physical as well as psychological details. A description of Mr Bounderby from *Hard Times* follows on page 209:

> ### Hard Times
>
> He was a rich man: banker, merchant, manufacturer, and what not. A big, loud man, with a stare, and a metallic laugh. A man made out of coarse material… A man with a great puffed head and forehead, swelled veins in his temples, and such strained skin to his face that it seemed to hold his eyes open, and lift his eyebrows up.
>
> *Charles Dickens*

Note how Dickens mixes the literal and the metaphorical possibilities of language to create a vivid presence. A plainer description appears in a novel written in the early 20th century by Willa Cather, *A Lost Lady:*

> ### A Lost Lady
>
> A well-grown boy of eighteen or nineteen, dressed in a shabby corduroy hunting suit, with a gun and a gamebag, had climbed from the marsh… he walked with a rude, arrogant stride, kicking at the twigs, and carried himself with unnatural erectness, as if he had a steel rod down his back.
>
> *Willa Cather*

You will notice that along with physical and emotional details, **actions** are incorporated into the Cather description. Some treatments of character will depend also on the inclusion of **gesture**, another convention of characterization.

A more recent example includes some physical description in conjunction with a minute gesture. Careful selection and combination by Richard Powers work here to deliver a character who is highly individualized. Notice, too, how important the convention of **names** is to enrich the portrayal of character.

> ### Plowing the Dark
>
> Spiegel assigned her a prodigy to call her own. A boy called Jackdaw – Jack Acquerelli. Jackdaw came fresh from California's largest computer science factory, although he looked barely old enough to mail in his own software registration forms. He was just her height, one of the reasons he'd taken up with computers in the first place. He might have been attractive, except for the steady diet of Doritos and the inability to abide much human contact without flinching. Adie took to him at once, if only for mocking his last name. Each time she met him she unbuttoned the top button of his habitual plaid flannel shirt, until she trained him to do so, all by himself.
>
> *Richard Powers*

Activity

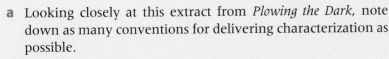

a   Looking closely at this extract from *Plowing the Dark*, note down as many conventions for delivering characterization as possible.

b   What do you infer about Jack from what is written here?

There are two other techniques that have become conventional in creating characters in novels and short stories. One of the most common and important is, of course, **dialogue**. Very often, we learn about characters through what they say and through what others say about them.

One of the interesting challenges for writers is to make dialogue sound like human speech without exactly replicating human speech, with its stutters, changes of direction, meaningless tags and hesitations. Additionally, there are the problems of putting speech on the page without using repetitive phrases. As the novel has developed, such indicators as "She said" or "He thought" have been used in various ways, and in some writers have even disappeared completely. This latter practice often demands very focused attention in order to know who is speaking.

Dialogue in *Hard Times* and *A Lost Lady* uses **conventional phrases** as well as spacing to indicate both who is speaking and in what tone:

Hard Times

"This is a very obtrusive lad!" said Mr. Gradgrind, turning and knitting his brows on him.

"We'd have had a young gentleman to meet you if we had known you were coming," retorted Master Kidderston, nothing abashed.

Charles Dickens

A Lost Lady

Mrs. Forrester nodded at him from her end of the table. "And now tell us your philosophy of life, – this is where it comes in," she laughed teasingly.

The Captain coughed and looked abashed. "I was intending to omit that tonight."

Willa Cather

These are passages you would easily recognize as dialogue if you opened the novel at random, and it's clear to see both who is speaking and to whom.

In the 20th century, the conventions of presenting dialogue have changed. It is even possible to have at least a short story that includes no dialogue at all, for example Nadine Gordimer's early story, *Is There Nowhere Else Where We Can Meet?* (1951).

Still, Gordimer, in her early fiction, uses conventions that are much like those of Dickens and Cather, and then in her later works follows the pattern of omitting the conventional phrases indicating speakers and tones, so that her characters often speak without identification of any kind. The dash becomes an indicator of changing speakers. Here is an example from a later novel, *Burger's Daughter*:

> **Burger's Daughter**
>
> – You'll do what the white man tells you –
>
> – Listen. Listen, a minute, man – if my boy wins a big fight overseas –
>
> – So what? You'll make a lot of money and he can show his medal with his pass when he gets back –
>
> *Nadine Gordimer*

So what we have with the convention of dialogue is another set of practices that affect how a story is presented on the page, and a convention that has undergone some changes since novels and short stories were first written.

The second interesting convention often used by writers to provide information about characters is by connecting them to **lists** such as lists of books, or other items they possess, such as clothing, collections of art, etc. Lists are an efficient way for writers to tell the reader a good deal about a character. Here is a brief example:

> **The Unfinished Game**
>
> An agitated young woman, with shocking red lips and excess baggage (two suitcases, three handbags, two plastic bags stuffed with odds and ends) kicks my foot and thrusts herself forward.
>
> *Goli Taraghi*

Conventions of time, space and structure

The final set of conventions we are going to look at in this chapter has to do with:

- the way that **time** is involved in narratives
- the **place** or **space** where the sequence of events takes place.

Narratives and time

Abbott offers the interesting observation that "narrative… gives us what could be called the shape of time" (Abbott 2002), a sense of where we are in the space where we exist. It is a commonplace observation that stories help us to understand who we are and our relations to others.

We also might consider narrative time as opposed to clock time, because another distinction is often made about the representation of human life in art as opposed to the linear clock time in which we live our lives, at least at one level.

We know that we have to be places at certain clock times. If we want to meet someone, it will be no good if we are unclear about where or when. However, narratives have the power to operate with both clock time and narrative time, where things can be speeded up or slowed down. As novelists, we can get the man to the plane in two sentences or in 40.

We also need to consider that there are different times operating simultaneously when we're reading a novel. One kind of time is going on in the narrative and another is going on with us. We are taking time out of our life to read the novel and that might be an afternoon or a month. Likewise, the time in the novel might be years or a day. *Ulysses* by James Joyce is a novel of 644–1000 pages (depending on the edition) and covers one day in the life of Leopold Bloom in Dublin, Ireland. Sometimes, in fact, we are so lost in a novel that we become immersed in the time that it covers. All of these aspects have to do with our experience of such 'fictions'.

There are generally two conventional ways in which writers present the passage of time: either in **chronological order** (as events are imagined to happen), which tends to present the narrative in a linear fashion – a timeline – or in a **disrupted** or **disjointed order**. The earliest novels, even those that were constructed of letters written among characters (a genre known as the **epistolary novel**) tended to present events in roughly chronological order.

Within these timelines, very often a secondary story – or several – will be included. Subplots are a convention we all recognize from both novels and films. They are, of course, secondary stories. If you look at a variety of definitions of this feature of plots, you will discover such words to describe their function as "contribute interest", "add complexity", "give impetus to action", "add zest and relief" (Harmon and Holman 1999); "mirror, enhance, or intensify" (Quinn 1999) and "parallel and contrast" the main plot (Baldrick 1990). When, as in a Dickens novel, you can have as many as 75 characters, it's very likely that you will have some of these secondary stories.

Later novels, starting in the early 20th century, began to disrupt or disjoint the narrative sequence. Events yet to come would also be included by a convention known as **prolepsis** or **flash forwards** and, at other moments, characters or the narrator would include **flashbacks** (or **analepsis**) to return to events or happenings that precede the narrative.

Naturally, these disruptions would have an effect on another convention – **pace**, or the speed with which events unfold. In turn, **suspense** (a very important element for readers) is affected both by chronology or disruption, as well as the leaping forward and looking backward.

Place or space

The final aspect of novels and short stories we are going to consider in this chapter is most often called the **setting of the narrative**. Both the time in which the novel or short story is set and the place or places form the context for events and affect our perception of both people and events.

Writers can either foreground the setting, even to the point of making a place begin to seem like another character, as in the novels of Thomas Hardy, for example. Or they can make it so vague that we are barely aware of it, or feel the events could be taking place just about anywhere.

Settings can also contribute significantly to the mood or atmosphere of narratives. Dark and shadowy places work well for mystery, the unexpected and the violent. Open spaces can be intimidating or liberating.

In all cases, it is wise for you as a reader to take account of the **physical** as well as the **cultural** aspects of both time and space in your works in this genre.

13 Prose other than fiction: the autobiography

Objectives
- to learn about autobiography as a genre
- to examine the development and varieties of autobiography
- to understand the conventions of autobiography

"Reflection trained on mystery."
Barrett John Mandel

*"Self-knowledge?
A contradiction in terms."*
E. M. Cioran

Self-portrait of Frida Kahlo

Self-portrait of Hokusai

Self-portrait of Saluum

Self-portrait of Artemisia Gentileschi

The visual representations above remind us that the aim of autobiography is to portray the self. Sometimes the style and attitude of such portrayals convey that the artist intends to communicate to the best of their ability exactly how they see themselves and their evolution in life; at other times, the artist adds touches of irony or imaginative distortion. As viewers, we do our best to discern the nature of what we are seeing. The same holds true when we are reading the self-portraits known as 'autobiographies'.

Looking at the word 'autobiographical' in the 21st century, it can be observed to have taken on a wide variety of meanings over the years, including such traditional forms as diary, memoir and autobiographical fiction. In addition, with the wide usage of the internet, blogs and social networking sites have also become places where people create 'autobiography'. In studying autobiography in the IB literature course, you will ordinarily be looking at book-length accounts of someone's experiences – their presentation of self.

Definitions/descriptions of what is understood by 'autobiography'

Almost universally, 'autobiography' is defined or described as the story of a person's life written by that person.

The French writer Phillip Lejeune is often referred to when the study of autobiography as literature is discussed. His conception of autobiography is straightforward but includes some ideas worth pursuing: "A retrospective prose narrative (story) that a real person creates about his or her own existence when he emphasizes individual life, particularly the history of his own personality" (Lejeune 1974).

There are several things worth noting here. Most often, autobiography is written in **prose**, but can be written in poetic form. *The Prelude*, written by William Wordsworth in the 19th century, is certainly considered to be a part of autobiography in verse. Here is a short selection from 'Childhood and Schooltime':

Childhood and Schooltime

. . . .My seventeenth year was come;

 And, whether from this habit rooted now

So deeply in my mind, or from excess

In the great social principle of life

Coercing all things into sympathy,

To unorganic natures were transferred

My own enjoyments; or the power of truth

Coming in revelation, did converse

With things that really are; I, at this time,

Saw blessings spread around like a sea.

The Prelude: Book II

William Wordsworth

Here, we see the speaker, very likely Wordsworth himself, considering his close alliance with the natural world.

In 1960, the British poet John Betjeman composed a verse autobiography, 'Summoned by Bells'. 'Lives of X' (1971) is another autobiography in poetry rather than prose by the American poet John Ciardi. So there are other possibilities, but the usual expectation is that autobiography will be delivered in prose.

Story or narrative points us in the direction of the aspects of narration that are at the heart of other forms, the novel and short story. In fact, autobiographies often include those old standbys of fictional narratives, plot, character and setting. All of these become conventions of the autobiographical form as well.

Plot

The narrative usually (but not always) unfolds in a chronological way, as lives are believed to occur. In Ondaatje's account of his early life in Sri Lanka, *Running in the Family* (1982), he includes dialogues, photographs, poems and reflections along with separate historical accounts, although there is an underlying narrative line of his coming to terms with the lives of people in his family, particularly his parents. While 'plot' is more complicated, usually, than the linear narrative of a life, the way Ondaatje presents his account takes on the complexity we tend to associate with a plot.

Character

Character is certainly an element of autobiography. Often, there are many minor and some major characters other than the 'I' subject of the autobiography. In *Down and Out in Paris and London* (1933), Orwell offers memorable sketches of people he encounters, Paddy and Bozo, other men 'on the road' – a life Orwell chose to follow for a while. Ondaatje's portrait of his grandmother, Lalla, is constructed in several different scenes, perhaps most notably her death. Here is the conclusion of the extract that describes Lalla's death by drowning:

Running in the Family

Below the main street of Nuwara Eliya the land drops suddenly and Lalla fell into deeper waters, past the houses of 'Cranleigh' and 'Ferncliff'. They were homes she knew well, where she had played and argued over cards. The water here was rougher and she went under for longer and longer moments coming up with a gasp and then pulled down like bait, pulled under by something not comfortable any more, and then there was the great blue ahead of her, like a sheaf of blue wheat, like a large eye that peered towards her, and she hit it and was dead.

Michael Ondaatje

While it is often the history of the writer's own **personality** that lies at the center of autobiographical accounts, other people, who may in fact become quite memorable, enter the narrative.

Setting

Setting is also an important element in autobiography; indeed, some autobiographical writing seems almost as interested in conveying a sense of the social and cultural backdrop as the personality of the subject of the autobiography. In Orwell's account of life 'on the road', he conveys a vivid sense of the 'spikes' or hostels where nights are spent; in Paris, his accounts of the restaurants where he works range from the comic to the horrifying:

Down and Out in Paris and London

In the kitchen the dirt was worse. It is not a figure of speech, it is a mere statement of tact to say that a French cook will spit in the soup – that is, if he is not going to drink it himself. He is an artist, but his art is not cleanliness. To a certain extent he is even dirty because he is an artist, for food, to look smart, needs dirty treatment. When a steak, for instance, is brought up for the head cook's inspection, he does not handle it with a fork. He picks it up in his fingers and slaps it down, runs his thumb around the dish and licks it to taste the gravy, runs it round and licks again, then steps back and contemplates the piece of meat like an artist judging a picture, then presses it lovingly into place with his fat, pink fingers, every one of which he has licked a hundred times that morning. When he is satisfied, he takes a cloth and wipes his fingerprints from the dish, and hands it to the waiter. And the waiter, of course, dips <u>his</u> fingers into the gravy – his nasty, greasy fingers which he is for ever running through his brilliantined hair.

George Orwell

216

In Alexandra Fuller's *Don't Let's Go to the Dogs Tonight: An African Childhood* (2003), an account of her girlhood in Rhodesia (now Zimbabwe), one comes away from the autobiography with a strong sense of both the backdrop and the trials and adventures of growing up in an unstable political situation.

Don't Let's Go to the Dogs Tonight: An African Childhood

Dad says, "Okay, kids, that's enoughtofthat."

So we sit there on each side of the back seat with a big hole in the middle where Olivia should be and watch Mum's eyes go halfmast.

We are driving through a dreamscape. The war has cast a ghastly magic, like the spell on Sleeping Beauty's castle. Everything is dormant or is holding its breath against triggering a land mine. Everything is waiting and watchful and suspicious. Bushes might suddenly explode with bristly AK47s and we'll be rattled with machinegun fire and be lipless and earless on the road in front of the burned out smoldering plastic and singed metal of our melting car.

The only living creatures to celebrate our war are the plants, which spill and knot and twist victoriously around buildings and closed down schools in the Tribal Trust Lands, or wrap themselves around the feet of empty kraals. Rhodesia's war has turned the place back on itself, giving the land back to the vegetation with which it had once been swallowed before people. And before the trappings of people: crops and cattle and goats and houses and business.

Alexandra Fuller

In both Orwell's and Fuller's extracts, we get some sense of another element from Lejeune's description of autobiography, "A real person['s]… existence" gets back to the issue of truth and invention in autobiography, and this is indeed a point of much discussion when people talk and write about autobiography.

Generally, it is presumed that there is what Lejeune calls an 'autobiographical pact' between the writer of autobiographies and the reader. The writer tells something that is presumed to represent his 'individual life' and the reader presumes they are receiving a fair representation of that life.

However, much depends, of course, on how far writers even *want* to convey the truth about themselves with any exactitude and how far they *can*. Memory is not a fully reliable archive, and so many things – fantasy, desire, self-protection and guilt, for example – can intrude upon the writer's intention. We tend to re-write our lives at different stages of our life, and that is only one of the elements that is in play when a writer sets out to deliver autobiography. Indeed, that is why some contemporary critics prefer the term 'life narratives' or 'life writing' to autobiography. These terms seem to leave more room for the inexactitude of memory and the variability of the impulse to 'tell the truth' about the self, and the personality of the writer. How does one objectively convey the history of one's 'own personality'?

So when we enter the world of autobiographical writing, we are in uncertain territory. We expect, surely, some truthful account of a person's life and experiences, but it is also wise to be wary; we will only learn from the person what the speaker chooses to deliver and omit.

Some of the related issues about 'autobiographical writing' that arise in this study

Fiction or autobiography?

One issue is the frequency of works most often called 'autobiographical novels' or 'fictional autobiographies'. In these forms, the life of the writer and, usually, the central character are often conflated or blended. It is easy, with a little research, to discover that certain events in the novel are very close to actual experiences of the writer. Such is the case with Sylvia Plath's *The Bell Jar*. Here is one description that is clearly based on the year Plath was herself a guest editor at *Vogue* magazine:

The Bell Jar

There were twelve of us at the hotel.

We had all won a fashion magazine contest, by writing essays and stories and poems and fashion blurbs, and as prizes they gave us jobs in New York for a month, expenses paid, and piles and piles of free bonuses, like ballet tickets and passes to fashion shows and hair stylings at a famous expensive salon and chances to meet successful people in the field of our desire and advice about what to do with our particular complexions.

Sylvia Plath

What we have here is a somewhat fictionalized but fairly accurate reflection of what occurred in Plath's life. However, as her work proceeds, there is always likely to be a mixture of what has 'really happened' and what is developed in a novelistic fashion of highlighted or exaggerated moments and representations of what the writer thought on a particular occasion.

As George Misch, the German scholar, points out in his study of this kind of writing, *Autobiography in Antiquity* (2003), autobiography itself is a genre unlike any other form of literary communication, since its boundaries are so fluid. Works such as *The Bell Jar* create real problems of 'naming'. Is this work to be called a novel, a work of fictional autobiography or 'autofiction'? Sometimes, the subject of the work is even referred to in the third person. But the borders of almost every genre are perhaps equally susceptible to being permeated so that, in cases like *The Bell Jar*, the reader is free to choose how to read and 'receive' the work. There are no easy answers, nor is there ever universal agreement about either the labels or particular works – *The Bell Jar* represents some of these problems.

Feminist views of autobiography as a developing form

Another interesting angle on the genre of autobiography is the work of various feminists discussing this form. Jill Ker Conway, in her work *When Memory Speaks: Reflections on Autobiography* (1998), takes the view that men's and women's autobiographies differ in significant ways. Men, she says, have often written biographical works that test the hero on a journey, while women, having little say over their lives and fates for many years, tend to cast their stories in terms of the quest for property and social mobility through finding a mate (with the exception of those women in religious communities like Hildegard of Bingen or Teresa of Avila, who told stories of their spiritual odysseys). You may want to test this theory by comparing the works you are studying in this genre.

A brief history of autobiography

The autobiographical impulse has certainly been present in human experience dating back to classical times. The Greek roots of the word (auto – self; bio – life; graph – writing) suggest writing about one's own life. Some of the earliest autobiographies, such as the *Confessions* of St Augustine in the 5th century and the 15th-century autobiography/ travel narrative of Marjery Kempe, sought to represent spiritual journeys, while the autobiography of Benvenuto Cellini, an artist of the 16th century, called *Vita* (or life) provides an energetic account of Cellini's artistic life and such added exploits as murders and the conjuring of devils.

The autobiography of Benjamin Franklin, the American writer and diplomat, sheds considerable light on the social and political world of the new America of the 18th century, while Jean-Jacques Rousseau's *Confessions*, another 18th-century French autobiography, suggests the more personal direction autobiography would take in succeeding centuries. Rousseau promises to hide nothing ("a portrait in every way true") but also admits that not everything will be unerringly factual. In so speaking, Rousseau again raises the question of what is 'true' and what is invented, distorted or poorly remembered, or included to make a particular political or didactic point.

In the 20th and 21st centuries, autobiographical writing has taken a great many forms, with the result that the line between the 'vertical pronoun' of autobiography – the 'I' – can appear in many forms. In the 16th century, the autobiographical inclusions that the French writer Montaigne makes in *Essais*, a combination of the essay form with autobiographical reflections, can be seen to predict that autobiography will take various forms. In so many ways, Montaigne also predicts the expectations readers will continue to embrace when they hear the term 'autobiography'; he states of his work: "It is myself I portray." Nevertheless, it is not uncommon in the 20th century for the portrayal to be done by a writer who is not the subject, as in Alex Haley's role as recorder of *The Autobiography of Malcolm X*. There are clearly many diverse ways of approaching the autobiographical, including the 'celebrity autobiography' and even works that are more than minimally invented.

Some recent works, such as Primo Levi's *If This is a Man* (an account of his years in Auschwitz) and Tim O'Brien's *If I Die in a Combat Zone, Box Me Up and Ship Me Home,* deal with a particular segment of a person's experience, and may sometimes have a political or didactic intent, whether the horror of the Holocaust or the gut-wrenching experience of being a soldier. Likewise, both George Orwell's *Down and Out in Paris and London* and Michael Ondaatje's *Running in the Family* treat only a

Here's an interesting way of contrasting early autobiography and more modern versions of this genre. Jonathan Goldberg, in his study of Cellini's *Vita (Vita and the Conventions of Early Autobiography*, 1974), proposes that there are characteristics that differentiate the two:

- Early autobiographies often see a **universal design** and **recurring patterns** of which the subject is a part. These works tend to be depersonalized and public. An early autobiography like St Augustine's *Confessions* situates itself within a context of the devout life of a Christian.
- Autobiographies after Montaigne are more likely to emphasize the **uniqueness** of the subject, and what is **personal** and often **private**. If you are studying autobiographies from very different time periods, say one by Thoreau and one by Maya Angelou, you might make a point of comparing the place of the personal and the private in the two works, even though neither goes back as far as Cellini's.

certain period in the writer's life. In these cases, as in many autobiographies, the writer conveys a sense of enlightenment, or a moment of **epiphany** that is common in autobiography. Such enlightenment may occur in the actual ongoing life of the person. This seems to be the case with Orwell's account of Paris, or, retrospectively, with Ondaatje's revisiting of his childhood in Sri Lanka. Additionally, in the final pages of his account of England, Orwell takes a rhetorical or didactic approach to the lives of people who live on the road.

Activity

Compare the following two insights (the first from Ondaatje and the second from Orwell) in terms of what they convey of a moment of awakened consciousness through their language, tone and content.

Ondaatje:

Orwell:

Words such as *love, passion and duty* are so continually used they grow to have no meaning – except as coins or weapons. Hard language softens. I never knew what my father felt of these 'things'. My loss was that I never spoke to him as an adult. Was he locked in the ceremony of being 'a father'? He died before I even thought of such things.

It is altogether curious, your first contact with poverty. You have thought so much about poverty – it is the thing you have feared all your life, the thing you knew would happen to you sooner or later; and it is all so utterly and so prosaically different. You thought it would be quite simple; it is extraordinarily complicated. You thought it would be terrible; it is merely squalid and boring. It is the peculiar *lowness* of poverty you discover first; the shifts it puts you to, the complicated meanness, the crust-wiping.

The conventions of autobiographical writing

In studying this genre and preparing to write about it in Paper 2, you may expect questions that will focus on the conventions of the genre you have read. If this genre is autobiography, you will see that many of the conventions of narratives such as the novel will also be involved in your works. We have mentioned that **plot**, **character** and **setting** are often elements found in autobiographies. Since some of the works you study may blend into the territory of the fictional, other conventions such as **flashbacks** and **flash forwards** may also be relevant.

Although it might be expected that the life story will follow a **chronological order**, there are also possibilities for a **disrupted narrative**. An autobiography might even be structured in **circular** fashion, tying together an event that is briefly related in the opening and more elaborately examined at the end. **Suspense** can certainly appear in autobiographies, as the reader waits to learn how a decision or an event will conclude for the good or ill of the subject.

Very often, the construction of a **personal** or **archetypal myth** (hero, victim, pariah) will be apparent in a work studied. The autobiographer will sometimes work to construct an overall profile of a life in this way, which can fit into one of the archetypal life stories. Another factor in differentiating one autobiography from another, which will have a substantial impact on the reader's perception of the work's subject, will be the **tone** in which the writer speaks about their experiences and judgments. How the writer conveys their attitude will matter a great deal to the reader's impressions, as will that all important factor, **diction**, or the choice of words.

Anecdotes that elaborate the understanding of the 'I' subject are also very common in autobiographies. Particular experiences that mark the stages of the evolution of the character recur frequently enough in autobiography to be considered an important element of the form. In the *bildungsroman* or 'growing up' narrative, as in other autobiographies, moments that mark a move from **childhood understanding to adult** are conventional. Accounts of **schooling** and **stages of intellectual development** are other conventional aspects of these works, as are **romantic relationships** with their anticipations, consummations and broken hearts.

This list does not comprehensively cover all the stylistic aspects of autobiography, but it will give you an initial sense of some strategies used to convey the story of a life to readers.

Activity

You have now taken a brief survey of aspects of the autobiographical form. In the extracts that follow, three writers (one from Morocco, one from Nigeria and one from Canada) recall a basic and recurring human experience, bathing. All are telling about their own experiences in three different settings.

Read through the three extracts carefully. What can you say about each of them in terms of:

- **descriptive qualities**: what is included, what is left out?
- **position**: what is the position of the speaker in relation to others in the extract? How does this affect your judgment of both the speaker and the actions described?
- **tone**: how does the speaker convey their attitude to the events?
- **language**: what features of the language help you to understand this autobiographical moment?
- **similarities and differences**: looking at the extracts comparatively, what can you say about their similarities and differences? They are all about childhood/early adolescence, but do they all convey the same thoughts and feelings?

Dreams of Trespass: Tales of a Harem Girlhood

Our traditional *hammam* ritual involved a "before," a "during," and an "after" phase. The phase before the *hammam* took place in the central courtyard, and that was where you made yourselves ugly by covering your face and hair with all those unbecoming mixes. The second phase took place in our neighbourhood *hammam* itself, not far from our house, and that was where you undressed and stepped into a series of three cocoon-like chambers filled with steamy heat. Some women got completely undressed, others put a scarf around their hips, while the eccentrics kept their *sarwals* on, which made them look like extra-terrestrials after the fabric had gotten wet. The eccentrics who entered the *hammam* with *sarwals* on would be the target of all sorts of jokes and sarcastic remarks, such as "Why don't you veil, too, while you're at it?"

The "after" phase involved stepping out of the misty *hammam* into a courtyard where you could stretch out for awhile dressed only in your towels before putting on clean clothes. The courtyard of our neighbourhood *hammam* had inviting wall-to-wall sofas placed on high wooden tables so you were protected from the wet floor. However, since there were not enough sofas to accommodate everyone who frequented the *hammam*, you were supposed to take up as little space as possible and not linger long. I was so happy that those sofas were there, because I always felt terribly sleepy after leaving the *hammam*. In fact, this third stage of the bathing ritual was my favorite, not only because I felt brand-new, but also because the bath attendants, under instruction from Aunt Habiba (who was in charge of *hammam* refreshments), distributed orange and almond juices, and sometimes nuts and dates too, to help you regain your energy. This "after" phase was one of the rare times when grownups did not have to tell children to sit still, for all of us would be lying half-asleep on top of our mothers' towels and clothes. Strange hands would be pushing you here and there, sometimes lifting your legs, other times your head or hands. You heard the voices, but could not raise your fingers, so delicious was your sleep.

At a certain time of the year, a rare heavenly drink called *zeri'a* (literally, "the seeds") was served at the *hammam* under the tight supervision of Aunt Habiba, so as to insure equal distribution. *Zeri'a* was made of melon seeds that were washed, dried, and stored in glass jars specifically made for the *hammam* drinks. (For a reason I still cannot understand, that wonderful drink was never served anywhere else but in the *hammam*.) The seeds had to be consumed quite quickly or they would spoil, which meant that *zeri'a* could only be tasted during the melon season, never more than a few weeks a year. The seeds were crushed and mixed with whole milk, a few drops of orange-flower water, and a pinch of cinnamon. This mixture then sat for a while, with the pulp inside. When it was served, the jug could not be disturbed too much, so the pulp would remain at the bottom and only the liquid would be poured. If you were too sleepy to drink after the *hammam* and your mother loved you very much, she would always try to pour a taste of *zeri'a* down your throat, so you would not miss out on that special event. Children whose mothers had been too absent-minded to do this would start screaming with frustration when they awoke and saw the empty jars. "You drank all the *zeri'a*! I want *zeri'a*!" they would howl, but of course, they would not get any until the next year. The melon season had a cruelly abrupt end.

Fatima Mernissi

Ake: The Years of Childhood

She advanced, sponge in hand, 'Joseph lets me do my face,' I persisted.

'Mama says I should bathe you, that is all I know. She didn't divide your body into bits, some for you and some for me.'

Her left hand now dipped the bowl into the bucket, scooped up the water and moved to douse my head. I ducked.

'Look at you! You are wasting water. You know what Mama is going to do to you when I tell her?'

I moved to the corner of the bathroom. Too late, I realized I was trapped.

Even so, I fought for my life. As the bowl looped over my head with its contents, I reached out and deflected it. Nubi was drenched and it seemed to make her angry.

'Now you see what you have done!' The movement was so fast, I had no time to protect my face. From out of nowhere a huge wad of moistness slammed into my face, traversing every pore rapidly but most especially blocking my nostrils.

Her fingers dug into my skull, pressing it down while she scrubbed my face without once letting in air. When I tried to bite I only got a mouthful of the sponge, so I did my desperate routine, let my knee buckle and, in that brief respite, butted her in the stomach. I heard her scream, 'O pa mi o' and the next moment there were cries of 'Tani yen?' from all over the house.

'Tani lo' gun nbe yen? Tani?' And then there were running feet.

Hastily wiping off soapsuds with both hands, I blinked my eyes open and saw Wild Christian framed against the opening. She shook her head from side to side, baffled as always. Now I was really scared that she was going to take over.

'She has finished,' I said. 'I have had my bath.'

'He butted me with his head,' Nubi complained, clutching her stomach.

'Stop exaggerating,' Mama snapped.

'Yes Ma.' And Nubi straightened up at once.

'Screaming down the whole house. Are you trying to scare everybody?'

'No Ma. But he wouldn't let me scrub his face.'

'You've scrubbed it,' I reminded everyone at large. 'You've done nothing but scrub it since I came to have my bath. You've nearly scrubbed it to death, what more do you want to scrub? Tinu is still waiting for her bath.'

Suddenly I felt secure; there was a smile on Wild Christian's face. She said to Nubi, 'All right, call Tinu. In any case they are both old enough to start bathing themselves now.'

'Yes, yes. I've said it before. I don't need her or Joseph.'

'But you must bathe in their presence, so they can make sure you do a proper job.'

I nodded. It seemed a little enough concession to make. Just the same, I added, 'I don't really need them. In fact I have scrubbed myself before when Joseph was too busy. Joseph inspects me afterwards and he says I am quite clean.'

'All right then. Although I can never understand how you come to be so afraid of water, you, a July-born.'

I was now rinsing off the rest of the soap. 'But I am not afraid of water,' I protested.

'No? Just look at the way you are rinsing yourself. There is soap all over your face but you haven't even touched it.'

I quickly threw the next bowlful over my head. As usual, something went wrong. It usually did when water was cast over my head or face. The next moment I was spluttering and fisting the stinging rivulets off my face, fighting for breath.

Even through the wasps' nest that had erupted about my ears as the water commenced its habitual torture of my senses I heard Wild Christian laughing as she walked away.

Wole Soyinka

How I was bathed

We are having a formal dinner. String hoppers, meat curry, egg rulang, papadams, potato curry. Alice's date chutney, seeni sambol, mallung and brinjals and iced water. All the dishes are on the table and a good part of the meal is spent passing them around to each other. It is my favourite meal – anything that has string hoppers and egg rulang I eat with a lascivious hunger. For dessert there is buffalo curd and jiggery sauce – a sweet honey made from the coconut, like maple syrup but with a smoky taste.

In this formal setting Gillian begins to describe to everyone present how I used to be bathed when I was five. She had heard the story in detail from Yasmine Gooneratne, who was a prefect with her at Bishop's College for Girls. I listen intently, making sure I get a good portion of the egg rulang.

The first school I went to was a girls' school in Colombo which accepted young boys of five or six for a couple of years.

The nurse or ayah in charge of our cleanliness was a small, muscular and vicious woman named Maratina. I roamed with my pack of school friends, usually filthy from morning to night, and every second evening we were given a bath. The bathroom was a sparse empty stone room with open drains in the floor and a tap to one side. We were marched in by Maratina and ordered to strip. She collected our clothes, threw them out of the room, and locked the door. The eight of us were herded terrified into one corner.

Maratina filled a bucket with water and flung the contents towards our cowering screaming bodies. Another bucket was filled and hurled towards us hard as a police hose. Then she strode forward, grabbed a child by the hair, pulled him over to the centre, scrubbed him violently with carbolic soap and threw him towards the opposite side of the room. She plucked another and repeated the soaping. Totally in control of the squirming bodies she eventually scrubbed us all, then returned to the bucket and thrashed water over our soapy nakedness. Bleary-eyed, our bodies tingling and reeling, our hair curved back from the force of the throw, we stood there shining. She approached with a towel, dried us fast and brutally, and threw us out one by one to get into our sarongs and go to bed.

The guests, the children, everyone is laughing and Gillian is no doubt exaggerating Yasmine's account in her usual style, her long arms miming the capture and scrub of five-year-olds. I am dreaming and wondering why this was never to be traumatically remembered. It is the kind of event that should have surfaced as the first chapter of an anguished autobiographical novel. I am thinking also of Yasmine Gooneratne, now teaching at a university in Australia, whom I met just last year at an International Writers' Conference in New Delhi. We talked then mostly about Gillian who had also been at university with her. Why did *she* not tell me the story – this demure woman in a sari who was "bath prefect" at Bishop's College Girl's School, who officiated over the cleansing of my lean five-year-old nakedness?

Michael Ondaatje

Prose other than fiction: the travel narrative

Objectives

- to get a sense of the travel narrative as a literary genre
- to acquire some sense of the development of the form
- to understand the conventions of this genre

Why We Travel

We travel, initially, to lose ourselves; and we travel, next, to find ourselves. We travel to open our hearts and eyes and learn more about the world than our newspapers will accommodate. We travel to bring what little we can, in our ignorance and knowledge, to those parts of the globe whose riches are differently dispersed… The beauty of this whole process was best described, perhaps, before people even took to frequent flying, by George Santayana in his lapidary essay, 'The Philosophy of Travel'. We "need sometimes", the Harvard philosopher wrote, "to escape into open solitudes, into aimlessness, into the moral holiday of running some pure hazard, in order to sharpen the edge of life, to taste hardship, and to be compelled to work desperately for a moment at no matter what."

Iyer, P. 'Why We Travel'. Saturday 18 March 2000. Salon.com.

Questions of Travel

Is it lack of imagination that makes us come
to imagined places, not just stay at home?
Or could Pascal have been not entirely right
about just sitting quietly in one's room?

Continent, city, country, society:
the choice is never wide and never free,
And here, or there… No. Should we have stayed at home,
wherever that may be?

Elizabeth Bishop

What do we mean by travel literature?

Looking into another vast field of written examples, it makes sense to open not only with this first question, but with other basic questions also:

- What kind of travel are we referring to?
- What's the difference between a traveller and a tourist?
- How is a guidebook different from travel literature?

225

These are not easy questions to answer. Since the genre of travel literature or travel writing has some strong similarities to autobiographical accounts, how they are distinguished from one another is another problematic query, along with: 'Who is the audience for travel literature?' This chapter will try to give you some help with both raising questions and finding answers so that, by the end of the chapter, you will be in a strong position to shape your own answers to these questions; there aren't any 'right' answers, only answers that can be thought through individually with advice from scholars who think about such matters.

We use the term travel 'narrative' because this term, which is often used for fiction, applies here also, for it is most often 'the representation' of a story – the story of someone travelling somewhere. Tourists travel but they don't always try to share their story with others in a carefully written form. Guidebooks certainly provide information about places, but their intention is primarily expository, informational and often evaluative.

Ancient gate of the Old Citadel, Aleppo, Syria

Activity

Two accounts of the citadel in Aleppo, Syria follow. Note that you are dealing with two very different approaches to travel writing: the first is a guidebook for travellers, and the second, which is subtitled "autobiography", is a traveller's account of visiting the same area.

1   Note as many similarities and differences as you can in the two writers' approaches, paying particular attention to purpose, tone and language.

2   Given that both writers are 'travellers' from the outside, consider the effect of their presentations on their likely audiences, as well as their handling of their outsider role.

Jordan and Syria: A Survival Kit

The citadel dominates the city and is at the eastern end of the souks. It is surrounded by a moat, 20 metres deep and 30 metres wide, which is spanned by a bridge on the northern side. Entrance to the citadel is through a 12th-century gate and behind this is the massive fortified main entrance. Although finely decorated on the outside, the inside is a succession of five right-angle turns, where three sets of solid steel-plated doors made a formidable barrier to any occupiers. Some of the doors still remain and one of the lintels of the doorways has carvings of entwined dragons, and another has a pair of lions.

Finlay, H. 1987. *Jordan and Syria: A Survival Kit*. Australia. Lonely Planet.

The Coast of Incense

I climbed down fifty high steps into an immense Byzantine hall on pillars, and then wandered over the Haram and the palace of the Egyptian Caliphs and the medieval precautions round the great gate, with secret posterns and holes to pour pitch down on the assailants. There is a horrid prison, deep down with no windows and a hole in the roof for letting good down – I always dislike going into prisons and offer a little prayer for all the unhappiness that must have been spent inside them.

I went all over this citadel with a Christian of Aleppo, an employee of the French delegation very anxious to tell me how anti-French he was, but as I was their guest and being particularly nicely treated I had to snub him promptly. He took me all over the bazaars which are the nicest I know in the East, all narrow vaulted with stone and little square openings in the vault letting down shafts of light. As you look at Aleppo from the citadel, you can see a green expanse in the middle and these are the bazaars.

Freya Stark

It is clear that much traditional travel literature is written with a consciousness of being read and appreciated by others, not just for its content, but also for its style. Its **genre boundaries**, as with so many other forms, are fluid and elusive. There are many examples of how travel literature blends, steps out of its 'bounds', and enters the territories of other genres.

One striking example of such mixtures would be the work *Luca Antara* by Martin Edmond, whose works range over travel, biography and poetry. Travel is certainly at the center of this work, as Edmond examines the story of a Portuguese servant, Antonio da Nova, who is sent out in the 1600s to discover more about Luca Antara, one of the islands believed to lie to the south. When da Nova's crew mutinies on the west coast of Australia, da Nova is rescued and led across Australia by Aboriginal people. This work of Edmond's is such a mix of autobiography, travel writing and fiction that it has puzzled critics and reviewers. Nonetheless, it is able to be included when travel literature is considered. In any study of travel writing, the same problems are likely to be encountered. However, even though its boundaries are unclear, there are certain features that can be found in much of this literature

Some aspects of travel literature

1 One feature that travel literature shares with autobiography is its **voice**.

Most often, the travel narrative will be told by the 'I' who makes the journey. This **univocal** voice can sometimes be joined by another. Sometimes the voice takes on a **persona**, as in some essays by Samuel Johnson and Charles Lamb, for example.

Washington Irving in *The Adventures of Geoffrey Crayon* (1835) employs the persona of Mr Crayon to describe, among other things, a 19th-century American travelling in Europe. His is not a work of only travel writing, but includes short stories and essays also.

Combining two aspects, persona and **companion**, Mark Twain sets off to visit Europe with a fictional companion, Joseph Harris, whose views about their travels are often included. His work, *A Tramp Abroad* (1880), and Irving's are their own literary versions of the 'Grand Tour'. This name was given to the kind of travel regarded in the 17th and 18th centuries as an opportunity for mostly upper-class Europeans to acquaint themselves with classical roots and great art. It later became an idea embraced by artists and by Americans, though perhaps with less lavish resources.

Washington Irving

Mark Twain

2   The writing about travel can be presented in something as short as an essay or as long as a substantial novel.

3   Longer examples of travel literature can usually be described as having a defined **beginning**, **middle** and **end**. These narratives tend to be **circular**: they begin at home, embark on and pursue an itinerary, which may be highly organized or somewhat spontaneous, and are completed by a return home – the traveller departs and the traveller returns.

In *Passenger to Teheran,* written in 1926, Vita Sackville-West departs from a particular English train station and returns there:

Passenger to Teheran

One January morning, then, I set out; not on a very adventurous journey, perhaps, but on one that takes me to an unexploited country whose very name, printed on my luggage labels, seemed to distil a faint, far aroma in the chill air of Victoria Station: PERSIA.

In May of the same year, after a journey that included a route that circled south to Iran and Delhi and then back through Russia and Poland, the writer finishes her journey:

Was I standing on the platform at Victoria, I who had stood on so many platforms? The orange labels dangled in the glare of electric lamps. PERSIA, they said.

Vita Sackville-West

It's difficult to imagine a more precisely circled journey, perhaps one that is almost too neat in its balance (although the departure scene is not the opening of the book).

4 Another aspect to consider is the difference between travel literature that pictures an ongoing journey with stops and descriptions or reflections along the way, and one that involves a journey *to* a particular place in which the bulk of the work is centered on that place. While Sackville-West's work is an example of the former, William Dalrymple's *City of Djinns: A Year in Delhi* is an example of the latter:

City of Djinns: A Year in Delhi

After having visited the city of Delhi at the age of seventeen, mesmerized by the great capital, so totally unlike anything I had seen before…

And later, Dalrymple returns:

Five years after I had first lived in Delhi I returned, now newly married. Olivia and I returned in September. We found a small top floor flat near the Sufi village of Nizamuddin and there set up home.

William Dalrymple

---

5 The issues of subjectivity, objectivity, and whether an account is a mix of fact and fiction are also likely to arise when looking at travel writing. One of the earliest narratives, which tells of the travels of Sir John Mandeville (published between 1351 and 1357), is a complex tissue of personal experience, rather fantastic descriptions of customs and creatures and pieces of the travel accounts told by others. Below is a sample from his description of Egypt, a place he did not actually visit himself. Mandeville didn't always believe he had to visit a place in order to include it in his narrative.

At the deserts of Egypt was a worthy man, that was an holy hermit, and there met with him a monster (that is to say, a monster is a thing deformed against kind both of man or of beast or of anything else, and that is clept a monster). And this monster, that met with this holy hermit, was as it had been a man, that had two horns trenchant on his forehead; and he had a body like a man unto the navel, and beneath he had the body like a goat.

www.travellersinegypt.org

---

6 Finally, the **purpose** of travel that eventually becomes travel writing might be considered. In some cases, the writing impulse may be the strongest force of all, as may be the case of Twain's account of tramping through Europe. However, travel is undertaken for many purposes and many of these journeys end up being recorded in journals, diaries, and short accounts, as well as long narratives that the writers want to share with a wider audience. It might be useful to consider some of the purposes that have characterized travel writing over the years.

The purpose of travel writing
To find oneself

As Iyer notes in the epigraph to this chapter on page 225, some journeys are about finding something about oneself, or 'finding oneself'. Indeed, very often, the writer will reveal that the journey has elicited or pushed them to some new perception about their own life, choices and history.

Freya Stark writes in her combined autobiography and travel narrative, *The Coast of Incense*:

The Coast of Incense

It always surprises me to notice how short a time is taken by events that have been so slow in coming… Perhaps one of the advantages of my perpetual seesaw between illnesses and activity was the learning of this lesson: the saving up through long periods for some treasured enterprise which came and went like lightning, but illuminated the past and the future as it went by.

Freya Stark

In *A Fez of the Heart: Travels Around Turkey in Search of a Fez*, Jonathan Seal closes the book with an epiphany:

A Fez of the Heart: Travels Around Turkey in Search of a Fez

Looking back, I realized that the fez had been the means to an end, not an end in itself, for I had failed to trace this elusive hat to its origins… The end had been Turkey itself. The fez had guided me to the divisions that modern Turkey denied… but that made her intriguing, endlessly different, and finally the country she was.

Jonathan Seal

Che Guevara in *The Motorcycle Diaries* articulates the truism that the self that leaves home is not the same one that returns:

The Motorcycle Diaries

The person who wrote these notes passed away the moment his feet touched Argentine soil again. The person who reorganizes and polishes them, me, is no longer, at least I am not the person I once was. All this wandering around "Our America with a capital A" has changed me more than I thought.

Che Guevara

These three extracts above are only a tiny sampling of the many examples of the impulse not only to travel but to record travel.

Curiosity

Very early in the history of travel narratives, a great many accounts were driven simply by curiosity and fascination with places not yet experienced by outsiders or even described. Wanting to know, or even to understand, the 'other' certainly produces as vast an array of travel accounts as does the search for the self.

Whether it is Ibn Battuta, the Muslim traveller of the 14th century, setting out to visit all the countries of the Muslim world and covering 75,000 miles, or Mary Kingsley, travelling unaccompanied to West Africa in 1895, a desire to know the world beyond immediate horizons has continually been a strong motivation.

A modern, first-time travel writer, Jason Eliot, explains his impulse to go to Afghanistan in a way similar to Joseph Conrad's fascination with maps as a child and a determination to 'go there', a curiosity that eventuated in Conrad's novel, *Heart of Darkness*. In the first pages of *An Unexpected Light: Travels in Afghanistan*, Eliot tells a friend:

An Unexpected Light: Travels in Afghanistan

If I must look for a beginning, I have to go back to when I was twelve years old, my mind spinning from a turn-of-the-century account I'd just read of an explorer's travels through what was then Turkestan, to which the northern portion of what is now Afghanistan belongs. The names meant very little to me them, but I felt the living image of them nonetheless, and longed to know if the descriptions I had read were real.

Jason Eliot

Religion

Spiritual journeys also account for a good many travel narratives and these have had a long history. Very early travel accounts such as *The Book of Marjery Kempe* (written in the late 1340s) or the 17th-century Japanese poet Basho's descriptions of his travels embody such journeys, and there are many such 'pilgrimages' that have been recorded and, in turn, inspired others. Whether to the Christian Shrine of Compostela or on the Islamic *haj* to Mecca, travellers follow their devotional impulses and often record them.

The search for family roots

Another motivation for travel and for accounts of them arises from the desire to search out the roots of one's family and origins. Often, this search is allied with **genealogical research**, the study of family connections and beginnings. If you search under "travel for roots and family history" on the internet, you will discover a multiplicity of sites that give accounts of trips which are offered or journeys that have been made by people in search of their 'roots'.

Allied to this form is the 'return to roots' account, such as can be found in *Maximum City: Bombay Lost and Found* by Suketu Mehta. In this work, we are first introduced to the family roots he left behind at age nine and to which he returns 21 years later. Here is another example of the travel narrative that is not about moving along an itinerary, but a journey to a single place that will be carefully studied. Speaking of such a return, Mehta writes:

Maximum City: Bombay Lost and Found

I existed in New York, but I lived in India, taking little memory trains. The fields at dusk. Birds flying home overhead, your car stopping by the side of the road and you getting out. Noticing minute things again: the complexity of the gnarled peepal by the roadside, the ants making their way around it.

Suketu Mehta

Travelling to write in an informed way

To the motivations already listed should be added writing, which both involves travel and emerges from a political angle on the place visited, as in Elizabeth Hardwick's essay, 'Sad Brazil', from *Bartleby in Manhattan and Other Essays*:

Sad Brazil

I had been here in 1962 and now, 1974, I returned. Indeed it is impossible to forget the peculiarity and beauty of this rich and hungry country. Paradox is the soul of it. Droughts and floods, fertility and barrenness come to reside in each individual citizen, creating instability of spirit that is an allurement and a frustration, a mixture that was formerly sometimes thought of as feminine. It was the time of the installation of the new President, Geisel, under the military rule. Latin America's wars are, for the most part, of the internal kind, the kind beyond armistice. Heavy police work that gives the generals time to run the country. General, the word itself appears to be a sort of validation, a kind of Ph.D without which General Peron and General Pinochet might have appeared to be mere citizens presuming.

Geisel, the new President of this land of color – olive, black, mixed, European, Indian, reddish brown like dried flowers – turned out to be a lunar curiosity thrown down from some wintry, arctic celestial disturbance. He is thin and colorless, as ice is colorless. A fantastical ice, solid in the heat of the country. No claim to please, astonish, nothing of the cockatoo or macaw. Dark glasses shield the glacial face, as if wishing to filter the tropical light and darken the glow of the chaos of bereft persons, the insects, slums, French fashions, old ports at Bahia and Recife, the brilliant, irredeemable landscape.

Elizabeth Hardwick

Both Hardwick's essay and Mehta's detailed study of returning to Mumbai combine vivid and concrete impressions of place with acute political analysis, another variety of travel literature.

A brief history of travel writing

In order to set your reading of travel narrative in some sort of context, we have looked at some aspects and some purposes that characterize and generate, respectively, this very large body of writing. As Casey Blanton writes in her study *Travel Writing: the Self and the World*, "the texts, in the end, seem inexhaustible" (Blanton 2002).

Another way to look at travel writing in a superficial but global way is to divide its history into three periods: Medieval and Renaissance, 18th and

19th centuries, and the 20th and 21st centuries. We have, in fact, looked at extracts from some of these.

Medieval/Renaissance travel writing

Just as with autobiography, this form of writing has occurred since Greek and Roman times; in fact, both Homer's *Odyssey* and Vergil's *Aeneid* could be considered to fall under the umbrella of this genre.

We have already mentioned both Marjery Kempe and Sir John Mandeville. However, along with Ibn Battuta's *Rihla* (the account of his travels), we have the other striking journey of Marco Polo (1298). These men both travelled impressive distances, one for mercantile reasons, the other as a devotee of Islam. In them are represented three of the principal motivations for travel in these early centuries: curiosity, trade and religion. So much explorative travel was accomplished during these years that the 16th century is often called 'The Age of Discovery'.

If there was any doubt that many early travellers were both setting out on journeys and writing about them, Peter C. Mancall's 2006 anthology, *Travel Narratives in the Age of Discovery,* offers 37 documents relating travel in Asia, Africa, North and South America, and Europe written between the 15th and 17th centuries.

Activity

Look at the map of Ibn Battuta's and Marco Polo's trips.

1 What similarities and differences can you see in their routes?

2 Do you think their purposes in travelling can be discerned or guessed at from these routes?

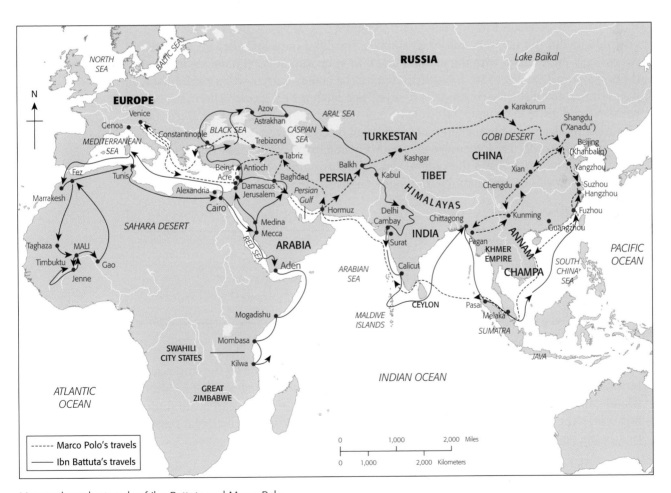

Map to show the travels of Ibn Battuta and Marco Polo

The 18th and 19th centuries

During these two centuries, travel became more and more available and accessible and the travel narrative flourished as well.

Other aspects of Samuel Johnson's work (the 18th-century essayist and critic) were his accounts of his travels in the Hebrides and in Wales. However, his colleague and biographer James Boswell seemed more suited to this kind of writing. Sir Walter Raleigh summed up Johnson's version as "the most ceremonious of diaries," but a sample of Boswell's work suggests a good deal more talent in this realm.

The Portable Johnson and Boswell

We rode on well till we came to the high mountain called the Rattachan, by which time both Mr. Johnson and the horses were a good deal fatigued. It is a terrible steep to climb, notwithstanding the road is made slanting along. However, we made it out. On the top of it we met Captain MacLeod of Balmeanach (a Dutch officer come from Skye) riding with his sword slung about him. He asked, "Is this Mr. Boswell?" which was a proof that we were expected. Going down the hill on the other side was no easy task. As Mr. Johnson was a great weight, the two guides agreed that he should ride the horses alternately. Hay's were the two best, and Mr. Johnson would not ride but upon one or other of them, a black or a brown. But as Hay complained much after ascending the Rattachan, Mr. Johnson was prevailed with to mount one of Vass's greys. As he rode it downhill, it did not go well, and he grumbled. I walked on a little before, but was excessively entertained with the method taken to keep him in good humour. Hay led the horse's head, talking to Mr. Johnson as much as he could; and just when Mr. Johnson was uttering his displeasure, the fellow says. "See such pretty goats." Then *whu!* he whistled, and made them jump. Little did he conceive what Mr. Johnson was. Here was now a common ignorant horse-hirer imagining that he could divert, as one does a child, *Mr. Samuel Johnson!* The ludicrousness, absurdity, and extraordinary contrast between what the fellow fancied and the reality, was as highly comic as anything that I ever witnessed. I laughed immoderately, and must laugh as often as I recollect it.

James Boswell

Joshua Slocum's *Sailing Alone Around the World* is another account of travel at the end of the 19th century (in this case sea travel) and is a lively and readable account of this voyage:

Sailing Alone Around the World

Early on the morning of July 20 I saw Pico looming above the clouds on the starboard bow. Lower lands burst forth as the sun burned away the morning fog, and island after island came into view. As I approached nearer, cultivated fields appeared, "and oh, how green the corn!" Only those who have seen the Azores from the deck of a vessel realize the beauty of the mid-ocean picture.

At 4:30 P.M. I cast anchor at Fayal, exactly eighteen days from Cape Sable. The American consul, in a smart boat, came alongside before the *Spray* reached the breakwater, and a young naval officer, who feared for the safety of my vessel, boarded, and offered his services as pilot. The youngster, I have no good reason to doubt, could have handled a man-of-war, but the *Spray* was too small for the amount of uniform he wore. However, after fouling all the craft in port and sinking a lighter, she was moored without much damage to herself. This wonderful pilot expected a "gratification," I understood, but whether for the reason that his government, and not I, would have to pay the cost of raising the lighter, or because he did not sink the *Spray*, I could never make out. But I forgive him.

Joshua Slocum

One particular travel narrative in the 18th century stands out as being quite different from accounts of people who decided that they would venture out to a different part of the world for pleasure and keep a record of it.

The travels of Olaudah Equiano, as they are reported in *The Interesting Narrative*, were published in 1789. His account is of something we could call 'forced travel', as he was captured in his homeland of Africa and recorded in his narrative that sea voyage in painful detail. Although, when he became a free man, Equiano embarked on voyages for commercial and even adventurous purposes later in his life, his searing account of travel in a slave ship could be counted his most powerful writing:

The Interesting Narrative

One day, when we had a smooth sea, and moderate wind, two of my wearied countrymen, who were chained together (I was near them at the time), preferring death to such a life of misery, somehow made through the nettings, and jumped in the sea; immediately another quite dejected fellow, who, on account of his illness, was suffered to be out of irons, also followed their example; and I believe many more would very soon have done the same, if they had not been prevented by the ship's crew, who were instantly alarmed. Those of us that were the most active were, in a moment, put down under the deck; and there was such a noise and confusion amongst the people of the ship as I never heard before, to stop her, and get the boat out to go after the slaves. However, two of the wretches were drowned, but they got the other, and afterwards flogged him unmercifully, for thus attempting to prefer death to slavery. In this manner we continued to undergo more hardships than I can now relate; hardships which are inseparable from this accursed trade. – Many a time we were near suffocation, from the want of fresh air, which we were often without for whole days together. This, and the stench of the necessary tubs, carried off many. During our passage I first saw flying fishes, which surprised me very much: they used frequently to fly across the ship, and many of them fell on the deck.

Olaudah Equiano

Looking back at the 20th-century extract from Pico Iyer on page 225, write a short commentary on how the three extracts from the 18th and 19th centuries reflect (or do not reflect) the kind of thinking about travel that this 20th-century man expresses.

The 20th and 21st centuries

Travel by both women and men ranged across the world during this period: at the turn of the century, Isabella Bird continued her writing, including works on Korea and China. Caroline Kirkland's *African Highways* continued the interest in that continent that had drawn Mary Kingsley to it. Mark Twain's adventures in the 1860s in the 'wild' west of America were reported in *Roughing It*. All of these writers were close precursors of the great range of exploration and of the styles of travel writing of the 20th and 21st centuries.

At the end of this chapter are included three examples of more recent travel writing, and you will be invited to look at certain stylistic conventions as they appear in these samples. Before we do this, it will be good to review some of the conventions that have been either implicitly treated in this discussion of travel literature or need to be explicitly identified.

Conventions of travel narrative

Again, the conventions we might identify as those of travel literature include the traditional trio of **plot**, **character** and **setting**.

The plot in many of these works is the story of **movement** and then of **discovery**. Whether the discovery is of a place, a people, or a deeper sense of the self, it is a likely element and expectation in travel writing.

The planning of a **goal** as well as an **itinerary** are both conventional parts of such narratives. Another stylistic choice involved here will be the choice of **structure** for the movement of the narrative: will it be linear or circular?

Who the **characters** of the narrative will be, and how many, are matters of the scope decided upon by the travellers. Do they hope to explore the landscape, the people and their ways of living, architecture, the influence of colonialism or imperialism and the possibilities for trade? There can be a multitude of such purposes. Whether purpose is established in advance of the journey, or used as a principle in retrospect, in order to give a frame or structure to the writing, is likely to be a question for the reader to consider.

Voice is a central matter in the construction of travel literature. Will the voice be singular, univocal? Will more than one voice be heard? There are many opportunities in travel literature for multiple voices to make their way into the story: companions in travel, people encountered, whose voices are woven into the writing. Previous travellers along the same route may be alluded to or they may be quoted.

Tone, so much a part of voice, will have a significant role in any travel narrative. There is a great range of possibilities here, and any consistent or changing attitudes about what the traveller sees and conveys will critically affect the reader's impressions and judgments both of the voice and of the treatment of 'the other'. Such tones, conveying these attitudes can cover a whole spectrum from admiration and wonder, to irony, self-deprecation, and even dismissiveness. Through tone and, of course, through choices of **language**, the writer may well convey a desire to identify, or at least empathize, with people they encounter, or they may objectify them. In addition, whether the narrative is written in the **present** or the **past tense** can affect the reception of the tale of travel.

Travel takes people places and so, of course, the handling of **setting** will be a crucial element to such narratives, whether the travel is to a single place or a succession of places. Within the place, will the self be foregrounded or will the speaker recede into the background and give way to the presentation of people and/or setting? Different people will also foreground different aspects. We have seen this earlier in the brief history of travel writing.

A final sampling of post 19th-century travel literature

"The whole object of travel is not to set foot on foreign land; it is at last to set foot on one's own country as a foreign land."
G. K. Chesterton

Activity

Read the following three extracts carefully. Make some notes about:

- what attitude the pieces reflect generally (dismissiveness, objectification, respect, for example)
- what particular aspects or conventions they include (persona, purpose, voice, for example).

Once you have completed your notes, write a short essay entitled: 'Style in modern travel writing.'

City of Djinns: A Year in Delhi

'Our village was famous for its sweets,' said Punjab Singh. 'People would come for miles to taste the jalebis our sweet-wallahs prepared. There were none better in the whole of the Punjab.'

We were sitting on a charpoy at International Backside Taxi Stand. For weeks I had been begging Balvinder's father to tell me the story of how he had come to Delhi in 1947. A stern and sombre man, Punjab would always knit his eyebrows and change the subject. It was as if Partition were a closed subject, something embarrassing that shouldn't be raised in polite conversation.

It was only after a particularly persistent bout of badgering, in which Balvinder took my side, that Punjab had agreed to relent. But once started, he soon got into the swing of his story.

'Samundra was a small and beautiful village in District Lyallpur,' he said. 'It was one of the most lovely parts of the whole of Punjab. We had a good climate and very fertile land. The village stood within the ruins of an old fort and was surrounded on four sides by high walls. It was like this.'

With his hands, the old man built four castle walls. From the details that he sketched with his fingers you could see he remembered every bastion, every battlement, each loophole.

'Our village was all Sikh apart from a few Hindu sweepers. Our neighbours were Mahommedan peoples. We owned most of the land but before 1947 we lived like brothers. There were no differences between us…' Punjab stroked his beard. He smiled as he recalled his childhood.

'On the 15th August 1947 the Government announced Partition. We were not afraid. We had heard about the idea of Pakistan, but we thought it would make no difference to us. We realized a Mahommedan government would take over from the Britishers. But in our Punjab governments often come and go. Usually such things make no difference to the poor man in his village.

'Then, quite suddenly, on the 10th of September, we got a message from the Deputy Commissioner in Lyallpur. It said: '"You people cannot stay. You must leave your house and your village and go to India." Everyone was miserable but what could we do? All the villagers began loading their goods into bullock carts. The old men were especially sad: they had lived their whole lives in the village. But we were young and could not understand why our grandfathers were crying.

William Dalrymple

Japan: Perfect Strangers

As I spent longer in Japan, I increasingly came to feel that the "empire of signs" was, as I had half expected, the most complex society I had ever seen, and to that extent, the most impossible to crack. If nothing else, its assumptions were so different from those of the West that to understand it seemed scarcely easier than eating a sirloin steak with chopsticks. The Japanese might drink the same coffee as their American counterparts, and their magazines might boast English titles. But how could one begin to penetrate a land where shame was more important than guilt, and where public and private were interlocked in so foreign a way that the same businessman who unabashedly sat on the subway reading a hard-core porno mag would go into paroxysms of embarrassment if unable to produce the right kind of coffee for a visitor? Japan defied the analysis it constantly provoked; Japan was the world's Significant Other.

By the same token, I also found that discussions among foreigners about the true nature of Japan continued endlessly, and fascinatingly, yet never seemed to come to anything new. Every foreign "explanation" of the country seemed finally to revolve around exactly the same features – a reflection of the place's homogeneity, perhaps, but also of its impenetrability. How every foreigner wondered (in unison), could a culture promiscuously import everything Western, yet still seem impenetrably Eastern? How did the place remain so devoted to its traditions even as it was addicted to modernity and change? What to make of a people with an exquisite gift for purity as well as an unrivaled capacity for perversity? And how on earth could a land of ineffable aesthetic refinement decorate its homes with the forms of cartoon kitties?

Japan, for the foreigner, was all easy dichotomies: samurai and monk, Chrysanthemum and Sword, a land, as Koestler wrote, of "stoic hedonists." If the test of a first-rate mind, as Fitzgerald once wrote, is the ability to hold two opposed ideas at the same time and still keep going, Japan had the most first-rate mind imaginable.

To me, however, all these familiar contradictions seemed finally to resolve themselves into a single, fundamental division: between Japan of noisy, flashy, shiny surfaces and the Japan of silence and depth. The first – the face of modern Japan – afforded a glimpse into a high-tech, low-risk future, a passage into the clean, well-lit corridors of a user-friendly utopia, where men glided on conveyor belts into technocentric cells that were climate-controlled, sweetly scented and euphoniously organized by a PA system. Here was society as a microchip, a tiny network of linked energies. Commuters functioned like computers, workmen like Walkmen. Every morning, armies upon armies of workers – men all in jackets and ties, women all in look-alike skirts and blouses – surged through the subways of Tokyo, undifferentiated, unerring and undeflected.

Pico Iyer

Round Teheran

Then the bazaars are full of surprises; in one place it is a sword stuck up to the hilt into the wall, Rustem's sword, they say, Rustem being their favourite heroic character; and in another place it is an open courtyard, shaded by large trees, where one can buy all kinds of junk, laid out in little chess-board squares on the ground, for a few farthings, every kind of thing from old sardine-tins to silver kettles pawned by Russian refugees. Nothing more tragic than this evidence of the Russian catastrophe; here is an old gramophone record, and here a pair of high button boots, very small in the foot, with a pair of skates screwed on; they speak, not only of present-day personal misery, but of a life once lived in gaiety; and all theoretical sympathy with Lenin vanishes at the sight of this human, personal sacrifice made on the altar of a compulsory brotherhood. Russia seems very near. Indeed, in Asia the different countries do seem nearer to one another, more mingled, than do different countries in Europe, by some contradiction, despite the enormous distances; here in Persia one cannot lose sight of the fact that China, Russia, Turkestan, Arabia, surround us, remote though they may be, and buried each in a separate darkness; perhaps because vagrants from out of these neighbouring regions find their way to the Persian bazaars, and wander with an air of strangeness, in different clothes that proclaim the country of their origin, an Arab in his burnous, a Russian in his belted shirt, a Turcoman in his shaggy busby, unlike Europeans, who differ from one another, if at all, only by their complexions. In the open courtyard of the bazaars, the green field as it is called, nationalities jostle, poking amongst the junk-stalls for some scrap of treasure, a buckle, or a collar-stud, while the vendors squat near at hand, with lacklustre eye, less concerned to sell than to see that nothing is stolen.

Such a desultory life I lead, and the life of England falls away, or remains only as an image seen in an enchanted mirror, little separate images over which I pore, learning more from them than ever I learnt from the reality. I lead, in fact, two lives; an unfair advantage. This roof of the world, blowing with yellow tulips; these dark bazaars, crawling with a mazy life; that tiny, far-off England; and what am I? and where am I? That is the problem: and where is my heart, home-sick at one moment, excited beyond reason the next? But at least I live, I feel, I endure the agonies of constancy and inconstancy; it is better to be alive and sentient, than dead and stagnant. "Let us", I said, as we emerged from the bazaars, "go to Isfahan."

Vita Sackville-West

Prose other than fiction: the essay

How is the essay defined?

You could, yourself, probably come up with a reasonable definition of this form of prose other than fiction. Below, however, are some 'professional' definitions of this form which, like so many of the other forms we have discussed, has highly fluid 'margins' or 'boundaries'. People use the essay for many purposes and the following is a brief history of the evolution, the variety of use and the conventions of the essay as used in the IB literature course.

In this chapter, our attention will focus on what can loosely be called 'literary' essays. These are written to be enjoyed and studied as texts, and may have some features that you might be asked to both admire and practise.

The definitions offered below are taken from collections of literary terms; their descriptions are designed to be relevant to artistic or literary essays.

    a "A moderately brief prose on a restricted topic."

    Harmon/Holman

    b "A prose composition usually from 2 to 20 pages, dealing with or taking off from a restricted topic."

    Quinn

    c "Any brief composition in prose that undertakes to discuss a matter, express a point of view, or persuade us to accept a thesis on any subject whatever."

    Abrams

In all three cases, these entries go on to discuss sub-categories and sometimes the history of the essay – we will look at these also.

As we look at some essays or extracts taken from them, you will note that the essay is similar to the autobiography and the travel narrative in the sense that it delivers the writer's view of the world and human behaviour.

1 Read the three definitions of 'essay' on the previous page. Choose the common elements found in them and create two descriptions or definitions of your own.

2 How would you define or describe the kinds of essays you are asked to create for your academic course?

3 How would you define or describe the kinds of essays you read in your literature course in periodicals, or even audio (and sometimes visual) essays that you hear in podcasts, or see and hear in vodcasts?

How long has the essay been around?

As you may guess, people have been writing essays for as long as they have been writing. Essays were written in classical Greece and Rome, but in the tradition of essays in English, you will almost always find that the first reference will be to the French writer of the 16th century, Montaigne, referred to as the "father of the modern essay". His *essais* gave rise to the modern form of the word 'essay'. The etymology of the French word *essayer* is said to arise from the Latin *exagere* (to weigh or sift something). In the case of the essay, that sifting and weighing is usually applied to a particular, sometimes even minute, subject.

Montaigne's most well-known successor in the English tradition, Sir Francis Bacon, covered a range of subjects in this form. Below is a sample of what the essay style looked like in the 17th century.

Of Studies

Studies serve for delight, for ornament, and for ability. Their chief use for delight is in privateness and retiring; for ornament, is in discourse; and for ability, is in the judgment and disposition of business… To spend too much time in studies is sloth; to use them too much for ornament is affectation; to make judgment wholly by their rules is the humor (temperament) of a scholar… Crafty men contemn studies, simple men admire them, and wise men use them, for they teach not their own use; but there is a wisdom without them, and above them won by observation.

Francis Bacon

You are not likely to find Bacon's essays easy reading, but he was considered a master of the style of the essay in his own time. As we look at further samples up to the 21st century, it is apparent that the style of the essay changes, although some of the same subject matter will be revisited.

Both the 18th and 19th centuries produced quite a number of significant influences on what the essay would become in the English language tradition. Samuel Johnson, who was also responsible for producing the first English dictionary, wrote some still-remembered critical essays on Shakespeare, and also wrote incisively about other writers. His 'Rambler' essays include two important aspects of the essay as they developed: the use of a **persona**, through which the writer speaks, and the use of the essay as a site for **moral** or **didactic speech**. The 'Rambler' is the

persona that Johnson uses to convey his views. There are over 200 of these 'Rambler' essays, and in his essay 'On Fiction' he takes a very dim view of the kinds of novels that we frequently read today.

On Fiction

There have been men indeed splendidly wicked, whose endowments threw a brightness on their crimes, and whom scarce any villainy made perfectly detestable because they never could be wholly divested of their excellencies; but such have been in all ages the great corrupters of the world, and their resemblance ought no more be preserved than the art of murdering without pain… Vice (for vice is necessary to be shown) should always disgust; nor should the graces of gaiety, nor the dignity of courage be so united with it as to reconcile it to the mind.

Samuel Johnson

Activity

Consider a novel that you have read where there is a protagonist who engages in one or many evil or violent acts.

a Clarify what Johnson says above about fiction.

b How do you and Johnson both judge the protagonist and his influence?

Shortly before Johnson's time, there were some other 18th-century essayists who had a significant influence on the development of the essay in English. Joseph Addison and Richard Steele were friends since childhood. Various downturns in their fortunes in the early years of the 18th century brought them together in providing a major force in developing the **periodical essay** – essays published in the magazines or newsletters of the time. Although both men were strict moralists, in the mold of Johnson, they developed an essay that was less didactic and less formal than his.

These two essayists ranged widely in topic, and included fashions, foolishness in social behaviour, along with literary and philosophical subjects. They were agents in pointing the essay towards a more informal style, particularly in the writing of Steele, although the modern reader might not recognize the style as particularly 'informal'. Their two periodicals, the *Tatler* and the *Spectator*, were precursors of the work of 19th-century writers such as Charles Lamb.

Both Addison and Steele had considerable influence in the development of the essay and the writing of effective prose. Johnson had the following to say about Addison's style:

Life of Addison

His prose is the model of the middle style: on grave subjects not formal, on light occasions not groveling; pure, without scrupulosity, and exact without apparent elaboration; always equable and always easy… Whoever wishes to attain an English style… must give his days and nights to the volume of Addison.

Samuel Johnson

In the 19th century, we find not only informal style, but also a focus that becomes increasingly personal. Charles Lamb wrote an essay entitled 'A Chapter on Ears'.

A Chapter on Ears

I have no ear – Mistake me not, reader, – nor imagine that I am by nature destitute of those exterior twin appendages, hanging ornaments, and (architecturally speaking) handsome volutes to the human capital. Better my mother had never borne me. I am, I think, rather delicately than copiously provided with those conduits; and I feel no disposition to envy the mule for his plenty, or the mole for her exactness, in those ingenious labyrinthine inlets – those indispensable side-intelligencers.

When therefore I say that I have no ear, you will understand me to mean – for music. To say that this heart never melted at the concourse of sweet sounds, would be a foul self-libel… I even think that sentimentally I am disposed to harmony. But organically I am incapable of a tune. I have been practising "God save the King" all my life; whistling and humming of it over to myself in solitary corners; and am not yet arrived, they tell me, within many quavers of it. Yet hath the loyalty of Elia never been impeached.

Charles Lamb

Activity

Looking back at the work of Bacon and Johnson on pages 241–2, try to identify the elements in Lamb's writing that are either similar or different to the earlier writers.

You will have noticed Lamb's use of "Elia". Just as Johnson chose to use a persona, so does Lamb. In fact, Lamb invented names for both himself and his sister, Mary, whom he includes in many essays as part of a **dialogic form** of the essay. Usually, **univocal** essays proceed with one voice; an occasional choice of two voices appears over time. Lamb was very attentive to Mary, who suffered a mental disability. She was treated with persevering care by Lamb. 'Old China' is an essay in which Lamb affectionately foregrounds the voice of Bridget (Mary) in reminiscing over their younger years, a contemplation set off by a form of **ekphrasis** – the portrayal of visual art in a piece of writing. In this case, the art is found in the scene on a china teacup:

Old China

Here is a young and courtly mandarin, handing tea to a lady on a salver two miles off… And here the same lady, or another – for likeness is identity on teacups – is stepping into a little fairy boat, moored on the hither side of this calm garden river, with a dainty mincing foot…

Charles Lamb

Alexander Theroux's *The Primary Colors: Three Essays* contains many examples of ekphrasis (the attempt to portray visual art in words):

The Primary Colors

Consider the vibrant blue watercolour wash of Childe Hassam's exquisite 'Yonkers from the Palisades' with its six or seven shimmering different tints of blue… Or the saturated hues of azure and royal blue in Winslow Homer's 1901 'Coral Formation', where he allowed the deep blue washes to dry in such a way as to suggest the crystal clarity of the deep water.

Alexander Theroux

If this phenomenon interests you, Oscar Wilde's *The Picture of Dorian Grey* and Willa Cather's *Song of the Lark* are two novels in which ekphrasis plays a significant role. Ekphrasis gives writers a chance to make their writing more colourful, concrete and vivid. It also affords an opportunity to exercise their skill with precise words to echo visual effects.

Activity

Choose one of the following pieces of visual art and try your essay skills with ekphrasis.

- *Tattoo and Haircut* by Reginald Marsh.
- *Duties* by James Cudjoe.
- *Black Arena* by Vivan Sundaram.

You will find reproductions of these art works on the internet, and you may want to choose another work that interests you.

By the 19th century, the essay had become a reasonably popular form. In the US, Ralph Waldo Emerson and Mark Twain were frequent practitioners of the **didactic** and the **satirical** essay, respectively, so it is clear the essay was developing on both sides of the Atlantic. However, we might ask, "Where were the women writing essays?" "Who was writing essays in Africa, New Zealand, Australia and in Canada?"

Since this is only intended as a very brief summary of the development of the essay in English, some of this research will have to rest with you, and with the syllabus studied in your class. However, there is a very interesting essay writer named Sui Sin Far, daughter of an English father and a Chinese mother. Far made a living at the turn of the century by giving voice to the experience of being of mixed parentage. Her essay is a blend of anecdotes of the trials of being Eurasian and her final evolution of thinking about her identity, which she offers as a conclusion to the essay she calls 'Leaves from the Mental Portfolio of an Eurasian' (1890). Clare Herlihy explains:

Far made a living for herself by writing articles and essays for numerous newspapers and magazines such as the *Montreal Daily Star, Montreal Witness, Dominion Illustrated, Los Angeles Express, Boston Globe, Good Housekeeping, The Independent* (NY), and *New England Magazine*. In spite of chronically poor health and a limited command of the Chinese language, she managed to travel all over the North American continent and communicate with Chinese American communities in Boston, New York, Montreal, and San Francisco, earning her a reputation as a well-respected reporter for the growing Chinese American community.

In her essays, Far describes her often painful struggle to come to terms with her identity as a bi-racial woman in a culture rife with anti-Chinese sentiment. 'Leaves from the Mental Portfolio of an Eurasian' (*Independent*, 21 January 1890) is her most well-known classical essay. Her writing is deeply personal and she tells her story with a well-crafted sense of irony.

Far was a pioneer, a voice for a people who were forced into relative silence by the cultural norms of the era in which she wrote. She never married or had children and died on April 7, 1914, two years after the publication of her most famous collection of fiction and nonfiction, *Mrs. Spring Fragrance and Other Writings*.

Clare Herlihy in Quotidiana, a website sponsored by Brigham Young University.

After relating some early childhood experiences in England and the US,
Far tells about the family's move to Canada:

Leaves from the Mental Portfolio of an Eurasian

The scene of my life shifts to Eastern Canada. The sleigh which has carried us from the station stops in front of a little French Canadian hotel. Immediately we are surrounded by a number of villagers, who stare curiously at my mother as my father assists her to alight from the sleigh. Their curiosity, however, is tempered with kindness, as they watch, one after another, the little black heads of my brothers and sisters and myself emerge out of the buffalo robe, which is part of the sleigh's outfit. There are six of us; four girls and two boys; the eldest, my brother, being only seven years of age. My father and mother are still in their twenties. "Les pauvres enfants," the inhabitants murmur, as they help to carry us into the hotel. Then in lower tones: "Chinoise, Chinoise."

For some time after our arrival, whenever children are sent for a walk, our footsteps are dogged by a number of young French and English Canadians, who amuse themselves with speculations as to whether, we being Chinese, are susceptible to pinches and hair pulling, while older persons pause and gaze upon us, very much in the same way that I have seen people gaze upon strange animals in a menagerie. Now and then we are stopt and plied with questions as to what we eat and drink, how we go to sleep, if my mother understands what my father says to her, if we sit on chairs or squat on floors…

Whenever I have the opportunity I steal away to the library and read every book I can find on China and the Chinese. I learn that China is the oldest civilized nation on the face of the earth and a few other things. At eighteen years of age what troubles me is not that I am what I am, but that others are ignorant of my superiority. I am small, but my feelings are big – and great is my vanity.

Much later, Sui Sin Far moves west for reasons of health and work:

I secure transportation to many California points. I meet some literary people, chief among whom is the editor of the magazine who took my first Chinese stories. He and his wife give me a warm welcome to their ranch. They are broadminded people, whose interest in me is sincere and intelligent, not affected and vulgar. I also meet some funny people who advise me to "trade" upon my nationality. They tell me that if I wish to succeed in literature in America I should dress in Chinese costume, carry a fan in my hand, wear a pair of scarlet beaded slippers, live in New York, and come of high birth. Instead of making myself familiar with the Chinese Americans around me, I should discourse on my spirit acquaintance with Chinese ancestors and quote in between the "Good mornings" and "How d'ye dos" of editors.

"Confucius, Confucius, how great is Confucius, Before Confucius, there never was Confucius. After Confucius, there never came Confucius," etc., etc., etc. or something like that, both illuminating and obscuring, don't you know. They forget, or perhaps they are not aware that the old Chinese sage taught "The way of sincerity is the way of heaven."

My experiences as a Eurasian never cease; but people are not now as prejudiced as they have been… So I roam backward and forward across the continent. When I am East, my heart is West. When I am West, my heart is East. Before long I hope to be in China. As my life began in my father's country it may end in my mother's.

After all I have no nationality and am not anxious to claim any. Individuality is more than nationality. "You are you and I am I," says Confucius. I give my right hand to the Occidentals and my left to the Orientals, hoping that between them they will not utterly destroy the insignificant "connecting link." And that's all.

Independent, 21 January 1890.

This essay looks forward to the much more **personal** style of essays in the 20th century. The emphasis on individual experience followed by a very sophisticated address of the problems of nation and nationality stands in contrast to the essays, largely by men, that have often been the focus of studies of the essay in English.

Activity

Phillip Lopate in the introduction to his collection of essays entitled *The Art of the Personal Essay* observes that the paucity of women writers in the earlier essays he selects can be attributed to two factors.

- Firstly, Lopate says that women writers often chose more lucrative forms for publication and kept essay writing for journals and diaries.

- Secondly, Lopate opines that the tone of the essay in its early history was one of an "easy gentlemanly 'natural' authority that comes from being in the world."

Lopate suggests that the traditional realm of women in the centuries before the 20th did not confer anything similar to what was "perhaps a certain masculine arrogance" that allowed men to confidently speak on almost any subject.

Re-read the extracts taken from Sui Sin Far's essay. Compare them to some of the earlier examples in this section in terms of subject, tone and style.

The essay in the 20th and 21st centuries

There are certainly far too many well-known writers of the personal, philosophical, didactic, satirical, or critical essay for us to cover in this brief survey of the essay as a form of prose other than fiction. The expansion of the 'essay' into both audio and video forms (podcasts from national media services like the BBC and NPR and video essays from YouTube, for example) has vastly extended the range of access to essays.

Looking at two of the most significant essayists in the 20th century can give us a sense of how differently from the earliest essays language and angle of vision were handled at this time. Virginia Woolf and George Orwell are writers who operated in several forms. Their novels are well known, but they also occupy a significant place in the history of the essay in English.

Virginia Woolf in both of her *Common Readers* offers selections from over 100 essays – book reviews and critical essays – between 1926 and 1931. One of her essays, addressed to the common reader – you and me – was originally read at a school she visited. In it you can see the great feeling she had for books, appreciating them from the point of view of both reader and writer.

How Should One Read a Book?

* A paper read at a school.

In the first place, I want to emphasise the note of interrogation at the end of my title. Even if I could answer the question for myself, the answer would apply only to me and not to you. The only advice, indeed, that one person can give another about reading is to take no advice, to follow your own instincts, to use your own reason, to come to your own conclusions…

It is simple enough to say that since books have classes – fiction, biography, poetry – we should separate them and take from each what it is right that each should give us. Yet few people ask from books what books can give us. Most commonly we come to books with blurred and divided minds, asking of fiction that it shall be true, of poetry that it shall be false, of biography that it shall be flattering, of history that it shall enforce our own prejudices. If we could banish all such preconceptions when we read, that would be an admirable beginning. Do not dictate to your author; try to become him. Be his fellow-worker and accomplice. If you hang back, and reserve and criticise at first, you are preventing yourself from getting the fullest possible value from what you read. But if you open your mind as widely as possible, then signs and hints of almost imperceptible fineness, from the twist and turn of the first sentences, will bring you into the presence of a human being unlike any other. Steep yourself in this, acquaint yourself with this, and soon you will find that your author is giving you, or attempting to give you, something far more definite.

Virginia Woolf

George Orwell's essay 'Politics and the English Language' (1946) is one of his best known. It is both **political** and **literary** inasmuch as he is concerned with the shaping of language and its implications for politics. In his essay 'Marrakech', we can see a blend of travel narrative and political musing, as Orwell writes from a personal point of view about what he sees in the Moroccan city as a white military man: the poverty, the inequity, the Senegalese army passing him as he watches and muses:

> **Marrakech**
>
> But there is one thought which every white man… thinks when he sees a black army marching past. "How much longer can we go on kidding these people? How long before they turn their guns in the other direction?"
>
> It was curious, really. Every white man there had this thought stowed somewhere or other in his mind. I had it, so had other onlookers, so had the officers on their sweating chargers and the white N.C.O.'s marching in the ranks.
>
> *George Orwell*

While the style of the essay has certainly changed since those of Johnson or Bacon, Woolf and Orwell show us that the style remains quite **formal** and conscious of the careful choice of language and sentence structure.

Later essays in the 20th century and into the 21st century are often written in the same vein, but also extend into new modes. Susan Griffin's *Eros of Everyday Life: Essays on Ecology, Gender, and Society* (1995) moves the reader into the realm of **feminist theory** and/or **eco-criticism**; a field of reflection and critique which can be found in essays of Aldo Leopold, Barry Lopez, Terry Tempest Williams and Gretel Ehrlich, to name only a few. On the other hand, Anne Carson's *Eros the Bittersweet* (1998) is a set of philosophical and literary essays exploring the concept of 'eros' in classical writing.

Other essays can be **autobiographical** or **historical**. Bharati Mukherjee has written of her journey away from India to a new identity as an "American" writer in a "Four-hundred-year-old woman"; Ariel Dorfman in 'Saying Goodbye to Pablo' marks the moment of Pablo Neruda's death. Forms, too, can vary. Margaret Atwood wrote an essay called 'The Female Body', which is divided into seven separate sections. The essay, like other forms, adapts itself to experiments and variations.

The conventions of the literary essay

Throughout this exploration of the essay, features that characterize the form have been highlighted. The term 'convention' is somewhat elusive in this wide-ranging literary genre, but it might be useful to close with a list of features that could be considered conventions of the form.

First, in the matter of **voice**, we have seen that it can be univocal, with a single speaker, or dialogic, with a dialogue that can be presented in various ways. Some essays will use the mask of a **persona**.

The **subject** is very often quite limited, even to the point of minute attention. The essay is not often used to provide a 'large' or comprehensive view of the subject. Neither does it necessarily invoke scholarly support or proof; many would suggest there is a lower standard of proof demanded of the literary essay than other forms of rhetoric.

The intention or **purpose** of the essayist can vary widely; some essays are didactic, some are philosophical or political. Some essayists focus on very common issues of daily life; others take on significant matters of human behaviour.

There are essays that intend to provoke change through **satire**. Irony and humour are often used to attract the interest of the reader.

The essay can be personal and informal, or adopt a magisterial, authoritative or formal tone. Ordinarily, the personal essay may be intimate but not sentimental.

Autobiographical elements often appear in the form of brief narratives or anecdotes.

To return to the beginning of the history of the essay, there is fair agreement that the impulse of the essay is exactly what the French word, *essai*, suggests: the essay seeks to explore, to experiment with ideas, to try them out.

Activity

As a final consideration of the essay, read through the essay below from a significant contributor to the essay form in the 20th century, Annie Dillard. Answer the questions that follow.

Living Like Weasels

A weasel is wild. Who knows what he thinks? He sleeps in his underground den, his tail draped over his nose. Sometimes he lives in his den for two days without leaving. Outside, he stalks rabbits, mice, muskrats, and birds, killing more bodies than he can eat warm, and often dragging the carcasses home. Obedient to instinct, he bites his prey at the neck, either splitting the jugular vein at the throat or crunching the brain at the base of the skull, and he does not let go. One naturalist refused to kill a weasel who was socketed into his hand deeply as a rattlesnake. The man could in no way pry the tiny weasel off, and he had to walk half a mile to water, the weasel dangling from his palm, and soak him off like a stubborn label.

And once, says Ernest Thompson Seton – once, a man shot an eagle out of the sky. He examined the eagle and found the dry skull of a weasel fixed by the jaws to his throat. The supposition is that the eagle had pounced on the weasel and the weasel swiveled and bit as instinct taught him, tooth to neck, and nearly won. I would like to have seen that eagle from the air a few weeks or months before he was shot: was the whole weasel still attached to his feathered throat, a fur pendant? Or did the eagle eat what he could reach, gutting the living weasel with his talons before his breast, bending his beak, cleaning the beautiful airborne bones?

I have been reading about weasels because I saw one last week. I startled a weasel who startled me, and we exchanged a long glance.

Twenty minutes from my house, through the woods by the quarry and across the highway, is Hollins Pond, a remarkable piece of shallowness, where I like to go at sunset and sit on a tree trunk. Hollins Pond is also called Murray's Pond; it covers two acres of bottomland near Tinker Creek with six inches of water and six thousand lily pads. In winter, brown-and-white steers stand in the middle of it, merely dampening their hooves; from the distant shore they look like miracle itself, complete with miracle's nonchalance. Now, in summer, the steers are gone. The water lilies have blossomed and spread to a green horizontal plane that is terra firma to plodding blackbirds, and tremulous ceiling to black leeches, crayfish, and carp.

This is, mind you, suburbia. It is a five-minute walk in three directions to rows of houses, though none is visible here. There's a 55-mph highway at one end of the pond, and a nesting pair of wood ducks at the other. Under every bush is a muskrat hole or a beer

249

can. The far end is an alternating series of fields and woods, fields and woods, threaded everywhere with motorcycle tracks – in whose bare clay wild turtles lay eggs.

So, I had crossed the highway, stepped over two low barbed-wire fences, and traced the motorcycle path in all gratitude through the wild rose and poison ivy of the pond's shoreline up into high grassy fields. Then I cut down through the woods to the mossy fallen tree where I sit. This tree is excellent. It makes a dry, upholstered bench at the upper, marshy end of the pond, a plush jetty raised from the thorny shore between a shallow blue body of water and a deep blue body of sky.

The sun had just set. I was relaxed on the tree trunk, ensconced in the lap of lichen, watching the lily pads at my feet tremble and part dreamily over the thrusting path of a carp. A yellow bird appeared to my right and flew behind me. It caught my eye; I swiveled around – and the next instant, inexplicably, I was looking down at a weasel, who was looking up at me.

Weasel! I'd never seen one wild before. He was ten inches long, thin as a curve, a muscled ribbon, brown as fruitwood, soft-furred, alert. His face was fierce, small and pointed as a lizard's; he would have made a good arrowhead. There was just a dot of chin, maybe two brown hairs' worth, and then the pure white fur began that spread down his underside. He had two black eyes I didn't see, any more than you see a window. The weasel was stunned into stillness as he was emerging from beneath an enormous shaggy wild rose bush four feet away. I was stunned into stillness twisted backward on the tree trunk. Our eyes locked, and someone threw away the key.

Our look was as if two lovers, or deadly enemies, met unexpectedly on an overgrown path when each had been thinking of something else: a clearing blow to the gut. It was also a bright blow to the brain, or a sudden beating of brains, with all the charge and intimate grate of rubbed balloons. It emptied our lungs. It felled the forest, moved the fields, and drained the pond; the world dismantled and tumbled into that black hole of eyes. If you and I looked at each other that way, our skulls would split and drop to our shoulders. But we don't. We keep our skulls. So.

He disappeared. This was only last week, and already I don't remember what shattered the enchantment. I think I blinked, I think I retrieved my brain from the weasel's brain, and tried to memorize what I was seeing, and the weasel felt the yank of separation, the careening splash-down into real life and the urgent current of instinct. He vanished under the wild rose. I waited motionless, my mind suddenly full of data and my spirit with pleadings, but he didn't return.

Please do not tell me about "approach-avoidance conflicts". I tell you I've been in that weasel's brain for sixty seconds, and he was in mine. Brains are private places, muttering through unique and secret tapes – but the weasel and I both plugged into another tape simultaneously, for a sweet and shocking time. Can I help it if it was a blank?

What goes on in his brain the rest of the time? What does a weasel think about? He won't say. His journal is tracks in clay, a spray of feathers, mouse blood and bone: uncollected, unconnected, loose leaf, and blown.

I would like to learn, or remember, how to live. I come to Hollins Pond not so much to learn how to live as, frankly, to forget about it. That is, I don't think I can learn from a wild animal how to live in particular – shall I suck warm blood, hold my tail high, walk with my footprints precisely over the prints of my hands? – but I might learn something of mindlessness, something of the purity of living in the physical sense and the dignity of living without bias or motive. The weasel lives in necessity and we live in choice, hating necessity and dying at the last ignobly in its talons. I would like to live as I should, as the weasel lives as he should. And I suspect that for me the way is like the weasel's: open to time and death painlessly, noticing everything, remembering nothing, choosing the given with a fierce and pointed will.

I missed my chance. I should have gone for the throat. I should have lunged for that streak of white under the weasel's chin and held on, held on through mud and into the wild rose, held on for a dearer life. We could live under the wild rose wild as weasels, mute and uncomprehending. I could very calmly go wild. I could live two days in the den, curled, leaning on mouse fur, sniffing bird bones, blinking, licking, breathing musk, my hair tangled in the roots of grasses. Down is a good place to go, where the mind is single. Down is out, out of your ever-loving mind and back to your careless senses. I remember muteness as a prolonged and giddy fast, where every moment is a feast of utterance received. Time and events are merely poured, unremarked, and ingested directly, like blood pulsed into my gut through a jugular vein. Could two live that way? Could two live under the wild rose, and explore by the pond, so that the smooth mind of each is as everywhere present to the other, and as received and as unchallenged, as falling snow?

We could, you know. We can live any way we want. People take vows of poverty, chastity, and obedience – even of silence – by choice. The thing is to stalk your calling in a certain skilled and supple way, to locate the most tender and live spot and plug into that pulse. This is yielding, not fighting. A weasel doesn't "attack" anything; a weasel lives as he's meant to, yielding at every moment to the perfect freedom of single necessity.

I think it would be well, and proper, and obedient, and pure, to grasp your one necessity and not let it go, to dangle from it limp wherever it takes you. Then even death, where you're going no matter how you live, cannot you part. Seize it and let it seize you up aloft even, till your eyes burn out and drop; let your musky flesh fall off in shreds, and let your very bones unhinge and scatter, loosened over fields, over fields and woods, lightly, thoughtless, from any height at all, from as high as eagles.

Annie Dillard

Activity

1 Can you discern any structural approach or principle in this piece? (If you can't put your finger on one, can you say that the essay is integral or coherent?)

2 What attitude(s) does Dillard express towards the weasel?

3 Who is foregrounded here, the speaker or the weasel? How is this done? How did you make your determination?

4 What particular language choices do you find admirable or effective in this essay?

5 What do you think is the purpose or aim of this essay?

How to write an essay for the Paper 2 exam

Objectives

- to clarify the demands of the Paper 2 exam
- to explore good revision and essay strategies for Part 3
- to understand the role of genre and conventions in your answers
- to examine sample essays and their evaluation

> *"A good essay must have this permanent quality about it; it must draw its curtain round us, but it must be a curtain that shuts us in not out."*
> Virginia Woolf

This chapter recognizes your need to get answers. The answers will be given differently by various writers and teachers of writing, but the materials of this chapter are designed to offer you some guidelines that have worked for other IB students. By 'worked' we mean that students who practise all or most of the following recommendations should be able to produce essays that will contribute substantially to their overall IB grade.

What is the nature of the exam?

In the Paper 2 exam, worth 25 per cent of the overall grade, you will be offered three questions related to the genre you have studied with your class. One of these questions must and may only be answered using works that you have studied in Part 3 of your course. It's very important that you are clear about which works are legitimate to use, as using other works from your IB literature course will result in the examiner having to apply penalties for the use of invalid works.

The works may very likely be ones you have most recently studied in class, but not always, so you want to be sure you are very clear about getting this right. Examiners find it painful to penalize a perfectly sensible essay for using erroneous works – those not studied in Part 3 – but they are required to do so. It's simply a waste of your efforts to make this kind of mistake.

You will also want to avoid choosing a question from a genre that is not part of your Part 3 list. You may be tempted to choose a question on characterization from drama when you have studied novels and short stories, but don't do it! Again, examiners will have to penalize your work.

Your teacher will provide you with the list of works that are included in Part 3 of your particular syllabus. Other students around the world will have different lists. This great variety of works in different genres creates the necessity for asking the questions in particular ways.

It may be helpful for you to look at exam style questions that may appear on a Paper 2 exam paper. Then, for your own situation, complete the activity that follows.

Examples of Paper 2 exam style questions

Answer ONE of the following questions using only works from Part 3 of your syllabus. You must use at least two works in your answer.

Drama
1 Extended speeches by individual characters, either alone on the stage or with others present, are used in plays with various purposes and outcomes. Using at least two plays you have studied, show how playwrights use such speeches to achieve purposes particular to their plays.
2 Plays employ various kinds of structural divisions such as prologues and epilogues, act and scene divisions, even carefully placed intermissions. Discuss the dramatic uses made of these divisions in at least two plays you have studied.
3 "A play should make you laugh or should make you cry." With reference to at least two plays you have studied, discuss the methods playwrights use to create heightened emotion in the audience.

Poetry
1 The metaphor, based on analogies between things, is a common and expected element of poetry. Show how at least two poets in your study have heightened meaning or interest in their poems by the use of metaphor.
2 Focusing on the works of at least two poets you have studied, explore how imagery is used to create an impact on the reader.
3 Light and dark, country and city: Contrasts of many kinds are used by poets to sharpen their expression of ideas or feelings. In the works of at least two poets you have studied, explore the way contrasts have been used to achieve particular effects.

The novel and short story
1 Writers of fiction do not always relate events in the order in which they seem to occur in the worlds of their novels or short stories. Choosing two works by writers you have studied, show how variations of chronological order can be seen to serve the purposes of the stories.
2 A writer once said that the reader should be able to return to the first pages of a novel or short story and find resonances of the entire work. With reference to at least two works you have studied, consider the importance of the beginning to the work as a whole.
3 Who tells the story is often an essential feature in how far a reader finds a novel or short story credible, but sometimes it seems not to matter at all. Using two works you have studied, say how far the impact of the voice which tells the story is important to the success of the work.

Prose other than fiction: essays, travel narratives and autobiographies
1 Separating various stages of an autobiography or travel narrative is a challenge for writers in these forms. Choosing two works you have studied, discuss the way the writers have structured their works to make their material clear and interesting to their audiences.
2 Personal history as well as the backdrop of events surrounding that personal history are both significant to many works of prose other than fiction. In two works of this kind, discuss the handling of these two realms of existence.
3 Choosing at least two works you have studied, discuss the ways in which particular places are presented as well as their significance to the works as a whole.

We will be returning to these exam style questions throughout the chapter to make certain points.

Perhaps now you can see that there really are only three questions out of 12 that are available for you to answer. Just to be sure you are clear, complete the following activity.

Activity

1   At the time of the exam, you may be tired, anxious or distracted. What would be a good strategy for ensuring that you do not stray into questions on the wrong genre?

2   Which is the appropriate set of questions for you to write about?

3   Are there any other specific directions that you need to pay particular attention to?

4   a   Looking at each of 'your' legitimate questions, rank them in the order in which you would be likely to choose them.

   b   With a partner, discuss your choices in relation to the works you are studying or have studied so far.

Preparing for the exam

Because students have studied the works about which they must write, they have the advantage of being in control of at least half of the demands of the exam: they can set themselves the task of carefully re-reading both the works and the notes and supplementary material provided in class. No one can do this for you; it's a very individual thing.

The sections which follow address issues that, if you think about them and put them into practice, will give you a considerable advantage in delivering a successful, even excellent, Paper 2 essay.

Step 1: beginning revision

At the end of your course, the materials that you will need to have in your head when you enter the exam are selected from those discussed in Chapters 10–15. You will have read, discussed and written about one of the following **genres** and their **conventions**:

Night Owl

www.cartoonstock.com

1   Drama.

2   Poetry.

3   The novel and/or short story.

4   Prose other than fiction, including autobiography, travel narratives or essays, or a combination of these.

At higher level, you will have read four works, and at standard level you will have read three. To avoid confusion, you need to understand that in genres 3 and 4 above, you may have read various combinations of works. So, for example, your higher level class may have studied two novels and one or two groups of short stories, or you might have studied two autobiographies and two travel narratives. At standard level, you will have one less work or group of works, but there could be various combinations from within these genres.

Probably the most important thing in this part of your syllabus is to read the works while your class is studying them. You may feel that an acceptable strategy – owing to the demand of other classes or other parts of your life – is to be present in the class, pick up what you can of the works from that, and then read some or all of the works just before the exam. **If you intend to succeed in Paper 2**, this is simply a bad idea. You may be able to come up with some rationalizations for this course of action, but you are probably deceiving yourself.

> Do I need to read all of the works in order to succeed in the exam?

The answer is, "Yes". You may argue, "But I only need to write about two." While this is true, you may well find yourself in the following scenario:

> I can answer this question really well using my knowledge of Work 1, but Work 2, which is the only other work I know well enough to write about, is barely going to work (if at all). If only I knew Work 3, I could write a good answer.

You need to have a range of choices; you need to have good options.

'Knowing' a work is going to involve reading and then re-reading (even, if you can imagine it, more than once). What you want to have available when you go into the exam is something like a tapestry, or a wall of tools that you are quite familiar with; when you have chosen a question that you would like to write about, you can turn to your resource and select the materials that are most relevant, the particular threads of the tapestry or the tools from the wall.

Examiner's criteria

The first descriptor (or criterion) examiners will use to mark your essay is one based on your 'knowledge and understanding' of the works you choose to write about. In order to gain high marks, both of these features need to be demonstrated.

Firstly, you need to show that you know and understand the works you are writing about, and, secondly, that the elements of the works you choose to discuss are clearly related to the question you have chosen to answer.

> Remember: you will not have copies of the works you have studied in the exam room.

> You can see the complete set of the descriptors for standard level and higher level at the end of this chapter on pages 268–72.

This last part of the descriptor is often misunderstood or ignored by candidates, particularly those who do not have that tapestry or set of tools available in their heads. These candidates, usually with only a vague or superficial knowledge of the literary works – which is likely to be paired with limited understanding of the works – tend to call up just about anything they know and wrestle it into some kind of hoped-for relevance to the question.

You may, for example, know one or two characters that interest you, but are very limited in your knowledge of what exactly happens to them, or can recall little more than one or two details of the area the travel narrative involves. However, if the question wants you to show the line of development of that character, or discuss the way the travel narrator chooses to describe nature, you won't have much luck in answering that question.

Therefore, the first rule of success is to know the content and details of works you have studied for Part 3 very well.

Step 2: focusing on genre and convention and a methodology of revision

Not only are you expected to know, in detail, the content of the works, but you need to be clear about both the genre of the works you have studied and the conventions that are operating in that work. You will find material on both of these in Chapter 9, but also more specifically in the chapter devoted to the particular genre your class has studied.

In preparing for your exam, you could take the following self-test to see where you stand in terms of convention and genre, as well as knowing the correct titles and authors of the works you are free to use in Paper 2.

Activity

1 From which genre are the works of Part 3 chosen for your class?

2 List the three (standard level) or four (higher level) works you may legitimately choose from for your Paper 2 essay. You can list them in one of two ways: in date order according to when they were written, or in order of preference.

3 List three conventions of the genre that you have studied.

4 Give an example of each of the conventions you have chosen, using three different works.

Completing this activity may show you that you have a fair amount of revising to do before you are ready to take on the exam paper. Everyone has a certain individual style of revising, but the following suggests various ways in which students take on this task. Above all, digging out the books and your notes the night before the exam will not be the best approach or make up for the time you should have spent reading, writing and attending your English classes.

Methods of revising

Revising does not need to consume your whole life! By choosing a system that best suits you and your habits, you should be able to do a more than adequate job with this part of your IB literature course. Here are a few suggestions that have worked for various students:

- As you are re-reading the works and discussing them in class, insert colour-coded sticky notes labelled with various conventions, such as epiphany, recurring or central metaphors, shift of narrator, flashback, etc.

- If the style of learning in your classroom involves note-taking, either by hand or on your computer, go through and make a systematic list or outline, reorganizing the points that are most meaningful and important for *you*. Try to get them into some form that will make it easy for you to review in the last week before the exam (and the night before the exam).

- Use some mind-mapping software from the internet and create a visual set of connections to conventions and to the places where they are found in the works. For some people, the visual effect is the strongest aid to memory.

- Using a large sheet of paper, lay out a comparative chart in which you can identify such elements of a text as the title and author (correctly spelled); character names and alternate names like nicknames; place names; features of structure (acts and scenes, chapters, stanzas or sections); turning points or crucial scenes or lines, etc. Then, set up a space for each of your three or four works and fill in the feature from each work. This chart can give you the comparative features of the works in an easy format for last-minute review.

- Make a chart of the conventions you have addressed in class; supplement it with the list of conventions for the appropriate genre in this book. Try to find at least one, if not more, example from each of your three or four works and record them in a way that is easy for you to remember.

In these suggestions, your actual writing or reorganization will itself provide reinforcement of the things you need to know.

These are only a few of the ways in which you can revise for the exam, and you will have others that suit you particularly. You will notice that, so far, there is no suggestion that you make a list of direct quotations from your works and we need to talk about this.

Revising detail

One significant way of demonstrating knowledge as well as understanding of your Part 3 works is by referring in detail to specific places in the works. Sometimes people understand this demand as requiring candidates to directly quote from the works they have studied.

It should be understood that **direct quotation is not demanded** in order to write a persuasive response to the questions. Students do not have their texts with them in the exam, so it would hardly be fair to demand such a thing.

However, it can not be argued that being able to quote exactly what Blanche Dubois says as one of her exit lines in *A Streetcar Named Desire* is a disadvantage to your essay. If the words are well embedded in the essay and tied carefully to a point in the argument, then it is very likely that the reference reinforces the evidence of knowledge and possibly even understanding of both the question and the play.

If you are writing about poetry, being able to show that the convention of end-rhyme is effectively used to reinforce a central idea in the poem is helped by being able to cite an example.

How should one approach this issue? For some questions, such as the climactic moment in a novel, you may need to do no more than refer very specifically to who is involved, and what events occur and in what sequence to be able to answer very commendably and then offer your analysis in terms of the question. If, however, there are significant words uttered at the climactic moment of the novel by one of the characters, the moment described can be delivered more vividly if some words of the narrator or character are remembered and included. When Hamlet says he will trust Rosencrantz and Guildenstern as he would "an adder fanged", we understand very clearly his conclusions about them.

Individual differences are involved here. Some students find it easy to recall the exact words of a line of poetry or a crucial event in a work; for others, it is very challenging.

What *you* need to aim for with most genres is the ability to cite, re-describe or paraphrase material you may want to use to support your points. If you choose to make a list of favourite lines and memorize them, that may function as an aid to your remembering detail. It also creates a 'reading' of the work that marks an individual response.

What you don't want to do is to decide on a set of lines as a whole class – chosen communally or by your teacher – and all memorize the same ones. There are two reasons for this:

- This practice tends to undermine your individuality as a responder to a question.
- There is the temptation to insert, indeed pound, those lines into your essay simply because you know them, and it seems to you a waste not to use them.

Bringing your knowledge to the questions

Having given some thought to how you need to prepare yourself for Paper 2 in terms of the literary works you will be using, there are quite a few other aspects of this part of your assessment that will be helpful to consider.

In this course, you will need to be aware that the emphasis is on your grasp of the **features of a particular genre** along with the **conventions** writers use to construct the particular works.

In many ways, one of the big challenges you will face is finding one of the three questions that, from your point of view, will fit the way you have read, understood and appreciated at least two of the works in Part 3.

The other challenge is to rightly estimate what the question is asking for. You and your class will need to practise these questions to gain both clarity and confidence to respond successfully.

Activity

The following questions expect you to use at least two of the works you have studied to provide an answer. Re-write or re-phrase each of the questions in a way that makes it clear to you what you would need to do to offer a satisfactory response. (The focus here is on grasping the way questions may be posed.)

1 In at least two plays you have studied, comment on the way the playwright uses exit lines by one or more characters to either offer a rounded or satisfying resolution to thoughts and feelings raised in the play, or to attempt to provoke the audience to do more thinking.

2 A turning point in a novel or short story is used in many ways by writers to evolve the plot or to reveal something crucial about a character. In at least two works you have studied, show how two writers have used a turning point in their narratives.

3 Poems always have at least one voice, sometimes more than one. In at least two poems you have studied, examine the ways that two poets have either foregrounded or subdued the voice that speaks in the poems and what effect that has on the power or impact of the poem.

4 In both autobiographies and travel narratives, the reader generally expects the progression to be a linear one, where growing up or going on a journey is told in the way events are likely to have happened. In order to add interest, sometimes writers interrupt or alter this chronological sequence. Discuss the choices at least two of your writers have made in this matter and the effects on the interest and credibility of the works.

5 Essays are written to express either thoughts or feelings or both in relation to some particular subject. In the essays of at least two writers you have studied, discuss the way the writers have used the conventions of the essay to either attempt to elicit thinking or feeling from their audience.

You will need to practise these questions and others in various ways; the next section gives you some practice strategies to help you.

Step 3: learning effective strategies for interpreting Paper 2 questions

One of the most common errors students make when looking at their choices of question is to read the question superficially, focusing on a familiar word like 'character' or 'dramatic tension' and then inventing the question they *wish* they had been asked.

Certain words such as these are going to appear over and over again in questions. It is important to know that there are two elements to these questions:

• A central or recurring element such as the one described above.

• A particular angle for this exam, one that includes the recurring element but asks for something specific to that element.

For example, two questions on the novel or short story might include character:

1　A writer in the genre of novel and short story has many tools at hand for developing character. In the characterization of two minor but important characters in two works you have studied, show how two conventions you consider important have been used to make the characters memorable in spite of being minor.

2　A major convention used by novel and short story writers in developing their characterizations is a moment of revelation or epiphany. In the works of two writers you have studied, examine closely such a moment and the effect it has on the creation of the character.

You will, perhaps, think, "Aha! I'll write about character in these two works." What you need to do is step back and ask yourself, "*What* about character am I being asked to discuss?" This will be the secret, or at least one of them, to your success in this exam.

There are various initial strategies for ensuring that you are able to create an answer that will merit high marks in the second descriptor the examiner needs to apply: 'response to the question'. What you should be aiming for is Level 5: "The student responds to the main implications and some subtleties of the question, with relevant and carefully explored ideas. An effective comparison is made of the works used in relation to the question."

If you only decide that you will write something about character or even characterization (without addressing its appropriate focus on the methods the author has used), you are only likely to make a basic response.

Strategy 1
- In the two questions above, make a list of *all* the elements included in each question.
- Identify both the center of each question (the recurring element) and the particular angle for this exam.
- Finally, make a list where you prioritize the elements of each question. What is central? What is secondary?

When you have practised these things, you will probably be on firm ground to begin making other decisions about writing this essay.

Strategy 2
Another strategy to make sure you start from a strong base in your essay is to re-write the question in other words. Very often this can help students to see the terms of the question from a more personal angle.

Now that you have had a little practice with this kind of question, we need to explore the nature of the essay you need to write in response.

Step 4: knowing what kind of essay you are expected to write and the strategies that may help you
One of the skills assessed in this part of the IB literature course is writing about two works you have studied in response to one of three questions. What you are asked to produce is a **comparative essay**.

Activity
Look back to the exam style questions on page 253. Choose one of the questions from the genre your class has studied. Use it to test out the two strategies opposite.

It is very important that you are clear about what this exam essay involves. Over the years, you may have done very different things when asked to write a 'comparative essay' and yet they all seemed to have satisfied the demand.

In order to write a good Paper 2 essay, you will need to:

- discuss both similarities and differences; the essay is an exercise in **comparison and contrast**
- 'take a position' on the material of the question, because the essay is not just a re-description or a listing of similarities and differences, but a view or an **argument** *about* the similarities and differences, and possibly even some evaluation of their significance.

Comparison and contrast

When you consult a source, whether book or web page, to check how to write a comparison/contrast essay, you will discover that it is a fairly standard academic demand – and not just for the study of literature. Many university subjects will ask you to construct a piece of writing that compares and contrasts the features of some aspect of human learning or experience. Here are a few titles of sample essays from various sources:

- 'Grant and Lee [American Civil War generals]: a study in contrasts.'
- 'Compare and contrast constructions built in two architectural styles: Baroque and Rococo.'
- 'Compare and contrast causes of the American and the French revolution.'

Both your teacher and a wide variety of sources will be available to offer you their most effective advice about how to proceed towards a successful comparison/contrast essay. These will range from lists to Venn diagrams, for example, as a preliminary stage and you should be able to find one procedure that works for you as an individual.

Essentially, however, you will need to know your literary works well enough so that you can effectively select some features that are similar and some that are different. All of these must be relevant to the particular topic and the particular angle that your exam question requests you address.

Let's take one of the exam style questions on page 253 (see below). First, decide what the **central topic** of the question is and, secondly, what **particular angle** on that question is required for your essay.

---

1 Extended speeches by individual characters, either alone on the stage or with others present, are used in plays with various purposes and outcomes. Using at least two plays you have studied, show how playwrights use such speeches to achieve purposes particular to their plays.

- **What does the examiner expect you to focus on in your answer?**

  Longer speeches by characters.

- **What particular angle is expected?**

In this question, you will be invited to look at "various purposes and outcomes". Depending on your point of view, this breadth of possibility may be an advantage or a hurdle. You can see that *you* will have to choose a purpose (or two) that you believe the playwright has in using extended speeches, and you will also want to consider the purpose and effect of those choices. So, what might be some possibilities for you to argue about your works?

1 Longer speeches are used to reveal something otherwise hidden.

2 Such speeches are used to add a new dimension to the characterization so far delivered by the playwright.

3 Longer speeches are used to introduce a new element of conflict.

4 The speeches are there to provide a concluding impression of the character.

These are only some possibilities; you are likely to think of others based on the way your class has studied such works.

One of the elements of the process of planning how you will answer this question will be helped if you train yourself to think of both similarities and differences in relation to the two plays. This will allow you more possibilities.

From the list above, you might want to choose point 1 and show how two playwrights handle that purpose in similar but significantly different ways. *Or* you might want to choose point 3 for one play and point 4 for a second play, showing that the same convention can be used in different ways with different effects.

There is simply no 'one size fits all' formula for how you will handle a question with the works you have studied. Even within your own class group, using the same works, different students will go in different directions.

The single biggest thing you want to think about and remember is that **differences** are just as important as **similarities**. Students writing Paper 2 essays tend to make one recurrent error: they build their whole essay around re-describing the similarities of a particular feature and leave it at that. This approach does not produce a successful IB literature comparative essay. We want you to aim for something more complex and interesting than re-describing similarities.

So what would be more interesting and complex?

Well, you might show that both playwrights have given the protagonist a long speech very close to the end of the play (a similarity), but that the speeches have very different effects on the people around them. The playwrights may use different effects to change the audience's impression of the character, resulting in a reversal of how the audience is likely to feel and what the viewers now think of the protagonist. The effects of these strategies could be quite similar or very different.

Choice of interpretation could make for a good display of your knowledge and understanding, as well as offer a direct answer to the question. You are also likely to be led into some evaluation of the playwrights' practices and their relative success.

You will probably have made an argument about how extended speeches are used in these plays. What does this mean?

An argument about literary works

Paper 2 requires that you write:

- a 'literary argument'
- comparatively.

Question: So what is a 'literary argument'?

It is constructed when you take a position on the way extended speeches, for example, are used by two playwrights.

It is about the way the play is constructed using the conventions of the genre, in this case extended or long speeches by individual characters, often called monologues. For example:

> Although Tennessee Williams gives most of the extended speeches to Tom in *The Glass Menagerie,* Tom's double role as narrator and character makes his speeches less compelling to the audience than the way Arthur Miller handles the longer speeches of Willy in *Death of a Salesman.*

This is a position or thesis that can be argued: we can agree with this notion of Tom or we might disagree and argue that his speeches are just as effective as Miller's assignment of speeches to Willy Loman.

An effective essay on this position should include the first three elements of the descriptors that the examiner who reads your essay will use for evaluation:

- Knowledge and understanding of the two plays.
- A response to the terms of the question.
- An appreciation of the convention(s) highlighted in the question.

Finally, the examiner will be looking for an easy-to-follow presentation of your ideas, which brings us to another big question relating to comparison/contrast essays: how will I organize my ideas about the two plays into a good essay?

Organizing an effective comparative essay

Again, your teacher will have some effective ideas and strategies for approaching this challenge – and it *is* a challenge. You will also find plenty of advice in writing manuals and other sources.

Essentially, you will need to:

- lead a reader through the relevant similarities and differences
- decide what you want to argue about and its particular angle
- keep the focus on the literary convention you are discussing.

This is quite a lot to handle, although all the elements tend to blend into one another as you put your thought processes on to paper. At the very least, you will want to decide on one of two approaches. These may be labelled and handled differently in your class but, whatever the approach, it must allow the reader to follow your argument easily.

Either:

a You will set out your introduction and then discuss the aspects of one work, use a transitional paragraph, and move on to discuss your second work. Some call this the 'block essay'.

Or:

b You will decide on perhaps two or three similarities and differences and discuss those in relation to each of the works. This format is sometimes called the 'topical essay'.

This set of distinctions is very broad but, above all, it should be an essay that is both easy to follow and, if you can manage it, interesting to your reader.

The fourth descriptor that the examiner will be using to evaluate your essay, as you can see from pages 269 and 271 is "Organization and development". The structure you use will be judged by this descriptor. Please also note the inclusion of the word "development".

You must not only cite points that will support your argument, but you must develop them. In other words:

● select your best evidence to support whatever claims you make

● develop the points to the best of your ability in the allotted time.

The final element of evaluation for your essays in this exam is, as in every assessment you will complete, your use of language. Review the materials on language in Chapter 2.

No one has any doubt, including your teachers and your examiners, that producing a good Paper 2 answer is a difficult task. Still, you will have been working within the frame of the IB English A literature course for two years, and many of the skills outlined above have been in a constant and incremental process of development. Before you enter the exam, you will have practised both with Paper 2 questions and with writing answers.

Rather than theorizing or advising you further at this point, it will be useful to look at two examples of essays that address the exam style question on page 253 on extended speeches. Even though you may not know well, or at all, the plays being discussed, it will be helpful for you to examine the essay for the following features:

1 Do we as readers know which plays are being discussed from the very beginning?

2 Do we see that the writer of the essay is 'taking a position' on the question?

3 Does that position provide a line of coherence throughout the whole essay?

4 Is the line of argument one we can follow?

5 Is the essay conscious of both similarities and differences?

6 Is the writer explicitly or implicitly conscious of the convention of long speeches or monologues?

7 Does the writer reveal detailed knowledge with direct evidence from the plays of both the existence and effect of the convention?

To accomplish all seven of these goals would perhaps result in the 'perfect' essay, something very difficult to achieve under exam conditions. Looking at the two following essays, use these seven points to decide to what degree you find the following essays successful.

The first essay is by a standard level student. It is important to remember that both standard and higher level students will be responding to the same set of questions. However, standard level students will have 90 minutes to complete their essay and higher level students will have 120 minutes.

---

1 Extended speeches by individual characters, either alone on the stage or with others present, are used in plays with various purposes and outcomes. Using at least two plays you have studied, show how playwrights use such speeches to achieve purposes particular to their plays.

Standard level student essay

In both *A Streetcar Named Desire*, by Tennessee Williams, and *Translations*, by Brian Friel, extended speeches by individual characters are used to advance the characterization of particular characters who reveal a fear of inadequacy.

In *A Streetcar Named Desire*, Blanche gives her first significant speech in Scene 10 where she shows her first outburst of desperation to Stella. This is only the first of many monologues given by Blanche as the play continues, though, for Blanche has many 'issues' which must be expanded on to the audience. For example, she gives a similar speech later in Scene 6 when she explains to Mitch her fallout with her first marriage. There she clearly demonstrates her neediness as a consequence of her traumatic past.

Blanche's monologue in the first scene also showcases, or introduces rather, her insanity. She speaks of the deaths of her parents and the loss of Belle Reve, both touchy subjects, with such vigour that manifests her traumatic life. Williams establishes this over-the-top energy by carefully placing his punctuation – the first seven sentences end in exclamation points to indicate Blanche's excitement, and they are followed by a few sentences ending in periods to show the change in tone as she moves on to accuse Stella.

This leads to the third point that is revealed through Blanche's first major speech: the demonstration of her arrogance and lack of sensitivity towards Stella. Blanche speaks to her sister with such condescension that she seems to attempt to portray herself as a heroine. This is evident in her simultaneous uses of both the first and second-person perspectives. The condescending "you" refers to Stella when Blanche accuses: "You just came home in time for the funerals, Stella…Where were you? In bed with your – Polack!" She then boosts her own self-esteem with the first person by claiming, "I, I, *I* took the blows…"

These three points help to characterize Blanche, who is a fully developed and dynamic character who runs the plot. Right from the opening, the audience begins to understand that these traits of Blanche which are introduced in the speech are aimed at demonstrating her less obvious feelings of inadequacy. The poor woman has lost her family, her home, her job, and her husband (whose suicide was her fault), so it is no wonder she develops a neediness so excessive that it leads her to insanity.

Similarly, in *Translations*, Friel uses the extended speeches of Yolland to characterize his feelings of inadequacy. However, Yolland does not exaggerate his emotions to the point of insanity as does Blanche. In fact, Yolland's extended speeches are necessary for any understanding of his character by the audience because he is so reticent.

In Act 2, Scene 1, Yolland explains to Owen that he was thanking Doalty for his kindness. This leads Yolland to acknowledge his lack of skill in speaking Irish. He says with such submission: "I suppose you're right: I suppose I couldn't live here…" This portrays Yolland's lack of self-esteem and insecurity.

At the end of his first expressive speech, Yolland confesses to Owen the real reason he is in Ireland: his father sent him to India, but he missed the boat. He was so embarrassed that he was unable to face his father and had no better options. This is the epitome of his feeling of inadequacy, for he has failed to please his father. I believe this serves as an archetypal situation which models a common father-son relationship as a side-embellishment to the play (aside from the language/colonization conflict).

Also, Yolland's regretted attempt to win his father's approval foils the attempt of Manus to prevent his father's guilt. Both convey a sense of servitude to their fathers, but Manus does so out of care for Hugh's feelings and conscience. We can assume that Yolland only does so for the personal praise of a job well done and for the approval of his father.

It is especially important that Yolland conveys these feelings through his extended dialogue with Owen, because he is otherwise too shy to speak so deeply in front of the other characters. While Blanche does not seem to have this problem, it is clear that the two are both demonstrating feelings of inadequacy and neediness. Williams and Friel successfully chose these traits to characterize in these speeches perhaps because of their ability to resonate with the audience. Hence, by further developing this archetype of insecurity, the playwrights provide a stronger connection for the audience.

This second essay, in response to the same question, is written by a higher level candidate:

Higher level student essay

Although Ariel Dorfman uses extended speeches much more in *Death and the Maiden* than Tennessee Williams does in *A Streetcar Named Desire*, the effects of these speeches are similar in these two plays. As the only characters to give extended speeches in these two dramas are women who have been abused in some way, the expression of their experiences and feelings through monologues is both powerful and important to the development of the plot. These extended speeches allow Dorfman and Williams to develop the personalities of the protagonists, create tension and advance the storyline of their respective plays without the use of excess dialogue between characters.

It is important to remember that the plays in question were written for performance. In a play, the easiest and most common way to give the audience information is through dialogue. Dorfman avoids long and arduous conversations between characters by having Paulina explain much of what the audience needs to know through an extended speech. In Act 1, Scene 4 (pages 19–22), Paulina ties and gags Roberto and proceeds to have a one-way conversation with her captive. By allowing Paulina to speak freely, without interruption, Dorfman succeeds in passing a great deal of information on to the audience that would have normally taken an excessive amount of dialogue to convey.

Because Roberto is present but unable to speak, Paulina gives the impression that she is talking to herself. She rambles and speaks to Roberto in a very conversational way that, under different circumstances, would be humorous. This leaves the audience feeling confused. Roberto, a Good Samaritan and helper of Gerardo, is trussed to a chair with a gun to his head, and yet Paulina is acting like it's a picnic in the park. This forces the audience to question Paulina's sanity, and, while this speech gives the audience a lot of information, it also keeps the result of the situation hidden: who knows what this crazy woman is going to do? Paulina's speech seems light and happy: "But here I am chatting away when I'm supposed to make breakfast, aren't I, a nice breakfast? Now you like – let's see, ham sandwiches, wasn't it?" (Page 20.) The very nonchalant way that Paulina addresses Roberto gives a sinister feeling to the scene. The audience may ask: what is there to be light and happy about? As a result, a feeling of slight apprehension plagues the reader. This is definitely intentional, as it keeps the audience on their toes, wanting more.

The audience learns a lot about Paulina through her extended speeches. In total, she gives three of these speeches. They become more serious as time progresses: the first, as mentioned above, is fluttery with a sinister feeling. In the second speech (pages 29–30), Paulina mentions some of the things that happened to her, and starts accusing Roberto. In her last extended speech (pages 57–60), she recounts the horrible story of her capture and torture. Through these three monologues, the audience gleans a lot about her character. The way in which she tries to hide her pain in the first speech shows the audience how she has been holding in her feelings: trying to cover them with a fake, flowery façade. The ease with which Paulina watches Roberto sweat and suffer under interrogation also suggests that she is hurt, or crazed, enough to go as far as it takes. Dorfman uses extended speeches to allow Paulina to show her character to the audience. When she is the only person talking, she reveals much more about herself then when her husband is present, or when Roberto is able to speak.

It is interesting how Dorfman uses extended speeches to transport the audience from the present to either the past or the future. When Paulina 'converses' alone with Roberto for the second time, she recounts much of her and Gerardo's history. While she is speaking in the present tense, most of what she is talking about is from the past. Another example of this comes in Act 3, Scene 2, when Paulina's story becomes Roberto's confession. They each talk about atrocities that happened several years ago, bringing the audience up to speed on past events. Dorfman uses dialogue between characters for developing situations that occur in the present. For example, after Paulina recites her second extended speech, she and Gerardo get into an argument about what to do with Roberto: "*Gerardo*: Paulina, this is intolerable. I must talk with you. *Paulina*: And who's stopping you? *Gerardo*: Alone. *Paulina*: Why? The doctor used to discuss everything in my presence, they –" (page 33). In her speech, Paulina has revealed

information about her past and yet as soon as she starts conversing with her husband, she moves back into the present. To fill in the back-story, Dorfman transports the audience from the current plot to the past through the use of extended speeches. In *Death and the Maiden*, the only way the audience finds out about what has happened to Paulina is through these extended speeches.

The effects of extended speeches are similar in *A Streetcar Named Desire* and *Death and the Maiden*, especially in terms of character development. Both Williams and Dorfman use these speeches to give their audiences insight into their two traumatized protagonists: Blanche and Paulina. Both of these women dislike recounting or being questioned about past events. Paulina only reveals things about her past when she does not feel pressured: when she is the only one talking. Similarly, Blanche dislikes being questioned and usually hides behind a fake and 'ladylike' shield. Blanche reveals some of the most important things about her past when she is giving extended speeches, unhindered by anyone's prying questions. It is through these monologues that the audience learns about the real Blanche: the strong woman who has endured numerous hardships.

Throughout most of *A Streetcar Named Desire*, Blanche acts as if she is innocent and pure: untarnished by anything. Whenever she is conversing with someone, she puts on this show. Similar to Paulina, she only really comes out of her shell in extended speeches. In this case, Williams is using these speeches to develop Blanche's character. For example, when Blanche first arrives in New Orleans and meets Stella, she is excited and fluttery, all the while maintaining her air of innocence. However, when Belle Reve is mentioned, Blanche flies off the hook and becomes angry and defensive. In this long extended speech (pages 26–7), Blanche becomes a different person: she appears scared, nervous and even angry. In this example, Williams uses the extended speech to show a different side to Blanche. He develops the audience's knowledge of Blanche's character by having her express her thoughts and feelings in a long monologue.

If Blanche's superficial conversations were the only thing that the audience saw of Blanche, they wouldn't think much of her character. She usually appears flighty and air-headed, except when she is giving a long speech. These rare occasions are when the audience sees Blanche's intelligence. For example, in Scene 4 (page 72), Blanche goes on a long rant about Stanley. It is the day after he beats up Stella, and Blanche is appalled that her sister goes back to him so easily. While this long speech is very dramatic, Blanche uses very eloquent language and humorous comparisons to describe Stanley. While it really depends on how the actor is playing her, there is a certain decisiveness in Blanche's language in this excerpt that is not seen anywhere else. Williams uses her long speech to show the audience that Blanche is not just a superficial, flowery person, but that she can express her ideas intelligently.

Throughout most of this play, Blanche's history remains obscure. It is obvious that something has happened to her because of the way she acts, but the audience never finds out what it is until she gives an extended speech about it. Blanche avoids talking about her history during almost the entire play. When Stanley questions Blanche in Scene 2 (pages 37–44), she evades answering most of his questions. The audience learns of Blanche's history only when she decides to reveal it in a long speech. In this particular scene (pages 95–6), Blanche tells the heartbreaking story of how she discovered that her husband was gay. It is one of the only times in the play that Blanche leaves herself vulnerable. Yet again, this shows the audience a side of Blanche they have never seen before: sensitive, sorrowful and broken.

Both Tennessee Williams and Ariel Dorfman use extended speeches to develop the characters of their protagonists. Paulina and Blanche are both very good at hiding their emotions, and especially their pasts. In *Death and the Maiden*, Paulina's long speeches give insight into her history, transporting the audience from the present to her past. Blanche's monologues in *A Streetcar Named Desire* help the audience to understand why she is so nervous and superficial. In both cases, extended speeches allow the audience to see past the initial view of these two women, allowing the audience to better understand their actions through the use of this particular convention.

Paper 2 assessment criteria: essay (standard level)

Criterion A: knowledge and understanding
- How much knowledge and understanding has the student shown of the Part 3 works studied in relation to the questions answered?

Marks	Level descriptor
0	The work does not reach a standard described by the descriptors below.
1	There is little knowledge and no understanding of the part 3 works in relation to the question answered.
2	There is some knowledge but little understanding of the part 3 works in relation to the question answered.
3	There is adequate knowledge and some understanding of the part 3 works in relation to the question answered.
4	There is good knowledge and understanding of the part 3 works in relation to the question answered.
5	There is very good knowledge and understanding of the part 3 works in relation to the question answered.

Criterion B: response to the question
- How well has the student understood the specific demands of the question?
- To what extent has the student responded to these demands?
- How well have the works been compared and contrasted in relation to the demands of the question?

Marks	Level descriptor
0	The work does not reach a standard described by the descriptors below.
1	The student shows virtually no awareness of the main implications of the question, and ideas are mostly irrelevant or insignificant. There is no meaningful comparison of the works used in relation to the question.
2	The student shows limited awareness of the main implications of the question, and ideas are sometimes irrelevant or insignificant. There is little meaningful comparison of the works used in relation to the question.
3	The student responds to most of the main implications of the question, with relevant ideas. A comparison is made of the works used in relation to the question, but it may be superficial.
4	The student responds to the main implications of the question, with consistently relevant ideas. An appropriate comparison is made of the works used in relation to the question.
5	The student responds to the main implications and some subtleties of the question, with relevant and carefully explored ideas. An effective comparison is made of the works used in relation to the question.

Criterion C: appreciation of the literary conventions of the genre

- To what extent does the student identify and appreciate the use of literary conventions in relation to the question and the works used?

Marks	Level descriptor
0	The work does not reach a standard described by the descriptors below.
1	Virtually no literary conventions are identified, and there is no development relevant to the question and/or the works used.
2	Examples of literary conventions are sometimes correctly identified, but there is little development relevant to the question and the works used.
3	Examples of literary conventions are mostly correctly identified, and there is some development relevant to the question and the works used.
4	Examples of literary conventions are clearly identified and effectively developed, with relevance to the question and the works used.
5	Examples of literary conventions are clearly identified and effectively developed, with clear relevance to the question and the works used.

Criterion D: organization and development

- How well organized, coherent and developed is the presentation of ideas?

Marks	Level descriptor
0	The work does not reach a standard described by the descriptors below.
1	Ideas have virtually no organization or structure, and coherence and/or development are lacking.
2	Ideas have some organization and structure, but there is very little coherence and/or development.
3	Ideas are adequately organized, with a suitable structure and some attention paid to coherence and development.
4	Ideas are well organized, with a good structure, coherence and development.
5	Ideas are effectively organized, with a very good structure, coherence and development.

Criterion E: language

- How clear, varied and accurate is the language?
- How appropriate is the choice of register, style and terminology? (Register refers, in this context, to the student's use of elements such as vocabulary, tone, sentence structure and terminology appropriate to the task.)

Marks	Level descriptor
0	The work does not reach a standard described by the descriptors below.
1	Language is rarely clear and appropriate; there are many errors in grammar, vocabulary and sentence construction, and little sense of register and style.
2	Language is sometimes clear and carefully chosen; grammar, vocabulary and sentence construction are fairly accurate, although errors and inconsistencies are apparent; the register and style are to some extent appropriate to the task.
3	Language is clear and carefully chosen, with an adequate degree of accuracy in grammar, vocabulary and sentence construction despite some lapses; register and style are mostly appropriate to the task.
4	Language is clear and carefully chosen, with a good degree of accuracy in grammar, vocabulary and sentence construction; register and style are consistently appropriate to the task.
5	Language is very clear, effective, carefully chosen and precise, with a high degree of accuracy in grammar, vocabulary and sentence construction; register and style are effective and appropriate to the task.

Paper 2 assessment criteria: essay (higher level)

Criterion A: knowledge and understanding

- How much knowledge and understanding has the student shown of the Part 3 works studied in relation to the questions answered?

Marks	Level descriptor
0	The work does not reach a standard described by the descriptors below.
1	There is some knowledge but virtually no understanding of the part 3 works in relation to the question answered.
2	There is mostly adequate knowledge and some superficial understanding of the part 3 works in relation to the question answered.
3	There is adequate knowledge and understanding of the part 3 works in relation to the question answered.
4	There is good knowledge and understanding of the part 3 works in relation to the question answered.
5	There is perceptive knowledge and understanding of the part 3 works in relation to the question answered.

Criterion B: response to the question

- How well has the student understood the specific demands of the question?
- To what extent has the student responded to these demands?
- How well have the works been compared and contrasted in relation to the demands of the question?

Marks	Level descriptor
0	The work does not reach a standard described by the descriptors below.
1	The student shows little awareness of the main implications of the question, and ideas are mainly irrelevant and/or insignificant. There is little meaningful comparison of the works used in relation to the question.
2	The student responds to some of the main implications of the question with some relevant ideas. There is a superficial attempt to compare the works used in relation to the question.
3	The student responds to most of the main implications of the question with consistently relevant ideas. There is adequate comparison of the works used in relation to the question.
4	The student responds to the main implications and some subtleties of the question, with relevant and carefully explored ideas. The comparison makes some evaluation of the works used in relation to the question.
5	The student responds to all the implications, as well as the subtleties of the question, with convincing and thoughtful ideas. The comparison includes an effective evaluation of the works in relation to the question.

Criterion C: appreciation of the literary conventions of the genre

- To what extent does the student identify and appreciate the use of literary conventions in relation to the question and the works used?

Marks	Level descriptor
0	The work does not reach a standard described by the descriptors below.
1	Some literary conventions are identified but there is limited development relevant to the question and/or the works used.
2	Examples of literary conventions are sometimes correctly identified and developed, with some relevance to the question and the works used.
3	Examples of literary conventions are satisfactorily identified and developed, with relevance to the question and the works used.
4	Examples of literary conventions are clearly identified and effectively developed, with relevance to the question and the works used.
5	Examples of literary conventions are perceptively identified and persuasively developed, with clear relevance to the question and the works used.

Criterion D: organization and development

- How well organized, coherent and developed is the presentation of ideas?

Marks	Level descriptor
0	The work does not reach a standard described by the descriptors below.
1	Ideas have little organization; there may be a superficial structure, but coherence and/or development are lacking.
2	Ideas have some organization, with a recognizable structure, but coherence and development are often lacking.
3	Ideas are adequately organized, with a suitable structure and attention paid to coherence and development.
4	Ideas are effectively organized, with a very good structure, coherence and development.
5	Ideas are persuasively organized, with excellent structure, coherence and development.

Criterion E: language

- How clear, varied and accurate is the language?

- How appropriate is the choice of register, style and terminology? (Register refers, in this context, to the student's use of elements such as vocabulary, tone, sentence structure and terminology appropriate to the task.)

Marks	Level descriptor
0	The work does not reach a standard described by the descriptors below.
1	Language is rarely clear and appropriate; there are many errors in grammar, vocabulary and sentence construction, and little sense of register and style.
2	Language is sometimes clear and carefully chosen; grammar, vocabulary and sentence construction are fairly accurate, although errors and inconsistencies are apparent; the register and style are to some extent appropriate to the task.
3	Language is clear and carefully chosen, with an adequate degree of accuracy in grammar, vocabulary and sentence construction despite some lapses; register and style are mostly appropriate to the task.
4	Language is clear and carefully chosen, with a good degree of accuracy in grammar, vocabulary and sentence construction; register and style are consistently appropriate to the task.
5	Language is very clear, effective, carefully chosen and precise, with a high degree of accuracy in grammar, vocabulary and sentence construction; register and style are effective and appropriate to the task.

17 The extended essay

Objectives

- to make clear the position and nature of the extended essay in your IB Diploma Programme
- to define and clarify the process of producing the essay
- to provide some helpful advice to help you succeed in this IB Diploma Programme requirement

What, where, when and who? A quick summary

The IB Diploma Programme offers a clear definition, for both students and teachers, of the extended essay: "an in-depth study of a focused topic." These few words can be your best and clearest guide to what you will undertake with this IB Diploma Programme requirement.

This requirement for the IB Diploma Programme appears at the center of the **IB hexagon** along with your theory of knowledge course and your creativity, action, service (CAS) requirements. In the final evaluation of your IB work, the extended essay is evaluated in conjunction with your theory of knowledge performance to provide additional diploma marks to those you have earned in your courses.

The point at which you begin to work on your extended essay will be determined within your individual school. It is fairly typical to begin the process in the second half of your first year in the IB programme. Particular details will be given to your supervisor; in the case of an essay in English A literature, this will most likely be one of the teachers in your English department.

Decisions

You can choose the subject for your extended essay. You do not have to choose English; you may decide to write the essay on any of the subjects you are studying. When studying an IB Diploma Programme subject, the IB wants to see proof that you are:

- able to choose and define an appropriate topic
- capable of research in a particular discipline
- able to develop and present a piece of writing that reflects your competence in clear and well-organized formal writing.

Once you have decided on an essay in English, the next significant challenge will be to discover a question, in this case about literature, that you are interested to explore. The discovery of this **research question** may turn out to be one of your biggest challenges in the extended essay process.

At this point, you will undoubtedly need to find, and then consult with, the person who will be the supervisor of your essay. Your school will have a process for introducing you to the essay, but every extended essay must have a supervisor who helps the student through the process.

The role of the supervisor will be to:

- help you define your research question
- suggest materials and sources that may help you to focus on your question
- guide you in creating an outline and a first draft
- advise you on the format and presentation of sources
- read your final draft and conduct a *viva voce* (discussion).

Parameters for appropriate English A literature extended essays

First, you need to understand the scope of the literature permitted in this subject. There are three categories of literature that you may use:

- **Category 1**: studies of a literary work(s) originally written in English.
- **Category 2**: studies of a literary work(s) originally written in English compared with literary work(s) originally written in another language.
- **Category 3**: studies in language.

> It is important to note that in all categories you are permitted to range fairly widely in your choice of works about which to write: you may write about works by Shakespeare or about J. R. R. Tolkien. You can write about local and contemporary writers. Just remember that this is a **literary essay**, not one that focuses chiefly on sociological or other considerations.

Activity

1 With a partner, think about some possible topics, based on works you have studied in class, for extended essays in one, two or three categories. It will be helpful to have a general class discussion about these, as your teacher will be in a position to help you discern which topics are likely to work, or which could be improved upon to provide a good course of action.

2 After deciding as a class on three or four likely topics, reframe these as research questions.

For example: if one of the topics is 'Death in five poems of Emily Dickinson', the research question would both narrow down the topic and present it as a question to be explored:

"How does Emily Dickinson present death as both fearful and friendly in five of her most popular poems?"

Sample topics for categories 1 and 2:

Category 1:

- "The effect of additional chapters in the later version of Louise Erdrich's *Love Medicine*."

- "The presentation of motherhood in *Beloved* by Toni Morrison."
- "Black humour in Heller's *Catch-22* and Vonnegut's *Slaughterhouse Five*."
- "The role and significance of dance in Austen's *Pride and Prejudice* and *Emma*."

Category 2:

- "The unreliable narrator in Ford's *The Good Soldier* and Machado de Assis's *Don Casmurro*."
- "The techniques of characterization in three short stories by Chekhov and Flannery O'Connor."
- "Blindness handled in two distinct ways in Henry Green's and José Saramago's two novels of the same name."
- "Lermontov's *A Hero of Our Time* as a reflection of George Gordon Lord Byron's development of the 'Byronic hero' in his selected poetry."

What is the nature of a research question in English A literature?

- *A good research question* in this subject will be one in which you are able to convey some personal critical judgment about literature.

- *A good research question* is one that is finally shaped after examining some available critical comment on the writer and the work(s).

- *A good research question* is one that is sharply focused and possible to treat in no more than 4000 words.

Meeting these criteria is not an easy task. Often, we have a vague sense of something that would be interesting to discuss, but the process of making that clear in our own heads can be challenging. It can help to write out a proposal to discuss with your supervisor. It's one way for both of you to see whether what you are thinking about is viable.

Activity

Below is a first proposal presented to a supervisor for an extended essay in English A literature. Read it carefully and then explore the following questions:

a Into which category does the essay fall?

b Is this a legitimate choice of works?

c What do you understand the focus of the essay to be?

d Do you think the focus is sharply defined?

e Can you express the focus of the essay in a one-sentence research question?

English extended essay proposal

What role do children play in the two novels *The Kite Runner* and *A Thousand Splendid Suns* by Khaled Hosseini? How are such youths depicted, and how do they add to the general sense of complex emotion and underlying depth throughout the two storylines? As Hosseini makes clear, "there are a lot of children in Afghanistan, but little childhood". Why is this so? It seems that Hosseini enjoys portraying them as ironically innocent victims of their surroundings, but also characters that surpass their years in experience and subtle understanding. Whether it be Amir and Hassan in *The Kite Runner* or Aziza and Zalmai in *A Thousand Splendid Suns*, the kids are at first innocent, incorruptible, naïve – and then life happens. In the latter story, more characters start out young and grow older through the course of the tale, such as Mariam, Laila or Tariq, and this helps readers to see the changes in them as they age. The former tale, on the other hand, involves Amir as a child and an adult, but also speaks of Hassan's son Sohrab, who is still a child by the end

of the book. Sohrab is a boy who goes through so much he appears to have psychological trauma, and withdraws from the world around him – yet "despite everything, he [is] still just a child", as Amir realizes near the end.

In this way, it is clear that Hosseini uses children as tools to weave more emotion and depth into a story that otherwise is made of a stronger, harder fabric. Difficult themes, issues and ideas are dealt with in a more simplistic manner, utilizing kids' viewpoints as lenses through which the reader begins to see the world. The author also realizes that by allowing many of the main characters to be children, readers can relate to the tales in a more intimate manner – for each and every one of us has experienced childhood, and each and every one of us can never forget. The texts are made all the more powerful through this universal sense of understanding; we are haunted by the resonance it has in our minds for long after. An essay would thus be an appropriate medium through which to research and develop these ideas and further explore preconceived notions about the topic.

Indeed, children are explored in these two novels as part of a microcosm of the world itself. They are intense, different and absorbing of all their surroundings. For why else does Rahim Khan say that they "aren't coloring books"? Of course, "you don't get to fill them with your favorite colors". Whether you are good or bad is not the question; the question is: What experiences have made you into who you are today?

You may have observed some problems with this proposal. As shown here, it is often the case that students cannot quite decide exactly which particular aspect of a topic to pursue, as here with the topic of children. This means that you may need to make more than one attempt to narrow down and focus your topic. This is a step worth doing well and doing in a focused space of time. As anyone who has produced a major piece of writing such as a doctoral thesis or a book will tell you, the more time you allow between your work periods, the more effort it takes to recover your line of thinking and move forward.

Step 1: research question

Step 1 is to choose a writer or work(s) that interests you and get your research question to a state of being focused and clear. This does not mean that you will not do some minor adaptation as you go along – perhaps you will find that really close analysis means that you will have to draw in your ambitions a little. You really must have a sense of direction. The following chart may help you to work towards a good research question.

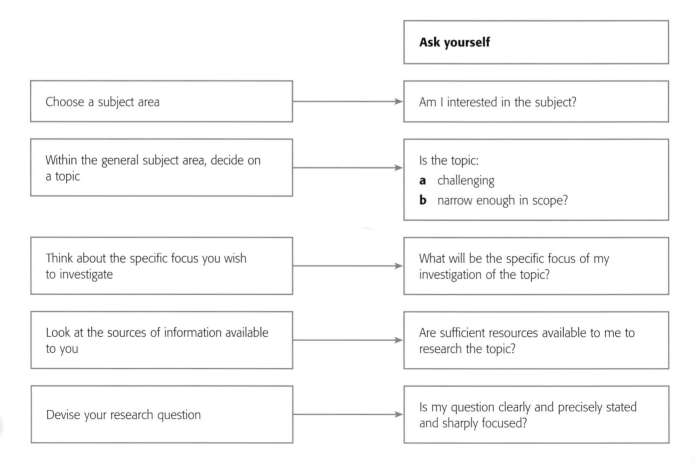

	Ask yourself
Choose a subject area	Am I interested in the subject?
Within the general subject area, decide on a topic	Is the topic: **a** challenging **b** narrow enough in scope?
Think about the specific focus you wish to investigate	What will be the specific focus of my investigation of the topic?
Look at the sources of information available to you	Are sufficient resources available to me to research the topic?
Devise your research question	Is my question clearly and precisely stated and sharply focused?

Step 2: outline

Step 2 will actually assist you in becoming clear and testing whether your idea will work: an outline. This stage involves laying out a plan for how you will treat the material. There are many systems of outlining or planning. Your school will likely have a format for this; if not, there are good written guides to outlines both in books and on the internet.

When you think you have a broad plan, you will need to discuss it with your supervisor. You are not bound to this plan, but it will help you to make Step 3 more productive.

Step 3: research

At this point, unless you are working with literature that is very familiar to you, you will need to read or re-read the work(s). Now that you have a question you are trying to answer and, thus, a focus, you will be more conscious of those aspects that are particularly relevant to your essay. It may seem unnecessary to re-read, but you will ultimately save yourself a lot of time by doing so: you will know where relevant details can be found, you will see the work in a new light and you will have an organic sense of the whole work from which to develop your essay.

It's a good idea to keep some notes during this reading, either by marking your texts or in a separate format. You can see that 40 hours to accomplish a good literary essay is not a liberal estimate.

Step 4: use of secondary sources

Your literary work is your **primary source** for research. However, you will want to consult some **secondary sources**, for instance some of the literary criticism relevant to your study.

A search of secondary sources is one that can be either very extensive or quite limited. There are pitfalls with both. On the one hand, you can get so addicted to seeing what other people have said that you lose your own sense of the work(s) you are planning to discuss. On the other hand, neglecting to explore a few examples of what other people have thought of the work(s), or even of something close to your own topic, deprives you of a larger sense of how the work has been received or thought about.

Some issues associated with secondary sources

1 Notes

You will want to take notes. These notes must be carefully handled. You will, again, save yourself a lot of time and frustration later if you:

- choose a system for taking notes. Older systems involve note cards or various other paper systems, but there are many systems available on the internet.

- take the time to set up a system and keep to it.

2 Quotations and paraphrasing

When you copy directly from another source (something someone else has written) you must indicate this with the use of quotation marks. You then need to make a note of the information for the source you have used. You will need this later for footnotes and the bibliography. On the issue of footnotes and bibliographies, there are many different acceptable systems. You need to use one system consistently throughout your essay. Your supervisor will have more specific advice for you and you can also consult the *Extended Essay Guide* (December 2010) provided by the IB. There will be a copy at your school.

When you write a phrase that does not quote but conveys the idea of someone else in your own words, you are creating a **paraphrase**. This, too, must be recorded in your notes; the idea may be a unique insight and if you use it in your essay, you will need to give credit to the person who loaned it to you.

So, again, record the exact information about the source. Later, your supervisor will need to help you decide about citation and inclusion in the bibliography. Your school is likely to have a clear practice about which formats to use, and your supervisor will advise you about the form you should use for your handling of footnotes and bibliography.

As you can see, the process of writing the extended essay is designed to provide you with a secure sense of what's involved in good academic research.

> It's not good scholarship to wander through other people's work, taking their ideas without acknowledgement. This is **plagiarism**. Your school and your teachers will have detailed information about this; carelessness and unclarity about it can lead to a loss of your IB Diploma.

Step 5: refining your outline

It's likely that the work you have done in re-reading and surveying secondary sources will have given you some further or different ideas about how you might refine your outline, and even perhaps slightly alter your research question. At this point, it will be useful to edit both of these to be sure they are clearly in line with each other and that when you finish this step you have a clear sense of direction. Both the research question and the outline will be important factors in moving to Step 6 of the process.

Step 6: composing a first draft

If you have followed the above five steps, you should be in a very strong position to begin a draft of your whole essay. Generally, you may want to think of the task in three parts:

- The **introduction**, in which your research question clearly appears.
- The **body** of the essay.
- The **conclusion**.

The introduction, in which your research question clearly appears

In the introduction, often your research question will appear as a statement rather than a question – a statement of your position about the question. Sometimes it is helpful to try out that statement by beginning with the word "Although". In addition to helping you clarify what it is you are going to argue, it also reminds you that a good literary essay needs to go beyond purely re-describing the contents of the work(s). It takes a position on some issue and argues the position with evidence from your primary and secondary sources.

Your introduction will also include a brief description of each of the works addressed in the essay. This, of course, may only be one work. The examiner has read the work(s) about which you are writing, so avoid plot summary. You do not need to address the biography of the writer(s), although in cases where the context is important to the topic a reference to biographical material may be relevant. As a basic minimum, at the end of your introduction the reader should know:

- what works you are addressing, who has written them and when
- what you are going to discuss, and what will be the angle or position through which you will discuss it.

> You may find that as long as you have a clear sense of your position or thesis statement written out at the beginning, you may prefer to leave the full development of your introduction until you have written the body and the conclusion of the essay – these are the next parts of the essay.

The body of the essay

In many ways, this 'fleshly' label is appropriate to what you will do next: the development and presentation of how the research question will be answered by you. While the introduction might be seen as the 'head' of the essay and the conclusion the 'feet', the real 'flesh and blood' of your essay will be in the paragraphs that come after the introduction and before the conclusion.

Look at your outline: now that it's time to write, does your outline seem logical and possible? If not, do a little adjusting and then begin to write immediately. It's best, again, to set aside some connected time to start on this task straight away, so you don't waste time having to re-read and re-think and getting back in the 'zone'.

There are many ways to organize the material in the body of the essay, but with your outline you have already made some tentative decisions.

The conclusion

Finally, you will want to bring your ideas around to a concluding statement or conclusion. Try to avoid a version of your introduction; this is neither very interesting for your reader nor very stylish. Presumably, the body of your essay has developed the proposal you made at the beginning and so you now have more to say.

Introductions and conclusions are not easy for any writer. You will undoubtedly want to look closely at yours before you present your first draft to your supervisor. You will want to write a complete introduction so as to practise for clarity and interest. This is a very important part of the essay and, in some ways, a test of whether or not you have a clear direction for the essay.

The supervisor may or may not ask you to have all of your notes and bibliographical references ready at this point. Sometimes the supervisor wants to be sure first that you have a topic that you are able to develop in a convincing way.

Activity

Read carefully through the following introduction and conclusion to an essay: "Fiction vs. prose other than fiction: stylistic approaches to writing about another culture." These are both fairly successful examples of each. What can you identify as features of a good introduction and conclusion?

Introduction

As a foreign journalist, it is a daunting task to write about situations in countries where the culture is very different from one's own. However, it is an important task because it increases awareness and may, if written well, inspire action on the part of the reader. To convey a message that will make a strong impact on readers, one of the most effective approaches is to present it in an emotionally moving way. This essay will compare the effectiveness of the emotional impact of two books written by foreigners about women in Islamic societies: *Nine Parts of Desire* by Australian journalist Geraldine Brooks, and *Honor to the Bride* by American journalist, Jane Kramer. While both books are written about the same cultural issue, the authors take very different approaches to presenting the issue. *Nine Parts of Desire* is a non-fiction work written in traditional journalistic style, compiling many different examples of the life of women in Islamic cultures. In contrast, *Honor to the Bride* is written as fiction, although the story is based on fact, and reads very much like a novel. Both books appear to be written with the intent of provoking thought and reaction in the public and, while each is effective in achieving this goal, I will argue that the fictional approach Kramer takes in *Honor to the Bride* is more effective because it makes a deeper emotional impact. Specifically, there are three aspects of the books that bear comparing: firstly, the scope of the topic covered and consequently the length of the book; secondly, the author's attitude towards the subject as revealed in the tone of the writing and, thirdly, the authorial commentary used.

Conclusion

The comparison of these three aspects – scope of topic, author's attitude as revealed in tone and authorial commentary – clearly shows that *Honor to the Bride* can be argued to be more effective than *Nine Parts of Desire* in its emotional impact. However, the argument about how this emotional impact affects the book's overall effectiveness cannot be complete without the consideration of the factors that influence reader reception of a book. The main factor in the case of these books is the publishing date. The fact that the books were published two decades apart means that they were written for very different audiences. This means that it is impossible to definitely judge the effectiveness of one book over another because each may have been the most effective for the audience the author was targeting at the time. For example, it is possible that while the fictional approach of *Honor to the Bride* might have been acceptable to Kramer's audience of the 1970s, Brooks' audience in the late 1990s might consider its humour and irony to be politically incorrect or even offensive… it is important to note that Kramer's audience was not very well exposed to, or interested in, the Islamic culture, so in *Honor to the Bride* Kramer was 'introducing' the world of Islamic women to her readership and needed an approach that would catch readers' attention. In contrast, Brooks' audience in the 1990s was likely to be already aware of, and even directly concerned about, Islamic culture and its treatment of women, so the heavily informative journalism in *Nine Parts of Desire* might have been exactly what the audience wanted and needed.

Therefore it is clear that a definitive argument about the overall effectiveness of either book is not possible because each was written for a different audience and the authors' specific intentions were not the same. However, I have concluded that, although *Nine Parts of Desire* gives a greater breadth of information, *Honor to the Bride* is more effective in communicating the conditions of women in Islamic societies because its message moves the reader emotionally, leaving a deeper impact.

Step 7: further drafts and final draft

If you have spent time on following all of the preceding steps, you should be close to finishing the process of writing your extended essay. Once you have discussed your first draft with your supervisor, you may wish to make some changes. Careful work up to this point may mean that your first and final drafts are very similar, although you may want to:

- add more detail to support your argument
- clarify certain things or expressions
- move some material into a slightly different order
- address a particular feature of grammar or punctuation that you regularly get wrong
- improve your introduction or conclusion
- check your word count does not exceed 4000 words.

You are largely finished with the basic work, and are ready to polish and correct and produce your final draft of the introduction, body and conclusion.

> You may find that you have so much material that you have written more than 4000 words. Examiners do not have to read beyond this word limit. You must prune your work to 4000 words or you will lose marks.

Step 8: the abstract

There is a little more to do, however. At this point, you will need to produce the scholarly feature of your essay called the abstract.

An abstract is a very brief account of:

- the research question
- the scope of your attention
- your conclusion.

For the IB, your abstract must be no more than 300 words. It will be the first thing the reader or examiner encounters. It must be clear and concise. The norms for this feature are clearly stated by the IB:

"The requirements for the abstract are for it to state clearly the research question that was investigated, how the investigation was undertaken and the conclusion(s) of the essay."

As you can see, there are three elements to the abstract. At the end of this chapter on page 297, you will be able to see an example of the assessment criteria.

A checklist for your abstract:
- Do not confuse the abstract with your introduction to the essay.
- Do not try to summarize your whole essay here.
- Do not explain why you have chosen the topic.
- Do not exceed **300 words**.

> You will perhaps note that this sounds more applicable to a research project in the sciences than a literary 'investigation'. However, the 'how' in your English extended essay is more likely to be how (and how well) your evidence supports what you have proposed. For example, how the **literary techniques** used by Emily Dickinson make death both friendly and fearful.

Step 9: putting the whole essay together

The following are the elements that the examiner should easily find and read when they receive the essay:

1 The **title page** with a title clearly indicating the focus of the essay. Obscure and metaphorical titles are not helpful. What the examiner

wants to know is: "What am I about to read?" The idea of a title is to deliver information, not to mystify. On this page, include your name, candidate number and the date.

2   The **abstract** comes next. It should be titled "Abstract" and printed on one page.

3   The **contents page** follows immediately. It should list the sections of your essay such as "Introduction", "Body", "Conclusion" and "Bibliography".

4   The **essay** itself, with headings that match what you have listed on the contents page.

5   **Endnotes** are only needed if you have not placed your footnotes throughout the essay.

6   The **bibliography**, which includes sources you have used to develop your essay.

7   An **appendix** or **appendices** are only needed if you must include some material that is not widely available, such as the work of a poet whose work may not be easily obtained by the examiner.

Step 10: the final check

This is where you must keep up your efforts before you breathe that final sigh of relief:

- Check that your essay does not exceed 4000 words. This applies to the essay itself, not including the abstract, table of contents, footnotes or endnotes, bibliography and appendices.

- Check the pages are numbered correctly.

- Check that footnotes and their numbers match and appear in the appropriate order and location.

- Check that titles, chapters, poems or essays are presented in the correct format.

- Finally, proofread**,** proofread and proofread! Yes, you will be rather tired of this material when you get to this stage. However, you will significantly improve your marks if you set aside a short period of time (when your head is clear and you are alert) and read your essay aloud. You are likely to hear things you don't see. Fix them!

As part of your final check, you may want to read the assessment criteria at the end of this chapter on pages 294–7. Getting an A in your extended essay is not easy, but if you follow the steps and advice in this chapter, you will be in a strong position to do so. Even more importantly, you will have practised some skills that you will find invaluable during the next steps in your life.

Viva voce

Your work with the extended essay may conclude with an interview with your supervisor during which you will both discuss the final product. The teacher may ask questions and you may make comments. This final interview can be used by your supervisor to help them in writing a final comment for the examiner.

Extended essay

To what extent was Charlotte Brontë successful in portraying a "plain and small", conventionally unattractive heroine, in *Jane Eyre*?

Candidate Name: Mariam Sameh Aziz
Candidate Number: 00654-013
Subject: Group 1 – English
Advisor: Ms. Leah Edens
Word Count: 3999

Abstract:

Charlotte Brontë's claim of creating an unconventional heroine in *Jane Eyre* has been subject to criticism; thus, this paper aims to analyze the character of Jane Eyre, in order to determine the extent to which Brontë was successful in creating a "plain and small", conventionally unattractive heroine, in *Jane Eyre*. In order to thoroughly analyze Jane's character, various aspects of the novel are examined. Jane's view of herself to be very plain, small, and simple seldom changes; however, when she thinks herself no longer plain, the criticism that Brontë did not completely defy convention is supported. Nevertheless, Brontë's foiling of Jane's character with those of Eliza and Georgiana Reed, and her portrayal of Jane's monotonous life, overshadow Jane's infrequent view of herself as anything but plain, small, and simple.

The physical setting is examined, where Brontë's insistence on creating an unconventional heroine is seen through her description of the physical setting, which portrays Jane's isolation, at the very beginning of the novel. Jane's nature is noted through the analysis of her relationship with Rochester and Mary and Diana Rivers, where she is found to be extremely impressionable. The investigation of Jane's character is further carried out by examining whether or not she is a "threat to the literary tradition of masculine heroism", analyzing the foil in character and performance between Jane and Blanche, as well as the foil between Rochester's treatment of both women. Despite the novel's ending in a Victorian conventional marriage, it is inevitable to conclude that Brontë was to a great extent successful in creating a "plain and small", conventionally unattractive heroine in *Jane Eyre*.

Explain. One character can be a foil for another but not 'inbetween'.

Table of Contents:

Introduction:

In rejecting "the convention of the beautiful heroine"[1] and trying to "show a heroine as plain and small as [her] self"[2], Charlotte Brontë, in the mid-1800s, wrote *Jane Eyre*, defying literary and societal convention; however, she grants the world a work that has changed the view of women ever since. Among the criticisms of the work, some critics have deemed it "uneasily balanced"[3] in that "the conventional aspects"[4] do not go well with the protagonist's "autonomy and control"[5], and that Jane "did not contradict Victorian values; she simply allowed a realistic conventional female perspective to the repressive time period"[6]; conversely, Brontë herself asserted that "unless [she, herself,] can have the courage to use the language of Truth in preference to the jargon of Conventionality, [she] ought to be silent".[7] Because of the lack of consistency in the view of *Jane Eyre*, as of all literary works, regarding Brontë's ability to successfully portray a "plain and small", conventionally unattractive heroine, assessment of this question is crucial in determining whether Brontë truly was one of the pioneers in portraying a true heroine in her work, or if her claims, and those of many of her critics, are to be disregarded as false.

Body:

Brontë presents Jane's simplicity and her low view of herself through Jane's thought of herself as ignorant, and her inability to take pride in her achievements. Despite Jane Eyre's education for six years at the Lowood Orphan Asylum, and her occupation as a teacher for two years, she reckons herself an ignorant woman, and cannot take pride in her achievements, thus viewing herself as a plain, small and simple being. Upon hearing Mr. Rochester and his guests speaking "of playing charades"[8], Jane comments to herself that it is because of her "ignorance [that she] did not understand the term"[9]. Brontë's choice of diction in using the word "ignorance" portrays Jane's simple and low view of herself, despite her extensive education; the absence of knowledge of a single word: "charades", makes Jane view herself as ignorant. The absence of pride even in her most valued accomplishments displays Jane's simplicity and plainness. While Rochester is occupied with surveying the pictures she has drawn, she is occupied with telling the reader "what they are... that they are nothing wonderful".[10] Again, Brontë uses negative diction when Jane describes her own work, as she sees it as "nothing wonderful"; her achievements she cannot acknowledge, even the paintings which she has spent entire vacations making, she seems unpleased with,

---

[1] http://academ ic.brooklyn.cuny.edu/english/melani/cs6/bronte.html

[2] http://academic.brooklyn.cuny.edu/english/melani.cs6/bronte.html

[3] http://everything2.com/title/jane%2520eyre

[4] ibid

[5] ibid

[6] ibid

[7] http://www.glencoe.com/sec/literature/litlibrary/pdf/jane_eyre.pdf

[8] Charlotte Brontë, *Jane Eyre* (Boarders Classics, 2006), p.179

[9] ibid, p.179

[10] ibid, p.123

not because of her vanity, on the contrary, because of the small view she has of herself and her work.

Jane's plain view of herself at the beginning of the novel seldom changes; however, when it does, it supports the criticism that Brontë did not completely defy convention, as Jane feels that her face "is no longer plain: there was hope in its aspect, and life in its color" after Rochester's proposal to marry her; conventionality is noticed in this scene, as like any other girl who is asked to marriage, she sees "hope" in her future, rather than the plainness she saw in her face every day. Jane's infrequent view of herself as hopeful and full of life is seldom portrayed in the novel, and only is when most necessary. Jane is a girl, like any other, who would be pleased at the thought of marriage; her low and simple view of herself however is consistent through the novel, as she cannot see beyond the small girl at Gateshead.

Tautology.

Brontë's insistence on portraying a "plain and small" heroine is evident from the beginning of the novel where she foils Jane's character with those of Georgiana and Eliza Reed, her cousins whom she lives with at Gateshead; however, she uses irony later in the novel to portray Jane's heroism as a result of her plainness, in contrast to Georgiana and Eliza's unpleasant futures, despite their beauty, and sophisticatedly enjoyable childhood. Living with her aunt at Gateshead, Jane's situation, even physical, was not good, as she felt her "physical inferiority to Eliza, John and Georgiana Reed".[11] Despite Jane's cousins' unmannerly behaviour, "Eliza, who was headstrong and selfish, was respected [and] Georgiana, who had a spoiled temper, a very acrid spite, a captious and insolent carriage, was universally indulged"[12], while Jane was abused by her cousin John Reed despite his being well mannered and having none of the flawed characteristics of Eliza and Georgiana. The foil between the "respect" and "indulgence" Eliza and Georgiana receive, despite their actions, and the "abuse" that Jane receives, portrays her horrid and violent childhood. Irony is used to portray Jane's heroic characteristics in foil with her cousins' vainness when Eliza tells Jane, on their parting after having met at Jane's aunt's death, that she wishes her well and that she has "some sense"[13], in contrast to her view of her sister, Georgiana, as a "vain and absurd animal".[14] Jane's note of her cousins upon her departure from Gateshead that "Georgiana made an advantage match with a wealthy worn-out man of fashion; and that Eliza actually took the veil", displays the irony in the three women's lives. On one hand, Georgiana and Eliza, after having lived a luxurious childhood, cannot find happiness, rather each escapes, Georgiana by marrying a "worn-out man", and Eliza by becoming a nun. Conversely, Jane Eyre, the poor small child who endures severe suffering during her childhood is the only one who finds happiness, through her independence, thus, becoming a heroine.

Escapes what? Happiness? Reality?

---

[11] Charlotte Brontë, *Jane Eyre*, (Boarders Classics, 2006), p.3
[12] ibid, p11
[13] ibid, p240
[14] ibid, p.233

Jane's monotonous life, evident through the external setting, which portrays the mental setting and characterizes Jane's childhood, and her first encounter with Rochester and with Mary and Diana Rivers, which portray how easily impressed she is, serves to depict her small, plain and simple nature. "The novel opens with a modest statement about the weather: 'There was no possibility of taking a walk that day.' It is winter, the weather is cold, dark, and rainy. Jane, taking refuge from the unfriendly Reed family, nestles on a window seat close to the glass, hidden by a heavy red curtain. There she reads a favorite book in search of comfort. In this emblematic description of the setting, Brontë quickly conveys one of the main themes of the novel – emotional isolation and the search for self-respect."[15] The weather, and Jane's isolation portray her plain and simple nature, which is later developed through the novel, however each is significant to the extent that Brontë portrays them in the very first sentence of *Jane Eyre*. "The bleak winter weather not only reflects Jane's inhospitable surroundings but also her lonely state of mind. Jane lives without the warmth of family or friends."[16] The physical setting does not only serve to portray itself, rather portray the mental setting as well. Brontë does this by using diction such as "cold", "dark", and "rainy", in describing the weather, to depict Jane's childhood, thus helping the audience to understand the formation of her character as plain, small and simple, as a result of what she goes through. "Jane Eyre describes her first encounter with Rochester as an event of 'no moment'. Her act of kindness in helping the fallen man to his horse is merely an 'active thing', significant only because it provides a welcome change to an otherwise 'monotonous life'". [17] Jane describes the effect of the incident, saying that "'The new face was like a new picture introduced to the gallery of memory; and it was dissimilar to all others hanging there'... Jane adds, 'I had it before me when I entered Hay and slipped the letter into the post office; I saw it as I walked fast down hill all the way home'... Jane's admission that this image, 'dissimilar' to all others mounted in her mental museum, represents her first encounter with a masculine figure 'dark, strong, and stern', evidences a young, impressionable woman ready for romance."[18] Jane's plain and simple life is evident through her first encounter with Rochester, as she describes the event as "an active" thing, portraying her quiet and "monotonous life". The fact that Rochester's image "haunts" her memory shows how she is inexperienced in love, depicting her "young and impressionable" nature. The fact that she is impressionable relates back to plain and small, as a person with such qualities is very easily influenced and impressed. Jane's impressionable nature is again seen through her encounter with Diana and Mary Rivers, especially Diana, who "had a voice toned, to [Jane's] ear, like the cooing of a dove. She possessed eyes whose gaze [Jane] delighted to encounter... It was [Jane's] nature of feel pleasure in yielding to

---

[15] http:///www.glencoe.com/sec/literature/litlibrary/pdf/jane_eyre.pdf

[16] ibid

[17] http://findarticles.com/p/articles/mi_qa3708/is_199707/ai_n8765444/
    pg_1?tag=artBody;coll

[18] http://findarticles.com/p/articles/mi_qa3708/is_199707/ai_n8765444/
    pg_1?tag=artBody;coll

an authority supported like hers: and to bend, where [her] conscience and self-respect permitted, to an active will."[19] Jane's finding the Rivers sisters to be of great interest and intelligence, and her delight to be in their presence portrays her belief of herself as inferior and emphasizes her simplicity, as she "could join with Diana and Mary in all their occupations, converse with them as much as they wished and aid them when and where they would allow [her]"[20], depicting her submissiveness and yielding to those who she perceives of higher education and better experience. Jane's impressionable nature, seen through her first encounter with Rochester, and with Mary and Diana Rivers, as well as the external setting at the beginning of the novel, vividly characterizes her life as isolated and monotonous, depicting Jane's simplicity and inexperience.

Simply re-writing secondary criticism.

Brontë's portrayal of a strong independent heroine has been thought to be a "threat to the literary tradition of masculine heroism", through achieving equality in love between Rochester and Jane. When Jane first arrives at Ferndean Manor where Rochester lives "there were no flowers, no garden-beds"[21], and the "parlor looked gloomy: a neglected handful of fire burned low in the grate; and, leaning over it with his head supported against the high, old-fashioned mantelpiece, appeared the blind tenant of the room."[22] The setting in which Jane finds the "blind tenant of the room" sitting is a very dull and gloomy one, which symbolizes Rochester's isolation and depression. However, later when they are married "most of the morning was spent in the open air. [Jane] led him out of the wet and wild wood into the cheerful fields: [she] described to him how brilliantly green they were; how the flowers and hedges looked refreshed: how sparklingly blue was the sky."[23] The setting portrayed in the scene after they were married strongly contrasts with that when Jane finds Rochester sitting alone in isolation; Jane's presence gives life not only to Rochester, but to the place as well, as can be seen through the contrasting imagery of the first scene, where there are no flowers and no garden beds, and the second scene, where "flowers and hedges looked refreshed". Jane's significance in Rochester's life portrays the importance of the female aspect for the survival of the male. "With Rochester as with everyone an urge to independence of mind possesses her to a degree that would be a handicap to the conventional Victorian marriage. Such independence is a threat to the literary tradition of masculine heroism – and, indeed, it is not surprising that when she does marry him, he is literally a cripple, reduced in manly strength, maimed and blind, forced to lean on her, to accept her guiding hand."[24] Rochester first meets Jane when she helps him after he has fallen from his horse. She is of great help to him later when his dangerous brother in law shows up at Thornton Hall and when his bed is set on fire. "Even in the time of their

This needs to be established. Why is it a threat?

---

[19] Charlotte Brontë, *Jane Eyre* (Boarders Classics, 2006), p.343
[20] Charlotte Brontë, *Jane Eyre* (Boarders Classics, 2006), p.350
[21] Charlotte Brontë, *Jane Eyre* (Boarders Classics, 2006), p.433–434
[22] ibid, p436
[23] ibid, p.442
[24] http://proquest.umi.com/pqdweb?did=936612&sid=3&Fmt=3&clientId=7003&RQT=309&VName=PQD

courtship when he is his full self, she makes it clear that though she called him "master"… she will not be a helpless parasite."[25] Furthermore, when Rochester tells Jane: "'my bride is here,' … again drawing [her] to him, 'because my equal is here, and my likeness,'"[26] Brontë's choice of diction in using the word "likeness" reaffirms the idea of equality of genders, through portraying a simple, yet authentic heroine, one whom the male character significantly relies on.

To portray Jane as an unattractive heroine, Brontë foils her and Blanche, through their performance and the response of other characters to them, as well as Mr. Rochester's different treatment of both women. As Blanche played the piano "her execution was brilliant; she sang: her voice was fine; she talked French… with fluency and with a good accent,"[27] she excited "not only the admiration, but the amazement of her audiors".[28] Whilst on the other hand, Jane's performance compelled Rochester to scream at her: "'Enough!' …'You play a little, I see, like any other English school-girl: perhaps rather better than some, but not well.'"[29] Whereas Blanche's performance was admirably exquisite, making her seem very beautiful, Jane's average performance foiled with that of Blanche's, adding to her unattractiveness and ordinariness.

How does this bear upon Jane's lack of self-esteem?

Through Rochester's treatment of both women, the audience can easily note the foil between their beauties. The tone Brontë uses when Rochester converses with Blanche is a respectful and honouring one, as he tells her: "Madam, I support you on this point, as on every other,"[30] portraying his admiration. While playing a game of charades with his guests, Rochester, on summoning "the ladies around him,"[31] to select those on his team, declared that "Miss Ingram is [his], of course."[32] The diction in choosing the words "of course" when Rochester selects Miss Ingram to be on his team shows his highly respectable treatment of her. Unlike Rochester's treatment of Blanche, which remains consistent throughout the novel, his treatment of Jane severely changes. Through the first period of their encounter, Brontë uses a very commanding and harsh tone when Rochester speaks to Jane, as when he tells her: "go into the library – I mean, if you please. (Excuse my tone of command; I am used to say, 'Do this,' and it is done. I cannot alter my customary habits for one new inmate.) Go then, into the library; take a candle with you; leave the door open; sit down to the piano, and play a tune."[33] When "Adele showed [him] some sketches… which she said were [Jane's]… [He didn't] know whether they were entirely of [Jane's] doing;" his questioning of the authenticity of her paintings is clear foil with his

---

[25] http://proquest.umi.com/pqdweb?did=936612&sid=3&Fmt=3&clientId=7003&RQT=309 &VName=PQD

[26] Charlotte Brontë, *Jane Eyre* (Boarders Classics, 2006), p.253

[27] ibid, p170

[28] ibid, p.176

[29] ibid, p.122

[30] Charlotte Brontë, *Jane Eyre* (Boarders Classics, 2006), p.176

[31] ibid, p179

[32] ibid, p.179

[33] ibid, p.122

praising of Blanche's performance. However, as time progresses, beginning with when Jane helps Rochester with Mason's injury, until the end of the novel, his treatment shifts completely, as Brontë's tone shifts from a commanding tone to a less commanding, soft and friendly one. This is indirect characterization of Jane, as it portrays her real self, which Rochester can now see clearly, as opposed to the plain and easily commanded girl he used to see in her. After having shouted at Jane to stop playing the piano early during the novel, Rochester later insists that Jane "must play the accompaniment."[34] As Brontë foils between Rochester's treatment of Blanche and his treatment of Jane, early in the novel and as events progress, she portrays Blanche's outer beauty which is admired by everyone, as opposed to Jane's inner beauty which is only admired by Rochester after he spends time truly knowing her.

Quote needed to support point.

Brontë does not only foil between Rochester's treatment of both women and between the obvious differences in their looks to portray Jane's unattractiveness, however, she also foils between both women's decisions, to portray the true heroine. During Rochester's guests' stay at Thornfield, Blanche treats Rochester with the utmost respect and complementation, as she believes he is a very wealthy man, who will make a suitable husband; as "Mr. Rochester led in Miss Ingram, she was complementing him on his acting."[35] As Jane is commanded by Rochester to be present at all times during his guests' stay, she closely observes Blanche and her relationship with Rochester, concluding that "Miss Ingram… was very showy, but she was not genuine: she had a fine person, many brilliant attainments; but her mind was poor… She was not good; she was not original… tenderness and truth were not in her."[36] Blanche's treatment of Rochester directly foils with Jane's treatment, as Jane's treatment is rather blunt and simple, as opposed to Blanche's complimentary, unauthentic treatment. She doesn't "call [him] handsome… though [she] love[s] [him] most dearly: far too dearly to flatter [him],"[37] choosing to remain genuine. Blanche Ingram's agreement to marry Rochester because of his wealth is in conformity with Victorian convention, as it was the norm for fair women, like Blanche, to marry wealthy and established men, like Rochester. Even Jane, who is deeply in love with Mr. Rochester, can understand the idea of their marriage; she "had thought him a man unlikely to be influenced by motives so commonplace in his choice of a wife; but the longer [she] considered the position, education, etc., of the parties the less [she] felt justified in judging and blaming either him or Miss Ingram for acting in conformity to ideas and principles instilled into them, doubtless, from their childhood."[38] Later, however, when Mr. Rochester "caused a rumor to reach [Blanche] that [his] fortune was not a third of what was supposed… the result… was coldness both from [Blanche] and her mother,"[39] Blanche's refusal to marry Rochester when she

[34] Charlotte Brontë, *Jane Eyre* (Boarders Classics, 2006), p.269

[35] ibid, p.182

[36] ibid, p.183

[37] Charlotte Brontë, *Jane Eyre* (Boarders Classics, 2006), p.258

[38] Charlotte Brontë, *Jane Eyre* (Boarders Classics, 2006), p.185

[39] ibid, p.253

finds out that he is not as wealthy as she had thought is in conformity with convention, however, her act is very un-heroine like. On the other hand, Jane refuses to marry Mr. Rochester when he first proposes, asserting that she has "an independent will,"[40] however, she later agrees to his proposal. When the truth of Rochester's marriage is revealed during the wedding ceremony, despite Jane's love for him and his high status, which although does not matter to her is a large factor in Victorian marriages, she leaves him and runs away. Upon the death of her uncle, Jane inherits a large sum of money, becoming a rich and independent woman. Despite her new status, she realizes that her love for Rochester has not died and that he was the man who had awakened her soul, therefore, she returns to him, and agrees to marry him, in spite of the situation she finds him in; Rochester himself is amazed at Jane's commitment to marry him. He tells her that "as [she is] rich, [she], no double, [has] friends who will look after [her], and not suffer [her] to devote [her]self to a blind lamenter like [him];"[41] defying all convention, Jane answers that she is now "independent… as well as rich." Jane is now her "own mistress,"[42] and will "certainly – unless [he] objects"[43] stay with him. Brontë's foil of Blanche's beauty and Jane's unattractiveness, Blanche's societal manners and Jane's bluntness, serves to portray that, ultimately, the heroine, Jane, is made, not through her beauty or lavishness, but through her heroic decisions, depicting Brontë's defiance of Victorian convention of the "beautiful heroine" which "unlike her sisters, Charlotte rejected."[44]

Need to define 'heroine'.

Needs explaining.

As Jane herself asserts, "most true is it that 'beauty is in the eye of the gazer'"[45], despite her unattractiveness, Rochester, after getting to know her, finds her extremely beautiful as opposed to his initial view of her as "not pretty any more than [he is] handsome,"[46] her view of herself however remains unaltered. As Rochester falls in love with Jane, he communicates to her his thoughts that she is "a beauty in [his] eyes; and a beauty just after the desire of [his] heart – delicate and aerial"[47] The tone used by Brontë when Rochester describes Jane in this scene is a very romantic one, and is supported by the use of romantic diction, such as "desire" and "delicate", portraying that it is the love spell Rochester is under that is causing his view to change, and that her beauty is not that of appearance, but one soul and heart. The major contrast between his initial and later view of her beauty is well depicted when he says: "'Jane, you look blooming, and smiling, and pretty,'" where Brontë uses positive diction to describe Rochester's later view of Jane. However, in relating her current beauty to the past, Rochester says, "truly pretty this morning. Is this my pale, little elf? Is this my mustard-seed?" Brontë uses negative diction when Rochester

Not very good examples of romantic diction.

---

[40] ibid, p252
[41] ibid, p.437
[42] ibid, p437
[43] ibid, p.437
[44] http://academic.brooklyn.cuny.edu/english/melani/cs6/bronte.html
[45] Charlotte Brontë, *Jane Eyre* (Boarders Classics, 2006), p.172
[46] ibid, p.130
[47] ibid, p.258

calls her "pale", "little elf", and "mustard-seed", portraying how beauty truly is "in the eye of the gazer,"[48] depicting Jane's inner beauty, which Rochester has come to see after knowing her well. Despite Rochester's new view of Jane as pretty, she herself cannot see that, and says that the "secret voice which talks to [her] in [her] own heart"[49] tells her that she is "not beautiful."[50] Brontë's portrayal of Jane as unattractive defies convention: however Brontë's courage to portray a true heroine fueled her to create such a plain and small character. ◁

Was Brontë portraying a true heroine or describing herself?

"Acknowledging the tendency of authors to make their heroines beautiful, Charlotte asserted she would create 'a heroine as plain and small as [herself], who shall be as interesting as any of yours.' The main character of Jane Eyre is not pretty. As the character herself says: 'I sometimes regretted that I was not handsomer: I sometimes wished to have rosy cheeks, straight nose and small cherry mouth; I desired to be tall, stately and finely developed in figure; I felt it a misfortune that I was so little, so pale, and had features so irregular and so marked.'"[51] ◁

Why can't this be a primary source?

Although Jane's marriage to Rochester contradicts conventional Victorian marriage, the novel ultimately ends with a conventional Victorian literary technique. "Although Jane Eyre is a love story that ends in marriage, everything Jane says about herself is calculated to show that she is not the romantic heroine for whom the marriage ending is a foregone conclusion."[52] Brontë's break off from conventional Victorian traditions is portrayed through the heroine's unattractiveness, her plain and simple nature, and her marriage in the end to a blind and crippled man. "To begin with, she is plain; her lack of requisite beauty of such a heroine is stressed continually… But she is also different from the romantic heroine in her rejection of the defect – seen as a grace – of female helplessness. She is threateningly intelligent, forthright to the point of bluntness, submitting herself mentally to no one, not even when she finally does improbably win a man's love."[53] The novel itself however ends in a traditional Victorian manner, as *Jane Eyre* ends with the recital of a prayer, as Jane says: "Amen; even so come, Lord Jesus!,"[54] speaking "to the fervent religiosity of the Victorian period."[55]

---

[48] ibid, p172

[49] Charlotte Brontë, *Jane Eyre* (Boarders Classics, 2006), p.154

[50] ibid, p.154

[51] http://www.glencoe.com/sec/literature/litlibrary/pdf/jane_eyre.pdf

[52] http://proquest.umi.com/pqdweb?did=936612&sid=3&Fmt=3&clientId=7003&RQT=309&VName=PQD

[53] http://proquest.umi.com/pqdweb?did=936612&sid=3&Fmt=3&clientId=7003&RQT=309&VName=pqd

[54] Charlotte Brontë, *Jane Eyre* (Boarders Classics, 2006), p.456

[55] http://www.victorianwe.org/authhors/dickens/ge/ripple17.html

Conclusion:

In an attempt to create a "plain and small" conventionally unattractive heroine in *Jane Eyre*, in challenge of the Victorian convention of beautiful heroines, Charlotte Brontë creates the unique feminine protagonist, portrayed through foil with her cousins, how "plain and small" she sees herself, the depiction of her impressionable nature through her monotonous life, and her "threat to the literary tradition of masculine heroism."[56] Brontë further portrays Jane's unattractiveness through her view of herself as such, Rochester's altered view of her after they fall in love, foiling her with Blanche Ingram's beauty, foiling both Mr. Rochester's treatment of the two women, and their treatment of him, as well as the decisions both women make, portraying Jane as the true heroine, despite her unattractiveness and plain, small, and simple nature. Brontë's depiction of Jane's plainness supersedes the rare portrayals of her as slightly sophisticated and pretty; thus Brontë establishes her as an independent woman, in defiance with Victorian convention. Because unattractive heroines and female independence have now become the norm in our societies, and thus in our literature, "it is hard for the modern reader to see the innovative aspects of this novel because they have become familiar to us."[57] Through analyzing this work, it is without difficulty that the audience can realize the success of Brontë in pioneering the creation of authentic heroines, through the character of Jane Eyre, whose unattractiveness and plain, small and simple nature, only serve to produce a heroine, unlike any other at the time, who has appealed to the audience for many years, making *Jane Eyre* an astounding literary classic.

---

[56] http://proquest.umi.com/pqdweb?did=936612&sid=3&Fmt=3&clientId=7003&RQT=309&VName=pqd

[57] http://academic.brooklyn.cuny.edu/english/melani/cs6/bronte.html

Bibliography:

Bell, Millicent. "Jane Eyre: The tale of the governess." Spring 1996
http://proquest.umi.com/pqdweb?did=936612&sid=3&Fmt=3&clientId=7003&RQT=309&VName=pqd

Brontë, Charlotte, Jane Eyre. New York: Ann Arbor Media Group, LLC, 2006.

"Charlotte Brontë 'Jane Eyre'" Brooklyn College.
http://academic.brooklyn.cuny.edu/english/melani/cs6/bronte.html

"Jane Eyre." Everything2. 18 Aug. 2000.
http://everything2.com/title/jane%2520eyre

Ripple, Zoe. "New Life, Old Love in Charles Dickens Great Expectations."
2004. Brown University
http://www.victorian web.org/authors/dickens/ge/ripple17.html

Starzyk, Lawrence J, "'The gallery memory': The pictorial in Jane Eyre." Summer 1997.
http://findarticles.com/p/articles/mi_qa3708/is_199707/ai_n8765444/pg_1?tag=artbody;coll

"Study Guide for Jane Eyre by Charlotte Brontë." Glencoe.
http://www.glencoe.com/sec/literature/litlibrary/pdf/jane_eyre.pdf

First examiner's comments

Lacks precision syntactically and intellectually when discussing one character as a foil for another. Over-reliance on secondary criticism (for observations that could easily arise from looking at the text). There is nothing particularly original here and several questions are not tackled. Was Brontë, for example, raising the standard for plain women, or merely writing about herself? Mrs Gaskell had something to say on this!

Second examiner's comments

I agree with the comments from the first examiner, especially the suggestion that with such a "well-worn" topic as this, the candidate needs to be able to offer more which is fresh and original. The conclusion indicates that with another draft a more robust discussion might have emerged. As it stands, the essay is much too reliant on secondary sources.

Assessment criteria	First examiner	Second examiner	Maximum available
A	2	2	2
B	1	2	2
C	2	2	4
D	2	2	4
E	2	2	4
F	2	2	4
G	3	3	4
H	2	2	2
I	3	3	4
J	2	2	2
K	2	2	4
Total	23	24	36

Extended essay assessment criteria

Criterion A: research question (Objectives 1 and 2)

This criterion assesses the extent to which the purpose of the essay is specified. In many subjects, the aim of the essay will normally be expressed as a question and, therefore, this criterion is called the 'research question'. However, certain disciplines may permit or encourage different ways of formulating the research task.

Achievement level	Descriptor
0	The research question is not stated in the introduction **or** does not lend itself to a systematic investigation in an extended essay in the subject in which it is registered.
1	The research question is stated in either the introduction or on the title page but is not clearly expressed **or** is too broad in scope to be treated effectively within the word limit.
2	The research question is clearly stated in either the introduction or on the title page and sharply focused, making effective treatment possible within the word limit.

Criterion B: introduction (Objectives 1 and 5)

This criterion assesses the extent to which the introduction makes clear how the research question relates to existing knowledge on the topic and explains how the topic chosen is significant and worthy of investigation.

Achievement level	Descriptor
0	Little or no attempt is made to set the research question into context. There is little or no attempt to explain the significance of the topic.
1	Some attempt is made to set the research question into context. There is some attempt to explain the significance of the topic and why it is worthy of investigation.
2	The context of the research question is clearly demonstrated. The introduction clearly explains the significance of the topic and why it is worthy of investigation.

Criterion C: investigation (Objectives 1 and 3)

This criterion assesses the extent to which the investigation is planned and an appropriate range of sources has been consulted, or data has been gathered, that is relevant to the research question. Where the research question does not lend itself to a systematic investigation in the subject in which the essay is registered, the maximum level that can be awarded for this criterion is 2.

Achievement level	Descriptor
0	There is little or no evidence that sources have been consulted or data gathered, and little or no evidence of planning in the investigation.
1	A range of inappropriate sources has been consulted, or inappropriate data has been gathered, and there is little evidence that the investigation has been planned.
2	A limited range of appropriate sources has been consulted, or data has been gathered, and some relevant material has been selected. There is evidence of some planning in the investigation.
3	A sufficient range of appropriate sources has been consulted, or data has been gathered, and relevant material has been selected. The investigation has been satisfactorily planned.
4	An imaginative range of appropriate sources has been consulted, or data has been gathered, and relevant material has been carefully selected. The investigation has been well planned.

Criterion D: knowledge and understanding of the topic studied (Objectives 3 and 7)

Where the research question does not lend itself to a systematic investigation in the subject in which the essay is registered, the maximum level that can be awarded for this criterion is 2. "Academic context", as used in this guide, can be defined as the current state of the field of study under investigation. However, this is to be understood in relation to what can reasonably be expected of a pre-university student. For example, to obtain a level 4, it would be sufficient to relate the investigation to the principal lines of inquiry in the relevant field; detailed, comprehensive knowledge is not required.

Achievement level	Descriptor
0	The essay demonstrates no real knowledge or understanding of the topic studied.
1	The essay demonstrates some knowledge but little understanding of the topic studied. The essay shows little awareness of an academic context for the investigation.
2	The essay demonstrates an adequate knowledge and some understanding of the topic studied. The essay shows some awareness of an academic context for the investigation.
3	The essay demonstrates a good knowledge and understanding of the topic studied. Where appropriate, the essay successfully outlines an academic context for the investigation.
4	The essay demonstrates a very good knowledge and understanding of the topic studied. Where appropriate, the essay clearly and precisely locates the investigation in an academic context.

Criterion E: reasoned argument (Objectives 1 and 4)

This criterion assesses the extent to which the essay uses the material collected to present ideas in a logical and coherent manner, and develops a reasoned argument in relation to the research question. Where the research question does not lend itself to a systematic investigation in the subject in which the essay is registered, the maximum level that can be awarded for this criterion is 2.

Achievement level	Descriptor
0	There is no attempt to develop a reasoned argument in relation to the research question.
1	There is a limited or superficial attempt to present ideas in a logical and coherent manner, and to develop a reasoned argument in relation to the research question.
2	There is some attempt to present ideas in a logical and coherent manner, and to develop a reasoned argument in relation to the research question, but this is only partially successful.
3	Ideas are presented in a logical and coherent manner, and a reasoned argument is developed in relation to the research question, but with some weaknesses.
4	Ideas are presented clearly and in a logical and coherent manner. The essay succeeds in developing a reasoned and convincing argument in relation to the research question.

Criterion F: application of analytical and evaluative skills appropriate to the subject (Objective 7)

Achievement level	Descriptor
0	The essay shows no application of appropriate analytical and evaluative skills.
1	The essay shows little application of appropriate analytical and evaluative skills.
2	The essay shows some application of appropriate analytical and evaluative skills, which may be only partially effective.

3	The essay shows sound application of appropriate analytical and evaluative skills.
4	The essay shows effective and sophisticated application of appropriate analytical and evaluative skills.

Criterion G: use of language appropriate to the subject (Objective 6)

Achievement level	Descriptor
0	The language used is inaccurate and unclear. There is no effective use of terminology appropriate to the subject.
1	The language used sometimes communicates clearly but does not do so consistently. The use of terminology appropriate to the subject is only partly accurate.
2	The language used for the most part communicates clearly. The use of terminology appropriate to the subject is usually accurate.
3	The language used communicates clearly. The use of terminology appropriate to the subject is accurate, although there may be occasional lapses.
4	The language used communicates clearly and precisely. Terminology appropriate to the subject is used accurately, with skill and understanding.

Criterion H: conclusion (Objectives 1, 4 and 5)

This criterion assesses the extent to which the essay incorporates a conclusion that is relevant to the research question and is consistent with the evidence presented in the essay.

Achievement level	Descriptor
0	Little or no attempt is made to provide a conclusion that is relevant to the research question.
1	A conclusion is attempted that is relevant to the research question but may not be entirely consistent with the evidence presented in the essay.
2	An effective conclusion is clearly stated; it is relevant to the research question and consistent with the evidence presented in the essay. It should include unresolved questions where appropriate to the subject concerned.

Criterion I: formal presentation (Objective 5)

This criterion assesses the extent to which the layout, organization, appearance and formal elements of the essay consistently follow a standard format. The formal elements are: title page, table of contents, page numbers, illustrative material, quotations, documentation (including references, citations and bibliography) and appendices (if used).

Achievement level	Descriptor
0	The formal presentation is unacceptable, or the essay exceeds 4000 words.
1	The formal presentation is poor.
2	The formal presentation is satisfactory.
3	The formal presentation is good.
4	The formal presentation is excellent.

Criterion J: abstract (Objective 5)

The requirements for the abstract are for it to state clearly the research question that was investigated, how the investigation was undertaken and the conclusion(s) of the essay.

Achievement level	Descriptor
0	The abstract exceeds 300 words **or** one or more of the required elements of an abstract (listed above) is missing.
1	The abstract contains the elements listed above but they are not all clearly stated.
2	The abstract clearly states all the elements listed above.

Criterion K: holistic judgment (Objective 1)

The purpose of this criterion is to assess the qualities that distinguish an essay from the average, such as intellectual initiative, depth of understanding and insight. While these qualities will be clearly present in the best work, less successful essays may also show some evidence of them and should be rewarded under this criterion.

Achievement level	Descriptor
0	The essay shows no evidence of such qualities.
1	The essay shows little evidence of such qualities.
2	The essay shows some evidence of such qualities.
3	The essay shows clear evidence of such qualities.
4	The essay shows considerable evidence of such qualities.

Glossary

Alliteration the repetition of the same consonant sound, especially at the beginning of words. For example, "Five miles meandering with a mazy motion" ('Kubla Khan' by S. T. Coleridge).

Allusion a reference to another event, person, place, or work of literature – the allusion is usually implied rather than explicit and often provides another layer of meaning to what is being said

Ambiguity use of language where the meaning is unclear or has two or more possible interpretations or meanings. It could be created through a weakness in the way the writer has expressed himself or herself, but often it is used by writers quite deliberately to create layers of meaning in the mind of the reader.

Antithesis contrasting ideas or words that are balanced against each other.

Apostrophe an interruption in a poem or narrative so that the speaker or writer can address a dead or absent person or particular audience directly.

Assonance the repetition of similar vowel sounds. For example: "There must be Gods thrown down and trumpets blown" ('Hyperion' by John Keats). This shows the paired assonance of "must", "trum", "thrown", "blown".

Atmosphere the prevailing mood created by a piece of writing.

Ballad a narrative poem that tells a story (traditional ballads were songs) usually in a straightforward way. The theme is often tragic or contains a whimsical, supernatural, or fantastical element.

Blank verse unrhymed poetry that adheres to a strict pattern in that each line is an iambic pentameter (a ten-syllable line with five stresses). It is close to the natural rhythm of English speech or prose, and is used a great deal by many writers including Shakespeare and Milton.

Caesura a conscious break in a line of poetry.

Cliché a phrase, idea, or image that has been used so much that it has lost much of its original meaning, impact, and freshness.

Colloquial ordinary, everyday speech and language.

Comedy originally simply a play or other work which ended happily. Now we use this term to describe something that is funny and which makes us laugh. In literature the comedy is not necessarily a lightweight form. A play like Shakespeare's 'Measure for Measure', for example, is, for the most part a serious and dark play but, as it ends happily, it is often described as a comedy.

Conceit an elaborate, extended, and sometimes surprising comparison between things that, at first sight, do not have much in common.

Connotation an implication or association attached to a word or phrase. A connotation is suggested or felt rather than being explicit.

Consonance the repetition of the same consonant sounds in two or more words in which the vowel sounds are different. For example: "And by his smile, I knew that sullen hall,/ By his dead smile I knew we stood in Hell" ('Strange Meeting' by Wilfred Owen). Where consonance replaces the rhyme, as here, it is called half-rhyme.

Dénouement the ending of a play, novel, or drama where "all is revealed" and the plot is unravelled.

Diction the choice of words that a writer makes. Another term for "vocabulary".

Didactic a work that is intended to preach or teach, often containing a particular moral or political point.

Dramatic monologue a poem or prose piece in which a character addresses an audience. Often the monologue is complete in itself, as in Alan Bennett's *Talking Heads*.

Elegy a meditative poem, usually sad and reflective in nature. Sometimes, though not always, it is concerned with the theme of death.

Empathy a feeling on the part of the reader of sharing the particular experience being described by the character or writer.

End-stopped a verse line with a pause or a stop at the end of it.

Enjambment a line of verse that flows on into the next line without a pause.

Epic a long narrative poem, written in an elevated style and usually dealing with a heroic theme or story. Homer's 'The Iliad' and Milton's 'Paradise Lost' are examples of this.

Farce a play that aims to entertain the audience through absurd and ridiculous characters and action.

Figurative language language that is symbolic or metaphorical and not meant to be taken literally.

Free verse verse written without any fixed structure (either in meter or rhyme).

Genre a particular type of writing, e.g. prose, poetry, drama.

Hyperbole deliberate and extravagant exaggeration.

Imagery the use of words to create a picture or "image" in the mind of the reader. Images can relate to any of the senses, not just sight, but also hearing, taste, touch, and smell. "Imagery" is often used to refer to the use of descriptive language, particularly to the use of metaphors and similes.

Irony at its simplest level, irony means saying one thing while meaning another. It occurs where a word or phrase has one surface meaning but another contradictory, possibly opposite meaning is implied. Irony is frequently confused with sarcasm. Sarcasm is spoken, often relying on tone of voice, and is much more blunt than irony.

Lyric originally a song performed to the accompaniment of a lyre (an early harp-like instrument) but now it can mean a song-like poem or a short poem expressing personal feeling.

Metaphor a comparison of one thing to another in order to make description more vivid. The metaphor actually states that one thing *is* the other. For example, a simile would be: "The huge knight stood like an impregnable tower in the ranks of the enemy", whereas the corresponding metaphor would be: "The huge knight was an impregnable tower in the ranks of the enemy". (See **Simile** and **Personification**.)

Meter the regular use of stressed and unstressed syllables in poetry.

Motif a dominant theme, subject or idea which runs through a piece of literature. Often a "motif" can assume a symbolic importance.

Narrative a piece of writing that tells a story.

Ode a verse form similar to a lyric but often more lengthy and containing more serious and elevated thoughts.

Onomatopoeia the use of words whose sound copies the sound of the thing or process that they describe. On a simple level, words like "bang", "hiss", and "splash" are onomatopoeic, but it also has more subtle uses.

Oxymoron a figure of speech which joins together words of opposite meanings, e.g. "the living dead", "bitter sweet", etc.

Paradox a statement that appears contradictory, but when considered more closely is seen to contain a good deal of truth.

Personification the attribution of human feelings, emotions, or sensations to an inanimate object. Personification is a kind of metaphor where human qualities are given to things or abstract ideas, and they are described as if they were a person.

Plot the sequence of events in a poem, play, novel, or short story that make up the main storyline.

Prose any kind of writing which is not verse – usually divided into fiction and non-fiction.

Protagonist the main character or speaker in a poem, monologue, play, or story.

Rhetoric originally, the art of speaking and writing in such a way as to persuade an audience to a particular point of view. Now this term is often used to imply grand words that have no substance to them. There are a variety of rhetorical devices, such as the rhetorical question – a question which does not require an answer as the answer is either obvious or implied in the question itself. (See **Apostrophe**.)

Rhyme corresponding sounds in words, usually at the end of each line but not always.

Rhyme scheme the pattern of the rhymes in a poem.

Rhythm the "movement" of the poem as created through the meter and the way that language is stressed within the poem.

Satire the highlighting or exposing of human failings or foolishness within a society through ridiculing them. Satire can range from being gentle and light to being extremely biting and bitter in tone, e.g. Swift's *Gulliver's Travels* or *A Modest Proposal*, and George Orwell's *Animal Farm*.

Simile a comparison of one thing to another in order to make description more vivid. Similes use the words "like" or "as" in this comparison. (See **Metaphor**.)

Soliloquy a speech in which a character, alone on stage, expresses his or her thoughts and feelings aloud for the benefit of the audience, often in a revealing way.

Sonnet a 14-line poem, usually with ten syllables in each line. There are several ways in which the lines can be organized, but often they consist of an octave and a sestet.

Stanza the blocks of lines into which a poem is divided. (Sometimes these are, less precisely, referred to as verses, which can lead to confusion as poetry is sometimes called "verse".)

Stream of consciousness a technique in which the writer records thoughts and emotions in a "stream" as they come to mind, without giving order or structure.

Structure the way that a poem or play or other piece of writing has been put together. This can include the meter pattern, stanza arrangement, and the way the ideas are developed, etc.

Style the individual way in which a writer/artist has used language/imagery to express his or her ideas.

Subplot a secondary storyline in a story or play. Often, as in some Shakespeare plays, the subplot can provide some comic relief from the main action, but subplots can also relate in quite complex ways to the main plot of a text.

Symbol like images, symbols represent something else. In very simple terms a red rose is often used to symbolize love; distant thunder is often symbolic of approaching trouble. Symbols can be very subtle and multi-layered in their significance.

Syntax the way in which sentences are structured. Sentences can be structured in different ways to achieve different effects.

Theme the central idea or ideas that the writer explores through a text.

Tone the tone of a text is created through the combined effects of a number of features, such as diction, syntax, rhythm, etc. The tone is a major factor in establishing the overall impression of the piece of writing.

Zeugma a device that joins together two apparently incongruous things by applying a verb or adjective to both which only really applies to one of them, e.g. "Kill the boys and the luggage" (Shakespeare's 'Henry V').

Index